AF352570

SACRED
AND
SOCIAL

SACRED AND SOCIAL

Theological Foundations
for Catholic
Social Teaching

KENNETH R. HIMES, OFM

GEORGETOWN UNIVERSITY PRESS / WASHINGTON, DC

The publisher is not responsible for third-party websites or their content. URL links were active at time of publication.

Library of Congress Cataloging-in-Publication Data

Names: Himes, Kenneth R., 1950- author.
Title: Sacred and social : theological foundations for Catholic social teaching / Kenneth R. Himes.
Description: Washington, DC : Georgetown University Press, 2025. | Includes bibliographical references and index.
Identifiers: LCCN 2024014059 (print) | LCCN 2024014060 (ebook) | ISBN 9781647125479 (hardcover) | ISBN 9781647125486 (paperback) | ISBN 9781647125493 (ebook)
Subjects: LCSH: Catholic Church—Doctrines. | Christian sociology—Catholic Church.
Classification: LCC BX1753 .H543 2025 (print) | LCC BX1753 (ebook) | DDC 261.8088/282—dc23/eng/20241107
LC record available at https://lccn.loc.gov/2024014059
LC ebook record available at https://lccn.loc.gov/2024014060

26 25   9 8 7 6 5 4 3 2   First printing

Cover design by Erin Kirk
Interior design by Westchester Publishing Services

With Gratitude for Their Faith and Action
To the Members Living and Dead of the
NOVA Community, Arlington, VA
Pax Community, McLean, VA
LFC Community, Danvers, MA
Bethlehem Community, Newton, MA
St. Vincent de Paul Community, Albany, NY

CONTENTS

ACKNOWLEDGMENTS

I wish to thank Tom Shannon, Steve Pope, and William McConville, each of whom read significant portions of the draft manuscript. Even where I resisted their advice, I benefited from their questions and suggestions. I am also indebted to the excellent librarians at Boston College who made access to necessary materials fast and convenient. Finally, my gratitude to the Jesuit community at Boston College and the Franciscan fraternity at Siena College (Albany, NY) for their support and hospitality.

1

CATHOLICISM, IMAGINATION, AND TRADITION

The theological dimension is needed both for interpreting and for solving present-day problems in human society.[1]

At the historic ecumenical council held in Rome in 1962–65, commonly known as Vatican II, the assembled bishops stated that the church "is at once a sign and a safeguard of the transcendence of the person."[2] The statement is significant because it is rooted in a religious claim about the reality of creation; as the biblical account of Genesis tells us, each human being is made in God's image.

The church must be able to fulfill this charge of being "a sign and a safeguard" of the human person without simply becoming another humanitarian organization or one more social welfare agency. So the conciliar bishops were equally committed to the claim that the church's mission is not political but religious: it is to be at the service of the reign of God.[3] At the same time emphasizing the religious mission of the church did not entail a dismissal of the importance of earthly life. For the power of God's reign must reach out to transform all aspects of human experience; God's reign cannot be reduced to some otherworldly realm apart from our temporal existence. At the council the attending bishops cited four areas where the religious mission would of necessity "spill over" into social concerns: a commitment to the defense of human dignity, the promotion of human rights, fostering unity among all members of the human family, and discerning the significance and meaning of human work and activity.[4] The impact of the church in those four areas has often been designated the social mission of the church, a dimension of its religious mission.

Though hardly the most important way the Catholic church has sought to further its social mission, the development of Catholic social teaching has played an important part in the church's life. Such teaching refers to statements issued by those who are members of the episcopal college, the clerical hierarchy within the Catholic church. The common term used in contemporary Catholicism to designate this official teaching office is the *magisterium*, literally the office of a *magister* or teacher. Since the nineteenth century the most influential format for official social teaching has been that of the papal encyclical, a circular letter sent by a pope to fellow bishops or, more recently, to a wider audience.

A debated issue of terminology to address is whether the appropriate description of the official hierarchical teaching is social doctrine. Several decades ago a French Dominican theologian, Marie-Dominique Chenu, wrote a book in which he used the term in a pejorative sense. For Chenu "social doctrine" was an ideology, meaning by that an abstract theory to be universally applied deductively, while ignoring inductive methods and any empirical evidence that would challenge the theory. He maintained that many of the social teachings of the nineteenth and twentieth centuries, prior to Vatican II, were infected by such an ideological approach. Chenu wanted to see changes in the method of Catholic social teaching that would move toward greater reliance upon an inductive reading of the signs of the times and the use of social sciences. Simply put Catholic "social doctrine" was a negative expression for Chenu.

During the papacy of John Paul II the expression "social doctrine" was used positively, sometimes in a way that appeared to be a direct rebuttal to the Chenu position. To make his case Chenu emphasized the discontinuity between pre- and post-conciliar social teaching, whereas John Paul II often stressed the continuity of the tradition and did not shy away from using the word "doctrine" since he was unwilling to accept Chenu's premise of discontinuity. Consequently, one finds the expressions "social teaching," "social doctrine," and a third term "social magisterium" used virtually synonymously in official church documents. Since "social teaching" is used both by those who favor and those who oppose the Chenu thesis, I consider it the most apt for use throughout this book.

CATHOLIC IMAGINATION

In the common way of understanding imagination, the word designates what is fantasy or unreal, fictitious in the sense of "you're just imagining you heard footsteps." Theologians, philosophers, and artists, however, may speak of imagination in a different way. In their usage of the term it refers to the creative faculty of the human mind. Imagination is the capacity to construct a world, to formulate an interpretive grid whereby we make meaning of our various experiences. In short imagination allows us to construe reality. It is the process whereby we order, interpret, and make sense of the reality that we encounter.

Nobody has experience plain and simple; we all interpret our experience of the world in order to make sense of it. Raw experience is always encoded through our imagination. Unlike the fictional detective Sergeant Friday on the old TV show *Dragnet*, who wanted "just the facts, please," we want to know what the facts *mean*. And when we seek to make meaning out of the facts, we employ our imaginations. The interpretive grid used to map our experience is often not a critically reasoned and comprehensive theory about reality but a constellation of images, metaphors, stories, and myths that provides each of us with an identity and situates us within the world we encounter.

For example a Christian believer confronts suffering with an image of a cross looming in her imagination; she is asked to contribute to a relief fund for hunger and recalls a parable about a Good Samaritan; or she reflects on the death of a friend with a story about the risen Christ, and moves through the day strengthened by a trust that her friend is now in the hands of a beneficent God. Other persons with imaginations shaped by different images and stories than this Christian woman may see suffering, human need, death, and daily life in very different ways.

Our imaginations both shape our experience and are shaped by experience. Being born in the twenty-first century, raised in a financially secure family of Asian immigrants living in the United States, shapes one's imagination differently than someone born in eighteenth-century Brazil within a financially impoverished family. Being raised in a family of devout Muslims provides a different imagination by which to interpret life's experiences than someone who has only known a polytheistic religious culture. "Through our ability to think imaginatively we develop a particular perspective or 'onlook' to see our reality,"[5] which brings certain features of experience to the forefront of our perception, underscores the importance of one or another aspect of experience, and relates present experience to similar past experiences.

To illustrate how imagination and experience interact, New Testament scholar Wayne Meeks describes the manner of a convert's entrance into an early church community as similar to how an immigrant becomes acclimated to a new adopted culture.[6] Much like the new immigrant who enters into and must learn a new culture that will become formative for his or her self-understanding, the recent convert is received into a new environment and undergoes a transformation process that entails taking on a new identity, embracing new role models, modifying one's value preferences, learning a new history, and engaging in activities that bring about novel experiences. The imagination of the new convert is absorbing a variety of elements that will transform how reality is to be interpreted, and that new imaginative "take" on reality has come about due to a range of experiences that accompanied the decision to undergo baptism.

It ought to be clear, then, that the imagination is not fixed but develops, and while some features of a person's imagination may stay relatively stable, it is always possible to undergo significant, even life-changing, alterations in one's imagination. Forsaking one set of stories and images for another is not uncommon as individuals move through their lives. Sometimes there is an intensification in the identity that was always present but previously carried little weight in a person's outlook. And in other individuals the basic perspective on life does not change dramatically, but a different set of stories, metaphors, or images reinforcing that perspective takes up residence in the imagination. The imagination is what allows us to make meaning in our lives, but it is not a fixed and determined process. There is freedom to exercise the imagination in ways that permit new frameworks of meaning to emerge.

I acknowledge that the imagination is a much-debated topic in philosophy and theology, both ancient and modern, with multiple definitions of the term and assessments of how the imagination operates. In this book I will use the term to convey the human capacity to interpret our experience as best we can grasp it, and construe or make meaning of the reality we encounter. There is a visual or perceptive aspect to imagination, as I use the term; we "see" the world through our imagination; it provides a lens through which we take a perspective on our experience. The envisioned world becomes our sense or reading of reality. We construe reality by seeing it though the lenses of the imagination. And the imagination also serves as the repository of images, narratives, and symbols by which we make meaning in our lives and our world.

To further understand the significance of imagination, we might rely upon David Tracy's work on the difference between the analogical and dialectical imaginations.[7] The dialectical imagination, characteristic of Protestant Christianity, "sets God over against the world and its communities and artifacts," while the analogical imagination, typical of the Catholic approach, "sees God's self-disclosure in such creatures."[8] Relying upon Tracy, the sociologist Andrew Greeley suggested, "The Catholic tends to see society as a 'sacrament' of God, a set of ordered relationships, governed by both justice and love, that reveal, however imperfectly, the presence of God. Society is 'natural' and 'good,' therefore, for humans and their 'natural' response to God is social." Protestants, on the other hand, tend to see the individual "over and against society and not integrated into it."[9]

To say the Catholic imagination is sacramental, whereby Catholics are inclined "to see the Holy lurking in creation,"[10] Greeley meant "the objects, events, and persons of ordinary existence hint at the nature of God and indeed make God in some fashion present to us."[11] Greeley's social science research suggested that among the major world religions, Catholicism "is the one most likely to see the transcendent lurking in the objects, events, and people of creation. It is the least likely to be afraid of contaminating God by using creation as a metaphor with which to describe Him."[12]

The analogical imagination also is linked to the topic of community; Greeley noted there is no serious challenge to the claim that Catholicism is a communal religion. In fact the main objection of the Protestant Reformers to Catholicism was "that it put a community of humans between the individual and God."[13] This Catholic approach to the church accords with a social vision in which God does not relate to us as isolated and autonomous individuals but rather as members of a people or community. Such communal networks, even small local ones, require some structure of leadership, not as an end in itself but as a means to the goals of the community. Thus it is unsurprising that Catholicism is characterized not only by sacramentality and community but also structure or institutionalization.

A final example of the Catholic imagination offered by Greeley is the role of Mary, the mother of Jesus, and her representation of tender, fertile, nurturing heavenly love. The metaphorical power of Mary is one of the distinguishing features of Catholic religious sensibility that differs from the other Abrahamic religions. It is Mary who "pushes the envelope of the Catholic imagination as far as it can be pushed by hinting that there is a maternal dimension in God as well as a paternal one."[14] For theologians and others familiar with feminist theology, the idea of seeing beyond the male imagery of God is widely accepted, but Greeley's point is that long before the formal reasoning now familiar after decades of feminist scholarship, there was a preconscious, imaginative grasp of a feminine dimension in the deity. And it was the imaging of Mary in countless paintings of nativity scenes, sculptures like Michelangelo's *Pieta*, and Madonnas by Raphael that fostered such a grasp of the feminine in the Catholic imagination about God.

By employing the language of imagination I will suggest the Catholic social tradition is not simply something to which one gives intellectual assent but is rather a complex of themes, images, metaphors, and historical experiences that forge a perspective whereby a Catholic may interpret and analyze social life. The social imagination, which gives rise to Catholic social thought and ultimately Catholic social teaching, is a lens through which a person sees and interprets the experience of reality.

Several caveats should be made about Greeley's thesis.[15] First, he did not claim the Catholic imagination, the way Catholics see the world, is better than other ways of imagining reality, just that it is different. Second, the institutional Church in its official teaching has not always understood or witnessed to the best aspects of the Catholic imagination. And third, not all individual Catholics are profoundly shaped by and operate with a Catholic imagination; Greeley only maintains "there is a propensity among Catholics to take the objects and events and persons of ordinary life as hints of what God is like."[16]

THE ROLE OF VISION

In addition to imagination a related term is vision. We commonly use the word "vision" as a descriptive report about an object or event. "But 'vision' is also used in another sense, as when one talks about an aesthetic vision or a religious vision. In this second meaning it is the imaginative, not the descriptive, element that is uppermost."[17] The outcome of an imagination that is shaped by a particular set of images, metaphors, narratives, and experiences is a way of perceiving the world, an architectonic vision, a comprehensive view of things whereby a person interprets the meaning of a particular object or event by putting it into the broad context of one's overall understanding of what reality is like. So two commentators on a specific political event may see the same occurrence but give it two quite distinct meanings due to the differing visions of life that reside in their imaginations.

This brings up an important lesson that postmodern theologies and philosophies have taught: "what counts as reasonable is shaped in important ways by the background beliefs, including the religious beliefs, of those doing the reasoning. . . . There is no *pure* reason or *uninterpreted* experience."[18] Each of us has a way of looking at life; we all interpret reality, each of us develops a framework for making sense of our experience. As we go about the process of interpreting, sorting out, and seeking to make sense of experience, we start out with a perspective, a vision each of us has for interpreting reality. And this can be a defining element in our lives, for our basic vision shapes our entire way of understanding and responding to the reality we encounter. An individual's "rationality is shaped by convictions one already holds."[19]

Now because "we all have a tint to our lenses that colors how we see and engage in the world,"[20] that does not mean the imagination is predetermined and fixed. By virtue of our personal histories—family, ethnicity, nationality, class, early education, religion—we are born into a certain view of life, in the sense that defining features of our imagination will be shaped prior to our making conscious choices about what we believe and value. Yet human development allows for individuals to move beyond, even reject, their early history. We are not fated to be mere copies of our parents or our classmates or members of our religious community. Still, as we come to critically appraise the vision that has been nurtured within us, we do that not from some Archimedean point of neutrality. We are merely adapting or moving from one point of view by means of adopting another imaginative vision.

This book will examine formal Catholic social teaching, but it is also concerned with the vision of life out of which the teaching emerges. In the next two chapters I will propose a theologically informed vision that has shaped and influenced those who have developed and accepted Catholic social teaching. That vision, standing behind the formal teaching, is an understanding of the human person, an understanding partly determined by several theological commitments that run through the social thought of the Catholic tradition. Those commitments and that understanding of the person provide the foundation for the moral vision of society that finds expression in Catholic social teaching. The official teaching has both shaped and been shaped by a distinctive vision of social life.

The import of the foregoing for a book on Catholic social teaching is that many of the themes and ideas of the Catholic social tradition may well seem less persuasive or even reasonable to people whose imaginations have been shaped by a different set of influences than those found in the Catholic tradition. And Catholic social teaching will be more readily acceptable to someone already attuned to a Catholic vision of social reality. That vision is the consequence of having an imagination shaped and tutored by the images, metaphors, symbols, rituals, and myths that have been generative of, and generated by, Catholicism as a faith tradition.

TRADITION AND TRADITIONS

Like any religion Catholicism claims "to speak not about a part of reality, but about the Whole." It wants to make known the ultimate mystery we call God by exploring "the experiences of death, estrangement, the absurdities of existence, the trust and wonder invited by the world, the simple sense of 'something more' to reality, and the experience of a love which knows no restrictions or conditions."[21] By focusing on these experiences, certain symbols, metaphors, images, and stories will be deemed particularly helpful by those wishing to communicate the religious meaning embedded in the elemental facets of human living.

When Catholic believers look for ways to express the religious interpretation of human existence, they return again and again to the story of the Jewish people as it is narrated in the Old Testament and to the individual story of a particular Jew, Jesus of Nazareth, and his life, death, and resurrection. These two sources of insight are believed to be unique instances of God's self-disclosure; by adopting these sources as revelatory of God, the Catholic steps into a "living frame of reference that is called Tradition."[22]

When the word *tradition* is popularly used, it can simply mean certain customs or norms, institutions or practices, that reflect the "way things are done around here." But theologians use tradition to suggest both the process of transmitting the Christian faith and the content that is being handed on. In the latter sense of the term, tradition includes the Bible, the teachings of the patristic era, the liturgical life of the church, and the lived faith of disciples throughout the centuries.[23] There is, after all, no thought or act that lacks a context. How we think and act is influenced by thoughts and actions that may have long preceded us. Any vision we have is in debt to the social contexts in which we have lived and in which we presently exist.

There is a tradition of Catholic social thought that led up to Catholic social teaching; to examine that tradition helps us to understand the background out of which the teaching developed. Catholic social teaching is a distillation, a synthesis of the broader and longer history of social thought that emerged from the scriptures and writings of the early church on down to the present time. Understanding the influence of that history on Catholic social teaching helps us not only to understand the teaching better but to grasp how central to the life of the Catholic church is its social mission.

There are three important points to note about the Catholic social tradition. First is that it has never been "purely" Christian. From the beginning Christian thinkers and writers drew upon sources of wisdom shared with others, whether it be covenant theories of the ancient Near East or philosophies of Greek and Roman thought. The use of pagan philosophy was not done uncritically, but over a period of centuries there was a process of incorporation of what was deemed sound and rejection of what was judged unreconcilable with Christian thought. The idea of humanity as essentially social, the distinction between perfect and imperfect societies, the view of a common good that was not merely the aggregate of individual goods, the value of the political order with regard to human flourishing, a good life as one lived in accord with reason—these were ideas that could be readily adopted. The social tradition of Christianity has never been unalloyed.

Second, the tradition is not monolithic; there have always been varied strands that may be woven together and strands that remain distinct as a leitmotif to the dominant theme. Different gospel narratives, the divergences between Greek and Latin church fathers, variances among the churches of North Africa and the Germanic tribes, the disparity found amid monastic and lay outlooks—all these varied inputs have shaped the tradition. And yet despite being diverse from the beginning, the third point is that the tradition is not shapeless. As Wayne Meeks suggests, "there are important family resemblances" because at work throughout the tradition are "root metaphors that have proven to have vast generative power."[24]

Third, a helpful way to think about tradition is as the collective memory of a people. Communities "in an important sense . . . are constituted by their past—and for this reason we can speak of a real community as a 'community of memory,' one that does not forget its past."[25] A person who grows up in and is formed by such a community of memory hears on multiple occasions those crucial stories that the community believes are core to its identity; the person not only is told how the community came to be and what it values but also participates in the various practices—rituals and moral activity—by which the community enacts the narrative that defines it.[26] As Yves Congar, the French Dominican theologian whose work was so important at Vatican II, put it: "Tradition is like the consciousness of a group or the principle of identity which links one generation to another; it enables them to remain . . . the same people as they go forward through history."[27]

Part of what a community does is preserve and hand on the sources of identity and renewal for its membership. To be a community entails forming a source of common unity, a shared set of beliefs, values, and commitments. Preserving the wisdom of the historical roots of the group as well as maintaining fidelity to those roots, even while adapting and developing them for new contexts, is a crucial task for the church. This last point suggests the importance of historical consciousness when examining and appropriating the biblical, liturgical, and theological resources of the community. To recall an adage of the historian Jaroslav Pelikan, "tradition is the living faith of the dead; traditionalism is the dead faith of the living." He went on to say, "I should add, it is traditionalism that gives tradition such a bad name."[28] The Catholic imagination, if properly formed, values tradition, not traditionalism.

As the formative narrative of the community is retold and passed on to succeeding generations, it must remain faithful to the founding of the tradition. For example, if a Christian community no longer tells a story about the message of Jesus regarding the availability of God's mercy and forgiveness; about the need to die to self in order to find new life; about the necessity to assist the poor, comfort the grieving, and give hope to the dying; about the centrality of the church's proclamation of the death and resurrection of Jesus—if such elements are forgotten or glossed over, then that Christian community has lost its memory. As Richard Gaillardetz has observed about the Catholic community, "an authentic appeal to tradition is an appeal to a living faith with long historical roots reaching back to the testimony of the apostles."[29]

At the same time, the community's memory must be remembered and re-presented in such a way that it addresses the historical context of the people who are its recipients. This is the point of Pelikan's distinction between tradition and traditionalism. The Catholic tradition cannot become a moment in history frozen in time forever. It must be able to develop and evolve while keeping faithful to its origins. A common image is that of a healthy tree which has limbs that emerge and grow, altering the size and shape of the tree over the course of the seasons, while remaining in touch with the roots that give life to the tree. A tradition must remain rooted in its founding source of life while growing and adapting to the environmental context in which it finds itself.

The account of the Catholic social tradition presented in this book will not be exhaustive but selective. I will suggest how the Catholic social tradition has been shaped by an account of the human person as being both sacred and social. These are the lynchpin themes upon which much of later Catholic social teaching depends. The political and economic ideas espoused in Catholic social teaching are, to my mind, largely derived from the theological anthropology, the foundational view of the human person, that has developed over time within the Catholic social tradition.

A DISTINCTIVE TRADITION

Throughout this volume I use "Catholic" as a qualifier of "Christian." Given that many Christian believers may share in the insights of the scriptures and early church thinkers, it can fairly be asked, what is so distinct about the social tradition being discussed that it is Catholic and not simply Christian? There is, of course, no desire to belittle the importance of how other Christian churches have developed a social tradition in my use of Catholic; nor should the word "distinct" be equated with "unique." Catholicism shares many of its fundamental beliefs with other Christian bodies, so uniqueness is not the point. Yet Catholicism configures those shared beliefs in a way that is different and distinctive. An example borrowed from Richard McBrien may help to clarify the point.[30]

There are many characteristics of the flag of the United States that are shared with other nations' flags. The US flag is tri-colored, but so, too, are the flags of Australia, Belgium, Botswana, Colombia, the United Kingdom, France, Germany, Ireland, and Italy. The three colors are red, white, and blue; but so, too, are the flags of Burma, Cuba, Czechoslovakia, France, the Netherlands, Panama, the United Kingdom, and New Zealand. The US flag has stars in its basic design. The same is true for the flags of Australia, China, Honduras, and Venezuela. Finally, the US flag has horizontal stripes, as do the flags of Aruba, Costa Rica, Cuba, Greece, Malaysia, Thailand, Togo, Uganda, and Uruguay. Yet despite the many shared features, no other national flag is quite the same or readily confused with the US flag (although Liberia does have a close resemblance). "What is *distinctive* about the United States' flag is not any one of its several *characteristics* but the precise *configuration* of those characteristics."[31] The same can be said about the Catholic social tradition with regard to the social views of other Christian churches.

Regarding the theological characteristics of Catholicism there is, as noted earlier, fairly widespread agreement that nothing is more characteristic of the Catholic tradition than sacramentality (with a small "s"). By that is meant the conviction that God is present in and through the visible things of creation. It is the tangible, historical, and visible that are the carriers of the divine presence. This expands the narrower idea of sacrament as identified with rituals, seven in Catholic teaching, such as baptism and eucharist. Rather all creation is potentially sacramental, that is, all created things may be visible signs of invisible grace. A sacramental consciousness is a faith perspective whereby the world in which we live is the place where God's reign is coming to be as divine grace works through all humanity and throughout history. Jesus Christ is the great sacrament (the creature in whom the Creator was fully present), the church is the sacrament of Christ (the ongoing body of his presence in history) and the customary seven Sacraments (with a capital "S") of Catholic spirituality are the rituals through which one encounters Christ within the life of the church community.

A correlate of sacramentality is mediation, an appreciation of the historical transmission of religious experience through the persons, events, and artifacts of this-worldly existence. The divine is not only signified by the creaturely but is made manifest by the temporal. God's love, mercy, justice, and healing come to us through individuals, groups, events, and institutions. We experience divine love through the love of a parent, spouse, friend, sibling, or stranger. Divine love is mediated love coming to us through our encounter with the created world and its creatures.

Accompanying mediation is an awareness of the centrality of community. God comes to us in the context of being part of a people. Abraham and Sarah were not called for their own sake but the sake of a people. Moses and all the great prophets were not given a message by God for their own salvation but to go to the Jewish people and call them to fidelity to Yahweh. Jesus called disciples not to establish an elite sect but to send them out to all the towns and villages with the message of the gospel. Throughout the Bible God calls a people, and the divine call to any individual is precisely so that individual can speak to the people. Community is central to the Catholic imagination and includes the recognition that communities must be institutionalized if they are to survive over time. The development of a community's structures and leadership requires both care and criticism—care because the community's survival necessitates some level of structure and leadership to continue; criticism because no human structure or leadership is without flaw or beyond the requisite of ongoing reform.

By way of a summary, I suggest six elements that are essential for the Catholic understanding of the Christian tradition:

1. an acknowledgement of the importance of a community of memory for preserving tradition and for the formation of personal identity (rootedness);
2. recognition that communities must be institutionalized if they are to survive over time and that the structural development of a community's way of life requires both care and criticism (communitarian);
3. appreciation of the historical transmission of religious experience through the persons, events, and things of this-worldly existence (mediation);
4. the centrality of a sacramental consciousness for the ability to perceive and celebrate the mediated revelation of God as this is found in a paradigmatic way through the history of Israel, the event of Jesus of Nazareth, and the ongoing life of the community which gathers in Christ's name (sacraments with a small "s" as distinct from the seven rituals called Sacraments with a capital "S");
5. the emergence of an analogical as distinct from dialectical imagination in epistemological method (seeking similarity amid difference);

6. appropriation of historical consciousness when examining the theological, liturgical, and scriptural resources of the community (tradition not traditionalism).

The distinctiveness of the Catholic imagination is comprised by the manner in which it combines certain characteristics like sacramentality, meditation, community, and tradition. In so doing it forms a social vision that is inspired by powerful root metaphors like *imago Dei* or the body of Christ, as well as central creedal beliefs like the Trinity and the Incarnation. The next two chapters will "unpack" a few of these metaphors and beliefs for their significance to the Catholic social tradition.

CATHOLIC SOCIAL TRADITION

The official social teaching of the Catholic church is an exercise of what is called the ordinary, authoritative magisterium as distinct from the extraordinary exercise of infallible teaching. Catholics owe such ordinary teaching a respectful hearing or reading, a sincere attempt to understand the teaching, and a presumption in favor of its truth. It is also important to understand that within the documents of Catholic social teaching there are varying levels of competence at work. That is, popes and bishops have more competence regarding judgments made about moral values and principles and not nearly as much on specific matters of political or economic detail. It is one thing to insist that on the basis of human dignity each person has a fundamental claim to the basic necessities of life. It is quite another to state that the best strategy for securing those necessities is through the payment of a just wage for labor; and it is yet another matter to state what dollar amount constitutes a just wage.

Along with the church's social *teaching* there is a larger body of reflection that may be called Catholic social *thought*. Throughout history many Catholic men and women have been engaged in thinking, preaching, teaching, and writing about social issues from the perspective of their faith. As to be expected from such a sizable and diverse segment of humankind, some of what Catholics have thought has become outdated or was even flawed at the time. However, much Catholic social thought has been useful and sometimes even brilliant. There is much to be learned from the historical record of Catholic social thought, whether it be Augustine's *City of God*, Aquinas's treatise on law from the *Summa Theologiae*, Thomas More's *Utopia*, Francisco Suarez's *Laws and God the Lawgiver*, or more recent authors like Barbara Ward on development economics or Dorothy Day on nonviolence and the works of mercy. There have been countless works written from a faith perspective that have brought genuine insight into the culture, politics, and economics of various societies.

Catholic social thought is not, however, to be equated with Catholic social teaching since this latter term has a narrower range, referring to the formal teaching of the Catholic hierarchy. Throughout this book, I understand the Catholic social *tradition* to include two parts, Catholic social *thought* and Catholic social *teaching*.[32]

Catholic social teaching is simply an attempt by church leaders to explicate how the religious convictions of a particular Christian church provide a way to make sense not only of one's personal life but also one's social life. It is an effort to move religious belief beyond a narrow concern focused solely on personal renewal and transformation and to include the fostering of societal change and development in ways that make human flourishing possible. Catholic social teaching does this by drawing out the implications of the Christian narrative—the metaphors, images, and stories of the faith community—so that the full meaning of Catholic belief becomes apparent; it then provides a series of normative judgments about what qualities and institutions should be in place for the attainment of a good society.

Such social teaching is not meant for the church alone. There is no need to restrict the wisdom within the Catholic social tradition to the internal life of the faith community. If Catholic social teaching reveals and/or underscores important truths about the human condition, then it can contribute to the good of a pluralist society. It does so not by being silent about its theological commitments but by being public about them. The aim of Catholic social teaching is not to dominate the will of anyone or coerce intellectual agreement but to bring the insights available in the Catholic social tradition to bear on matters affecting social as well as personal life.

The church can and should accept the standards of public speech in a pluralist society, engaging in dialogue that requires mutual listening and speaking. The dialogue must be free as well as open, allowing for genuine exploration of the meaning of the good life for individuals and the kind of society that makes the good life possible for all persons. Given the pluralism of American society and of global culture, it is necessary to practice intellectual humility and avoid overreaching claims about having the final word on a topic. However, it is possible to make a case that the Catholic tradition may speak a constructive and helpful word in the effort to build a more just, peaceful, and sustainable world. Catholic social thought and teaching aims to articulate a persuasive explication of a religiously inspired worldview as church members engage in public deliberation and conversation about social life.

Catholic social teaching was formed and will need continued reformulation through authentic conversation with others about the many understandings of the good life that have been achieved. In that conversation, Catholic social teaching can give voice to an imaginative outlook, rooted in Christian images, symbols, and narratives, that permit others to grasp the values and vision that motivate and communicate the Catholic church's social mission. If the church's social teaching can say something truthful about human persons and their communities, then there is no reason to presume that truth will not find resonance within the minds and hearts of people of good will, even if they do not share the entirety of the Catholic faith tradition. Receiving the insights drawn from other social traditions can also enrich the dialogue. The Catholic social tradition has deep and lasting roots at one end but is open to ongoing development and transmission at the other end. It can contribute to public conversation and debate about the sort of society we wish to create; it can also learn from other traditions—religious and secular—about what sort of society truly enriches the human person.

Nothing in what has been said up to now should lead the reader to conclude that Catholic social teaching has a monopoly on the social perspective educed from the biblical, patristic, and medieval eras. Nor do I wish to leave the reader with the idea that the Catholic church as an institution or Catholics as individuals have always lived up to the social teaching as proclaimed. No institution or individual fully lives up to its professed ideals, and very often it takes decades, even centuries, for a community like that of Catholicism to understand the full meaning of what it has actually taught. Think of how the citizens and government of the United States have struggled to understand the meaning and implications of the words of the Declaration of Independence that "all men are created equal" and "that they are endowed by their Creator with certain unalienable Rights." We can say more than we truly understand, and that is often the case when believers try to proclaim and teach the message of the Gospel.

How one moves from the imaginative perspective of the tradition to the formal articulation of the papal teaching is not easily explained. There is a discernment arising from an understanding as to what behavior is most fitting, given the way an individual pope sees reality and understands what is going on around him. Hence, despite the abundant confidence that popes have at times displayed in their judgments, it is not always possible to convincingly demonstrate a papal moral judgment to be the correct one. What Catholic social teaching can do is illustrate how the papacy or another member of the hierarchy sees a given matter in light of a particular understanding of reality, an understanding that draws upon the broader social tradition.

The resultant teaching may be more or less persuasive, depending on both the teacher and the recipients' appreciation for the tradition.

If one accepts that the Catholic social imagination existed prior to the more critically reasoned thought and teaching of the tradition, then we might conceive of a three-part process. It is possible to view the formal teaching of papal social encyclicals as a synthesis of a broader and longer tradition of social thought that emerged from the scriptures and writings from the early church continuing on down to the present. That history of social thought was, in turn, inspired and shaped by the Catholic imagination. As the esteemed church historian Roger Aubert suggests, it is a historical inaccuracy to see Catholic social teaching as coming from the popes beginning in the nineteenth century.[33] Leo XIII's encyclical *Rerum novarum* was not the beginning of Catholic social teaching but a culmination of much preceding thought and experience throughout the life of the church. The papal teaching was deeply dependent on the social consciousness of the Catholic community, which is far richer and older than the papacy of the last two centuries. Indeed, a fundamental claim of this book is that Catholic social thought is part of the very essence of the church's life, and without it modern papal social teaching would have been hard, perhaps impossible, to formulate.

In the ensuing chapters I will propose a theologically informed perspective that has shaped and influenced those who have developed Catholic social teaching. That perspective, which gave rise to the formal teaching, is an understanding of the human person determined by several theological commitments that run through the long and broad social tradition of Catholicism. Those commitments and that understanding of the person provide the foundation for the moral vision expressed in Catholic social teaching. I do not claim that the authors of the documents that constitute the literature of Catholic social teaching always consciously and specifically drew upon the theological themes I will present. Yet I do maintain that those theological themes are part of the Catholic social tradition.

COMMUNITARIANISM

Every political theorist, every economist, and every social reformer incorporates an understanding of the human person, either explicitly or implicitly, into their work. The church, too, rests its social tradition on a view of the person. Differences may arise among various social theories due to diverse ways of understanding the human, but Aristotle was correct in thinking that we must have some adequate and reasonably comprehensive vision of the person, what it means to be a human being, before addressing what sort of society we need and how that society can help human beings to flourish. Any seriously deficient rendering of the human person will inevitably lead to failed politics and economics. So starting with anthropology in examining a social tradition makes good sense.

The Catholic social tradition puts the human person at the center of political, economic, and cultural life. So in keeping with a loose band of social philosophies and theologies that may be labeled personalist, the Catholic social tradition, too, holds that the aim of any society is the enrichment and development of the person. The human person does not exist for the sake of society; rather society exists for the sake of the person. Equally true, however, is that persons cannot develop and flourish without social interaction and relationships. No human being can become his or her true self alone. Unlike other strands of social philosophies and theologies that see the individual as being so aggressive or sinful that society's role becomes that of a coercive restraint against the individual, the Catholic social tradition envisions society as a promoter of a common life that facilitates human development and well-being. Humans live in dense personal networks that create overlapping relationships, commitments, and involvements.

The theologian Michael Schuck has argued convincingly that even though the modern exposition of the tradition, as found in various papal encyclicals, has its major and minor motifs, there remains a unity: "the letters cohere around a shared—though variegated—communitarian understanding of the self and society."[34] I will use the term "communitarian" at several points in this volume, and at the outset I wish to explain how Catholic social teaching is expressive of a communitarian social perspective.

Community is very much at the heart of the Catholic social imagination. Humans take part in "a variety of relationships and associations with one another." When such relationships afford opportunities for people "to share common interests, intentions, purposes, sentiments, or understanding, and/or to participate in common activities," then we may call such group a community.[35] Community, therefore, in this usage is a dynamic that emerges when a group of people participate in common practices, depend on one another, make decisions together, identify themselves as part of something larger than themselves, and commit themselves to their own and the group's well-being. Community may be distinguished from society, since the former "is frequently taken to encompass bonds of affective and personal commitment among its members that enable their interactions and relationships to be conceived in terms that are less formally and institutionally structured"[36] than what is suggested by the word "society."

A person can belong to multiple communities—family, neighborhood, church, occupational, civic, and many others. Some communities may play a far greater role in the life of an individual than other communities. Some may be rather temporary, while others may be life-long. Those communities that offer a set of relationships which provide the "primary locus for the formation of a person's identity as a moral agent in relation to all others"[37] clearly carry greater significance than other communities. Catholicism aspires to be such a formative community for its adherents.

Catholicism's communitarianism may be understood as a reaction to the excesses of an individualism now characterized as "atomism." The communitarianism of Catholic social thought, as expressed in papal encyclicals beginning in the nineteenth century, was not a fully developed philosophy so much as a critical view of the extremes of liberal economics both in theory and practice. The arguments for the near absoluteness of property rights and the God-like wisdom of the invisible hand in unregulated free markets had by the mid-nineteenth century led to gross inequalities in power, wealth, freedom, and overall well-being between social classes. Papal social teaching emerged out of a communitarian vision that was sensitive to the social ills of economic liberalism.

Communitarianism gained currency in the English-speaking world sometime in the last quarter of the twentieth century. If classical liberalism as it emerged from the era of the Enlightenment can be understood as a response to the authoritarian and overbearing institutions of state, church, and society, then communitarianism may be viewed as a reaction to the excessive individualism of modern liberalism and its neglect of the common good, the infrastructure of community life, and the anomie of individualism. My use of communitarianism to describe the view of Catholic social teaching is not an endorsement of any particular author or movement that claims to represent communitarianism. I employ the term simply as a descriptor of Catholic social teaching's general dissatisfaction with the individualism of our time. In communitarianism attention is given to the responsibilities, conditions, and elements that are necessary for community life.

CONCLUSION

Catholic social teaching has sought to put into formal statements a basic vision of humankind being created in God's image, which means being created with dignity and fulfilled in loving community. The formal teaching articulates the vision which resides within the Catholic imagination.

Catholic social teaching puts into words what is already known deep within us, perhaps only dimly felt and fleetingly experienced, that we are sacred and social. Nothing explains Catholic social teaching better than it draws upon a theological tradition that holds a fundamental conviction about humanity: we are sacred and social. All the official teaching of papal encyclicals, conciliar statements, and pastoral letters of bishops can be traced back to that conviction.

Part I (Chapters 2–3) of this volume will consider two foundational aspects of Catholicism's view of the human person. Part II (Chapters 4–5) will delve into how the theological anthropology has been further developed in Catholic thought. Part III (Chapters 6–8) will present what I will call the "ethical coordinates" that Catholic social teaching distills from its foundational vision of the person and that provide the signposts for assessing what is needed to build communities and a society that upholds the dignity of the human person.

NOTES

1. John Paul II, *Centesimus Annus*, n. 25.
2. Vatican II, *Gaudium et spes*, n. 76.
3. Vatican II, n. 42.
4. Vatican II, ns. 40–43.
5. Philip Keane, *Christian Ethics and Imagination*, 90.
6. Wayne Meeks, *The First Urban Christians*, 12.
7. David Tracy, *The Analogical Imagination*.
8. Greeley, *Catholic Myth*, 46.
9. Andrew Greeley, 45. The word "tend" is used advisedly; Greeley is clear that one rarely encounters an imagination that is purely analogical or purely dialectical. The two modes of thinking usually exist side by side even if one predominates.
10. Andrew Greeley, *The Catholic Imagination*, 1.
11. Greeley, 6.
12. Greeley, 77.
13. Greeley, 123.
14. Greeley, 91.
15. The cautions noted here along with others are listed in Greeley, 16–20.
16. Greeley, 18.
17. Sheldon Wolin, *Politics and Vision*, 18.
18. David Hollenbach, "The Common Good in the Postmodern Epoch: What Role for Theology?" 15.
19. Hollenbach, 90.
20. Thomas Groome, *Faith for the Heart*, 215.
21. Stephen Happel and David Tracy, *A Catholic Vision*, 2.

22. Happel and Tracy, 4.
23. I am paraphrasing Richard McBrien, *Catholicism*, vol. 2, xlix.
24. Wayne Meeks, *The Origins of Christian Morality*, 216.
25. Robert Bellah, *Habits of the Heart*, 153.
26. Bellah, 154.
27. Yves Congar, *Tradition and the Life of the Church*, 8; as quoted in Gerald O'Collins and David Braithwaite, "Tradition as Collective Memory: A Theological Task to Be Tackled," 35.
28. Jaroslav Pelikan, *The Vindication of Tradition*, 65.
29. Richard Gaillardetz, *By What Authority?*, 72.
30. The next paragraph is a paraphrase of McBrien, *Catholicism*, vol. 2, 1172–3.
31. McBrien, 1173.
32. It might well be suggested that the Catholic social tradition also includes the activities of individuals and groups who have engaged in prophetic acts, social charity, and social justice. I do not question the vital role that such actions have played in the social mission of the church. In this study, however, I limit my focus to the ideas and teaching found in the Church's social tradition.
33. See Roger Aubert, *Catholic Social Teaching: An Historical Perspective*, esp. 75–96.
34. Michael Schuck, *That They Be One*, x.
35. Philip Rossi, "Community," in Judith Dwyer, ed. *The New Dictionary of Catholic Social Thought*, 206.
36. Rossi, 206.
37. Rossi, 207.

PART I

FOUNDATIONS

2

THE HUMAN PERSON IS SACRED

The belief that each person is created in the image and likeness of God is the foundational reason within the Christian tradition that every human person is understood as sacred. This belief, denoted by the Latin phrase *imago Dei*, is at the very center of theological anthropology in the Catholic tradition. This doctrine provides much of the basis for the claim that each person as sacred is to be treated with profound respect by all other persons. This chapter will present the Catholic understanding of two central beliefs: First, the human person is created in the image of God; and second, the Son of God became incarnate. Then I will examine the implications of those beliefs for the claim that human beings have a unique and special dignity deserving promotion and protection. This human dignity stems from belief in the sacredness of the human person created in the image of God, as well as the nature of humanity as the meeting place of Creator and creation. As we first look at belief in the imago Dei, we begin with the biblical testimony on the topic and will then investigate later development of the theme in the Catholic tradition. Following that we will discuss the significance of the Incarnation for an appreciation of the sacredness of the human person.

GENESIS: THE OLD TESTAMENT'S NARRATIVE OF CREATION

There is a single verse in the first chapter of the book of Genesis that plays a massive role in the formation of the Catholic social vision: "Then God said, 'Let us make humankind in our image, according to our likeness; and let them have dominion over the fish of the sea, and over the birds of the air, and over the cattle, and over all the wild animals of the earth, and over every creeping thing that creeps upon the earth" (Gen 1:26).[1] For the moment, let us focus on the first half of the verse, leaving the issue of dominion till later. Humankind is created in the image and likeness of God, or as later generations came to refer to it, the doctrine of the imago Dei. There are several points to note.

First, the creation of the human is presented differently than the divine acts of creation up to that point; the passage is set off by its own introduction, "Let us make humankind." As scholars have pointed out, this can be explained by recognizing that Genesis 1:26–31 was originally an independent narrative about the creation of humanity and was only later integrated within the Priestly account of the creation of the cosmos that makes up chapter 1.[2] It serves as a parallel to Genesis 2:4b–24, which provides the Yahwist account of the creation of humankind. When those two accounts are compared, a difference is immediately obvious: "ch. 2 tells how the event happened," while 1:26–31 puts the process of humanity's creation "very much in the background; not a word is said of the process," or the material out of which "man and woman were made. The emphasis is on what was created and for what purpose."[3] The human holds a special place in the plan of creation, which can be seen by the first characteristic of the human, being made in the image and likeness of God.

In making that claim about human beings, the author of Genesis is, in part, evoking an idea that was found in various cultures of the ancient Near East, that the king is the image of God on earth. "Babylonian creation texts describe the king as the image of a god, clearly a belief designed to enhance royal authority, while human beings in general are created to be slaves of the gods."[4] Since the Genesis passage is part of the Priestly account within the Pentateuch, which was given final shape during the period of exile, it is safe to say that the Babylonian creation story, the *Enuma Elish*, was known to the Hebrew authors. The Genesis text, however, "is distinctive in extending the notion of the imago Dei to include all" of humanity.[5] Hence the Genesis account may be seen as a "daring democratization, even contradiction, of this royal theology—every human person him/herself is God's image."[6]

The "democratization" influence is seen in that Genesis "denies that rulers are any more in God's image than are their subjects."[7] There is a fundamental equality between human persons, irrespective of social roles. The "daring" aspect of the Genesis account is that "it appears at first sight to go against the Second Commandment, which forbids images of the Divine." The language of "image and likeness" in the Old Testament is normally associated with idols. Yet the Genesis text may actually have served in an anti-idolatrous manner, "in the sense that the attention of early Near-Eastern man and woman was turned away from the statues . . . and turned toward the living persons around them."[8] Human beings ought not make any statues of God, "rather, the human being himself/herself is God's *statue*, i.e., God's representation on earth."[9]

This reading of the Genesis text, that as God's image and likeness a human being is God's representative on earth, is similar to the way that ancient kings erected statues of themselves in regions of their realms where they could not be personally present. There is, in short, an exalted role designated for the human that is different from the other creatures made by God. Each human person represents God. This theme is picked up later in the story when God affirms his covenant with Noah after the flood. "For your own lifeblood I will surely require a reckoning: from every animal I will require it and from human beings, each one for the blood of another, I will require a reckoning for human life. Whoever sheds the blood of a human, by a human shall that person's blood be shed; for in his own image God made humankind" (Gen 9:5–6). Because each human being is an image of God, there is accountability before God for any destruction of the divinely imaged human person. Human life is considered sacred because it was created and valued by God in a distinctive way.

An important second point about the Genesis text goes beyond the historical-critical background to consider its meaning for us today. Westermann suggests that the meaning must derive from the entire event of creation. "What God has decided to create must stand in relationship to him. The Creator created a creature that corresponds to him, to whom he can speak, and who can hear him."[10] For Westermann, this is the crucial difference between the religious and secular view about dignity, for the Genesis narrative "says something not only about human worth but also about the meaning of human existence"; to be a human person is to be "created for this purpose: namely, that something may happen between him and God and that thereby his life may receive a meaning."[11]

That "something" is the desire of God to enter into relationship with what the divine creator has fashioned. This is why humans have been graced with both intelligence and freedom, in order to be a partner in the dialogue between creator and creation. On this thoroughly theocentric reading of Genesis, the dignity of the human is not the consequence of some personal quality that we possess, but rather that we are the creature who God has not only created but addressed and invited into a relationship, or what will later in Genesis be called a covenant.[12] At the heart of the Genesis creation narrative is the desire God has to forge a relationship with the human; following the pre-history of chapters 1–11 there are the narratives of Abraham and other ancestors called by Yahweh to enter into a covenant so that "I will be your God and you will be my people."[13] So the imago Dei is not just about human worth; it is about the very meaning of our human existence.

A third aspect of the imago Dei is its applicability to both men and women. In the older account of the Yahwist tradition found in chapter 2 of Genesis, we are told that when the human is created as a lone individual "it is not good" (Gen 2:18). After the creation of other living creatures, there remains the sense that the human is incomplete (Gen 2:20). Only when another human is fashioned who is perceived as truly "bone of my bones and flesh of my flesh" is the person satisfied. To be human is not just to be in an I–Thou relationship with God, but humans are made for I–thou relationships with other human beings.[14]

Here we see a clue into the nature of moral experience. A person walks into a room where I am sitting. Once I am aware of the presence of this other, a response from me is unavoidable. I may wave, smile, say "hello," grunt, bury my face in a book, walk out of the room—but all of these are responses. Even saying or doing nothing is a response. In the presence of the other, I cannot help but respond; about that, I have no choice. What remains for me to choose is the kind of response to make—friendly, rude, indifferent, polite. My choice is limited to making an appropriate or inappropriate response, but I do not have a choice whether or not to respond. The mere presence of the other person evokes and requires a response. To borrow an expression from the philosopher Martin Heidegger, we are "beings-in-the-world-with-others."

Since the other is a human being made in the image of God, a "thou" who stands before me as a creature of worth like myself, there is an ethical dimension to this experience. The presence of the other is accompanied by an ethical demand due to the nature of human life, which is life together. In the midst of others, I must discern the morally appropriate response to the experience of the value of the other. The presence of a "thou" implies a moral call, by which I mean that the "I" has the capacity to react to the value or worth of the "thou" who is present.[15] To put it another way, the source of the moral call is the foundational moral experience we have of the worth of persons. It is from that primal data that we then proceed to ethical reflection about what is the appropriate response. "Ethics exists as an effort to see what does and does not befit persons in all their marvelous and compelling valuableness and sacredness."[16] Out of the experience of reverence for what God has created, we enter into a sense of obligation or ought in response to the creature before us. Moral theology follows upon the experience of the value of the other; it emerges in response to the encounter with the other who calls out for recognition and respect. Without the foundational moral experience of the value of the other, one simply has not yet entered into the world of moral beings, since moral growth is all about learning how to think and behave as a human being with other human beings whose value is not created by me but perceived and acknowledged by me.

This underscores the claim that "God intends humanity as a 'being-in-relationship.'"[17] As Lisa Cahill proposes, "the image of God implies that humans are created with the capacity for relationship with God, but also able to function analogously to God and on behalf of God within created relationships."[18] It is precisely in our ability to initiate and sustain relationships with others, which is imitative of God's way of relating to us, that we image God. The imago Dei is best not thought of as a noun but a verb;[19] we "perform" the image of God by the way we relate to others with compassion, generosity, mercy, and justice. The image of God is not a quality or trait of the human but "consists in human bonds and communal relations."[20]

Fourth, the relational nature of the imago Dei points toward the reality that the imago can be marred almost beyond the point of recognizability by the quality of our life together. The origin of evil in the Genesis account of the Fall is the denial that humanity is created in the image of God and the rejection of the goodness of being a human creature. And the first result of this sin is the collapse of the human relationship between the inhabitants of the garden. When God comes into the garden, the man and woman hide from their Creator. And the human person who rejoiced at the sight of the second human now blames her for the fault of eating fruit from the tree of knowledge of good and evil. They are alienated from God and quickly from each other. Not long after comes the story of Cain and the murdering of his brother Abel (Gen 4:1–15), and then humans find themselves in mutually alienated groups, symbolized by the story of the inability to communicate in the tower of Babel narrative (Gen 11: 1–9).[21] Of course, Adam, Eve, Cain, and Abel were not actual persons but symbols of realities that are universally experienced in the human story—we have become estranged from God, from other humans, from the communities around us, and even from ourselves. It is an estrangement of our doing, and it creates blindness to the presence of God's love all about us.

Furthermore, the nature of the imago suggests how to restore its clarity after sin; by building or rebuilding relationships and communities where humans may once again live with each other in such a way that God's gracious love and mercy are made present in creation. Since everything that exists is a result of God's will to enter into relationship with creation, the task of imaging God is about the establishment of relational bonds embodying the love and communion found at the origins of the created order. The Catholic tradition emphasizes that we do not accomplish this on our own, but in response to the gift of mercy and reconciliation made available to us by the ongoing self-gift of God in the person of Jesus and the power of the Spirit.

Fifth, the focus on the I–thou nature of moral experience clearly should not be equated with a morality of individualism. The "I" is shaped by the communities that have been formative for one's sensitivity to the value of the other, as well as the ability to reflect upon the experience of the other. And the other may well be plural, an intimate group of others such as a family or close friends, or perhaps a large and more impersonal group such as business customers, fellow citizens, or distant nations. As a creature of time and space, the "I" must determine the proper response to the "other," given the circumstances of the relationship, the competing demands for time and resources from additional valued others, and additional factors that come with finitude and the inability to do all that we might wish for other persons. "There can be no reduction of all interpersonal moral situations to the face-to-face, I-thou (or -you) situation of two individuals."[22] For example, the encounter between the self and others can be mediated through various social structures and institutions such as property laws, trade policies, electoral voting, the judicial system, and human rights practices.

Sixth, at the beginning of chapter 5 of Genesis, one reads: "When God created humankind, he made them in the likeness of God. Male and female he created them, and he blessed them and named them 'Humankind' when they were created" (Gen 5:1–2). There is no distinction between the sexes regarding this topic; both men and women are made in the divine image and likeness. "In creating the human race 'male and female,' God gives man and woman an equal personal dignity."[23] There is not a gradation of dignity among humans due to gender, race, ethnicity, social standing, or even wrongdoing. The imago Dei assumes a fundamental equality among the entire human race.[24]

Seventh, in light of the equality within the human family, a comment is important when verse 26 is taken in its entirety. The second half of the verse has God saying about humans, "let them have dominion over the fish of the sea, and over the birds of the air, and over the cattle, and over all the wild animals of the earth, and over every creeping thing that creeps upon the earth" (Gen 1:26b). The equality of dignity among humans is not shared with the rest of creation. History is replete with examples of how the creation story in Genesis has been used to legitimate the use and abuse of all creation that is not human. More recently, however, scholars have reminded us that the idea humans have "dominion" is not to be equated with domination. Instead, the statement regarding being created in the image of God, which distinguishes humans, is accompanied by a statement of responsibility. "Humans are told to participate in God's stewardship over creation and therefore have an active and responsible role." This charge as given by God, "rather than implying empowerment to exercise dictatorial rule over the rest of creation," is meant to indicate a rule "that is harmonious and mutually beneficial" for all creation.[25] That is what it means to act in accord with what the divine image entails. God invites humankind to assume responsibility and to be held accountable for how the rest of creation fares under humanity's care.

In the ancient world the king was not only responsible for the realm but was the one who mediated divine blessings for the realm entrusted to him. Hence, the human person "would fail in his royal office of dominion over the earth were he to exploit the earth's resources to the detriment of the land, plant life, animals, rivers, and seas" that are entrusted to him by virtue of bearing God's image.[26] Being made in the divine image entails acting as the divine Creator acts. To rule over creation as God rules over it means blessing it as good and caring for it. In sum, humanity's role is not to be understood as an exercise of control over other creatures or as the freedom to act in an arbitrary manner toward the rest of creation but is linked to playing the role of faithful steward, being the creature who tends to the rest of creation. The perspective of Genesis is that being human is tied up with service, protection, and care, not power, control, and exploitation. Humans may have a unique role in the created order, as verse 26 makes clear, but as creatures themselves, humans have a duty to act out that role of dominion in a way that accords with God's purposes in the story of creation, that is, to care for creation as its steward. Human dignity does not entail absolute dominion; only God has that with regard to creation.

An eighth point, important to grasp, is that the Old Testament claim that humans are made in the image and likeness of God has to do with the ancient Hebrew understanding of the holistic integrity of the person. In Genesis 2:7 we read: "Then the Lord God formed man from the dust of the ground and breathed into his nostrils the breath of life and the man became a living being." The human person is formed from clay and the taking in of the breath of life. According to biblical scholars this is a traditional story known centuries before it was written down; the author uses it to make his intended point that the human being "receives his existence from God and human existence is nothing else but created existence."[27] In Hebrew the expression for this vital element is *nephesh hayyah*, translated as living soul. However, "it does not mean that a 'living soul' is inserted into the human body; it means rather that man is created into or as a living soul, that is, into a living being."[28]

The Semitic world did not know of the divisions that we make today between mind, body, spirit, personality, brain, character, intellect, and the like.

It is the entire person, the whole human creature, who is made in God's image and likeness. There is no highlighting of some specific property of the person. Certainly, there is no evidence of a philosophy of the human that sees the person as consisting of "higher" or "lower" elements, an immortal soul inside a corruptible body. To ask, as later commentators would, which particular feature of the human establishes the basis for designating the person as the image of God is a misguided question arising from a nonbiblical view.[29] It is not our intellect, nor our freedom, nor our conscience, nor our soul or body, that warrants the claim about the imago Dei. It is the entirety of the human creature; "the human person as a whole is the bearer of the divine image."[30]

Ninth, despite the status given to the human person in the creation narratives, the biblical witness provides a caution. Genesis 1:27 states, "So God created humankind in his image, in the image of God he created them, male and female he created them." Biblical exegetes point out that this verse likely predates the creation story we have in Genesis into which it was inserted by the writers of the Priestly account when they produced the finalized version we now have. The earlier insertion only employed the Hebrew word for image (*Selem*) and did not use the Hebrew term (*dᵉmût*) for likeness to describe the creation of humankind. Image conveys the sense of "an exact copy or reproduction," whereas likeness connotes "resemblance or similarity."[31] The use of "image" suggests "an immediate relationship between human beings and God—there are no intermediary beings between them."[32] Verse 26, which has the addition of "likeness" in its text, "hints at the difference between God and human beings and shows that though being closely related to each other, God and human beings are not the same."[33] Thus, as we saw previously in the words of Yahweh to Noah, human persons, although made in God's image, are still accountable to God for how they behave. The Priestly account included the earlier version that only spoke of "image" and conveys intimacy in the relationship between divine and human. However, the Priestly writers also included verse 26 with its language of image *and* likeness so as to make clear that despite the intimacy between God and humanity there remains a vast difference between Creator and creature.

Finally, for all the importance that the language of the imago Dei holds in the Catholic social imagination, it may seem surprising that "after the opening chapters of Genesis, the Bible nowhere repeats the doctrine of creation in God's image and gives no explanation of it beyond what can be gained from these verses."[34] Upon reflection, however, it should be remembered that the Priestly account of the Pentateuch was the last of the major traditions to be blended into the body of the Torah. Biblical scholars theorize that it was not until the period of the exile in the sixth century BCE that the Genesis narrative would have been put into its more or less final formulation. Thus, most of the rest of the Old Testament texts would already have been composed. So, it is not surprising that the language of image and likeness does not appear throughout the Old Testament. Indeed, one commentator has suggested that "Genesis 1 is the outcome of prophetic religion, rather than the source of it," with its anti-idolatry language and emphasis on the sacredness of all persons, even the weak and vulnerable.[35]

NEW TESTAMENT PERSPECTIVES: PAUL

We turn then to post-Old Testament reflections on the imago Dei, beginning with an examination of how the theme is treated in the New Testament. All told there are seven passages in St. Paul's works that employ the word "image" when discussing the relationship of human persons and God.

> Christ is the true image of God (Greek: *eikon tou theou*; 2 Corinthians 4:4, Colossians 1:15) to whom Christians should orient themselves. They are Christ's image (Romans 8:29: image of the son of God) or they are transformed to God's image (Colossians 3:9–10) or to Christ's image through the Holy Spirit (2 Corinthians 3:18) . . . they are created as spiritual beings in his image (1 Corinthians 15:49). . . . St. Paul warns, however, that if they turn away from God, they can lose the quality of being God's image (Romans 1:23).[36]

There are two fundamental takeaways from the Pauline understanding. First, "St. Paul uses the imago Dei specifically for the person of the redeemer and does not dwell on it as a property of every single human creature."[37] Second, the image of God in Paul's use suggests a dynamic spiritual understanding of the image of God that entails a transforming power within human persons that is identified as the Holy Spirit.[38]

Already, therefore, in the New Testament period one can see an expansion in the way that the imago Dei is understood. "God is not only the ground of the imago in the sense of establishing human beings' functional value in creation, but also that it is God alone in the person of Jesus Christ, who can fulfill the telic potential of the imago after the Fall."[39] The "telic potential" means that the image of God is not simply a static notion, but there is a dynamic sense to the idea as found in the theological tradition. As humans we grow into the imago Dei through the working of the Holy Spirit (grace) within us. In the person of Jesus we have a historical embodiment of what Christians mean by the word "God." Simply put, Jesus is God in human terms, so if one wants to know what it means to be created in the image and likeness of God, look at Jesus. If one wants to know what true humanity is, look at Jesus. The New Testament portrayal of Jesus as truly human presents a normative model for disciples who seek to bring their being created in the image of God into sharper and settled focus. So the New Testament presents the imago as something of a goal (*telos*) into which a person grows or is transformed.

The Imago Dei and Redemption

The author of Colossians writes that disciples of Jesus can share in the divine image because those who have been baptized "have clothed yourselves with the new self, which is being renewed in knowledge according to the image of its creator" (Col 3:10). Each individual is to be conformed to this new image of God through redemption and following the way of the Son. That way entails passing through Christian baptism so as to turn away from sin and embrace the redeemed life offered by Christ. In the earlier hymn included in chapter 1, it is clear that no other heavenly spirit or being comes before Christ; he is preeminent, and "all things have been created through him and for him." Christ is "the head of the body, the church" and through him alone we are reconciled with God (Col 1:16–20). So the image of God in humans is seen not only in our creation by God, as in Genesis, but now also by our redemption in Christ.

Thus, Paul's treatment of the image of God leads to Christology and the role of Christ as redeemer. What is the relationship between belief in humanity's creation in the image and likeness of God and belief in the role of Christ as redeemer of humanity? The story of the Fall in Genesis chapter 3 raises a question that has been debated often in the Christian tradition. What does the reality of sin as part of the human condition mean for the imago Dei? Does sin destroy or erase the image of God in the human person? Centuries after Paul there was a rupture between Catholic and Protestant theologians regarding the answer to those questions. Today, however, the majority of Catholic and Protestant exegetes agree that the imago Dei cannot be totally destroyed since it defines the entire nature of the human person. Generally speaking, the Catholic tradition has maintained that "while the *imago Dei* is impaired or disfigured, it cannot be destroyed by sin."[40] Sin, as a rupture in the human person's relationship with God, disfigures the imago Dei and "salvation entails the restoration of the image of God by Christ."[41]

The image of God is impaired by sin in the sense that the human person no longer is capable of being properly oriented to Christ as the perfect realization of the image of God. Being made in God's image, we are constitutively relational, meant for union with God; but sin prevents the human person from fulfilling the dynamism of the orientation first given in God's creation. And so, Paul sees the redemption brought by Christ as a new creation (2 Cor 5:17), a saving transformation of humankind by virtue of Christ into the fullness of the image and likeness of God. Once again, humans are offered the opportunity to enter into covenant, to respond to God's loving plan of communion between creator and creature.

However, the ongoing consequences of sin within the human condition necessitate that no human person can undergo that transformation or fully realize the orientation to the divine without the healing, strengthening, and empowerment of God's grace. "It is Jesus Christ who reveals" to each person the fullness of being human, "in its original nature, in its final consummation, and in its present reality."[42] Without the revelation of Christ we would not know what it means to be truly human, which is what the imago Dei originally meant for humanity in the first creation. Now through our re-creation in Christ we are restored to the capacity for reflecting and achieving the imago that was the divine intention all along.

The Christ-event also reveals what the human person will be in eschatological fulfillment. It is by Christ's revelation that we understand the nature of our present struggle to be transformed into our final end. For Paul the present process of transformation is the work of the Holy Spirit acting within the deepest core of each person. Human beings, through baptism, enter into the death and resurrection of Christ[43] that is experienced as a process of conversion,[44] becoming the image of Christ.[45] Since Christ is the true image of God, becoming Christ-like is really being transformed into the imago Dei we were created to be.

Paul's treatment of the imago Dei exhibits some of the same proleptic or anticipatory eschatology of Jesus's preaching of the reign of God. On the one hand, the reign of God is present and at work in the world; on the other hand, the reign of God is a future reality that is yet to be fully manifested. So, for Paul, the image of God in the human person has been disfigured by sin and has been restored by Christ; yet the image of God remains to be fully exhibited only as the person is transformed into the imago of Christ. This somewhat paradoxical perspective was further explored by Christian theologians who came after Paul.

THE IMAGO DEI IN LATER CHRISTIAN TRADITION

Examining the post-apostolic authors of early Christian literature, the belief in the imago Dei continued as a theme in their theological anthropology. However, "patristic and medieval theology diverged at certain points from biblical anthropology, and developed it at other points."[46] There are three aspects to the later development to comment upon. First, the majority of patristic and medieval authors did not stay true to the holistic biblical understanding of the image of God as identified with the entire person. Instead, the tendency was to identify some particular capacity or quality of human beings with the imago Dei. Second, another aspect of the tradition was the tendency in some authors to focus on the "likeness" between God and humankind in a way that emphasized moral concerns. And third, there is the sad history of the full meaning of the imago Dei not being universalized in the treatment of every individual person.

The Imago Dei as an Aspect of Human Personhood

"Biblical anthropology clearly presupposes the unity" of the human person and "central dogmas of Christian faith imply that the body is an intrinsic part of the human person and thus participates in being created in the image of God." Nonetheless, when discussing the imago Dei many authors focused on a particular capacity of the human person as being the image of God, rather than seeing "the human person as a whole" as being the "bearer of the divine image."[47]

Already by 336 CE, Eusebius of Caesarea refers to God having "impressed a character on the mind of man according to the image and likeness of God."[48] This way of understanding the "image" became the dominant one as first Augustine and then centuries later Aquinas accepted the idea that the image of God in humankind was related to the intellect. Humans imaged God insofar as they are rational beings, capable of self-awareness with an ability to engage with others in relationship.

The influence of Augustine and Aquinas within the tradition was such that it became a commonly held conviction that human rationality is what permitted us to participate in the life of God. For Aquinas and earlier writers, it is because of our intellect and rationality that we are *capax Dei*, having "a dynamic orientation to the divine."[49] The human can know God because there is an analogy between divine and human reason. Furthermore, the image cannot be destroyed by human action or inaction for it is our very nature to be rational creatures.

"The age of scholastic philosophy was characterized by a deliberate choice for the intellectual-rational value of the image of God."[50] The focus was on the human ability to know oneself and God. For example, in the *Summa Theologica* of Aquinas the image of God is realized mainly by an act of intellectual contemplation: "Since man is said to be the image of God according to his intellectual nature, he is the most perfectly like God according to that in which he can best imitate God in his intellectual nature."[51] Not all scholastic writers were in agreement with Aquinas; some located the imago Dei mainly in the will rather than intellect, but the dominant viewpoint was an emphasis on the intellect as the element in the human that reflected God's image.

Our capacity for reason permits us to know something of God's reason through the study of the nature of the created order, including the nature of humans. For example, Bonaventure would speak of God's revelation being found not only in the books of the Bible but also in the first book, that of creation. God's act of creation was purposeful, and by studying and contemplating what God has created it is possible to learn something of the divine purpose. The natural law philosophy of the Catholic tradition stems from this foundational belief in the ability of the human intellect to perceive the divine purpose and plan of creation through critical reflection on reality.[52]

A downside to identifying the image of God with a given quality or capacity of the person is that other qualities or capacities may be given lesser status in describing the human. For example, emphasis on God's image as being found in the intellect led to underappreciating the body; seeing God's image as primarily a spiritual reality allowed the physical dimension of the human person to be given short shrift. The biblical view of the human person as being a unity of body and spirit was lost sight of to the extent that the image of God could be overly identified with but one dimension of the human. Also, as will be discussed shortly, equating the imago Dei with a given human quality or attribute can lead to questioning whether a person has God's image when they are judged as deficient in that attribute, for example intellect or freedom.

"Likeness" and Moral Conversion

Looking at the broad sweep of patristic literature, there are two trends evident, one that distinguished between the concepts of "image" and "likeness" and the other that effectively identified the one with the other.[53] Irenaeus of Lyon in the second century introduced the distinction between image and likeness, with image being viewed as denoting "an ontological participation" in God's life, while likeness was associated with "a moral transformation."[54]

Irenaeus's understanding of the divine likeness was connected with the Christological interpretation of the human person. A person might have been created in God's image, but because of the impact of human sin, the person has to grow into the likeness of Christ. Because of sin, the human likeness to Christ as the perfect image of God might be seriously disfigured. Human beings now must struggle to be transformed by grace into their true selves, to be made anew into the likeness of Christ.

Unlike Irenaeus, for Augustine, image includes likeness; nothing which is the image of something is unlike that thing. But likeness does not entail being an image; for something can be like another thing, for example, two eggs are alike, but one is not necessarily the image of the other. Augustine posits that what makes an image-likeness different than any other kind of likeness is the element of dependence; the image depends on the original, as an image in the mirror depends on the original thing that is pictured in the mirror.[55] What is different about humanity's image and likeness to God and Christ being the image and likeness of God is dependence. The Son is equal to the Father; the creature is not equal to the creator. Both the image and the likeness are there at creation, both are there after the exile from Eden, and both are there at the end of temporal life. What changes over time is "the degree of likeness between the image and the original." The image of God in the human person, since it is an image, is like God; but due to human sinfulness the likeness is distant and deformed and needs to be brought into closer focus to God. "Likeness does not 'add anything' to the idea of being an image; closer likeness does 'add something' to the idea of a deformed and distant image."[56] So even if Augustine did not follow Irenaeus in quite the same way when he treated the distinction between image and likeness, he still ends up with the belief that transformation must occur so that the human likeness to God comes into clearer focus.

Roger Ruston notes, "The doctrine of the image of God can be used in either an active or a passive sense. Earlier Christian theologians emphasized the active sense in that they were concerned with its implications for the way in which a person should conduct his or her life on this earth."[57] This is illustrated by Augustine in his commentary on Genesis 1:27: "The pre-eminence of man consists in this, that God made him to His own image by giving him an intellect by which he surpasses the beasts. . . . Given this honor, if man does not understand it and lives a good life in accordance with it, he will be on a level with the same beasts over which he has been placed."[58]

Whenever human morality is being discussed, there is always, at least, the implicit need to engage with human freedom. If there is no genuine freedom of the self, then there cannot be moral responsibility or accountability. So for

Irenaeus, and all subsequent Christian commentary on how humans are the likeness of Christ, there is a challenge to become authentically human, presuming that people are free to become more or less Christ-like. Consequently, a good deal of the writing on the doctrine of the imago Dei moved from a concern about what constitutes the basis for claiming humans are made in God's image to a focus on how humans ought to behave if they are to grow into the likeness of God as revealed in Christ. Hugh of St. Victor in the twelfth century speaks of "reason as image and love as likeness of God."[59] It was precisely by learning to love both God and neighbor as Christ did that a person was transformed into the likeness of God. Bonaventure in the thirteenth century used the term "likeness" (*similitudo*) to denote what humans can attain if they cooperate with God's grace and also used the even stronger term *deiformitas* for God-likeness.[60]

In Aquinas, the active sense of the imago doctrine is evident in his moral theology where "the human being as the acting image of God supplies the basic framework."[61] In his *Summa*, Aquinas states that human beings are in the image and likeness of God because, "like God the human being has intellect, free will, and the power of self-determination."[62] One may see here the intellect as the element associated with the image, while the exercise of freedom and self-determination (the realm of morality) is associated with the likeness.

The positive moral implications of the doctrine of imago Dei are clear: humans are to love God, and other humans, since other persons are the image of God. So, too, the potential negative aspect of the imago Dei is evident: if individuals are deemed not to adequately reflect the image of God, they can be treated as less than fully human. This has led to the dehumanizing practices of slavery, colonialism, racism, sexism, and ethnocentrism in the history of the Catholic communion.

Denying the Imago Dei as Universal

The imago Dei can also be understood by contrasting it with that which does not reflect the image and likeness of God. If the "image" in humans is reduced to rationality, then our definition of rationality could be used against those who evidence a different kind of rationality. Or if "likeness" requires a determined level or measure of moral transformation, then those with moral failings of a certain kind may be judged as a subclass of human beings, lacking the capacity for moral reflection and growth. In sum, there is a way of talking about the doctrine of the imago Dei that enables one group to belittle the humanity of another group. It is this unfortunate use of the biblical language that has led to Christians becoming accustomed to slavery, colonialism, sexism, racism, and other social sins.

For example, it is clear from Genesis 1:26–27 that "no ground exists for differentiating between men and women in respect to the image: the text implies that male and female are equal in their likeness to God, and consequently in their natural abilities and in their dominion over the rest of creation."[63] However, later commentators did not take that statement at face value. "Because of the near-universal fact of men's dominion over women, it was widely assumed that maleness was God-like and femaleness was not, with the inevitable conclusion that men are naturally more apt at representing God than women."[64] Note that the biblical text did not challenge the prevailing social ideology and system; rather the governing social environment led to a reinterpretation of the biblical text. Genesis could not really mean that men and women are equally created in the image and likeness of God; all one had to do is observe what the social reality looked like to conclude that "men are naturally more apt at representing God than women." One might say that the facts on the ground, that women everywhere in the known Christian world were subordinate to men, led to belief that this was the "'natural' order of things, which must somehow be traced to creation."[65] That, at least, was the conclusion reached by centuries of Christian, as well as other, thinkers.

The Genesis text makes a statement about the universality of the imago Dei in all human persons created by God, "without any restrictions regarding origin, sex, or religious belief."[66] But it is a text that has had to overcome deep-seated historical biases that too often have been identified with the original divine plan for creation because they were thought to be "natural." In our own time, there remain significant obstacles, not only of a practical nature, to attaining the full meaning of the biblical vision. Yet the Catholic tradition acknowledges, "'In creating the human race "male and female," God gives men and women an equal personal dignity, endowing them with the inalienable rights and responsibilities proper to the human person.' Man and woman are equally created in God's image."[67]

Something quite similar can be said about the Catholic tradition on the question of slavery, "a social institution from the ancient world was so powerfully entrenched in people's minds that the basic human equality and commitment to natural freedom" present in the imago Dei doctrine "was for a very long time powerless to challenge it."[68] Even worse, in the case of the African slave trade and the treatment of indigenous peoples throughout the New World, the social evil was so blinding that not only was the full sense of the imago Dei denied, but also the claim of being fully human was questioned. Excluding whole peoples from the human family was justified by seeing the image of God as located in human reason and denying that certain groups evidenced proper rational thought and action. The alleged deficiency in reason among non-Europeans legitimated their enslavement and degradation. For every missionary like Las Casas drawing on the Catholic tradition to defend non-Europeans there was a philosopher like Sepúlveda challenging their equal humanity.[69]

RECENT REFLECTIONS

The Swedish scholar Göran Collste has suggested that there are six different ways of thinking about the imago Dei in the Christian tradition: (1) God and humanity share ontological similarities, (2) humanity serves as God's steward over creation, (3) Christ defines the true meaning of being in God's image, (4) the Christian disciple defines what it means to be in God's image, (5) the male of the species defines what it means to be in God's image since females are derivative from males, and (6) growth in sanctification leading to union with God is being in God's image.[70] At least one of these approaches, number five, is a misinterpretation of the biblical witness even if it has had significant influence among Catholics and other Christians. The other interpretations of the imago Dei doctrine all have continuing support within the Catholic tradition, although I would add that the second understanding requires great nuance if it is to be useful in our present age. However, it is clear that "there is no univocal meaning of what it means to be made in the image and likeness of God" within the faith tradition.[71]

The 2004 statement of the International Theological Commission acknowledges the variety of ways in which the imago Dei is described. "The *imago Dei* consists" in the human being's "fundamental orientation to God," the capax Dei theme of Aquinas. It is humankind's "being made in the image of God" that supports its "sovereignty within the cosmos" along with the person's "knowledge and love of the Creator." Further, "it is Christ who is the image of the invisible God" and as the perfection of humanity "restores the divine likeness to the sons and daughters of Adam," a likeness "wounded by the first sin of the first parents."[72]

The ITC approvingly notes the claim that there is an "intrinsic value" in the creation of the human person in God's image. There is also the belief that the revelation of Christ does "not involve the suppression of the human reality in its creatureliness but its transformation and realization according to the perfect image of the Son." Therefore, "the *imago Dei* can in a real sense be said to be still in the process of becoming." And an element of that "becoming" is the person's orientation "to the pursuit of the good" in human action.[73] The idea of the imago Dei entailing moral transformation is evident here.

Reading the ITC summary of how the Catholic tradition has understood the meaning of the imago Dei, it is reasonable to conclude that within the Catholic theological tradition, "the *imago* exists ontologically in human beings, and that, while sin has 'wounded' this ontological goodness, it has not wholly corrupted or destroyed it." Here the distinction of Irenaeus, noted earlier, between image and likeness can be seen. Finally, human beings "also retain some of the normative functioning of those unique capacities that make us human, especially the normative exercise of freedom in relation to God and other human beings."[74] The tendency in the theological tradition to name a particular characteristic of the human person as bearing the imago Dei is again evident.

In its statement the ITC pointed out that various modern viewpoints pushed the imago Dei doctrine off to the side, even within Catholic thought. Science undercut the classical idea of our world being the center of the cosmos and the human as the center of that world reigning as God's image, and philosophy promoted a view of the human person as an autonomous agent responsible only to the self in attaining fulfillment instead of a distant or even absent deity.[75] While never denied by the church, the centrality of the imago Dei doctrine to Catholic discussions of the human person lost its prominence in certain eras.

Vatican II returned the doctrine of the imago Dei to a more central role in theological anthropology. Chastened by the horrors of two world wars, the *Shoah*, atomic bombings, and other bloody degradations of human dignity in the first half of the twentieth century, the bishops assembled at the council wanted to put forward a theologically grounded vision of the human person that could restore humanity to its proper place in God's plan for creation. In the Pastoral Constitution on the Church, known by its Latin title *Gaudium et spes*, the bishops cited Genesis 1:26 when asserting that the human person is created in the image of God, capable of knowing and loving the divine Creator. For the council fathers, that is a brief portrayal of humanity's "true situation," the simple answer to the question, what is the human person?[76]

After that opening, the entire first chapter of the Pastoral Constitution was devoted to unpacking the meaning and related themes of the claim that humanity is made in the image and likeness of God. The bishops acknowledge the reality of human sinfulness and accept that "all of human life, whether individual or collective, shows itself to be a dramatic struggle between good and evil, light and darkness."[77] Yet, the Catholic tradition regularly affirms that the image of God is not lost within the human because of sin. The conciliar text then comments upon several important aspects of how the imago is to be understood in the contemporary world. There is a clear affirmation that the entire person—material and spiritual—is a unity, and that holistic view applies to the imago within the human.[78] The bishops also place emphasis on the human intellect as the capacity that permits a person to explore, analyze, and understand the material universe but also transcend observable data to search out truth and pursue wisdom about the meaning of existence.[79] A third theme given attention is the significance of moral conscience in the human person. The voice of conscience summons a person "to love good and avoid evil, the voice of conscience can when necessary speak" to the human heart in a more specific manner: "do this, shun that." Conscience is described as the "most secret core and sanctuary" of a person where the individual "is alone with God."[80] The realm of conscience underscores the intrinsically moral nature of human existence and the divine call to choose love of God and of neighbor throughout one's life.

All the foregoing are themes that one might expect the Catholic tradition to hold up when discussing the various dimensions of the human person as a bearer of the image of God. Another theme, while always present in the tradition, was given renewed attention at the council and figures centrally in documents besides the Pastoral Constitution. "Only in freedom" can the human person be directed "toward goodness." Indeed, the bishops assert that "authentic freedom is an exceptional sign of the divine image" within the human. Each person must be free to act "according to a knowing and free choice." It is not truly human to act "from blind internal impulse nor from mere external pressure."[81] Human freedom operates at a level deeper than simple choice between consumer goods; it is freedom that permits each person to determine the proper response to God's grace and enter into the process of being transformed into Christ-likeness, to become the true image of God.

Writing more than fifty years after Vatican II, a well-respected theologian could sum up the contemporary Catholic viewpoint by describing the imago Dei as the "fundamental article of Christian theological anthropology," which functions as "the basis for every ethical evaluation."[82] It is foundational to the Catholic vision to see and grasp that every human being is created in the image of God. That vision is attested to by numerous commentators on Catholic social teaching. One of the best treatments of that topic in recent years expresses the consensus: "The dignity or sacredness of the human person in the larger Catholic tradition rests on the understanding from Genesis that the human person is created in the image and likeness of God."[83]

However, as vital as the doctrine of the imago Dei is for talking about the sacred nature of the person, it is the Incarnation that most clearly reveals the sacredness of the human person. Christ's humanity is the image in whose image we are created. We turn now to an understanding of the Incarnation and the role of this doctrine in developing Catholic social thought.

INCARNATION AND THE SACRED NATURE OF THE HUMAN PERSON

When the Creator decided to enter into creation, when the Eternal became subject to time, when the Son of God became something other than God, he became human. That humanity is the place in the created order where its Creator could unite with it is a profound indication of the sacredness and worth of the human person. But appreciation for the claim that Jesus was truly God and truly human took time to develop and was attained only after much debate and experience of Christian discipleship.

There is an adage that a mature mind is one that can hold two truths in tension, not losing sight of one for the sake of holding onto the other. In many ways that adage can be used to describe the situation of the early church. The tension is evident in the efforts to formulate the teaching on the nature of Christ as both truly human and truly divine. Indeed, one could examine the evolution of the church's understanding of Christ as a series of corrections whenever various parties promoted a view of Christ that eased the tension by slighting either Christ's humanity or his divinity.

The formulation of doctrine is an attempt to express adequately in words the lived experience of Christian believers. Doctrines are not identical with the Gospel message but are the work of reflection upon the meaning of the Gospel's message. The New Testament sought to communicate the disciples' experience of Jesus, and the evangelists offer portrayals of who Jesus was, what he preached, what he did, and what happened to him. Without question, the reason that there was any interest in Jesus after his death is that members of the early church experienced Jesus as risen and alive. Without that experience of and belief in the resurrection, it is hard to imagine Christianity being anything other than some fond memories of a prophetic teacher and martyr to a vision of life. The convictions that we find in the Acts of the Apostles and in the letters of Paul and other New Testament writers would be impossible to sustain without the belief that Jesus was not dead but risen in glory. And that belief was founded upon the experience of a number of disciples who encountered the risen Jesus. What that risen state was like, how it ought to be described, is less crucial than the claim that Jesus is risen. If that claim is factually true, later speculation would consider how we should understand what reality is like in order to accommodate such a claim.

When the Acts of the Apostles tells us of the ascension of Jesus into the heavens (Acts 1:9–11), of Peter's preaching at Pentecost that Jesus was raised to the right hand of God (Acts 2:32–33), and of Stephen's vision at his martyrdom that Jesus is standing at God's right hand (Acts 7:55), we are hearing the early church confess its belief in imagery familiar to people of the time, that Jesus has a special relationship with God. An ancient king would put next to his right hand only a trusted individual who embodies the king's ideals and values. If Jesus has that role, then it must be that Jesus reflects the character, purpose, and will of God.

For those who knew the historical Jesus in the flesh, the challenge was to understand how the humble Galilean prophet rejected by Israel's leadership could be the exalted one at God's right hand. That Jesus was a man there was no doubt among the earliest disciples who knew him. For the next generation of disciples, however, the challenge was shifting: How could the Son of God be a modest laborer who wound up dead from crucifixion? It was Paul, as well as others, who came to understand that God's power operates differently than human conceptions of power. God's power is seen in weakness and humility; God's power is revealed in Jesus,

> who, though he was in the form of God,
> did not regard equality with God
> as something to be exploited,
> but emptied himself,
> taking the form of a slave,
> being born in human likeness.
> And being found in human form,
> he humbled himself
> and became obedient to the point of death—
> even death on a cross. (Phil 2:6–8)

Precisely because of Jesus humbling himself,

> God also highly exalted him
> and gave him the name
> that is above every name,
> so that at the name of Jesus
> every knee should bend,
> in heaven and on earth and under the earth,
> and every tongue should confess
> that Jesus Christ is Lord,
> to the glory of God the Father. (Phil 2:9–11)

This two-fold conviction of the early church, that Jesus was both divine and human, became the source of numerous debates and was on the agenda of several of the early councils that codified what became orthodox Christian belief.

Councils and Heresies

Our English word "heresy" is derived from the Greek *hairesis*, which meant a decisive choice or strong opinion. Originally, it did not carry a negative connotation but was simply a term applied to a viewpoint held by an individual or shared by a group. In time, it developed the negative sense of a viewpoint that was divisive, standing opposed to the belief of a larger group and creating a minority sect or party. In the context of the church, with its strong emphasis on unity within the body of Christ, a heresy was seen as a poison infecting the church that had to be corrected or denounced. In a sense the existence of heresies was invigorating rather than threatening for the Christian community, because distinguishing proper belief from the various errors that arose became the means whereby the church was able to articulate its essential creed.

Among the earliest heresies was Docetism, the belief that Jesus was not truly human but merely appeared to be so for the sake of communicating with humanity. For the Greek mind, God was necessarily transcendent and remote, incapable of feeling emotion, experiencing suffering or death, or even having a real body with its physical limitations. The Docetists were Greek gentiles who accepted the message of Jesus but sought to understand Jesus from within their already existing philosophical categories about the nature of divinity. Rather than understand Jesus as revelatory of God, the Docetists understood Jesus in light of their philosophy about God. God could not become human because God for the Greek philosopher was impassible, that is, nothing outside of God could act upon or influence God. Hence, Jesus could not have truly become human but only seemed to be human or acted *as if* he were human.

More serious and longer lasting was the heresy of Gnosticism. Again, influenced by Greek philosophy's conception of God as remote and transcendent, the Gnostics believed in an array of demi-gods or divine emanations that mediated between the supreme God and earthly creatures. Jesus was adopted as the chief mediator who offered salvation from the world of matter and imperfection. This salvation came not through faith but through secret knowledge (Greek: *gnosis*) that allowed the human soul to escape the unhappy state of historical existence. Resistance to Gnosticism came from early patristic figures like Irenaeus who insisted on the doctrine of the Incarnation and the belief that Jesus redeemed material creation, including humanity's bodily condition. Salvation came not from knowledge but from faith, that is, trust in God's love as revealed in the life, death, and resurrection of Jesus.

On the other side of the Incarnation debate were those who supported "adoptionism," the idea that Jesus lived with such authenticity and integrity that God adopted him in a special sense as a divine Son. This way of thinking takes seriously that Jesus was truly human and by living as he did, he revealed something of God's nature. The problem with this approach is that it does not take seriously the belief that by the Incarnation, God willed to reveal the divine self; that in Jesus we encounter not a good man who shows something of God but that in Jesus we encounter God's very self. The fullness of revelation was not contingent upon someone eventually living so well that God might adopt the person. Instead, God willed to reveal the divine self in creation.

What these heresies illustrate is the difficulty involved in holding onto two truths at once: Jesus is both divine and human. Up to a point, the Christian church was content to push back against inadequate attempts to describe the nature of Christ, those that were too feeble in their support of the true divinity or true humanity of Jesus Christ. In time, however, it became necessary to say something positive about *how* Christ could be both human and divine. Various explanations—Apollinarianism, Nestorianism, Eutychianism—each had their moment but were finally rejected. At the Council of Chalcedon in 451, the Church formulated a creed that allowed a measure of latitude within the bounds of orthodoxy. Both the Alexandrian and Antiochene schools, the former stressing the divinity and the latter the humanity, could find room to expound their views. Chalcedon did not determine a theory of how divinity and humanity were united in Christ but maintained that they were united. "Thus the Definition stands for a principle rather than for a theory; and it permits the formulation of theories provided that the principle is safeguarded in them."[84]

Within the theological tradition there have been developments that have helped advance our understanding of how both truths about Christ, that he is human and divine, may be adequately held together. Two of these developments will be noted here. First is the medieval formula *homo capax Dei*, that is, the human person is capable of God. There is something about the human condition that opens us to receiving the divine in a way that is different from the rest of creation. Bearing the image of God in a unique way from the rest of creation, the human is made for God. The medieval

Franciscan, Bonaventure, suggests that there is a two-fold dimension to the Incarnation. The first is that the very nature of God is a "triune mystery of self-communicative love" and the second is the possibility of God becoming a creature. Bonaventure argues that when humanity's capacity for a relationship with God is actualized, "the created order finds its highest form of fulfillment" in the union of divinity and humanity. "Christ is the purest actualization of a potential that lies at the heart of the created order." Thus, when the eternal Word becomes the incarnate Word, we have the union of the uncreated with the created, the divine and the human, the infinite and the finite.[85]

A second development, one often associated with Bonaventure's fellow Franciscan John Duns Scotus, is the idea of the primacy of Christ. Though given prominence by Scotus, this viewpoint can be found in earlier theologians and is concerned with the motive behind the Incarnation. Essentially, what the Scotistic theory posits is that since the Incarnation is the absolute high point in God's communication with creation, the fullest expression of divine revelation, it seems odd that such a divine action was contingent upon human sin. That is, the mode in which Christ appeared, as savior or redeemer, may be due to our bondage in sin. But the divine intention behind the Incarnation must have been the Creator's will to communicate in the most intimate manner with creation by becoming part of it. If the Incarnation is the original divine intention, then all the claims about the imago Dei are derived from that original purpose: we are made in the image of the incarnate Son. Sin interferes not with the imago but with humanity's capacity for both reflecting and achieving it. From the beginning of the event of creation, human nature was created with God's intention already established, that humanity be the means whereby the divine self could be united with the world of creation. Humanity was conceived by God as the meeting place between Creator and creature.

The developments of Bonaventure and Scotus suggest a path forward in Christology, one which modern Catholic theologians such as Karl Rahner, Edward Schillebeeckx, and Walter Kasper have followed. Namely, the aim is to overcome the lasting influence of Greek thought that saw a huge chasm between God and humankind, for God's transcendence and impassibility made divinity seem distantly remote from anything human and material. Today we can ask: If the Incarnation was real, might it suggest that God and humanity may be closer to each other than Greek thought imagined? Substances that are completely and entirely unlike can never forge an organic union. Yet if God was incarnate in Jesus of Nazareth, then there must be something within the nature of a human person that permits the human to be essentially capable of union with the divine. Humanity truly is capable of the infinite; homo capax Dei.

If God incarnate is human nature perfected, then it is possible for a person to be both divine and human. If Jesus is truly God and also expresses the fullness of humanity, then Jesus of Nazareth was the way that God could be most fully revealed within creation, and the distance between creation and Creator is not as great as those theologies shaped by Greek presuppositions presupposed. This does not mean that the difference between God and humanity does not exist. Even if the human person is made in God's image and human nature is not utterly separated from divine nature, God is still God and humans are still creatures. Finite and infinite, temporal and eternal, sinful and holy are not simply collapsed by this way of thinking.[86] But acknowledging that Greek thought exaggerated the gulf between God and creation permits modern theologians to envision a way of holding the Chalcedonian principle of two truths together.

Seeing the truths together is also assisted by reconsidering the nature of humanity. Some approaches to the human condition stress the commonality of creatures. Stress on finitude and materiality that unites us with other creatures can obscure those aspects of the human condition that mark us unique—freedom, the drive for truth, the quest for beauty, the longing for intimacy and relationship. These features of the person indicate an openness and incompleteness, a drive to go beyond our present situation to a transcendence that makes space for humanity's capacity to receive God. The incarnation, in short, not only reveals God to humanity but reveals what is truly human to humanity. There is a value and worth to the human condition that is affirmed in the doctrine of the Incarnation. We are capable of receiving the infinite because from the outset human nature was intended to be the locus of the union of God and creation in the person of Jesus Christ. Sin never destroyed that basic affirmation of humanity's meaning and worth.

Christian Humanism

The hallmark of Catholic Christianity is its incarnationalism; that is, the theological conviction that the Holy Mystery at the source of all that exists, what we call God, has been fully revealed in the life, death, and resurrection of a human being named Jesus of Nazareth. The Catholic tradition sees Christianity as authentic humanism. In his first encyclical, *Redemptor hominis*, John Paul II wrote: "In reality, the name for that deep amazement at the human person's worth and dignity is the Gospel, that is to say: the Good

News. It is also called Christianity."[87] The Christian tradition's claim about Christ is not simply a juxtaposition of divinity and humanity; Jesus is not divine and also happens to be human. Rather, Catholic Christology maintains that in the human person, Jesus of Nazareth, we see the revelation of true divinity in so far as we see authentic humanity, and that we see true humanity in so far as we see authentic divinity.

The crucial point to understand is that humanity and divinity are not in competition. Indeed, not only are humanity and divinity not in competition, but the former is the sacrament of the latter. The human person was created for the exact purpose of receiving the self-gift of God to creation. The more truly human we become, the more Christ-like we become, which means the more we become the image of God. Only by becoming more and more truly human can a person become more like God; for God not only created humanity in the divine image, God became a human being, Jesus of Nazareth. In the hymn of Philippians cited previously, it is proclaimed that the One who is in the form of God does not strive to hold onto divine status but wills to be a human being like all other human beings. It is hard to imagine a stronger claim about the goodness and value of creaturely life than what the Christian tradition made in that hymn—the Creator chose to become a creature; God chose to become a human person. That is what is meant by John Paul II's statement that the Christian tradition is a "deep amazement at the human person's worth and dignity." To be a human, male and female, is to be "created by God, addressed by God, called by God, accepted by God."[88] The human person is capable of being God's partner in a dialogue, in a covenant, and is able to receive the fullest self-communication of God to creation through the incarnation of the Word as Jesus of Nazareth.

CONCLUSION

This chapter presented a Catholic understanding of two core beliefs: first, every human person is created in the image of God; and second, that the Son of God became a human creature. Then I examined the implications of those claims, namely, that human beings have a unique and special dignity that stems from belief in the doctrines of creation and Incarnation.

To bring this reflection on those themes to a close, I draw upon an essay by David Hollenbach, a distinguished commentator on the Catholic social tradition. Concerning the claim made in the title of the chapter, Hollenbach asserts, "Persons possess a worth that deserves to be treated with the reverence shown to that which is holy. As made in God's likeness, human beings possess a sacredness analogous to the holiness of God."[89]

When parsing the meaning of the imago Dei, Hollenbach proposes a three-fold framework. First, there is a substantialist version, so called because the image of God is associated with "aspects of the very substance of the person and inherently present within the person," namely the transcendence of the mind, or the essential freedom of the person.[90] Second is a relational interpretation, which "sees the image of God in persons as a reflection of the fact that the God in whom Christians believe is a Trinitarian union of three persons."[91] Hence, humans made in the image of such a God are also profoundly relational; that is, we are called to intimacy and community with others. Finally, the image of God also has a "functional interpretation'; that is, humans have been given a special charge to watch over the rest of creation, "being delegated by God to exercise the kind of care for creation that God's love for all creatures leads to"; for example, human dignity is linked to environmental integrity and sustainability.[92] All three of these interpretive strands have found a place within the Catholic understanding of the human person as a consequence of being made in God's image.

While this chapter has discussed the first and third strands, the second one that Hollenbach calls the relational has been purposefully omitted in this chapter. That is because the next chapter's focus will be an examination of the social nature of the person and how a Trinitarian understanding of the imago Dei has shaped the Catholic social vision. Following the third chapter, subsequent chapters will develop the implications of the theological anthropology presented in this and the next chapter, that the human person is both sacred and social.

NOTES

1. All references to biblical quotations will be included in the text using standard abbreviations for the biblical books. Biblical texts will be taken from the New Revised Standard Version (NRSV) unless quoting from another author using a different translation.
2. Claus Westermann, *Creation*, 47.
3. Westermann, 47.
4. Roger Ruston, *Human Rights and the Image of God*, 277.
5. International Theological Commission (ITC), "Communion and Stewardship: Human Persons Created in the Image of God," n. 8.
6. Ruston, *Human Rights and the Image of God*, 277.
7. Ruston, 277.
8. Ruston, 278.

9. Sigrid Müller, "Concepts and Dimensions of Human Dignity in the Christian Tradition," 25. All italics are to be found in original texts unless indicated otherwise.
10. Westermann, *Creation*, 56.
11. Westermann, 60.
12. "God shared his nature with human persons by creating them intelligent and free. But, I venture to say, it would hardly make sense for God to create such beings without wanting to meet them. In fact, we read in the Scriptures that from the first moment of human beings' consciousness God was conversing with them." Ladislas Orsy, "The Divine Dignity of the Human Person in *Dignitatis humanae*," 16.
13. For example: Genesis 17:7; Exodus 6:7; Ezekiel 36:28; Jeremiah 7:23, 31:33.
14. Westermann, *Creation*, 73.
15. Enda McDonagh, *Gift and Call*, 5–6.
16. Daniel Maguire, *The Moral Choice*, 73.
17. Douglas John Hall, *Imaging God: Dominion as Stewardship*, 113; as quoted in Lisa Cahill, "Embodying God's Image," 62.
18. Cahill, "Embodying God's Image," 64.
19. Alastair McFadyen, "Imaging God: A Theological Answer to the Anthropological Question?"
20. Cahill, "Embodying God's Image," 67.
21. Paul Ricoeur, "The Symbolism of Evil," 248–49, fn. 8.
22. McDonagh, *Gift and Call*, 22.
23. John Paul II, *Familiaris consortio*, n. 22.
24. Of course acknowledgement of the full implications of the Genesis texts about the imago Dei has been and continues to be a long and sad narrative marred by sins such as sexism, racism, imperialism, and other ideological denials of human equality. Tragically, the church among both its leaders and other members has too often not exhibited any greater sensitivity to the equality in dignity of all persons than other human communities.
25. McKeown, *Genesis*, 27, fn. 12
26. Westermann, *Creation*, 52.
27. Westermann, 77.
28. Westermann, 77.
29. See Westermann, *Genesis 1–11: A Commentary* (London: SPCK, 1984), 148–55 for an example of multiple interpretations of what makes the human the image and likeness of God.
30. ITC, "Communion and Stewardship," n. 28.
31. Maly, "Genesis," 11.
32. McKeown, *Genesis*, 26–27.
33. McKeown, 27.
34. Ruston, *Human Rights and the Image of God*, 277.
35. Ruston, 278.
36. Müller, "Concepts and Dimensions," 28.
37. Junker-Kenny, "Human Dignity or Social Contract," 82.
38. Müller, "Concepts and Dimensions," 28.
39. Petrusek, "The Image of God and Moral Action," 78.
40. ITC, n. 46.
41. ITC, n. 47.
42. ITC, n. 52.

43. Romans 6:3–5:
    Do you not know that all of us who have been baptized into Christ Jesus were baptized into his death? Therefore we have been buried with him by baptism into death, so that, just as Christ was raised from the dead by the glory of God the Father, so we too might walk in newness of life. For if we have been united with him in a death like his, we will certainly be united with him in a resurrection like his.
44. Romans 6:6–14:
    We know that our old self was crucified with him so that the body of sin might be destroyed, and we might no longer be enslaved to sin. For whoever has died is freed from sin. But if we have died with Christ, we believe that we will also live with him. We know that Christ, being raised from the dead, will never die again; death no longer has dominion over him. The death he died, he died to sin, once for all; but the life he lives, he lives to God. So you also must consider yourselves dead to sin and alive to God in Christ Jesus. Therefore, do not let sin exercise dominion in your mortal bodies, to make you obey their passions. No longer present your members to sin as instruments of wickedness, but present yourselves to God as those who have been brought from death to life, and present your members to God as instruments of righteousness. For sin will have no dominion over you, since you are not under law but under grace.
45. Romans 8:29:
    For those whom he foreknew he also predestined to be conformed to the image of his Son, in order that he might be the firstborn within a large family.
46. ITC, "Communion and Stewardship," n. 15.
47. ITC, ns. 28, 29, 31.
48. Eusebius of Caesarea, "From a Speech for the Thirtieth Anniversary of Constantine's Accession," in O'Donovan and O'Donovan, *From Irenaeus to Grotius*, 61.
49. ITC, "Communion and Stewardship," n. 48.
50. Autiero, "Human Dignity in an Ethical Sense," 16.
51. Aquinas, *Summa Theologica*, I, q. 93, art. 4.
52. We will return to this theme of the role of reason when we discuss natural law theory in chapter four.
53. R. A. Markus, "'Imago' and 'similitudo' in Augustine," 126.
54. ITC, "Communion and Stewardship," n.15.
55. Markus, "'Imago' and 'similitudo,'" 125.
56. Markus, 142.
57. Ruston, *Human Rights and the Image of God*, 269.
58. Augustine, *The Literal Meaning of Genesis*, Book 6, Ch. 12, n. 21, 193. As quoted in Ruston, *Human Rights and the Image of God*, 269.
59. Müller, "Concepts and Dimensions," 37.
60. Müller, 38. The author notes that Bonaventure used "likeness" not as the Genesis author did to emphasize the distance between God and humans but to signify a closer unity if the creature empowered by God's grace is formed into Christ's image. See fn. 61 in Müller.
61. Ruston, *Human Rights and the Image of God*, 269. The author suggests that the "passive" sense of the doctrine refers to how the imago Dei "says something about how persons bearing this image should (or should not) be treated by others." Ruston thinks this passive usage of the doctrine came into modern usage only with the antislavery debates of the nineteenth century.

62. Thomas Aquinas, *Summa Theologica*, IaIae, Prologue.

63. Ruston, *Human Rights and the Image of God*, 280.

64. Ruston, 280.

65. Ruston, 280.

66. Müller, "Concepts and Dimensions," 27.

67. ITC, "Communion and Stewardship," n. 36, quoting John Paul II, *Familiaris consortio*, n. 22. Note that women are accorded equal *personal* dignity, which may be understood as not granting equal social dignity.

68. Ruston, *Human Rights and the Image of God*, 288.

69. Lars Kirkhusmo Pharo, "The Council of Valladolid."

70. Göran Collste, *Is Human Life Special?*, 37. I am drawing upon Petrusek's summation of Collste as found in his essay, "The Image of God and Moral Action," 63.

71. Petrusek, "The Image of God and Moral Action," 63.

72. ITC, "Communion and Stewardship," n. 22.

73. ITC, n. 24.

74. Petrusek, "The Image of God and Moral Action," 79.

75. ITC, "Communion and Stewardship," n. 19.

76. Vatican Council II, *Gaudium et spes* (Pastoral Constitution on the Church in the Modern World), n. 12.

77. Vatican II, n. 13.

78. Vatican II, n. 14.

79. Vatican II, n. 15.

80. Vatican II, n. 16.

81. Vatican II, n. 17.

82. Autiero, "Human Dignity in an Ethical Sense," 16.

83. Curran, *Catholic Social Teaching 1891–Present*, 131–32.

84. Alan Richardson, *Creeds in the Making*, 84.

85. Thomas Shannon, "Bonaventure and Human Dignity," 17–18.

86. Richardson, *Creeds*, 89.

87. John Paul II, *Redemptor hominis* (Judith, Redeemer of Humanity), n. 28.

88. John Dwyer, "Person, Dignity of," in Dwyer, ed. *The New Dictionary of Catholic Social Thought*, 725.

89. David Hollenbach, "Human Dignity in Catholic Thought," 252.

90. Hollenbach, 253.

91. Hollenbach, 253.

92. Hollenbach, 255.

3

THE HUMAN PERSON IS SOCIAL

The human person is made in God's image, but who is this God who is the original for the human as image? What do we know of God? What can we say about God that might assist us in understanding what it means for humans to be made in the divine image? At the very outset, it is important to be intellectually modest about what we claim to know about God and not identify even our best images of God with God. And so it is important to remember that whatever we think of when we think of God is likely to be in error, at least in part if not totally. For "God" is simply a shorthand designation for the mystery that creates, sustains, and fulfills all that we call reality.

Still, with that caution in mind about the inadequacy of any conceptualization of God, the very nature of theology (*theos–logos*) is to speak about God. The Catholic tradition has done so relying upon a number of images, metaphors, similes, and stories. I suggest there are two fundamental ways of talking about God that have been most significant in the Catholic social tradition for understanding what it means to be created in the image of God. The first way, noted in the previous chapter, is the human made in the image of God, who is the Holy Mystery. Therefore, the human person is holy or sacred, and that implies the human person has a dignity, as we will discuss in the next chapter, that ought to be acknowledged in the way that we reverence whatever is genuinely holy or sacred.

The second way of talking about God that is fundamental to how the Catholic social tradition understands the human person is to say that God is Trinitarian. The God in whose image we are created is not the "Alone" or "Solitary" but a Trinity of persons equally participating in the divine nature.

The main point of the previous chapter was to explore the implications for Catholic social thought of various theological convictions about the sacredness of the human person. Just so this chapter will explore the implications for Catholic social thought that arise due to beliefs that God is a Trinity, that disciples are called to love one another, and that believers are united as one in the body of Christ. And the very first implication of those claims is that humans are essentially social. As the teaching of Vatican II makes clear, humans are "not made for life in isolation, but for the formation of social unity." Indeed, the Council fathers went on to point out that the history of salvation testifies that God has chosen people "not just as individuals but as members of a certain community."[1] Human beings are made for relationship; we enter into relationships in order to be truly human, and without relationships we could not be our true selves. In a phrase employed by the US Catholic bishops in their pastoral letter published in 1986: "Human dignity can be realized and protected only in community."[2] This chapter aims to make clear why it is imperative we understand the human person is not only sacred but essentially social. I will do so by examining the doctrine of the Trinity, the centrality of love and community in the practice of Christian discipleship, and the importance of the metaphor of the body of Christ.

THE TRINITY

The doctrine of the Trinity emerged within the Christian church as a consequence of holding onto two seemingly contradictory claims about God. The first claim, owing to the Jewish roots of Christianity, was the consistent belief in monotheism. "There is one God" was a statement no early Christian believer disputed. The second claim, owing to the experience and testimony of the first generation of Jesus's disciples, was a confession of faith that "Jesus is Lord." How to hold those two claims simultaneously was the driving force behind the early Church's working out of the unique relationship that Jesus has with the God he addressed as Father.

The New Testament rarely says explicitly that Jesus is God, because that would have confused Jesus with the Father in the minds of the earliest Christians, who were almost exclusively Jewish. Yet within the New Testament there are a variety of instances where Jesus, the Son of God, is seen as divine. Already in the early baptismal hymn that Paul includes in the second chapter of his letter to the Philippians, Jesus is understood to be pre-existent in the realm of the divine (Phil 2:6–11). Throughout the synoptic gospels, Jesus is portrayed as being the bearer of the reign of God, such that acceptance or rejection of Jesus is tied to being a participant in or outside of God's reign. Jesus is Lord of the Sabbath and is worshipped in communal prayer at the earliest assemblies of believers. Jesus is also described as possessing the fullness of the Spirit. However, nowhere in the New Testament is the relationship between the Father, Son, and Spirit explained. The one who sees Jesus sees the Father; the Father sends the Son and the Spirit into the world; Jesus departs in order that the Spirit might come into the community of disciples. A relationship between Father, Son, and Spirit is alluded to, but the nature of the relationship is not explained in the New Testament.

Further, the New Testament witnesses to the effect that the Trinitarian God had upon the early church. To employ language that was developed later in the tradition, the Christian scriptures reveal the "economic" Trinity, that is, God acting for us in the history of salvation. There is no revealed insight into the "immanent" Trinity, that is, the nature of God and God's inner life. Centuries would pass during which the Christian church developed its understanding of the nature of the Trinity before it came to appreciate that the "immanent" and "economic" Trinity were one and the same.[3]

Speaking about Mystery

Today, traditional language about the Trinity can be misleading because the meaning of words changes over time. Perhaps most misleading about the Trinity is the statement that Catholics believe there are three persons in one God—misleading because a great deal depends on what is meant by "person." Those who formulated and affirmed the Church's teaching about the Trinity in the third and fourth centuries "did not mean by 'person' what we mean by it today—a separate individual personality."[4] If they had meant that, we would be talking about tri-theism rather than Trinitarianism.

In Latin the word "*persona* originally meant a part played in social life, the social function of an individual in society, and then the occupier of such a role, part of a function. Thus, it was used of a role in a drama, or of the actor in that role."[5] The word was often employed in legal language, and it was the lawyer and theologian Tertullian who popularized the formula "one substance, three persons" to describe the Trinity.

In the eastern half of the empire, the corresponding Greek word to persona was *prosopa*, which was problematic. In earlier debates over modalism, prosopa was used to denote a temporary manifestation of the divine essence. Therefore, the role of Father, Son, or Spirit was not described as being an ongoing set of distinctions within the divine essence but an external appearance or manifestation that could be dropped or changed at the divine will. "Thus in the East another word *hypostasis*, properly the equivalent of the Latin *substantia* (substance), came to be used for each of the Three Persons of the Godhead, in the same sense as persona in the West."[6] This caused some linguistic confusion at times, but eventually the Eastern formula of "one substance in three hypostases" was seen as equivalent to the Western formula of Tertullian's "*Una substantia, tres personae.*"

In English there is no word similar to the exact meaning of persona or hypostasis. Those terms indicate something midway between abstract substance (the Latin substantia and Greek *ousia*) and concrete individual being. However, it is quite clear that "the modern English word 'person' suggests too much the idea of separate individual personalities," which is not what persona or hypostasis mean, while the words *mode, manifestation,* or *aspect* are too close to the heretical modalist viewpoint.[7] We simply do not have a modern English word that captures the patristic formulation of Trinitarian belief. It is imperative, however, that one keeps in mind that the language of hypostases was meant to avoid tri-theism (the danger of using "person" in the modern sense) as well as modalism (God assuming a temporary pose or function). God is one but is relational, permanently so, not just as a time-conditioned characteristic of God, and not merely functional—Creator, Redeemer, Sanctifier—but relational; hence the language of Father, Son, and Spirit. There is a lover, beloved, and the bond of love between them.

Perhaps we might think of the three "persons" of the Trinity as three eternal activities rooted in the one divine essence. God is eternally a loving Creator and parent, God's character is eternally that of Jesus Christ, and the Spirit's action is to be eternally inspiring, guiding, sustaining, and present in the world. This avoids modalism for these distinctions within the Godhead are not temporary nor simply related to the economic Trinity; this formulation is also less tri-theistic than what most believers mistakenly hold to be the orthodox teaching. In any event, "The historical doctrine of the Trinity commits us therefore to belief in the 'hypostatic' existence of Fatherhood, the character of Jesus and the activity of the Holy Spirit within the Godhead."[8] It does not commit us to belief in three persons in the modern sense of the word "person." What the church was doing in its efforts to speak about the Trinity was not to define or capture the Divine Mystery in human language; rather the aim of church doctrine was to eliminate misleading ways of talking about the Trinity, that is, modalism and tri-theism.

As much as there was unity among the early Church fathers on the Trinity "there is also a discernible difference between the theology of the Greek Fathers and the theology of the Latin Fathers."[9] For the Greek authors the focus was on the economic Trinity, God as experienced in salvation history, whereas the Latin patristic authors were prone to discussing the immanent Trinity, the inner life of God, the interrelation of Father, Son, and Spirit. Augustine fully exemplifies this latter approach. The problem was that by separating the economic from the immanent Trinity, the discussion, at least in the Western Church, became "a matter of abstract speculation alone, of no real pastoral importance" with little preaching or teaching on the topic in the life of the everyday Church.

The medieval scholastics, including Aquinas, did little to move understanding of the topic beyond the Augustinian position. Perhaps the major exception to this was the Victorine school led by Richard of St. Victor in the twelfth century. Rather than focusing on the divine nature, Richard examined the relationship of the "persons" and how humans might reflect that as images of God. The unselfish love of human beings bonded by friendship was posited as a reflection of the love between the Father, Son, and Spirit. Put simply, "in God there is one unselfish love and three infinite lovers: lover produces beloved, and lover and beloved are the productive principle of an equal co-beloved."[10] The Franciscans, Alexander of Hales and Bonaventure, took up the Victorine idea by talking about the inner life of God as characterized by perfect charity and that goodness shares or expands itself. Bonaventure emphasized expanding goodness and mutual love as the underlying principles of God's dynamism and plurality.

While holding onto the belief that there is one divine essence or substance, the Franciscan school also promoted the idea that because there is a unity of essence, there is a mutual indwelling of the hypostases or "persons." This idea, first introduced in the Eastern Church and called *perichoresis* in Greek, came to be known in the Latin West as *circumincession*. "Each one is in the other through an infinite communion, the common good of which is strictly and absolutely the proper good of each."[11] What is meant by "God" in the Catholic tradition is an eternally ongoing outpouring of the divine self (by the Father), an ongoing process of giving that is accepted and returned in a continual gift (by the Son), and the union of the Lover and Beloved is love, that is, *agape* (the Spirit). This is why the Catholic tradition maintains that in Jesus of Nazareth is seen the incarnation or embodiment of God. Jesus is God in human expression. If one wants to understand what Catholicism means by the word "God," look to Jesus of Nazareth.[12]

The significance of understanding the Trinity as a communion of self-giving love and its impact on relational thinking for the Catholic social imagination is difficult to overstate. As the International Theological Commission has written: "Created in the image of God to share in the communion of Trinitarian life, human beings are so constituted to be able freely to embrace this communion."[13] The emphasis on relational imagery in the Trinity has led to recent theological treatments named the "social model" of the Trinity.[14] This is a reflection on the mystery of God as self-giving love as revealed in the very nature of God as Trinitarian. The social model of the Trinity focuses on a theology of relationship, exploring "the mysteries of love, relationship, personhood, and communion within the framework of God's self-revelation in the person of Christ and the activity of the Spirit."[15] As Benedict XVI wrote in his encyclical on human development: "The Trinity is absolute unity insofar as the three divine Persons are pure relationality. The reciprocal transparency among the divine Persons is total and the bond between each of them complete, since they constitute a unique and absolute unity. God in Jesus desires to incorporate us into this reality of communion as well in his prayer: 'that they may be one even as we are one' (John 17:22)."[16]

A social theology of the Trinity highlights that the foundation and meaning of existence is to enter into communion with others. "In this regard, the Trinity is not just the origin and root of our existence, but also the ground, space and model of our social being."[17] To be a Christian is to live out the pattern of self-giving and mutual love that is at the heart of God's nature as a Trinity of Persons in one divine substance. As the bishops at Vatican II made clear, by our "innermost nature" humans are social beings, and unless we enter into relationships with others we cannot live well or develop our potential.[18]

The Trinity and the Imago Dei

Within the Christian tradition, any imaging of God must take as its starting point that God is Trinity. Christian belief in God as one and triune has direct repercussions for how we think about ourselves as humans. Since humans are made in the image of a Trinitarian God, then humans must be understood as made for communion with others. "That our God is a Trinity of Divine Persons points to our own communality; otherwise, we would not image our God."[19] And if our truest self-identity is that we are creatures made in the imago Dei, then we attain our truest and most authentic self by entering into and sustaining loving relationships with others, both God and fellow creatures.

Pope Francis captured what the image of God means for human life once it is understood that our God is Trinitarian.

> The divine Persons are subsistent relations, and the world, created to the divine model, is a web of relationships. Creatures tend towards God, and in turn it is proper to every living being to tend towards other things, so that throughout the universe we can find any number of constant and secretly interwoven relationships. This leads us not

only to marvel at the manifold connections existing among creatures, but also to discover a key to our own fulfillment. The human person grows more, matures more and is sanctified more to the extent that he or she enters into relationships, going out from themselves to live in communion with God, with others and with all creatures. In this way, they make their own that trinitarian dynamism which God imprinted in them when they were created.[20]

To be human is to be relational; there is no genuine human person who is not a person in relation. Therefore, it is essential for Christians to focus on both the range of their relations with others and what quality should characterize the way Christians relate to others.

LOVE AS THE CENTRAL QUALITY OF CHRISTIAN RELATIONSHIPS

The previous chapter showed that the early church came to understand that Jesus, the incarnate Son, was the true image of God. The disciple Philip wished to see the Father and was told by Jesus, "whoever has seen me has seen the Father. . . . Do you not believe that I am in the Father and the Father is in me?" (John 14:9–10). The faith of the early Christians was that Jesus was the clearest image of the living God. So after his conversion Paul develops an "insatiable thirst for knowledge about Jesus."[21] One feature of Paul's preaching about Jesus that differentiates him from other apostles is that he emphasized the way that Jesus died. Preaching in the early church regularly talked about the death of Jesus and the salvific meaning of that death "but remained resolutely silent on how Jesus died."[22] To preach a Messiah who had died the death of a traitor—crucifixion—must not have seemed the best way to invite new disciples. Yet Paul made the crucifixion the heart of his message.

It might be that Paul saw an issue that others did not grasp. "If Jesus was the Messiah, he should not have died."[23] Pious Jews did not expect the Messiah to die. When the Messiah came it would be for Israel the glorious climax to history. There was no speculation about what came next. So belief in a dead Messiah, one who died in such ignominy, would be a complete shock to the Jewish imagination. What Paul came to understand is that if death did come to a Messiah upon whom death had no claim, "then that person must have *chosen to die*."[24] Human beings understand that death comes to us all; we cannot avoid it. For Paul, however, what marks Jesus's death is that it was chosen, even though it was not necessary for God's Messiah. After Paul came to peace with the idea that Jesus's death was a freely chosen act of self-sacrifice, then "a dead sinless Messiah ceased to be a problem."[25]

It is noteworthy that Paul twice cites and augments liturgical hymns in his letters. In Philippians 2:8 he quotes, "he humbled himself and became obedient to the point of death," and then Paul added his own words, "even death on a cross." Then in Colossians 1:20 he cites another hymn, that "God was pleased to reconcile to himself all things" through Christ, which Paul interprets as meaning "making peace through the blood of his cross." Paul knew that in Judaism's history there had been many wise teachers of ethics and many wonder-workers who had performed healings. Jesus, however, was set apart from all these people for whom death was inevitable. "Thus Jesus' death became the key to the meaning of his life. It revealed to Paul that what makes a person genuinely human is the self-sacrificing love shown by Christ."[26] The nature of agape as love that seeks the good of the other is what Paul had in mind when in 1 Corinthians he wrote that "faith, hope, and love abide, these three; and the greatest of these is love" (1 Cor 13:13).

If the perfect image of God, Jesus, was the embodiment of self-sacrificing love, then that must be true of God as well. In the first letter of John, we read the claim, "God is love, and those who abide in love abide in God, and God abides in them" (1 John 4:16). This claim is repeated often throughout the New Testament, but perhaps most vividly and memorably in the parables of Jesus such as the story of the Prodigal Son (Luke 13:11–32), which, it has often been noted, is really the parable of the loving Father.

The story recounts a young man who asks for money from his father's estate and then goes off to squander his money in "dissolute living." Later, however, having fallen on hard times and reduced to working on a farm slopping pigs, "he came to himself" and realized that he would be better off working as one of his father's hired hands, for they "have bread enough and to spare, but here I am dying of hunger." And so the young man returns and seeks to be taken back as a worker. The father will have none of that abasement, and Luke tells the reader that "while he was still far off, his father saw him and was filled with compassion; he ran and put his arms around him and kissed him." The story continues with the father's directive to servants to fetch fresh clothes and sandals for the son, along with a ring for his finger, and then to prepare a celebratory feast. Readers will remember that Luke does not end the story there but moves onto the next scene in which the older brother returns from work and is angry that his ne'er-do-well brother has returned and been welcomed back so lavishly. The elder sibling is so angry that he refuses his father's invitation to enter and join the feast. This is, of course, a serious breach of etiquette and sign of disrespect toward his father, since in the ancient Near East for a person of lesser status to refuse an invite from a person of greater status was simply not done. Yet even in the face of such rude treatment the father speaks to his older child, "Son, you are always with me, and all that is mine is yours," but a celebration was necessary for your brother "was lost and is found."

The parable tells of two children, both of whom insult their father. The first, presuming he had a claim that as the younger son he did not legally have, says: "give me the share of the property that will belong to me." The son takes from the household's wealth what he had no proper claim to. Then he eventually returns, not motivated by remorse but by simple self-interest, because his father's workers got better treatment than he was receiving. Finally, the older brother engages in a public tantrum, no doubt seen by the servants, refusing to even enter his father's house. Luke makes the point that in both cases, the father goes out to both sons—running to embrace the younger, leaving the house to plead with the older. The father does not stand on protocol or social expectations of how sons should treat a father; the father speaks words of love and joy, forgiveness and compassion. Note, too, that the father does not argue with his elder son about the justice of his complaint; he merely brushes it aside because the father is uninterested in debating what is just. What the father is deeply interested in is love, agapic love of being a self-gift without tallying up who deserves this or that.

Recall, too, the context of Luke's parable: "the Pharisees and the scribes were grumbling" about Jesus's practice of table-fellowship with sinners (Luke 15:2). In reply to their challenge, Luke has Jesus tell the parables of the lost sheep and lost coin, and then the parable of the loving father. The point of all three stories is that Jesus acts the way he does toward "public sinners" because he has compassion and care for those that others would dismiss. And the reason he acts in this way is because that is how the Father acts toward sinners. The parable is a defense of Jesus's ministry to love those whom others consider unworthy of love.

The Lukan parables are a narrative telling of the teaching of Jesus found in Matthew's gospel in the Sermon on the Mount. Correcting the old teaching, "You shall love your neighbor and hate your enemy," Jesus says, "Love your enemies and pray for those who persecute you" (Matt 5:43–44). If his listeners wonder why they should adopt such a challenging teaching, Jesus encourages them to "be children of your Father in heaven; for he makes his sun rise on the evil and on the good, and sends rain on the righteous and on the unrighteous" (Matt 5:45).

Matthew's own parabolic telling of the nature of the Father's love is the story of the vineyard workers (Matt 20:1–16). A landowner goes out and hires workers at the beginning of the workday, and there is agreement on a fair daily wage. However, the landowner goes out on several other occasions during the day and hires more workers. When the time comes to pay the workers, the landowner starts with the most recently hired and gives them a full day's wage. Naturally, those at the back of the line, those who worked a full day, see this and expect to get a greater wage than the wage they had agreed to in the morning. Yet, to the consternation of those who had worked all day, they get the day's wage that had been mutually accepted. Complaints arise about working longer and harder, but the landowner does not back down: "Did you not agree with me for the usual daily wage? Take what belongs to you and go; I choose to give to this last the same as I give to you. Am I not allowed to do what I choose with what belongs to me: Or are you envious because I am generous?" (Matt 20:13–15). Arguments that try to restrict the generosity of the Father's love simply will not be accepted.

Love of God and Love of Neighbor

It is not only the broad scope of the Father's love that Jesus reveals in his ministry and preaching, but also the linkage of love of God with love of neighbor. Here the parable of the Good Samaritan in Luke's gospel (10:25–37) is a centrally important text. A lawyer asked Jesus what must be done to inherit eternal life, and Jesus replied with his own question, "What is written in the law? What do you read there?" The young man answered, "You shall love the Lord your God with all your heart, and with all soul, and with all your strength, and with all your mind, and your neighbor as yourself." Jesus commends him for this reply, but the young man pushes further, "and who is my neighbor?" Luke then has Jesus launch immediately into the parable of the unfortunate traveler from Jerusalem who fell among robbers on a trip to Jericho and was stripped, beaten, and left half-dead on the side of the road. Jesus tells of a priest and then a Levite who have the same reaction, crossing to the other side of the road to give the victim a wide berth as they passed. But a Samaritan, the hated distant cousin of the Jews, stopped to help the man and after bandaging his wounds took him to a place of safety and rest, paying for the expense of the care. Luke ends the story with Jesus asking the lawyer, who of the three on the road acted as neighbor to the victim, and the man's reply, "the one who showed him mercy." Jesus sends the lawyer off with the exhortation, "Go and do likewise."

Because this parable is among the best-known passages of the entire New Testament, there is a temptation to acknowledge the obvious lesson—the neighbor is everyone in need to whom we show compassion—and move on. But several other points about the story are worth noting. First, why mention the first two people who came upon the victim? And why add the detail that one was a priest, a religious leader, and the other was a Levite, an assistant in the temple? Second, what about the detail that both men passed by on the other side of the road? Third, what point is served by specifically mentioning that the story occurs on the road between Jerusalem and Jericho? The story's lesson about who is the neighbor could have been communicated if the robbery happened on any road, or if there were one or more passersby who were Jewish, or if they stepped over the man rather than cross the road. Might it be that there is another lesson to be learned from the parable?

The detail about the road being the one from Jerusalem to Jericho alerts Jesus's listeners to the fact that the priest and Levite on that road would have been going to or coming from the great temple in Jerusalem. Of course, that meant they either had or were about to offer worship to God. Why cross the road? Because the victim was bloodied, possibly dead. Touching or coming into physical contact with that bloodied body would have rendered the priest and Levite unclean, ritually impure, and incapable of participating in the temple's rites without purification. Now remember that the story is preceded by the dialogue between Jesus and the lawyer about the two great commandments to love God completely and to love the neighbor. The priest and Levite do not stop to help the victim because they are worried that such an act of neighborly love would pose an obstacle to their religious worship. The Samaritan does not have such religious scruples and cares for the victim. Certainly, the parable challenges us to expand our definition of who is our neighbor; but it also teaches us that anyone who thinks that they should avoid loving their neighbor because it would interfere with proper worship of God does not know who God is.

God is love; that is the revelation of Jesus about his Father. The two commandments are really one, as the writer of 1 John knew: "How does God's love abide in anyone who has the world's goods and sees a brother or sister in need and yet refuses to help?" (1 John 3:17). And later in the same letter: "Whoever does not love does not know God, for God is love" (1 John 4:8). The Johannine community knew the lesson of the parable of the Good Samaritan in Luke that defined the neighbor, but the community also knew the lesson that there is a union of love of God and neighbor in the teaching of Jesus. Lest a Christian disciple dismiss this second lesson as making too much of one parable, we can turn to another Gospel writer and another passage that has played a major role in the Catholic social imagination: the judgment of the nations found in Chapter 25 of Matthew's gospel.

In this pericope from Matthew's eschatological discourse, the Son of Man comes in glory to sit on the throne of judgment, separating the sheep from the goats. The criterion for distinguishing the two groups is made clear. The sheep are told by the Son of Man that "I was hungry and you gave me food, I was thirsty and you gave me something to drink, I was a stranger and you welcomed me, I was naked and you gave me clothing, I was sick and you took care of me, I was in prison and you visited me" (Matt 25:35). The goats, on the other hand, neglected to do all these things. What does *not* distinguish the one group from the other is any awareness that it was the Son of Man who was being treated with love or neglect. Not just the goats, but the sheep also ask, "When was it that we saw you hungry or thirsty or a stranger or naked or sick or in prison?" (Matt 25:44). The decisive factor was not directly serving the Lord in love but caring or not caring for "the least of these" with whom the Lord identifies. In other words, it is love of neighbor that is simultaneously and truly also love of God. The two commandments are one.

It is then more than a bit surprising when reflecting on Matthew's judgment scene that there is no overtly religious practice that is related to the judgment about membership in the sheep or goats. No question about church attendance, no query about whether one was married before a priest, no request to produce a baptismal certificate—nothing of that sort is determinative. The basis for judgment is agapic love: Did individuals give of themselves to those in need that they encountered? And the sheep did this not for the sake of Jesus, for they did not recognize his presence in the needy neighbor any more than the goats did. The test is simply, does one love one's brothers and sisters?

THE REIGN OF GOD AND THE NEW COMMUNITY

The central religious message of Jesus was his preaching and witness to the onset of the reign of God. In the first chapter of the first gospel, Mark recounts, in what exegetes call a summary verse, "Jesus came to Galilee, proclaiming the good news of God, and saying, 'The time is fulfilled, and the kingdom of God has come near; repent and believe in the good news'" (Mark 1:14–15). This brief text encapsulates the preaching of Jesus as he began his Galilean ministry: the reign or kingdom of God is at hand, and listeners ought to reform their lives and believe in the message of Jesus.[27]

Many who have studied the New Testament are aware of the two Greek words used for "time." There is time in the sense of the passing minutes, hours, and days that is designated as *chronos*, from which we get English words like *chronological* and *chronicle*. The other Greek word for time is *kairos*, and this is time in the sense of a moment that is pregnant with significance, a moment of decision, a time of existential choice. Kairos is a time of opportunity which must be faced, an action taken (or not) that will be decisive or determinative for one's life in some way. When Jesus spoke about the "time of fulfillment" in his preaching of the reign of God, the Greek word was kairos. The action to be taken in the kairos of Jesus's preaching God's reign was *metanoia* or in English, conversion. There are those who push the time of decision off to a later date, like those in the parable of the wedding feast who are invited but find various excuses for not attending, they "made light of it and went away, one to his farm, another to his business" (Matt 22:5). The fate of those who do not respond to Jesus's proclamation of the reign of God is clear: "everyone who hears these words of mine and does not act on them will be like a foolish man who built his house on sand" (Matt 7:26). When the bad weather comes, the house collapses and is ruined.

In Jesus's preaching there are parables for those who seize the kairotic moment as well. "The kingdom of heaven is like treasure hidden in a field, which someone found and hid; then in his joy he goes and sells all that he has and buys that field" (Matt 13:44).[28] Or again, "the kingdom of heaven is like a merchant in search of fine pearls; on finding one pearl of great value, he went and sold all that he had and bought it" (Matt 13:45–46). The persons portrayed in these parables have recognized the crucial moment in which they find themselves; they know the value of the reality that is before them and react appropriately—they give up all that they have to gain the object they have found. So, too, must all those who have been presented with the invitation to enter the reign of God: grasp the urgency of the moment of kairos and act.

Less well-known than the importance of understanding time for a disciple of Jesus is the significance of place in his message of God's reign. Yet just "as the reign of God has its kairos, its proper time, it also has its own *topos*, its place." The reign of God "is not a u-topia, which means 'no place, nowhere.'"[29] Rather, the reign of God must be made visible and manifested—it cannot remain an idea; it must be a historical reality in time *and* space. "That place is the people of God."[30] For Jesus that meant the people of Israel. God's reign extends over all the earth, indeed all creation, but God's rule "is revealed in Israel. It never manifests itself to the nations independently of Israel but always in connection with Israel and through Israel."[31]

In order for the reign of God to be a liberating experience, God cannot force or compel people to enter into it. That decision must be a human choice. And so "God 'starts out small,' beginning at a single place in the world. There must be a place—visible, comprehensible, subject to examination—where liberation and healing begin, that is, where the world can become what it is meant to be according to God's plan." And what will motivate and spur people to embrace this new reality is not moral pressure or human fear or magical fantasy, "but only the fascination of a world transformed."[32]

This method of inducing conversion was not lost on the early disciples. Paul's approach to instruction is similar in design. He does not demand obedience to law or commandment when speaking or writing in the imperative. Instead, he appeals to example, holding up a better way to live. An illustration of this is seen in the letter to Philemon regarding the runaway slave Onesimus. Paul writes, "though I am bold enough in Christ to command you to do your duty, yet I would rather appeal to you on the basis of love" (Philemon 8–9). Paul knew he had the authority within the community to compel Philemon to accept his demand that Onesimus be freed, yet he makes his teaching method clear: "but I preferred to do nothing without your consent, in order that your good deed might be voluntary and not something forced" (Philemon 14). This practice of holding up a more attractive way of life than the present one is the means to encourage transformation, and it stems from the conviction that seeing Christian community in practice will have an impact that will lead people to choose the better way of their own free will rather than by appeals to authority or law. Paul suggests to Philemon, "perhaps this is the reason he was separated from you for a while, so that you might have him back forever, no longer as a slave but more than a slave, a beloved brother—especially to me but how much more to you, both in the flesh and in the Lord" (Philemon 15–16). The new way of life must be chosen; even as Paul points out the benefit of having a "beloved brother" rather than a slave, it is for Philemon to choose that new way due to his changed heart and mind. "The constraint of a command makes a free choice impossible. If Philemon is to love Onesimus, the decision must be entirely his."[33]

The Old Testament, the only Bible Jesus knew, witnesses to the divine plan of finding a time and place where God's presence must become manifest. Following the cosmic prehistory of Genesis 1–11, the biblical narrative begins with the story of one individual, Abraham. No longer is the focus upon all of humanity, as in the Flood narrative or the tower of Babel story. "God begins to transform the world by starting anew, at a particular place in the world, with a single individual."[34] That individual will not be single for long, because along with Sarah he will be the origin of a great nation. The "end result must be a new society because redemption, salvation, peace, blessing have also—and indeed, primarily—a social dimension. At the very end of the Bible, we will find the image of the 'holy city,' the 'new Jerusalem' (Rev. 21)—and the city, the polis, was in antiquity the proper image of society."[35]

By the time of Second Isaiah, written at the period of the Babylonian captivity in the sixth century BCE, there is the dawning of an awareness that Israel was not chosen by God for Israel's own sake; instead it was chosen from the great number of nations, many more impressive and larger than the Hebrew nation, for the sake of those nations. This is the "burden of election" that lays with Israel. Israel exists for the sake of witnessing to the rest of the nations what God has in mind for all people: God's reign will extend over all the earth.

Has that election been voided in the New Testament? Has the unique and special role of a chosen people been replaced by "a vague and placeless universalism" that reveals God's presence in the world?[36] To think so is to overlook what the devout Jew, Jesus of Nazareth, did in his public ministry. A highly symbolic moment was his choice of the Twelve, "a demonstrative sign-action showing that Jesus cared about the twelve tribes of Israel. The Twelve are a visible sign and, of course, also an 'instrument' of his will to gather all Israel."[37] Jesus begins his ministry to the reign of God by creating a new people, a community of disciples within Israel. The visible embodiment of the reign of God begins with gathering the Twelve and will in time morph into the community of disciples that is the church. The church would be the "sacrament of the reign of God," a sign that would be a specific community, "a visible, tangible, graspable, definable, identifiable reality"[38] that bodied forth the presence of God in the world.

Early Christians and the Practice of Neighbor Love

The Christian community accepted the challenge of embodying the reign of God by adopting various practices that reflected the commitment to perform neighbor-love. As mentioned previously, when hearing the parable of the Good Samaritan there is a temptation to acknowledge the obvious lesson that the definition of the neighbor is everyone in need to whom we should show compassion and then move onto other thoughts. But we should not miss the important point of the centrality of the love commandment in the life of the disciple. And we might begin by considering first how surprising this commandment would have been to the vast majority of those living in the Roman Empire in the early decades of the church's life. Second, we should realize how vital was the Christian witness to that command for the growth of the Christian community within the empire.

On the first point, the social scientist Rodney Stark contrasted the love ethic of Christianity with pagan religion at the time and argued for the novelty of Christian belief that God cared for humans and cared about humans caring for each other.[39] "The simple phrase 'For God so loved the world ...' would have puzzled an educated pagan. And the notion that the gods care how we treat one another would have been dismissed as patently absurd."[40] Much of classical philosophy looked at mercy and pity as improper emotions that rational people ought to avoid. Indeed, "since mercy involves providing *unearned* help or relief, it was contrary to justice," reflecting a defect of character in the merciful.[41] Yet in such a moral environment, Christians believed and taught that mercy was a key virtue.

The belief that God loves humanity generated the corollary belief that Christians were not in right relationship with God unless they loved one another. And Stark suggests, "the principle that Christian love and charity must extend beyond the boundaries of family and tribe" and "even extend beyond the Christian community" was revolutionary.[42] A distinctive note that began with Judaism, "the linking of a highly *social* ethical code with religion,"[43] became even more influential due to Christianity's missionary evangelization that spread the message into the world of pagan Gentiles.

The gods of Greek and Roman religion did not issue or enforce ethical obligations among humans; "humans offended the gods only through neglect or by violation of ritual standards."[44] For a pagan worshipper, the concern was what service the god might supply if coaxed to do so by sacrifice. There was no expectation that God would feel love in response to the offering. The Greeks and Romans had an ethical code of virtues, but the virtues did not originate with a divine command and were not reinforced by divine order.

In a chapter entitled "Epidemics, Networks, and Conversions," Stark relates the impact of two major epidemics upon the Roman Empire. In the middle of the second century, during the reign of Marcus Aurelius, between a fourth to a third of the entire population of the empire—including the emperor—died in what medical historians believe was the first appearance of smallpox in the West. This was followed by a second devastating epidemic in the middle of the third century—this time possibly measles—which led to significant mortality in rural as well as urban areas. Through his careful study of both the patristic authors and pagan historians, Stark demonstrates that "pagan communities did not match Christian levels of benevolence during the epidemics, since they did not even do so in normal times when the risks entailed by benevolence were much lower."[45] What accounts for this difference? Stark's reading of the literature at the time suggests that Christian values had from the outset encouraged moral norms of charitable service and communal solidarity. And this was due to the surprising claim of Christians regarding their God. What was new, according to Stark, was "the notion that more than self-interested exchange relations were possible between humans and the supernatural."[46]

On the second point regarding the impact of the love ethic of the early church on Christianity's growth, there were at least three reasons why this growth was the consequence of the behavior of disciples. First, during the epidemics, Christians had lower mortality rates than the general population because of their care for one another. Second, there is evidence that there was an increase in conversions to Christianity among pagan survivors of the epidemics in a spirit of gratitude for the charitable work of the Christian community in saving them. Finally, there was also an increased esteem among the general population for the kindness and care of Christians, whose witness increased interest in the gospel message.[47] Stark does not maintain that Christian behavior during the epidemics was the single or even most important cause for the growth of Christianity, but he makes a good case that the seriousness with which early disciples practiced the love commandment had a real impact across the Roman Empire.

There is also evidence that Christians understood that their witness to certain values, like mercy, made an impact on the wider culture around them. The author of 1 Peter wrote to several Christian communities, mainly Gentile, scattered around Asia Minor: "Live such good lives among the pagans that, though they accuse you of doing wrong, they may see your good deeds and glorify God. . . . For it is God's will that by doing good you should silence the ignorant talk of foolish people" (1 Peter 2:12, 15). The author maintained that the behavior of Christians "will be observed by others as illustrative of what one can expect in a Christ assembly."[48]

The gospel of John's portrayal of the Last Supper of Jesus with his disciples has no account of the institution of the eucharist but contains the dramatic scene of Jesus washing the feet of his disciples and then speaking to them about how they are to live by underscoring his service and love for them. "A new commandment I give you: love one another. As I have loved you, so you must love one another. By this everyone will know that you are my disciples, if you love one another" (John 13:34–35).

This emphasis on mutual love and service as a hallmark of Christian community continued beyond the apostolic age into the patristic period.

Justin Martyr, writing in the middle of the second century, offered a defense of Christianity to the Roman emperor, Antoninus Pius, that included the contributions to the empire made by Christian practices. "We, who loved above all else the ways of acquiring riches and possessions, now hand over to a community fund what we possess and share it with every needy person."[49] And Tertullian, writing later in the second century, reflects the vitality of the North African church in his appeal to the emperor Septimius Severeus for legal toleration of Christianity: "Our care for the derelict and our active love have become our distinctive sign before the enemy. . . . See, they say, how they love one another and how ready they are to die for each other."[50] As Peter Phan has observed, "Both from Christian and pagan sources, it is clear that the practical exercise of charity towards a needy brother in the faith or towards a pagan afflicted with illness or misfortunes was an undeniable title of glory in the early church."[51]

In his recent detailed study of the way that small associations of Christians operated in the empire, Kloppenborg gives support to Stark's assessment of Christian behavior during epidemics: "Christians did not flee the city as many others did, but remained to take care of the sick, including their pagan neighbors. Those pagans who had been aided and survived not only would have had a strong demonstration of 'costly signaling' but would have been morally indebted to Christians."[52] The significance of the foregoing citations is not to argue that Christians had a simple monopoly on virtue but to propose that "central doctrines of Christianity prompted and sustained attractive, liberating, and effective social relations and organizations" throughout the Roman Empire.[53] There was a clear and determining connection between what Christians believed and what they understood was expected of their behavior. Perhaps one of the most powerful doctrines for shaping Christian behavior was the belief that all disciples were joined together as part of one faith community that foreshadowed and anticipated what ought to be true for all people.

The Body of Christ

"[I]t is no longer I who live, but it is Christ who lives in me. And the life I now live in the flesh I live by faith in the Son of God, who loved me and gave himself for me" (Gal 2:20). Here we see the same theme noted earlier, that Paul saw in Jesus a Messiah who chose to die in order to express the self-sacrificial nature of Christian love. Because that is the nature of Christ's fidelity, when Paul engages in agapic love he is making Christ present in the world. This is true for all faithful disciples because by baptism the disciples have been clothed in Christ and have become one in Christ.

According to Murphy-O'Connor, "this insight was a radical breakthrough in Paul's understanding of the relationship between Christ and his followers."[54] It led to Paul developing and highlighting the metaphor of the Christian community as the body of Christ. "For just as the body is one and has many members, and all the members of the body, though many, are one body, so it is with Christ" (1 Cor 12:12). This unity of the body of Christ also leads to Paul's insistence that there is equality among the baptized since "in the one Spirit we were all baptized into one body—Jews or Greeks, slaves or free—and we were all made to drink of one Spirit" (1 Cor 12:13). There are no degrees of being baptized: there is one baptism shared by all. Finally, the initial insight of Paul also reveals the mission of the Christian community in the world. Christians are to be the very body of Christ in the world, bringing into temporal existence the compassion, forgiveness, inclusivity, and loving service that Jesus himself preached and embodied during his life walking on the earth.

Reading the Pauline letters, it is evident that the Apostle used the metaphor of the body of Christ in several ways, referring to the physical flesh of Jesus, the eucharistic presence, and the Christian assembly. "In the last sense it is a figurative way of expressing the corporate identity of Christians with Christ." Fitzmeyer points out that this usage first appears in 1 Corinthians where Paul appeals to the local Christian community to overcome its divisions. "The symbol of unity is the figure of the body with its members."[55] In that context, it appears that Paul used the image as a claim for moral unity striving for a shared good (1 Cor 12:7). However, in other places within the letter Paul appeals to another sense of the term. In 1 Corinthians 6:15 he writes about defilement of the body due to sexual license and that the believer's union with Christ is more than moral but entails becoming "one flesh." Fitzmeyer asserts that "Paul is not speaking merely of members of a society governed by a common objective, but of members of Christ himself; their union is not only corporate, but somehow corporal." Something similar comes up in the tenth chapter of the letter where Paul discusses the unity arising from the eucharist; it entails more than a "union effected by cooperation to attain a common good."[56] Later authors in the tradition would call this meaning of the body of Christ the "mystical body," but that is not an expression that Paul used. "The ontological reality that is the basis of the union is the possession of the Spirit of Christ: 'We have all been baptized in one Spirit to form one body' (1 Cor 12:13; Rom 8:9–11)."[57]

In the letter to the Colossians, one finds further development of the body metaphor. In the hymn that is central to the first chapter, the theme introduced is that "Christ is the head of the body, the church," (Col 1:18a), which is "the logical extension of the insight of Galatians"[58] that believers "are all one in Christ Jesus." It would seem the author of Colossians very much had his words to the Galatians in mind in light of the "extremely close parallel"[59] between verse 3:28 of Galatians and Colossians 3:11 where we read, "there is no longer Greek nor Jew, circumcised and uncircumcised, barbarian, Scythian, slave and free; but Christ is all and in all!"

In the letter to the Romans, Paul's most systematic presentation of his thought, he discusses the meaning and implications of the Christian community as the body of Christ. The body is one and yet diverse: "For as in one body we have many members, and not all the members have the same function, so we, who are many, are one body in Christ, and individually we are members one of another. We have gifts that differ according to the grace given to us" (Rom 12:4–6a). The body's unity is found in its fidelity to live as Christ did. Its members should "love one another with mutual affection." They are called to "live peaceably with all." They are to love their enemies, "if your enemies are hungry, feed them; if they are thirsty, give them something to drink" (Rom 12:10, 18, 20). The motive for such a life of loving service is simple: "We do not live to ourselves, and we do not die to ourselves. If we live, we live to the Lord, and if we die, we die to the Lord; so then, whether we live or whether we die, we are the Lord's" (Rom 14:7–8). The body of Christ, the community of disciples, "should be animated by the self-sacrificing love that Christ showed on the cross."[60]

The source of Paul's use of the "body" metaphor is not certain. There had been a long tradition in Greek political philosophy of society as the body politic. Yet one commentator suggests, "it is psychologically impossible" that Paul would employ as a description of the church the same term used to characterize a society that he thought of as deeply divided by all sorts of distinctions of class, ethnicity, gender, religion, political status, and philosophies.[61] After all, it was fidelity to self-giving love that was the hallmark of Christian community in his mind. Perhaps Paul was jolted into thinking of the church as a "body" by reflecting on the most memorable feature of the temples of Aesclepius that were to be found all about the region of the Eastern Mediterranean.[62] These temples dedicated to the Greek god of medicine were a consequence of a cult that grew up around Aesclepius and his gift of healing.

The various sites usually had areas for exercise, baths, healthy foods, and consults with physicians. We might think of them as centers of holistic medicine. As the cult grew, more temples were built, and they became study centers for aspiring physicians. A common feature of the temples was ceramic representations of various parts of the body that had been cured. The sight of these reproductions of limbs could have moved "Paul to the realization that a leg was truly a leg only when part of a body. Believers, he inferred, were truly 'alive' only when they 'belonged' to Christ as his members. The body of Christ metaphor captured Paul's belief that being caught up in one's own egocentricity and isolation was a form of death but to be part of the body of Christ was to be engaged in a life of shared existence."[63]

While the metaphor of the body of Christ is distinctively Pauline, it points to a reality that was accepted by other New Testament writers. In the opening verses of the fifteenth chapter of John's Gospel there is the allegory of the vine and the branches. "Abide in me as I abide in you. Just as the branch cannot bear fruit by itself unless it abides in the vine, neither can you unless you abide in me. I am the vine, you are the branches" (John 8:4–5a). This mutual indwelling of Jesus with his disciples is a theme that appears in several of the extended addresses of Jesus in John's gospel; "mutual love and unity … are the focal points of the discourses."[64] The Johannine vine and branches imagery shows that decades after Paul's use of the body of Christ, the theme of Christ's relationship with his disciples as being one of loving union remained in the Christian imagination.

THE EXPERIENCE OF COMMUNITY IN THE EARLY CHURCH

The New Testament scholar Wayne Meeks has written about "the grammar of Christian practice." By that expression he means the social practices that "shaped and reinforced and gave meaning to the moral sensibilities of the early Christians."[65] Meeks groups the social practices of early Christianity into four categories: rituals, admonitions and sanctions, hospitality and control, and almsgiving.[66] In this sub-section I will discuss these categories, but will focus mainly on the importance of rituals, two in particular. Rituals are quintessentially social acts. Meeks proposes that we understand ritual as "a condensed action" the purpose of which is "to focus and concentrate meaning so that what is done in this nexus of sacred time and space ripples out onto all prior and subsequent doing" in the world beyond the community.[67]

Baptism in the Christian Community

The most oft-cited ritual throughout the literature of early Christianity was baptism. It was the ritual that, according to Paul, transformed Christians in their identity and life.

> Do you not know that all of us who have been baptized into Christ Jesus were baptized into his death? Therefore we have been buried with him by baptism into death, so that, just as Christ was raised from the dead by the glory of the Father, so we too might walk in newness of life. . . . We know that our old self was crucified with him so that the body of sin might be destroyed, and we might no longer be enslaved to sin. For whoever has died is freed from sin. (Rom 6:3–4, 6–7)

At the very earliest stage of Christianity's development, a rite of passage was created that symbolized a convert's separation from his or her earlier life and place in society to a new way of living and the entry into a new social nexus; a convert left the family of birth and became part of a new family with new brothers and sisters and with a new divine Father.

Meeks employs the examples of an immigrant who leaves behind homeland and existing relationships and must assimilate into a new homeland or a child who undergoes the process of enculturation into a family.[68] The Athenian Christian Aristedes wrote a defense of Christianity in the 130s or 140s describing his fellow Christians as an *ethnos*, a people or nation. Clearly, they were not a nation in the literal sense of ethnos, but the description stuck not only with critics of Christianity but also with Christians themselves. Christians did understand themselves as a distinct group, a community unlike others, with its own way of perceiving reality and living in a distinctive manner or way.[69] Indeed, "the way" was an early term for Christianity. Christians also referred to themselves as a *politeuma*, a term used to denote "an organized body of immigrants, resident aliens, for example Jews in a Greek city."[70]

Too often modern portrayals of conversion see it as an individual forging a new set of beliefs or values that involves a lonely struggle. However, the research of the religious sociologist Rodney Stark has suggested that more often conversion entails a person entering into a new set of relationships that lead to new self-understanding. People develop new loyalties and attachments and conform their beliefs and actions in order to maintain the acceptance, approval, and benefits that come with the new relationships.[71] Early Christianity provided social networks that offered "a structure of direct and intimate interpersonal attachments"[72] that effectively created a change in a convert's "primary reference groups" by "resocialization into an alternative community."[73]

Early Christian communities brought about a new baptismal identity for converts by processes of pre- and post-baptismal catechesis and preparation. Meeks suggests that when one examines the description of these processes its looks less like the moral reformation of individuals and more like the entrance into a cult. The difference is that in pagan cults what was protected were the sacred rites and space. "In Christian initiation, what is to be kept pure is the *community*."[74] And purity is viewed not only in terms of belief but also in moral terms. So when Paul includes moral exhortations in various letters, they are not ethical norms selected without any context but are teachings that arise out of the Christian convert's experience and the relationship Paul's readers have with him, each other, and the wider Christian movement. The question of morality is treated as a question of loyalty to a community.

By the time that Paul wrote Romans, likely in the summer of 56 CE or a bit later, "baptism is presupposed as a universal identity marker in Pauline assemblies."[75] Again and again, Paul will remind those who received his letters that they have undergone a conversion and been baptized into the death and new life of Jesus. One sees the language not only in Romans, but also in 1 Corinthians where he recounts the old lives led by members of the community—robbers, drunkards, adulterers, slanderers, and so on—and then adds, "this is what some of you used to be. But you were washed, you were sanctified, you were justified in the name of our Lord Jesus Christ and in the Spirit of our God" (1 Cor 6:11). Similar ideas and language can be found in the letters to the churches in Colossae and Ephesus. "All these letters are filled with language that recalls the ritual of baptism, with its images of transformation or rebirth, the restoration of primal unity, the taking off of the 'old human' with the vices thereunto adhering, and the putting on of the 'new human' characterized by the virtues that belong to one who is being remade 'after the image of the creator,' or, in the idiom of 1 Peter, the making of the people of God out of a 'nonpeople.'"[76] Throughout Paul's writing, baptism is treated not as an individual experience but as a rite that "marks the individual's *entry into a corporate identity*. Paul speaks of being baptized *into one body*, which creates a new identity."[77]

Eucharist and the Christian Community

If baptism is the ritual of conversion, then the other great ritual for Christians was eucharist, the sacrament of group integration. Baptism was a one-time ritual, but the Lord's Supper was a ritual celebrated regularly and, therefore, an ongoing means of fostering the identity appropriate to believers. The ideal acting-out of who Jesus is—the self-revelation of God—is found in the sacrament of the eucharist: Jesus is the one who gives himself away fully and without condition. The eucharist reveals Jesus as the one who will be body broken and blood poured out for others. By participating in the eucharistic ritual, Christians come to know who Jesus is, the perfect revelation of who the Father is: agape or self-giving love. The Johannine texts make it abundantly clear; God is love; "everyone who loves is born of God and knows God. Whoever does not love does not know God, for God is love" (1 John 4:7–8).

Sound eucharistic theology tells us that the sacrament is not something to be stared at, but an event in which to participate. Entering into the eucharistic ritual means participating in the very acting out of the nature of God, as pure self-gift. That is what the tradition means when it says that the Spirit of God dwells within us. "The Spirit does not dwell in us as in a box or container." We are not inert or passive if we genuinely participate in the sacrament of the eucharist; rather, "the spirit energizes, the Spirit is what activates"[78] the power of agapic love in the lives of all those who join in the ritual of becoming the body and blood of Christ.

From the onset when Christ told his disciples at the Last Supper to "Do this in memory of me," the Christian community has relived his death and resurrection in the eucharistic ritual. And that remembering of the Paschal mystery is also a "re-membering" of the body of Christ, a reconstitution of the body that was broken and the blood that was shed for the life of others. As members of Christ's body, disciples are meant to be the expression of his Incarnation, his life, death, and resurrection in the world. Disciples participate in the eucharist not only by receiving the blessed elements of bread and wine but by becoming the Body of Christ that is consumed; the Christian community is to embody the same pattern of giving one's life for others as Christ did.

In his scholarly research on the nature and role of associative practices throughout the classical world, Kloppenborg observes, "Communal meals are perhaps the most commonly attested practices of associations, including Christ assemblies."[79] In 1 Corinthians 5:11 Paul speaks of the communal meal as the place to draw the distinction between who is a true member of the community and who is not.[80]

Interestingly, even among non-Christian associations, the ritual of eating together was central for promoting social interaction and group identity.

In most cases the menu was simple bread and wine, for the purpose of the meal was not the menu but the practice of eating together. "The point of the meal was not to dine sumptuously but to *see oneself* as dining with the group and to *let others see it*."[81] In many associations, not only those who were Christian, putting on an expensive banquet would have limited the number of times the group could meet. The modest nature of the menu underscores that something else was going on besides dining. The aim of the meal ritual was "to draw attention to the performance itself, performance in which all participate and everyone has a role to play. Eating becomes an orchestrated *communal* practice that recasts an ordinary human activity as a ritual of belonging."[82]

Among groups that would have been constituted by people of various ethnicities, different gender, and unequal social status, it was particularly important to have a ritual of a common table shared by "people who otherwise would not dine together."[83] The Antioch church suffered from religious divisions between Jew and Gentile, but the Corinthian church was also divided, in its case by social status.

> Now in the following instructions I do not commend you, because when you come together it is not for the better but for the worse. For, to begin with, when you come together as a church, I hear that there are divisions among you; and to some extent I believe it. Indeed, there have to be factions among you, for only so will it become clear who among you are genuine. When you come together, it is not really to eat the Lord's supper. For when the time comes to eat, each of you goes ahead with your own supper, and one goes hungry and another becomes drunk. What! Do you not have homes to eat and drink in? Or do you show contempt for the church of God and humiliate those who have nothing? What should I say to you? Should I commend you? In this matter I do not commend you! (1 Cor 11:17–34)

Apparently, this was not a situation unique to the Christians in Corinth. The letter of James also has a sharp critique of gatherings where the wealthy are treated better than the poor when they assemble as a community (James 2:1–60). Such action undercuts the very purpose of the meal ritual, for "communal meals functioned as performances of belonging, making the group visible to itself, articulating who belonged and who did not."[84] In sum, the most common ritual of the early Christian assembly was a meal together that encouraged members to see each other as one, united together as members of the body of Christ celebrating a memorial Last Supper at which Jesus declared his body was to be broken and his blood shared as an act of self-giving love.

Additional Practices of Christian Community Building

In addition to rituals, Meeks notes other important elements of everyday life that Christians engaged in, which taught them about self-identity and moral practice. Admonitions and sanctions were practices that aimed at reducing behavior that went against community standards and expectations. Christianity was a movement of letter writers, and the preponderance of those letters were exhortatory in whole or in part.[85] Moral exhortation was hardly unknown in the classical world, but in the philosophical schools it was addressed to students by teachers. Among Christians the practice was mutual. Ordinary people would address one another in Christian communities; exhortation was not restricted to elites. Just as in households there would be moral training and advice passed on from adults to children, so in household churches of urban Christianity it was seen as natural to offer moral admonitions. The difference was that such moral instruction did not come from the male head of the household or the hired tutor of children, for "the glimpses of Christian meetings that we get from the letters show us communities of mutual admonition."[86] So, too, were the sanctions imposed of a communal nature, the most severe being the practice of the group shunning a person who was resistant to correction and reform.

Christianity was, of course, a missionary religion. There was a divine mandate to spread the gospel message to all nations that Paul and other itinerant Christian preachers and teachers took to heart. It would have been extremely taxing for Christian itinerants to sustain their work if they could not depend upon being welcomed by Christian communities on their journeys. Hospitality is an important virtue in any culture where being an outsider or alien leaves one beyond the ordinary circle of protection and care. Among Christians the virtue of hospitality was especially prized because it allowed settled communities to support the missionary work of those who were welcomed, but also because it established ties between fellow Christians beyond the local church.

An additional expression of solidarity both beyond and within the local church was the routine custom of almsgiving. An excellent illustration of this practice, done in the context of table fellowship, is found in Justin Martyr's description of a typical Sunday eucharist.

> When we have finished the prayer, bread is brought, and wine and water, and the president similarly sends up prayers and thanksgiving to the best of his ability, and the congregation assents, saying the Amen; the distribution, and reception of the consecrated [elements] by each one, takes place and they are sent to the absent by the deacons. Those who prosper, and who so wish, contribute, each one as much as he chooses to. What is collected is deposited with the president, and he takes care of orphans and widows, and those who are in want on account of sickness or any other cause, and those who are in bonds, and the strangers who are sojourners among [us], and briefly, he is the protector of all those in need.[87]

The crucial importance of giving alms beyond the local church is abundantly attested to in Paul's writing regarding the collection for the Jerusalem church. The poverty of Jerusalem was well-known throughout the Jewish world, with as many as two-thirds of the population supported by charity, either public or private. During his visit to Jerusalem in 51 CE, Paul was asked by James, Cephas, and John to continue to provide a subsidy from the church in Antioch.[88] Although Paul had broken with that community over the influence of the Judaizers, he resolved to continue financial assistance to Jerusalem by appealing to other churches he founded.

The idea of taking up a collection within occupational guilds, ethnic or immigrant associations, and other communal organizations was common in antiquity. Paul, however, was doing something different than what Gentile Christians would have known in their culture. First, collections were typically not "organized for the benefit of residents of a city or members of an association other than that of the donors themselves." Second, collections were not "normally framed as relief for 'the poor'"; such a special collection would have been curious to many Greeks. Finally, Paul made a point that the collection was not just for the 'poor,' but "as a collection for members of a *different* ethnic group."[89] In other words, collections as they were known in the world at Paul's time did not cross boundaries of geography, ethnicity, or class. Yet, early Christians practiced almsgiving in ways that did just that. The Jerusalem collection was transgressive, violating "boundaries of several cultural practices current in the Greek world . . . [the collection] functioned as a way for individual groups to perform membership in a broader identity."[90]

Communal Identity and Membership in the Early Church

The themes of identity and membership are important for understanding the powerful attraction of early Christian communities. Christianity arose at a time when many people of the classical world were experiencing the disorientation that came after the collapse of the Greek city-states and then later, the Roman Republic. The ideals of the city-state had become somewhat irrelevant with the demise of those political centers and the rise of empires like Alexander's. Even after his death, the various kingdoms overseen by his generals were far larger and less human scale than what prior generations had known. When the Roman Republic was transformed into an empire, it then included a broadly diverse population of multiple languages, religions, histories, customs, and ethnicities. People now had to learn how to live without the intense civic participation of the city-state or without the personal interaction of a republic but within a massive empire in which the lone individual seemed very small and of no account.

In such a social context, the philosophy of Stoicism had appeal as a counter to the feeling of isolation in a vast, impersonal world. People felt as if they faced the world alone and looked for a sense of belonging in a large world. But now, because there was little sense of nationality or locality, people found themselves reflecting on their shared or common condition as individual persons. Stoicism suggested that there was a "Great State" to which all belonged and emphasized the idea of personal morality as a responsibility of being a member of the human community.

Of course, stoicism arose among the Greeks, but by the time it had filtered into the Roman Empire, the movement had abandoned the city-state as the locus for political theory with its provincialism and rigid distinctions between citizens, foreigners, and slaves, as well as a notion of citizenship restricted only to those who would participate in actual governance. It reinterpreted political ideals to fit the new context of the "Great State" by outlining a worldwide sense of humanity, united by an understanding of justice broad enough to encompass all and holding up the idea of natural equality among people. So the "Great State," no less than the intimate city-state had a claim upon the loyalty of people and was not just a creature of force and coercion.

This revised stoicism of the Roman kind preserved the best of Roman ideals defined by a broad sympathy, good will, and gentleness of reason and moderation. This spirit that the Romans called *humanitas* is a corrective to a crude view of Rome drunk with power and conquest, with little regard for taste or the world of ideas. Hence, stoicism was music to the ears of the Roman nobility and the political elites of the empire.

At the same time a variety of religious movements within the ancient world sought to address the new situation in a vein similar to Stoicism. From this arose a sensibility of a human nature that was more or less the same for all. People were invited to reflect upon what united them with one another rather than what set them apart. Such a context helps us understand the popular appeal of Christian community. As Kloppenborg suggests, "conversion is better understood as a social phenomenon and has more to do with the realignment of *social* connections than it does with individual psychology. Conversion is not just a matter of the soul or mind but of one's social and affective alignments."[91] What membership in the early church offered was "connectivity: the creation of a social space in which people unrelated by blood could be connected with peers, with people of higher station via patronage, with people of different ethnic identities, with people of differing legal statuses, and with other locales either within a city or in other cities."[92]

Apart from the profoundly religious dimension of Christian gatherings, there was a very human need for social networks. This need was intensely felt in the first century CE. Without assuming that all social networks operate in the exact same manner, it remains true that one of the most important aspects of a social network is that it builds social capital, a sense of belonging and of worth. "But most importantly, the connectivity that is intrinsic to network membership creates trust among members because of shared values and pursuits."[93]

This last point reminds us that the virtue of faith had a connotation in the early church that has largely been lost. Today, we tend to equate faith as belief in some doctrine, a propositional content associated with the belief system. That "stands in marked contrast to the conception of *pistis/fides* at least before Augustine in the fifth century. *Pistis* in Greek and *fides* in Latin had the primary connotations of the 'loyalty' that was basic to relationships within families, between citizens and their leaders, between the army and the emperor, and between people and their gods."[94] Without denying that in the usage of Christian communities there was a substantive content to pistis/fides, it remains true that in those assemblies, "*pistis* is not just a matter of affirming 'I believe that x is true,' but rather of showing faithfulness or loyalty."[95] Membership in a network of relationships that built and maintained social trust among the group was a richly attractive dimension of Christianity's appeal to people in the ancient world.

An additional note about the language of the early Christian communities was the use of familial expressions. In the Pauline communities there was frequent language referring to Christians as children of God and also of the apostle. Although the terms for "brother' and "sister" occur more often in Paul's letters, they did show up in much of early Christian literature.[96] "James, 1 Clement, and 2 Clement show that the members are routinely addressed with the vocative, *adelphoi*."[97] There is also constant reference to God as "father" and Christians as adopted sons and daughters or heirs. Without denying the problematic consequences of so closely linking God-language with male imagery in the imagination, there was a positive aspect to the practice. "For one thing, relatedness itself is valued; to become a Christian was to be adopted into a new family or even to be 'born anew' with a divine parent and new siblings."[98]

The commitment to connectivity, to the life of a community, to a personal relationship with God and neighbor was at the center of early Christian understanding. It is both reflected in and instilled by a series of communicative practices that reinforce a way of self-understanding in the believer. The practices are communal, and "they are means of reminding individuals even when alone that they are not merely devotees of the Christian's God, they are members of Christ's body, the people of God.[99] The reality of community played a vital role in the social imagination of the early disciples.

CONCLUSION

The Catholic church maintains that it has been constituted by the action of the Spirit. Baptism is the ritual whereby one moves into a new set of relationships, acknowledging communion with the Trinity—the baptismal formula includes the invocation of the Father, Son, and Holy Spirit—along with communion with other believers and brothers and sisters in faith. Just as God is constituted as three persons in one, so the disciple is constituted by the grace of baptism to be in communion with the entire Body of Christ. Through participation in the life of that Body it is possible to grow in virtue and human flourishing through membership in a communal infrastructure that shapes personal identity and moral values.

One consequence of the communitarianism in Catholic social teaching is that disciples are encouraged to give attention to the responsibilities, conditions, and elements that are necessary for community life to flourish, with the assumption that successful community promotes the well-being of individual persons. Communities also provide an orientation to the moral world. Christians do not so much *seek* a social vision as they *encounter* one through their relationships with other people who are already participants in the life of the Body of Christ.

To use a metaphor of the distinguished political philosopher Sheldon Wolin, community functions as "the connective thread"[100] in the Catholic tradition that brings together an array of ideas about social life along with guidance for the emphasis that ought to be placed on those ideas. Indeed, Wolin suggests that "Christianity succeeded where the Hellenistic and late classical philosophies had failed, because it put forward a new and powerful ideal of community which recalled men to a life of meaningful participation." It is not that everything about that ideal always worked for the good of political thought in the West, but the ideals of solidarity and membership embedded in the Christian vision of community "were to leave a lasting imprint."[101] That the lasting imprint profoundly shaped the tradition of Catholic social thought will be demonstrated in the following chapters.

NOTES

1. Vatican II, *Gaudium et spes*, n. 32
2. National Conference of Catholic Bishops, *Economic Justice for All*, 1986, Pastoral Message, n. 14.
3. A helpful and clear treatment of the theology of the Trinity is found in Chapter 10 of Richard McBrien's *Catholicism*, vol. 1, 343–365.
4. Richardson, *Creeds*, 58.
5. Richardson, 60.
6. Richardson, 60.
7. Richardson, 61.
8. Richardson, 64.
9. McBrien, *Catholicism*, 348.
10. McBrien, 349–350.
11. Jacques Maritain, *The Person and the Common Good*, 58.
12. Here something must be said about the language commonly used in Trinitarian theology. As Wayne Meeks has written: "That Yahweh was the father of Israel was a firm element in Israel's covenant tradition," and it is "no wonder" that the word 'Father' came easily to the minds of early Christian authors. It was, indeed, the common way that Jesus spoke of God. Beyond the Hebraic background, "the patriarchal household of the Greco-Roman cities" provided the common models of authority, power, and leadership that Gentile Christians knew (Meeks, *The Origins of Christian Morality*, 170). The negative dimension of patriarchal imagery for God in the Christian tradition has become ever clearer in our contemporary experience, and the problem of sexist language for God and the adoption of a patriarchal perspective within Catholic social thought is a damaging consequence that remains to be satisfactorily addressed.
13. ITC, "Communion and Stewardship," n. 44.
14. Anne Hunt, *Trinity*, 177.
15. Hunt, 178.

16. Benedict XVI, *Caritas in veritate*, n.54.

17. Severine Deneulin and Augusto Zampini Davies, "Life Lived to the Full," 11.

18. Vatican II, *Gaudium et spes*, n.12.

19. Thomas Groome, *Faith for the Heart*, 190.

20. Francis, *Laudato Si'*, n.240.

21. Jerome Murphy-O'Connor, *Paul*, 34.

22. Murphy-O'Connor, 34.

23. Murphy-O'Connor, 35.

24. Murphy-O'Connor, 36.

25. Murphy-O'Connor, 36.

26. Murphy-O'Connor, 37.

27. The kingdom or reign of God is an expression referring to God's rule over creation. Perhaps the word *presence* conveys the intention of the reign of God; God is present in the inner life of the individual, in the experience of communities, and throughout the world; a presence that blesses, heals, frees, and redeems. The reign of God is both a process and the goal toward which the process is directed. I prefer to use "'reign" instead of "kingdom" not only to avoid the gendered term but also because the language of "reign" is more dynamic or active in its meaning.

28. The substitution of "heaven" for "God" in the verse about the kingdom reflects the Jewish piety of Matthew and his audience who prefer respectful circumlocutions rather than overuse of God's name.

29. Gerhard Lohfink, *Jesus of Nazareth*, 40.

30. Lohfink, 40.

31. Lohfink, 44.

32. Lohfink, 45.

33. Murphy-O'Connor, *Paul*, 119.

34. Lohfink, *Jesus of Nazareth*, 45.

35. Lohfink, 46.

36. Lohfink, 47.

37. Lohfink, 47.

38. Lohfink, 56.

39. Rodney Stark, *The Rise of Christianity*. The word *pagan* is used in a nonpejorative sense by Stark (and myself). Christianity was mainly an urban movement. Hence, the Latin word *paganus* meaning a country or rural inhabitant came to be the term referring to non-Christians.

40. Stark, 211.

41. Stark, 212.

42. Stark, 212.

43. Stark, 86.

44. Stark, 88.

45. Stark, 84.

46. Stark, 86.

47. Stark, 91–94.

48. John Kloppenborg, *Christ's Associations*, 326.

49. Justin Martyr, *Apologia*, 1.14 as quoted in Peter Phan, *Social Thought*, 21.

50. Tertullian, *Apologia*, 39 as quoted in Phan, 21.

51. Phan, 21.

52. Kloppenborg, *Christ's Associations*, 326.

53. Stark, *Rise of Christianity*, 211.

54. Murphy-O'Connor, *Paul*, 137.

55. Joseph Fitzmeyer, "Pauline Theology," 1409, n. 122.

56. Fitzmeyer, 1410, n. 123.

57. Fitzmeyer, 1410, n. 124.

58. Murphy-O'Connor, *Paul*, 153. I closely follow the author's exposition in this and the subsequent paragraphs.

59. Murphy-O'Connor, *Paul*, 153.

60. Murphy-O'Connor, 204.

61. Murphy-O'Connor, 154.

62. Murphy-O'Connor, 154.

63. Murphy-O'Connor, 154.

64. Pheme Perkins, "Reading Guide to John," 448.

65. Wayne Meeks, *The Origins of Christian Morality*, 91.

66. Meeks, 91–110.

67. Meeks, 92.

68. Meeks, 12.

69. Meeks, 9–10.

70. Meeks, 13.

71. Stark, *Rise of Christianity*, 16–20.

72. Stark, 20.

73. Meeks, *Origins of Christian Morality*, 26.

74. Meeks, 33.

75. Kloppenborg, *Christ's Associations*, 143.

76. Meeks, *Origins of Christian Morality*, 34.

77. Kloppenborg, *Christ's Associations*, 143.

78. Michael Himes, *Doing the Truth in Love*, 21.

79. Kloppenborg, *Christ's Associations*, 146.

80. "But now I am writing to you not to associate with anyone who bears the name of brother or sister who is sexually immoral or greedy, or is an idolater, reviler, drunkard, or robber. Do not even eat with such a one."

81. Kloppenborg, *Christ's Associations*, 147.

82. Kloppenborg, 149.

83. Kloppenborg, 149.

84. Kloppenborg, 151.

85. Meeks, *Origins of Christian Morality*, 102. The writer cites the work of Stanley Stowers, *Letter Writing in Greco-Roman Antiquity*, 15 and passim.

86. Meeks, , 103.

87. Justin Martyr, 1 Apologia, 67: 5–6 as quoted in Meeks, *Origins of Christian Morality*, 107.

88. Murphy-O'Connor, *Paul*, 106.

89. Kloppenborg, *Christ's Associations*, 260–261.

90. Kloppenborg, 263–64.

91. Kloppenborg, 11–12.

92. Kloppenborg, 55.

93. Kloppenborg, 56.

94. Kloppenborg, 14–15
95. Kloppenborg, 15.
96. Meeks, *First Urban Christians*, 86–87
97. Kloppenborg, *Christ's Associations*, 205.
98. Meeks, *Origins of Christian Morality*, 171.
99. Meeks, 110.
100. Sheldon Wolin, *Politics and Vision*, 23.
101. Wolin, 87.

PART II

THEOLOGICAL ANTHROPOLOGY

$$4$$

HUMAN DIGNITY
IN COMMUNITY

In his survey of the way that the word *dignity* has been understood in Western culture, the philosopher Michael Rosen observes, "History shows the existence of significant distinct strands in the meaning of dignity, strands that come together and move apart at different times."[1] Indeed, looking at the literature on the topic even within the Catholic tradition, one finds a variety of means for discussing and categorizing the meaning of dignity. This chapter will first provide a sketch of how human dignity has been understood over the course of centuries within Catholicism. Besides the dignity of the human person, an equally important and related claim is that the person is made for community and achieves human flourishing only by giving expression to his or her social nature. And so this chapter will also present important background on the central role of community in the Catholic social tradition and how the two themes of human dignity and human community are interwoven in the Catholic viewpoint.

THE MEANINGS OF DIGNITY

The moral theologian Antonio Autiero sees three separate perspectives that may inform one's understanding of human dignity. The first perspective entails what he calls "an 'ontological' approach (which can also be defined as 'natural law')." For Autiero, "the essence of the person is mainly expressed in the fundamental law that is incumbent upon it, a law that derives from its nature as a person." Seen in this manner, "human dignity is nothing other than the fullness of being; the *telos* of the person that is already within her, through natural law." Some authors advocating this perspective, especially those in the ancient and medieval eras, may have employed a theoretical and deductive method in determining that *telos* or end. However, Autiero acknowledges that today many advocates of this perspective follow an "'inductive-ontological' method . . . with due consideration for a positive and relevant meaning of experience, historicity, and the space-time, cultural-environmental conditioning" of our grasp of the essence of a person.[2]

The second perspective in understanding the meaning of human dignity is what Autiero calls, "the transcendental-philosophical approach as formulated by I. Kant." Following this approach, human dignity is "based on the moral self-determination of the human being, on his moral autonomy." To use a famous term coined by Kant, persons in their actions "must abide by the dictates of a categorical imperative which concerns and grounds" human dignity. It is this capacity of giving oneself "moral directives" that are obligatory, which constitutes the dignity of a person.[3] Autiero rightly notes that "dignity does not depend on the concrete realization of the moral imperative," since we all fail morally to some degree. Rather, "it is only the predisposition and the inclination towards the good that establishes the dignity of the person, not the realization of good acts."[4] Our dignity is grounded in our unique capacity for moral autonomy.

The third perspective outlined by Autiero "is immediately related to the basic lines of a theological anthropological approach." This, of course, is the perspective shaped by belief in "the creation and salvation of the human being by God." The Creator "imprints on the human being" the divine image and likeness.[5] In his comments on this perspective, Autiero emphasizes that he endorses the more holistic and biblical understanding of the imago Dei rather than the later reduction of the imago to human rationality.

Another framework on human dignity is considered by the theologian Sigrid Müller. She maintains that Christian beliefs support the idea of human dignity, even though there have been times when that support has "been obscured, and even suppressed."[6] Müller also proposes that the diversity within the tradition is such that "we should not speak of identical elements" in the tradition but something along the lines of "corresponding ideas and intentions."[7]

There are "four dominant dimensions of human dignity that are distinct but related."

First, there is "human dignity as an *anthropological* principle signifying the intrinsic worth of human beings." A second dimension of human dignity is its role "as a *moral* principle, namely as the foundation of morality, moral rights, and duties." The third dimension of human dignity is "as a *legal* principle, namely as a formal or material basis for the legislation of human rights." And Müller's fourth dimension is "human dignity as a *practical* principle, namely as the *object* and *aim* of a practice-oriented virtue ethics or normative ethics."[8]

Finally, the American Catholic moral theologian Darlene Fozard Weaver has examined official statements of Catholic teaching on human dignity and, like Müller, sees a fourfold meaning to the term. First is "an affirmation of human worth"; second is "an encapsulation of the human good"; third is "a moral criterion that constrains and entitles"; and lastly, "a moral expression of Christian humanism."[9]

The first meaning refers to the "moral status of human beings qua human. Human beings have inherent, noncontingent worth." This is an affirmation of "a kind of equality among all human beings that endures despite forms of inequality in abilities, accomplishments, or assets."[10] Fozard Weaver also sees dignity operating "as a shorthand for a Catholic understanding of the human good." This meaning connotes a sense of dignity as "a potential capable of fulfillment." It is not at odds with the first meaning of dignity; but whereas the first meaning highlights dignity as something humans inherently possess, this second meaning underscores "a potential way we may actualize or enact" our pursuit of the ideal of authentic humanity.[11] The third meaning of human dignity is its role as "a moral criterion" that "applies to particular actions or practices and to social conditions and systems." It is moral dignity as a standard that "entitles human beings to the conditions necessary for a manner of life consistent" with the first two meanings.[12] And the fourth version of human dignity, according to Fozard Weaver, has to do with its linkage to an overall theological anthropology. It is "humanistic in its attentiveness to features of human existence and in its rejection of a reductionistic view of humanity." These features "both warrant and give content to dignity as a universal human attribute and a cross-cultural principle."[13]

Autiero's, Müller's, and Fozard Weaver's methods of categorizing how we are to think of human dignity are not simply identical, but there are clear family resemblances or, to borrow the phrase used by Müller, there are "corresponding ideas and intentions" in the various schemata proposed. The influence of Kant is evident, the idea that dignity functions as an ethical standard is present in all our authors, and the heritage of the biblical witness is also represented in the portrayal of how human dignity is to be understood. The impact of the liberal tradition and its focus on individual liberty has also influenced our understanding of what human dignity entails. One thing that is evident is the popular use of various meanings ascribed to human dignity has waxed and waned over the course of time. The following subsection will briefly survey some significant stages in the evolution of a

Catholic understanding of human dignity and what is meant when the tradition defends and promotes human dignity.

THE CHANGING FACE OF HUMAN DIGNITY

In the New Testament there are a variety of ways of accounting for human dignity. There is human dignity due to God's making humankind in the divine image and likeness, a protological account of dignity. There is human dignity owing to our likeness to Jesus who is truly human, a Christological account. Then there is the dignity of the person who has been redeemed and called into a new, graced existence, an account that draws upon soteriology. Finally, there is the dignity of the person who is to live eternally in the experience of perfect love known as the Trinity, an eschatological account.[14] While distinct, these accounts do not contradict one another; they are complementary, and each adds a particular emphasis or insight into what we mean when we discuss human dignity. What the differing accounts witness to, however, is that too rushed an effort to define human dignity may lead us to underappreciate some rich aspect of the expression.

A second point to be taken from the diverse biblical accounts is that both Jewish and Christian scriptures maintain there is a sanctified or sacred dimension to the human person; that the Holy Mystery named God is intimately related to the human through the events of creation, incarnation, redemption, and salvation. For Christians, it is this sacredness of the human that generates belief in human dignity. Reference to belief in the imago Dei was central to a theological definition of human dignity.[15]

In his historical survey of the way that the word "dignity" has been understood in Western culture, Harvard professor Michael Rosen proposes that dignity "originated as a concept that denoted high social status and the honors and respectful treatment that are due to someone who occupied that position." That view of dignity is also found in the Old Testament, indicating "'elevation' or 'majesty.'"[16] According to Rosen, it is a concept that can be found in a variety of ancient cultures beyond the Hebraic. Still, the sense of dignity already had begun to evolve in the classical world. With the arrival of empires and the loss of the independent city-state, Greek Stoicism taught that human beings should see themselves as citizens of the world, of a *cosmopolis*, not simply a *polis*. The point is that what matters is not only the "position some individual or group occupies in relation to other beings in a particular society, but what position human beings as a whole occupy in the order of the universe."[17] Cicero adopts this theme in *De Officiis*, written in

44 BCE. Cicero certainly knew that *dignitas* was a conventional term for status, but in his treatise on moral living, he discusses "the dignity that human beings have solely because they are human, not animals."[18]

Rosen notes the Latin dignitas also developed another meaning that would become politically significant only later, that is, dignitas entered the vocabulary of art and rhetoric. Dignitas was used along with *gravitas* "to characterize speech that was weighty and majestic." And dignitas "was applied not just to the style of a speech but to the speaker." It is an instance of the early use of dignity's being identified with what is dignified in manner or bearing.[19] This is associated with Cicero's point about dignity having to do with how one lives out one's life.

Christian belief in the imago Dei became central to its understanding of human dignity. Several patristic writers proposed that Christians, once they recognized their own dignity, had to adopt a new way of life in dealing with other persons, whether fellow Christians or not. It became common to argue that the neighbor had dignity and had to be treated with respect and even love, an acknowledgement of the image of God present in the person. Christian moral teaching drew upon the dignity of a shared common human nature to promote the cause of neighbor love.

There was also an evolution in the understanding of dignity due to the Christian experience of persecution and martyrdom in the Roman Empire. Believing that they might have to suffer and lose their temporal lives, persecuted Christians held onto the hope that they would be saved and enter eternal life. "They recognized that human dignity had an interior character, and contrasted it with the exterior, social honor, to which the Latin term *dignitas* referred."[20] Thus Cyprian of Carthage in the first half of the third century CE used the term dignity "to emphasize the inner worth of the martyrs which corresponds to their eternal glory."[21]

The later Christian author, Lactantius, writing on the topic of social morality, developed a "relatively complete, organic and coherent doctrine, based upon the dignity of the human person."[22] That dignity is founded upon being made in God's image, and one of the consequences of that view of dignity is the "fundamental equality" among human beings.[23] In his writing, Lactantius blends his Christian faith with Roman philosophy and law in order to enhance two elements of theological anthropology. Through his understanding of the person in the biblical accounts of creation and in natural law theory, combined with the duty to practice the virtue of humanity, he underscored the importance of "a universal claim of the intrinsic worth of human beings." And second, his view of the role of human freedom "as a necessary condition for religious self-determination" enriched the idea of personal freedom as the capacity to engage in "conscientious moral decision-making."[26] So the idea of human dignity is related not only to the imago Dei but also to the claim of the intrinsic worth of every person—and the centrality of freedom in Christian writings.

In the fourth century the Cappadocian Fathers added to the Christian theological tradition not only by their work on the Trinity and Christology but also by including elements of social theology. Gregory Nazianzus endorsed the equality of all humans as reflective of the divine plan for creation. The God "who rains on the just and unjust and makes the sun rise on all equally" has put the goodness of creation "at the disposal of all and abundantly," so that God "honors by equality of the gift the equality of nature" in humankind.[27] Later in the same discourse, Gregory encourages his fellow Christians who are wealthy and powerful not to deny in practice their basic equality with the less well-off in their midst: "look at the primitive equality, not at the later distinction, not at the law of the powerful, but at the law of the Creator."[28] Gregory, in language reminiscent of Lactantius, believes "compassion or humanity is a duty derived from the fact that we share a common human nature."[29]

Gregory of Nyssa based his social thought on his theological anthropology, and he is clear that the human person is, as Genesis describes, the image and likeness of God. Consequently, the human being enjoys the highest dignity among earth's creatures. Peter Phan observes that for Gregory, "This dignity is the foundation for the respect that is owed to human beings in social life."[30]

Ambrose of Milan writing in the second half of the fourth century echoes the earlier idea of Cyprian of Carthage "that dignity does not depend on exterior honor but is present in situations of poverty and persecution."[31] Looking at the life of Jesus, Ambrose reflected that as Christ lived poorly, was persecuted and put to death, but never lost his dignity then, too, his disciples would not be without dignity even in hardship and suffering.

Augustine set the course of theological reflection in the West on this topic. For him, the imago Dei is found in every human person as the capacity to receive God, and while this capacity may be damaged by sin, it can never be eradicated. That is because "not human nature as such, not even the rational nature of the human soul, but the capacity to host the divine spirit makes human beings true images of God."[32] While other created beings have a likeness to God, it is human beings alone who receive the divine image by God's direct creative action. As a result, "there is no one in the human race to whom love is not due, either as a return of mutual affection or in virtue of his share of our common nature."[33]

Later developments in the theological tradition draw upon many of the ideas found in the patristic authors. For instance, Alcuin of York in the 700s sees the imago Dei doctrine as the basis for human dignity and sees human dignity as related to the human capacity to know and love God. Thus, God and humankind are so intimately related through the image of God in the human soul that "whoever does not love other human beings does not love God."[34]

In the medieval period, a variety of voices engage the topic of dignity. Bernard of Clairvaux in the early twelfth century suggests that the imago Dei includes freedom and human dignity and consists in the transcendent freedom of human beings that marks them as unique among earthly creatures. In the next century Alexander of Hales sees human persons as being of the "highest dignity because they are moral beings."[35] Bonaventure, with his tendency to utilize trinitarian classification, employs the imago Dei doctrine to propose "three different layers of human dignity." The "ontological, universal dignity of the human soul" beginning at creation is the trace of God (*vestigium*) in the person; the capacity of the soul to recognize and love God is the image of God (imago Dei); while the human ability to cooperate with divine grace permits the human to "reach similarity (*similitudo*) with God."[36] For Bonaventure, humanity is not the image of God in a general sense but is specifically made in the likeness of the Son who is both human and divine. The human imaging of the divine is perfectly captured in Jesus of Nazareth so that through Jesus not only is God revealed to us, but what it means for us to be human is also revealed. The very nature of human beings is to become Christ-like, and our capacity to become so through freedom and grace reflects our dignity as creatures. Albertus Magnus sees human dignity in the independence of thought, willing, and action that marks a human individual.[37] His student, Thomas Aquinas, maintains that "dignity signifies something's goodness on account of itself."[38] Here Aquinas uses language that is akin to stating dignity has to do with something's intrinsic or inherent value or worth. As Rosen suggests, this is an important strand of the Catholic tradition's viewpoint on dignity. The Thomist view is not limited to *human* dignity. Human beings do have dignity, but dignity is not restricted to human beings. "The world is composed of many things, all of them ultimately created by God and thus having their own dignity" by virtue of fulfilling their own place within the divine plan of creation.[39]

Still to be resolved, with reference to the last point, is the matter of what kind of dignity do human beings have, and is it distinct from the dignity of other creatures? There is also the question of, on what basis does anything have dignity? And does the level of dignity vary between humans or other creatures? Basing dignity on the imago Dei settled many matters as long as the Christian faith was culturally dominant, but later thinkers would have to return to the foundation of dignity—human or otherwise—once the age of secularity emerged.

Grounding human dignity on the image of God was also a way to distinguish it from that of other creatures, since although created by God and viewed as good, no other creature bears the imago Dei. The Genesis text is clear that humans alone have been made in the divine image and likeness.

Regarding variance about levels of dignity within humanity, the thrust of the imago paradigm lent itself to talk about equality in dignity. However, as Christian writers sought to locate the "home" of the imago Dei, there was a move away from the holistic vision of the biblical witness and an embrace of various features of the human that were identified with the image of God.

The danger of associating the imago with rationality, or freedom, or the capacity for relationship with God made it possible to ask if those failing a certain standard of rationality, or freedom, or faith, might not as fully bear the image of God as others. The debates over the dignity of indigenous people in the New World or Africa and the obligations of the colonial conquerors toward such people reflect the variations in how dignity was understood.

A text of particular importance for understanding dignity was that derived from an oration of the Italian Renaissance philosopher Pico della Mirandola. Reflecting much of the spirit of his time and culture, Pico, in the late fifteenth century, maintained that what is truly distinctive about humans is that we do not simply live out fixed or predetermined roles. Rather, human beings choose their own destinies, for God has given each person the wherewithal to shape the self, "according to a range of possibilities not available to other creatures."[40] Here dignity is not a matter of social station for the elite of a society but a common feature of humankind, linked to our ability to be self-determining. So Pico's answer to the question of what kind of dignity a human being has is that humanity has a dignity that puts it above the rest of creation by virtue of our freedom for self-determination.

Bishop Jacques-Bénigne Bossuet, the theologian and preacher in the court of Louis XIV, spoke of the dignity of the poor. No egalitarian, Bossuet did not think the poor and the French nobility were on a par, but he did believe that each had a dignity owing to their place within "a properly ordered hierarchy,"[41] rejecting Pico's emphasis on self-determination. It is important to note that Bossuet was well within the Catholic tradition with his conviction that though there are degrees and kinds of dignity, every creature, even a nonhuman creature, has dignity since each has a place within creation's order. The idea that human dignity is but one form of dignity is an important theme in the Catholic tradition, as will be seen when we discuss the views of recent popes regarding the environment.

Blaise Pascal, whose *Pensées* were published after Bossuet, agrees with Pico's view of human dignity as exceeding that of the rest of creation, but

Pascal lodges that dignity not in freedom but in thought. It is only the human that brings thought into the created universe. Still, Pascal, like Pico, does not accept Bossuet's emphasis on a divinely ordered hierarchy with individual dignity stemming from one's place in that hierarchy.

Later Roman Catholic Views on Dignity

The Catholic Church had a largely negative attitude toward the French Revolution for a variety of reasons. The revolution in France, "the eldest daughter of the Church,"[42] was, in part at least, a revolt against her mother. Turning the Cathedral of Notre Dame in Paris into the Temple of the Goddess Reason and raping a prostitute on the altar is bound to get the attention of a pope, and not in a positive way. Thus, it was unsurprising that there was a backlash by the Church to the calls for *liberté, égalité, et fraternité*, which continued even into the present age in certain Catholic circles.

As the Catholic tradition gradually accepted the concept of human dignity, it did so with a non-egalitarian meaning. For Aquinas, dignity meant the value some entity has by its place within the divine order of creation, an order that was hierarchical. So Bossuet, as noted previously, could acknowledge the dignity of the poor in France while also accepting the social hierarchy in place during the age of Louis XIV. That understanding of an ordered hierarchy in society fit well with a theological understanding of an ordered cosmos, in which differences in dignity were not only of kind (between humans and other animate creatures) but also of degree (between different roles in a society).

Leo XIII is commonly cited as the pope who began modern papal social teaching with his 1891 encyclical *Rerum novarum* on the rights of labor. But thirteen years earlier, he authored *Quod apostolici muneris*, an attack on socialism as an erroneous social philosophy primarily for its emphasis on egalitarianism and rejection of legitimate authority of rulers. Leo pointed out that God had created the cosmos in an ordered hierarchy, citing the distinctions among the heavenly choirs of angels as well as the various offices of the church as illustrative of the divine plan. He continued: "so also has He appointed that there should be various orders in civil society, differing in dignity, rights, and power, whereby the State, like the Church, should be one body, consisting of many members, some nobler than others, but all necessary to each other and solicitous for the common good."[43] Even "though Leo, Pius X and Benedict XV acknowledge the elevated status of human beings as the imago dei, this is not a claim around which their social teaching revolves. Rather the Leonine period popes' controlling moral insight is a cosmological vision of a communal hierarchy of being."[44] Hence, when Leo wrote about the dignity of labor in *Rerum novarum*, he was not arguing for social equality among people, but that labor had a proper place in the social order and should be recognized as such. The equality of persons in their dignity as created in the image of God, which Leo affirmed in paragraph five of the same encyclical quoted previously, did not translate into equality in social standing, even if Leo believed that at the time the laboring class was being denied its proper social standing.[45]

To grasp the dramatic nature of the Catholic social tradition's evolution, it is necessary to acknowledge just how long and deep was its resistance to egalitarian ideals in its various guises: liberalism, democracy, feminism, and socialism. The imagery of a hierarchically ordered plan of creation was dominant in the teaching of Catholicism. After Leo it would take several more decades and popes before the papal social tradition made its peace with at least some versions of those social movements and reject to some extent the ideal of a divine hierarchy in creation.

It was Pius XI who spoke of a kind of justice he called social justice; this understanding of justice identified what individuals and groups must do to promote the common good. When Pius XI discussed a just wage amid the worldwide depression of the early 1930s, he did not wish to place the entire burden on employers who were struggling merely to preserve their business. Instead, Pius, by use of social justice, directed attention to the need for "the reorganization of economic society so that a worker could in fact produce the economic equivalent of such a wage. Only at this stage would it be possible to assert that an employer, in justice, was obliged to pay such a stipend."[46] In other words, wage levels were not simply a matter of commutative justice between employer and employee; there was the element of social justice. This, then, led to the challenge of constructing a social order that facilitated the economic component of the common good. Pius used social justice to call for efforts to reform the economic structures of societies in the era of the Great Depression. The clear implication was that human dignity demanded social change on a structural level, going beyond Leo's presumption of a rather static, hierarchical social order. And this led to a dilemma not fully addressed till later in the development of the tradition.

Pius XII in his Christmas radio address of 1944 added the element of political democracy to discussions of human dignity. Speaking at a time when Nazism and fascism were denigrating the dignity of people in varied and severe ways, Pius proposed the right of the people to participate in the political process to limit the abuses of authoritarian regimes. Referring to the Christmas "feast day which commemorates both the benignity of the

Incarnate Word and the dignity" of humankind, the pope distinguished between "the people" and "the masses." The latter he saw as a shapeless mass of individuals within a given territory who are "inert of themselves" and directed by state authority. But "in a people worthy of the name, the citizen feels within the consciousness of his own personality, of his duties and rights, of his own freedom joined to respect for the freedom and dignity of others."[47] And so the ideal of participation in communal decision-making became an indicator of human dignity in the political realm.

John XXIII continued in this vein, situating much of his treatment of human dignity within the context of the common good, which "embraces the sum total of those conditions of social living, whereby men are enabled more fully and more readily to achieve their own perfection."[48] In 1963, John stated that "a civic society is to be considered well-ordered, beneficial and in keeping with human dignity if it is grounded in truth." And the attainment of the truth that we are tied to one another "will be accomplished when each one duly recognizes both his rights and his obligations toward others."[49] In *Pacem in terris*, John provides an extensive list of human rights and duties that flow from human dignity.[50] These rights were understood to be derived from the divine order that "the Creator of the world has imprinted in man's heart," an order that is in harmony with the attainment of human well-being and flourishing.[51] So some of Leo's successors in the twentieth century continued to speak about a divine order within creation, but they did so in a way that allowed for greater social reform, more equality, and increased moral agency on the part of people to fashion and shape that social order.

Even with Leo's rather static and hierarchic perspective we should not lose sight of a positive aspect to the Catholic vision of a divine order in creation. And this benefit distinguished Catholic thinking about dignity from Kant and his philosophical descendants. The foundation for dignity in Kant was the reality of morality, a moral code or law that lives within the human person. Since only human beings have the capacity for morality, because only human beings have true freedom, dignity is limited to the human. There is only one kind of dignity—human dignity. That mindset lends itself to an anthropocentrism and a radical separation of the person from nature that in contemporary times has been revealed as undercutting appreciation for the value of nonhuman creation. Here the Catholic insistence that all creation is reflective of the goodness of the Creator offers a corrective, although today it will require a different grounding than that of a hierarchical universe.

To say that the Catholic theological tradition has a rationale for upholding the dignity of all creation, not just human dignity, is not to claim that the tradition has been prophetic in its defense of the natural environment. Overall, the tradition operated in an anthropocentric way that led to environmental abuses, particularly in the modern era. But once an environmental consciousness began to develop in the present age, the Catholic tradition had the resources to incorporate the insight of the dignity of creation to strengthen its ecological agenda. This is because, as noted in Chapter 2, the Christian tradition had an important thread about the dignity of all creatures that was never simply forgotten even if it was pushed to the background. Yet to acknowledge the dignity of all creatures is not the same as saying that all creatures have equal moral standing; the Christian tradition does not support a species egalitarianism that refuses to recognize any difference in dignity between human persons and other living beings.

Returning our focus to human dignity, there is common ground between Catholicism and the Enlightenment perspective. Human dignity is intrinsic; there is a value to each person that is not dependent on the approval or even acknowledgment of other creatures. Although they may differ in their interpretation of what makes up the "inner transcendental kernel" of dignity in each human being, both Kant and the modern papacy maintain there is such a kernel.[52] Further, human dignity is inalienable; it can be neither given away nor taken away. A person's dignity can be violated, but it cannot be eradicated.

In summary, it took time for Catholicism to accept that human dignity was linked to certain rights and egalitarian social systems. These important implications of a strong sense of human dignity would eventually enter the mainstream of the Catholic social tradition, but it was not until well into the twentieth century that the papacy made the connections between dignity, egalitarianism, and rights. A series of twentieth-century social cataclysms far more tragic and violent than the French Revolution pushed the Catholic tradition to embrace the implications of human dignity that it had avoided. World Wars I and II along with the rise of oppressive regimes of national socialism, fascism, and communism opened the eyes of many Catholics to the significance of movements defending human rights, equality, democracy, and other dimensions of a humane social order, and which fed growing interest in promoting human dignity.

Human Dignity under Threat

For many Europeans, World War I both embodied and led to a great crisis, one that challenged those who conceived of modern Western civilization as being marked by progress and enlightenment. The brutal horrors of the war were especially disillusioning for Catholics who saw the war as a moment when a continent that had been profoundly shaped and informed by Christianity had seemingly thrown off its religious heritage.

In addition to the slaughter and death of so many, the destruction and impoverishment of the lives of the survivors, and the wreckage and ruin of entire landscapes, there was also an apparent loss of meaning and value. Traditional Christianity seemed to no longer give meaningful answers for such catastrophic loss. This vacuum began to be filled by a philosophical outlook of positivism and empirical science. From this perspective, agnosticism and atheism appeared to offer more appropriate answers than traditional Christianity.

For believing Catholics, the achievements of science—theoretical and applied—were not deemed troubling, but rather the problem was the exaggerated claims that the scientific method was the only means to true knowledge. This led to the view, in some quarters, that humans were simply matter—perhaps complex matter in its evolution, but still just matter.[53] For several Catholic thinkers the era of "The Great War" reflected the loss, or at least eclipse, of the spiritual dimension of human life. And that, in turn, led to false ideologies that presented skewed views of the human person. Broadly speaking, these skewed views can be labeled individualism and collectivism.

One form of collectivism has been ascribed to the utilitarian thought of Jeremy Bentham, the social reformer in the nineteenth century. Bentham's formula of the greatest good for the greatest number was achievable at the expense of a minority. More relevant for early twentieth-century Catholics, however, were ideas like nationalism and communism, both of which seemed to promote the well-being of a nation, a class, or a party at the expense of individuals. For the sake of the group, the individual was expected to sacrifice or be sacrificed so that the cause of the collective might succeed. The individual, therefore, would find meaning and purpose only when united with others to save their class or country.

On the other hand, at the turn of the century voices of individualism such as Herbert Spencer in England and William Sumner in the United States were prepared, in the name of a pseudoscientific social Darwinism, to ignore any claims of the community on the individual. The blend of *laissez faire* economics, the absolute priority of individual liberty, and theories of natural inequalities among people led to a viewpoint where those at the lower end of the socioeconomic ladder were deemed unworthy of assistance. Indeed, it was alleged that efforts at social reform caused more harm than good since such projects only prolonged the suffering of those who were doomed to fail due to their inability to compete for economic gain or be recognized in a "proper" culture. Later extreme renderings of classical liberalism slipped into a libertarian posture that continued to devalue the role of the state doing anything other than protecting the rights of individuals, with little regard for the idea of a common good.

In reaction to these social views, Catholic intellectuals began a movement that has been called "personalism." Foremost in the minds of the leaders of the movement was the need to assert the "primacy of the spiritual," a phrase coined by Jacques Maritain and taken up by others.[54] Personalism, however, does not represent a coherent single philosophy so much as an array of theological, philosophical, literary, artistic, and spiritual ideas that sought to give shape to an alternative to individualism and collectivism.[55] "It was distinguished and separated from egocentric individualism by stressing the moral obligation to serve others and the community, but it did not fall into the collectivist orbit because, due to his intrinsic dignity, the person possesses an absolute and noninterchangeable value and a series of inalienable rights."[56]

The unease of many Catholic thinkers in Europe with the spirit of the time was further heightened with the rise of fascism and Nazism, along with the growth of communism. These political movements in Europe grabbed the attention of Pius XI and Pius XII, and a good deal of papal writing on social matters addressed topics related to the policies of Mussolini, Hitler, and Stalin. At the same time, there was also concern about the hardships of many workers and their families due to the lack of economic protection available in the aftermath of the Industrial Revolution. So, there was a critique of capitalism but usually in milder form than the language employed against socialism.

Following the horrors of World War II, the Shoah, and the expansion of Stalin's totalitarianism into many countries in Europe, it was clear to many Catholics that a fatal flaw behind much of the death, destruction, and depravity of twentieth-century life was the operative view of the person that had fueled the various "isms" of the age. Although harbingers of a revised Catholic social vision were present earlier, as in Pius XII's acceptance of democracy, it was Vatican II that placed a retrieval of the doctrine of the imago Dei and a revised understanding of human dignity at the center of Catholic social thinking, making the former an indispensable element for a theological definition of the latter.[57]

GAUDIUM ET SPES: DIGNITY AND COMMUNITY

Just as the personalist movement stressed the primacy of the spiritual, so, too, when the authors of Vatican II's *Pastoral Constitution on the Church in the Modern World* (*Gaudium et spes*) set about their work, they were aware that in their account of the human person they must begin "with a God who speaks and human beings who are addressed and who are in turn drawn into responding to God and addressing each other and the whole of creation."[58] Human beings are created to be in conversation with God; to use an expression of Karl Rahner, humans are constituted as "hearers of the Word." The human person is "God's conversation partner . . . addressable by God and addressing God."[59]

To put it simply, the human is constituted as a creature of transcendence. That fundamental quality gives Catholic social thought its distinctiveness. Transcendence as an essential dimension of the person is rooted, as was seen in Chapter 2, in the biblical account of creation whereby "from the outset the person must be understood as a relation; and that being-as-relation draws the human person into forms of communion with God and with other creatures."[60] To be human is to be a creature addressed by God and invited into a relationship with the Creator and all that is created. The call from God is to accept the divine love that brought creation into being and to be motivated and empowered by that love to love others and be in relationship with them. The call that is "constitutive of the human person is not a call to live in isolation; it is a call to communion and community, to find ourselves in existing with and for others." It is vital to add at this point that even though a person can only attain a full and flourishing life in community, that is not to say "the person exists only for the community and that the interests of the person must be subordinated to those of the community or the collective. Communities exist for the persons who are their members, and their purpose is the protection and promotion of human dignity."[61]

Humans must go out of themselves and enter into communion with the Other and others. The human person cannot fully be who he or she is called to be except through a sincere gift of the self. By so doing, the human person in giving his or her self away to others is thereby transformed in the image of Christ-likeness. This reflects the claim of the Council that "only in the mystery of the incarnate Word does the mystery of the human person take on light."[62] In giving oneself away one finds oneself; this is a hallmark of Christian transcendence. This, then, is the foundation of morality in the Catholic perspective, for the essence of moral obligation is to respond to the summons to recognize the concrete dignity of other persons. So, in accord with the views of Autiero, Müller, and Fozard Weaver summarized at the beginning of this chapter, human dignity functions as the criterion and norm of the moral life. David Hollenbach has insightfully explained how dignity functions in this manner.[63]

Following a neo-Aristotelian approach of inductive reasoning Hollenbach seeks "to determine what sort of respect is due to human beings" by "paying attention to the diverse religious, cultural, and political communities of our world, and observing how they believe persons should be treated." Despite the pluralism one finds in such an inductive process, he suggests "some common standards may emerge." He borrows a phrase from Margaret Farley to talk about "obligating features of personhood," that is, dimensions of human dignity "that indicate not only *that* we should show respect towards one another but *what* it will mean to show such respect."[64] Hollenbach argues that three features of personhood consistently appear in such reflections. These are certain crucial *freedoms*, essential *relationships*, and basic *needs* that generate "both negative and positive obligations in our interaction with each other."[65] It was respect for these three "features of personhood" that "were evidently seen as required by human dignity by the drafters of the Universal Declaration" of Human Rights on behalf of the United Nations. Those charged with writing the Universal Declaration did not see human dignity as "an abstract standard but as a way of referring to those inductively identified characteristics of personhood that make concrete demands for respect on other persons and on social institutions."[66] In seeking to enumerate what freedoms, relationships, and goods are obligated by human dignity, Hollenbach suggests that reflection on what was absent in the twentieth-century horrors of political, societal, and economic life can reveal what are the necessary freedoms, relationships, and goods "essential to the attainment of human dignity."[67]

As was noted previously in Chapter 2, there have been voices within the Catholic tradition that have proposed one or another feature of the human person as being the location of the imago Dei, such as reason or freedom. Gaudium et spes does not ignore or deny basic dimensions of the human person, but it places these within the context of relationality; for "humans develop themselves in relationship to fellow humans. A human only becomes human in a social connection."[68] So it is dignity and relationality that are key to understanding the human person within the Catholic tradition. In their 1985 pastoral letter on economic justice, the US bishops stated, "Human dignity can be realized and protected only in community." They make a point that is emphasized throughout this book, "the human person is not only sacred but also social."[69]

Recall in Chapter 3 the thesis of Rodney Stark that early Christianity promoted an ethic of mercy and concern for the neighbor. The moral theologian James Keenan has commented on Stark's work, "Christianity required the recognition of the stranger in need as neighbor and, *inevitably*, as sibling."[70] At this point in my examination of the Catholic understanding of the importance of human dignity and life in community, I would like to consider why Christians would come to look upon the stranger in need as a brother or sister. To grasp why, it is helpful to understand Christianity's debt to Judaism through the theology of covenant, election, and the role of the Jewish people in God's plan for history. These themes were influential in shaping the early church's self-understanding of its mission to be a community that practiced neighbor-love.

A PEOPLE OF FAITH

Christianity, of course, did not emerge in full bloom with the first generation of Christians. In fact, it is crucial for understanding Christianity that we realize the earliest Christians were almost without exception Jews. That reality was determinative in important ways for Christian social thought and practice. Jewish faith began with the belief that God called a *people* into existence and continued to develop a relationship with those people throughout history. The Torah is filled with narratives, laws, blessings, rituals, and creedal statements concerning the creation of the Jewish people by virtue of Yahweh's election of them as "my people." In Deuteronomy we find one of the early formulas of that faith, which was part of a rite for celebration of the harvest.

> A wandering Aramean was my ancestor; he went down into Egypt and lived there as an alien, few in number, and there he became a great nation, mighty and populous. When the Egyptians treated us harshly and afflicted us, by imposing hard labor on us, we cried to the LORD, the God of our ancestors; the LORD heard our voice and saw our affliction, our toil, and our oppression. The LORD brought us out of Egypt with a mighty hand and an outstretched arm, with a terrifying display of power, and with signs and wonders; and he brought us into this place and gave us this land, a land flowing with milk and honey. (Deut 26:5–9)

The statement begins in the third person, but then turns into a statement about "us" and "we" and "our" who were a great nation, afflicted and enslaved, liberated from oppression and brought out of Egypt by God into a land of milk and honey. The testimony is not simply about what happened to a group of people long ago, it is a story about each generation of Israelites who know themselves to be a chosen people.

Jewish identity was caught up with their election as God's chosen people with a special role in salvation history. The many shared experiences of hardship in Israel's history forged a strong sense of community and ethnic unity among the Jewish people. Called to be holy as their God was holy meant leading a righteous life in accord with the Mosaic law. That law bound them to God in a lasting covenant and to one another in a strong sense of solidarity. "Not only did their covenant make them personally and communally responsible to God, the Israelites realized they were likewise responsible to and for each other. All the biblical covenants with God are also a covenant among the people themselves, binding them together to care for each other; only thus can they live their vocation as a *people* of God."[71]

A widely held conviction among Jewish and Christian commentators is that the idea of covenant is at the heart of Israelite religion. It gave recognition to and helped create a communal identity that was more important than individual identity. Dan Finn summarizes well the Jewish attitude toward self, others, and God. "Israelites most fundamentally understood themselves as members of a family and a community in relationship with God. The moral requirements they faced, whether in culture or law, were not seen as impositions by some foreign power or distant deity but rather they were understood as expectations rising quite naturally out of relationship with a God whose fundamental characteristic was his care for Israel itself."[72] Again and again, the Hebrew prophets proclaimed the message that the test of the covenant was both fidelity to Yahweh alone as Lord and establishing right relationship with others as the sign of justice. One might add that the acid test of justice toward others was the treatment of widows, orphans, and resident aliens. In a patriarchal and tribal society that biblical triad represents those who will be especially vulnerable—a woman without her husband, a child without its father, and an outsider with no membership in the group. Thus, treatment of the marginal in Hebrew society was the true test of the justice required of a people covenanted with Yahweh, the just and merciful God.

By the time of the exile, Jewish faith had come to see that Yahweh was not only the God of Israel but the creator of the entire world, as the opening chapters of the book of Genesis attested, and that one day all the peoples of the world would come to know Yahweh as the Lord God and come to worship at the Jerusalem temple as Second Isaiah envisioned.

> And the foreigners who join themselves to the Lord,
> to minister to him, to love the name of the Lord,
> and to be his servants,

all who keep the sabbath, and do not profane it,
    and hold fast my covenant—
these I will bring to my holy mountain,
    and make them joyful in my house of prayer;
their burnt offerings and their sacrifices
    will be accepted on my altar;
for my house shall be called a house of prayer
    for all peoples.
Thus says the Lord God,
    who gathers the outcasts of Israel,
I will gather others to them
    besides those already gathered. (Is 56:6–8)

The same theme of the universality of Yahweh's Lordship comes up again in Chapter 60:1–7, where it is claimed of Israel, "Nations shall come to your light. . . . Lift up your eyes and look around; they all gather together, they come to you" (Is 60:3a, 4a). So, Israel is truly God's chosen people, but chosen not for its own sake alone, but as the means to reveal to all peoples that Yahweh is the Lord God: "I will give you as a light to the nations, that my salvation shall reach to the end of the earth" (Is 49:6b). Hence the communal bonds of the covenanted people of Israel would come to embrace all the nations, leading them to acknowledge Yahweh.

To be faithful to their election as the people belonging to Yahweh, the chosen people who will bring others into knowledge of the true and living God, the Hebrew people took to heart that they were in a covenantal relationship. "Theologically, being a covenant people . . . is radically to be a member of a community; religion is not merely vertical, 'me and God,' it is also radically horizontal. It is a community of mutually shared obligations, responsibilities, and gifts."[73]

As a devout Jew, Jesus's understanding of his identity and mission would have been informed by the scriptures that he knew. His earliest disciples would have understood him in light of their Jewish faith. One aspect of that faith, since the time of the exile and ongoing diaspora, was the hope that one day the scattered people of God would be once more gathered together. The prophets in the post-exilic period saw such a gathering as having a major role in the consummation of Israelite history. "Gathering Israel is often parallel to 'liberating,' 'saving,' 'healing,' and 'redeeming' Israel."[74] The process is always a divine initiative; the people will not gather themselves, but they will be gathered. "The background is the image of the shepherd who gathers his flock and leads them home."[75] Old divisions between the northern and southern kingdoms will be erased, rivalries among the twelve tribes will dissipate, and the united people will once again live in the land that was given to them by their God. So strong had this eschatological vision become in the Jewish imagination that by the time of Jesus a petition for gathering the scattered people of Israel was part of Israel's daily prayer.[76]

In his public ministry, Jesus should be understood as being conscious of the need to gather the scattered. By his calling of the Twelve from a larger group of disciples and sending them out "in pairs to proclaim the reign of God throughout the land," Jesus is engaged in a deliberate act of signaling the eschatological time is at hand. "The Twelve exemplify the gathering and restoration of Israel as the eschatological people of the twelve tribes that is now beginning with Jesus."[77] They will be the symbolic center of gathered Israel in the new age.

Jesus himself never left Jewish territory to preach and minister among Gentiles. So how will the message of God's reign reach all the nations? Israel had long before worked out the answer in the motif of the pilgrimage of the nations. And Jesus as a faithful Jew must have accepted the insight of earlier prophets.

> In days to come
>   the mountain of the LORD's house
> shall be established as the highest of the mountains,
>   and shall be raised above the hills;
> all the nations shall stream to it.
>   Many peoples shall come and say,
> "Come, let us go up to the mountain of the LORD,
>   to the house of the God of Jacob;
> that he may teach us his ways
>   and that we may walk in his paths."
> For out of Zion shall go forth instruction,
>   and the word of the LORD from Jerusalem. (Is 2:2–3)

The belief was that "first Israel must be saved, and only then can the Gentiles also be convinced of God's salvation." So, the focus of Jesus's ministry was to the lost sheep of the House of Israel in the belief that "God acts on the peoples of the world through the people of God."[78]

Ultimately, God intended salvation for all people, but the reign of God must begin somewhere and with some community of faith, and it was the descendants of Abraham and Sarah who were the people chosen for that role. However, "by the end of the first century, most Christian communities, at least outside of Syria and Palestine, were predominantly Gentile in their ethnic makeup and had no immediate sense of continuity with the Jewish people."[79] In light of that development, Christian thinking evolved on the role of Israel in God's plan.

JEWISH CHRISTIANITY AND THE ORIGINS OF THE CHURCH

A crucial aspect of the evolving Christian community was working out its relation to Israel, as is evident in the writing of Luke. He worked out his understanding of the role of the early church in the first eight chapters of the Acts of the Apostles, which focused upon the early Christian community in Jerusalem. That account "provides the hinge between the first rejection of Jesus (in the Gospel) and the account of the Gentile mission. By showing that in this first community there was a 'restoration of Israel,' Luke can subsequently describe the Gentile mission not as a replacement of Israel but as its legitimate continuation."[80]

Luke shares with Paul the belief that God's work in history is the creation of a people who would be faithful to the covenant, the bond between God and humankind and people with each other. The Acts of the Apostles paints a portrait of a restored people, how the Jews of Jerusalem came to accept the way of the Lord Jesus.

> They devoted themselves to the apostles' teaching and fellowship, to the breaking of bread and the prayers. Awe came upon everyone, because many wonders and signs were being done by the apostles. All who believed were together and had all things in common; they would sell their possessions and goods and distribute the proceeds to all, as any had need. Day by day, as they spent much time together in the temple, they broke bread at home and ate their food with glad and generous hearts, praising God and having the goodwill of all the people. And day by day the Lord added to their number those who were being saved. (2:42–47)

A few verses prior to this account, Luke describes the preaching of Peter on the day of Pentecost—when the Holy Spirit came down upon the Twelve gathered in the upper room—to a gathering of Jews that ends with their request for guidance about what to do and Peter's response that they should be baptized in the name of Jesus who is both Lord and Messiah. The ritual washing of repentance preached by John the Baptist became the ritual of initiation into the messianic community. Peter's preaching was well-received, and a number of his listeners accepted the call to baptism.[81] So Luke makes clear that Peter challenged his Jewish audience to accept what God had done in making Jesus the Messiah and Lord. The issue Luke presents is whether God's revelation will be accepted this time or whether the Jewish people would reject the message about Christ once again. Luke is concerned to show there is continuity in God's love for Israel despite the initial rejection of Jesus. Through his disciples the Jewish community is given a second chance, and this time there is a welcome response of repentance and baptism. "Day by day the Lord added to their number those who were being saved" (Acts 2:47).

Now in his description of the early community of Jewish Christians, Luke "wants to show continuing and consistent patterns of behavior."[82] The communion among these early disciples is not only a spiritual one, a shared faith, but also a material sharing. And the quality of their life together is a witness that brings goodwill toward the early community. Luke's description of the group is no doubt idealized, borrowing classical Greek and Roman ideas of utopian societies. He wants to make the point that through the gift of the Spirit working in the community the early church attained the aspirations of much human longing to live in a society of unity, peace, joy, and reconciliation with God.[83] In this "snapshot" of the Jerusalem Christian community, Luke is also appealing to the idea of a faithful remnant or *anawim* that will continue in Israel and keep faith with God. That group does not replace Israel but is the living embodiment of an eschatological hope that embraces not only all of Israel, but now also others beyond Israel.

Key in the evolution of the Christian self-understanding vis-á vis Judaism is the figure of Paul. It took time for Paul to work out the theological issue involved, namely, that if God had chosen the Jewish people, why does a Gentile majority worship God through Christ? Coming to the later years of his life, Paul writes in Romans 9:6, "It is not as though the word of God had failed." Rather, it is that the word was not addressed exclusively to Israel, "in the divine intention [it] had a wider audience. Now that it has been explicitly and clearly addressed to Gentiles, they have responded, as indeed some Jews have." So, Paul concluded that he was part of the faithful anawim of Israel, that remnant "which proclaimed salvation to the nations, thereby fulfilling the eschatological obligation laid upon Israel."[84]

Initially, in his missionary efforts, Paul adopted a strategy in Antioch-on-Orontes of a mixed community of Jew and Gentile Christians that permitted Gentiles to live as Gentiles and Jews as Jews. But when the Jerusalem community sent a Judaizer faction to Antioch, possibly with the support of James, a confrontation was inevitable. The Judaizers warned that Jewish Christians would be compromised by table fellowship with Gentile Christians. Because Peter was there at the time, the Antioch church looked to him for guidance. Paul's recounting of what happened reveals his bitter disappointment. Referring to Peter, he wrote: "For before certain men came from James, he used to eat with the Gentiles. But when they arrived, he began to draw back and separate himself from the Gentiles because he was afraid of those who belonged to the circumcision group. The other Jews joined him in his hypocrisy, so that by their hypocrisy even Barnabas was led astray" (Gal 2:12–13). Paul lost his struggle to maintain a mixed community that would celebrate eucharist together. For him, "Antioch had become a travesty of what a Christian community should be."[85]

At Antioch, and likely in other urban locales, the Christian community was composed of sub-units, the house-churches where Christian believers would meet in small groups for table-fellowship and eucharist. "The trend must have been towards the creation of separate Gentile and Jewish house-churches, which were grouped together under the umbrella of 'The Church of Antioch.' Unless the umbrella was to be a complete fiction, however, there had to be strong and regular links between the various house-churches."[86] Most important of the ties to bind the house-churches together would have been table fellowship. In the minds of their contemporaries, the language of community would have rung hollow if there were not regular gatherings at a common banquet.[87] But the distinction between Jewish and Gentile food and the division of the house-churches into Jewish and Gentile gatherings was still in Paul's mind a factor in the failure of the Antioch church to resist the teaching of the Judaizers.

From that point on, Paul was clear in his commitment, "Jews who wished to follow Christ would have to give up the observances in which their Jewish identity was rooted."[88] The church had to be one community without division. Later in his letter to the Galatians, Paul laid out his reasoning. "Abraham had first been blessed because he had accepted God's word. This act of faith was the basis of the fidelity that characterized the subsequent life of Abraham. Faith, therefore, was fundamental. All else was secondary, and in particular the Law."[89] Given the earlier covenant with Abraham, Paul questioned the necessity of the Law: "What I mean is this: The law, introduced 430 years later, does not set aside the covenant previously established by God and thus do away with the promise" (Gal 3:17). He employs rabbinic reasoning to argue that Jesus is the true descendant of Abraham. "The promises were spoken to Abraham and to his seed. Scripture does not say 'and to seeds,' meaning many people, but 'and to your seed,' meaning one person, who is Christ" (Gal 3:16). Therefore, all those who belong to Christ inherit the Promise since they are the true descendants of Abraham. Gentile Christians are in the same position as Jewish Christians, equal as inheritors of the covenant that God first offered to Abraham. It was faith in and fidelity to Christ that mattered, and nothing else needed to be added to the identity of the Christian.[90] No other identity marker could be claimed that overrode the fundamental reality that "all of you who were baptized into Christ have clothed yourselves with Christ. There is neither Jew nor Gentile, neither slave nor free, nor is there male and female, for you are all one in Christ Jesus" (Gal 3:27–28).

For Paul it was the experience of the Spirit that brought Christians into a relationship, because it was the Spirit who constituted the disciples as the church. It was by means of baptism in Christ that a diverse and growing population was transformed into a community, the body of Christ. Thus, Christians understood themselves not only as ministers to those in need, but at a deeper level, they were brothers and sisters to all who were children of God.

CHRISTIAN COMMUNITARIANISM

The emphasis on community within early Christianity continued throughout the patristic era. It is evident, for instance, in the stress that Christian authors put on acts of mercy and caring for the sick. Yet, there is one realm where the communal perspective of the Christian tradition is particularly striking, and that is the rationale offered for almsgiving and the duty of the Christian disciple to practice it. The Shepherd of Hermas uses the parable of the vine and the branches to promote solidarity between rich and poor.[91] Justin Martyr, possibly writing at about the same time as the Shepherd—mid-second century—also discussed the sharing of goods in the early church and the social impact of the Christian teaching on love as agape.[92]

Clement of Rome's teaching on possessions is closely linked to a communal outlook. "Every organism is composed of different elements; and this ensures the common good. Take the body as an instance. The head cannot function without the feet. Nor likewise, can the feet function without the head. Even the smallest of our physical members are indispensable and valuable to the whole body; yet all of them work together and are united in a single obedience to preserve the whole body intact." If there was any doubt as to why Christians must act always with an eye toward the community, Clement made an appeal that echoed Paul, "In Christ Jesus, then, we must preserve this corporate body of ours in its entirety."[93]

Over time, early Christian writers developed a sense of the social obligations that accompany ownership of property that was quite opposed to the Roman sense of property ownership as near absolute. Clement of Alexandria neither endorsed the alleged "communism" of the early church nor required the renunciation of property. He did, however, understand ownership as conditional. Writing at the end of the second century, Clement taught that wealth might be accrued by a disciple; however, it brings with it a duty of willingness to share. "God has given us the power to use our possessions, I admit, but only to the extent that it is necessary: He wishes them to be in common."[94] The theological justification for this viewpoint regarding possessions is made clear: "God himself has created human beings for communion or sharing with one another, by sharing himself first of all, and by sending his Word to all alike, and by making all things in common."[95]

Cyprian of Carthage in the first half of the third century wrote the first systematic work on almsgiving. For him "almsgiving is not simply an act of charity but a serious obligation of justice deriving from the duty of sharing the goods that God has destined for common use."[96] This understanding of almsgiving as a matter of justice became a commonplace in patristic writing. At the end of the third century, Lactantius integrated almsgiving into his teaching on the social nature of humans. "Whereas for Aristotle men must live together because they are weak and cannot survive by themselves, for Lactantius, man's sociability is something intrinsic to man's nature itself; we must live together because of our humanity."[97] God "wishes that men should live in society and that we should see in each human being our own nature."[98] Lactantius called the social consciousness of an individual the person's "humanity" and urged "we must always practice humanity. . . . What is practicing the virtue of humanity if not to love a man because he is a man, because he has the same nature as mine?"[99] And, of course, that nature entailed having been made in the image and likeness of God.

Basil the Great writing in the East also put great weight on humanity's social nature, meaning that humans are social animals, not solitary individuals who come together only because they are incapable of meeting needs by themselves. "Who does not know that man is a political and social animal, neither savage nor a lover of loneliness? Nothing, indeed, is so comparable with our nature as living in society and in dependence upon one another and as loving our own kind."[100] By the fourth century, the acceptance of the common nature of possessions, initiated by Cyprian, had led writers to embrace a new theme: Humans are simply stewards of God's creation, and there is no right to ownership that effectively denies temporal goods to those in genuine need. Basil preached, "You have been made the minister of a gracious

God, steward for your fellow-servants. . . . The wealth you handle belongs to others; think of it accordingly."[101] His fellow Cappadocian, Gregory of Nazianzus, asked his audience, "Do you think that kindness towards your neighbor is not something necessary, but free; not law but exhortation? I would wish and think it were so, were I not frightened by the possibility of being numbered among the goats on the left hand of the Sovereign Judge . . . not because they have done something forbidden . . . but their having failed to care for Christ himself in the person of the poor."[102] John Chrysostom was even more accusatory in his preaching on the parable of the rich man and Lazarus. John suggested that the rich man was a thief, not because he had robbed Lazarus but because Lazarus had been denied some of the rich man's possessions when in dire straits.[103]

The language of duty and obligation appear forcefully in Christian writing on almsgiving. The core insight is that the goods of the earth were meant by God for all people. While the practice of personal ownership is not forbidden and may even be a helpful way of organizing economic society, never to be forgotten is that personal ownership is relativized by the prior claim that all humankind has a share in the goods of creation.

If one turns from the Greek-speaking churches of the East to the Latin West, the outlook remains much the same. Ambrose of Milan in the late 300s pulled together several elements of the Christian rationale for almsgiving.

> When giving to the poor you are not giving him what is yours; rather you are paying back to him what is his. Indeed, what is common to all and has been given to all to make use of, you have usurped for yourself alone. The earth belongs to all, and not only to the rich; yet those who do not enjoy it are far fewer than those who do. You are paying back, therefore, your debt; you are not giving gratuitously what you do not owe.[104]

This quote weaves together several themes that reflect the social imagination of early Christians. First, the earth is meant for all; hence no claim to ownership of land or its produce is absolute. Second, the needy have a legitimate claim upon those who possess wealth; therefore, the giving of alms is not a matter of charity but of justice. Third, what came to be called the universal destiny of goods and the obligations of justice reflect what today is called solidarity, the idea that while human beings are bound together by ties of interdependence, they are united even more strongly by bonds of neighbor love.

Ambrose's mentee, Augustine, cast the longest shadow of the church fathers upon the Christian tradition. On this topic, however, he is not especially novel but falls in line with most of his predecessors. Among all earthly creatures, the human person "is pre-eminent, being made in the image of God . . . created as one individual; but he was not left alone. For the human race is, more than any other species, at once social by nature and anti-social by sin."[105] On this last point, Augustine's thinking here is very much in accord with what has been said earlier in chapter 3 about the Christian being called to enter into loving communion with God and neighbor. Such love requires freedom; it must be a communion that is sought and chosen, not imposed.

But with freedom comes the possibility of failing to use one's freedom to love, instead rejecting communion with God or with other creatures. "Sin is precisely this failure of freedom, this turning away from the divine invitation to communion."[106] This rejection of relationship need not be understood as an explicit turning away from the Creator or creature. Rather, it may be more a case of apathy than deliberate action: the lack of a response to the invitation to love or the half-hearted effort at building and sustaining a relationship. As James Keenan has put it, "sin is simply the failure to bother to love."[107] Or, as Stephen Pope has amended that claim, it may not be that we simply do not care or wish to bother; it may be that we love in a disordered way, choosing personal comfort over the urgent need of another. We are always motivated by something we love, however disordered. Augustine saw the problem was pride, we love ourselves wrongly and thereby come to love the neighbor wrongly.[108]

Regarding the issue of the social, rather than antisocial, dynamic in human nature, Augustine observed, "every human being is a part of the human race, and human nature is something social and possesses the capacity for friendship as a great and natural good."[109] The humanity we share leads Augustine to consider what we owe to one another as fellow creatures made by the same creator. Since we all have basic human needs, a person may possess those material goods necessary to human well-being. That sort of possession is legitimate, but if goods are misused or are superfluous, then the claim to ownership is weakened and the duty to share with others grows in weight. Consequently, a strict moral obligation to share one's superfluous goods with the truly needy follows. In fact, Augustine calls such a failure to share with the needy equivalent to fraud and theft.[110]

By the end of Augustine's life, the Christian faith had been the religion of the Roman Empire for more than a century. As Christianity became accepted by emperors and social elites, it attracted those interested in social advancement and there was a decline in the number of highly motivated converts with a corresponding concern among more fervent disciples about maintaining a standard of discipleship that appeared to be at risk. In reaction, there was a rise of interest in various movements of monasticism.[111] In the East, Basil the Great had written on the preference for communal monasticism over that of hermits. In the West, Augustine provided a rule for those who wished to live together in community that was used by clerics, nuns, and devout lay people. It is the oldest monastic rule in the West and eventually became identified closely with ordained clerics who lived together while engaging in pastoral work. Later in the sixth century, Benedict of Nursia wrote his rule that became the most influential text in the history of monasticism. He decisively moved monastic life away from rigorous asceticism and isolation, which had become practices in the East despite Basil's influence, and toward a shared life that practiced regular communal prayer, hospitality toward strangers, obedience, and labor. "His emphasis on the balance of work and prayer, his validation of community, and his regulation of monastic life . . . offered the witness of an alternative society governed by the spirit of Christ."[112]

The church's teaching on almsgiving illustrates the impact that the communitarian mindset had on early Christianity. Themes of the common use of the goods of creation, the common nature of humanity, the intrinsically social nature of the person, the bonds of compassion and love—all contributed to the doctrine on almsgiving. That communal outlook continued to be evident in later Christian authors and in practices of monastic and later mendicant religious. Clearly, the Catholic perspective on community is not based solely upon the need for others to assist in meeting bodily needs. It is not just that a society permits a division of labor or adds to the talent pool available for use. It is true that each of us alone is insufficient to secure physical well-being, given the hazards of disease, climate, violence, natural disasters, and other threats to our survival, no less our flourishing. But even so, the Catholic claim about the centrality of community for human life goes far beyond the need for cooperation in warding off threats to physical well-being. Rather, the tradition consistently reflected the belief that the drive to community is not an optional appendix to human nature but lies at the very heart of what it means to be fully human.

MORE RECENT CATHOLIC COMMUNITARIANISM

A standard reference on Catholic social teaching written prior to Vatican II emphasized that human persons are oriented to social life "as to the means for their realization as persons, that is to say, for their perfection."[113] Precisely by active engagement with others the human being can grow toward full stature; personal relationships are essential to human flourishing. The authors Calvez and Perrin point out that belief in the social nature of the person and the inherently personal character of society are conclusions reachable by philosophical thought.

Another influential pre-conciliar commentator on Catholic social theory, Heinrich Rommen, put the matter this way: "Sociality is as essential to human nature as is rationality."[114] Humans are "born by the lasting community of the family into social life." Over time, persons are "educated in that community" and mature within it. Every person is "formed by various communities" and, in turn, "forms them as a free agent." That social nature finds further "fulfillment in citizenship in the state" and in the family of humankind, "which is transcendent to the state."[115] The communitarian dimension of Catholic social thought is clear: people "achieve their happiness and their destiny not as separated individuals but as coordinated members bound by solidaric responsibility for one another."[116]

Catholic teaching, drawing upon divine revelation, has a lofty view of the social order. At the heart of the sociability of the human is the common origin shared by all persons. The church's teaching on creation not only underscores creaturely dependence upon the Creator, but also emphasizes that humans have a personal relationship with God as with a loving parent. And that awareness of care and intimacy with God leads to a sense of universal brotherhood and sisterhood in which all humanity is bound together.[117] That sensibility is meant to serve as a check upon a view of community turning into exclusivism and capable of xenophobia.

In addition to our common origin there is the doctrine of redemption, the belief that all humanity has been healed by the love of Christ, which, in principle, broke down the barriers between persons and called all to a sense of communion in his body. Finally, there is the bond among men and women that is shared by a common destiny to which all are called, eternal life within the loving embrace of the Trinity. Thus, the conviction of the Christian is that any adequate rendering of the human person, whether religious or philosophical, must account for the intrinsically social orientation of each and every person, namely that humankind is made for community. This is not simply an aspiration, but an existential condition of human life; we are made for communion.

Therefore, attention to the creation, maintenance, and promotion of the conditions necessary for human community is vital to the full development of individual persons. For those who adhere to belief in their membership in the body of Christ, this obligation to build and sustain community should be particularly evident. *The Dogmatic Constitution on the Church* issued at Vatican II states in its opening paragraph: "the Church is in Christ like a sacrament or as a sign and instrument both of a very closely knit union with God and of the unity of the whole human race."[118] Describing the Church as a sacrament of both "closely knit union with God" and "the unity of the whole human race" is simply a rephrasing of the gospel teaching that the two great commandments to love God and one's neighbor are not only interrelated but are substantially the same. To recognize that loving God is profoundly and intimately linked to love of neighbor is to be "not far from the kingdom of God" (Mark 12:34).

While surviving physically is one aim of human life, thinking and willing are of the essence of human life. And these acts often may have as their object another person, and a desire to communicate, to connect, to establish rapport and a relationship with the other. Human beings engage in acts of sympathy and empathy; the human is oriented to express love as the highest goal of social engagement. A necessity born of blind laws of nature does not drive and shape human sociality. Human community is not analogous to a beehive or anthill, but it is a work of human freedom whereby a person seeks fulfillment and a richer, more complete, and satisfactory form of life. Human life is transformed into a higher mode of existence through practices of self-devotion, self-giving, and love.

Of course, society is not all one type. Social relations may range in intensity from intimate interpersonal bonds to loose friendly contacts in voluntary associations to corporate bodies with legal regulations governing members' behavior. All are important and necessary, but the truest sense of community is found in those relations not characterized by legal forms but embodying qualities of loyalty, friendship, love, trust, faith, and self-donation. The underlying anthropology of such a perspective is one that opposes seeing the individual as a monad or that treats social bonds as accidental to human life.

When this vision of the person is employed to describe human society, it will emphasize the unity of persons bound together not only by needs but by human aspirations. As Johannes Messner, the author of yet another standard text of pre-conciliar political thought, wrote: "By reason of their inequality as individuals they are predisposed to pool their different endowments and faculties" in order to satisfy important needs; but "by reason of their equality of . . . [a] spiritual nature there is a human fellowship in common ends which lie beyond their physical existence in the realm of truth, goodness, and beauty."[119] Community is necessary for the biological, intellectual, moral, and spiritual well-being of the person. Fundamental to this view of society, therefore, is the importance of cooperative activities, "which bring into being something new, in which all members of society participate in the realization of their ends."[120] If the dignity of persons is only realized in community, and if the image of God in the human is Trinitarian, that suggests genuine humanity requires the existence of social relations that respect human freedom, assist in the meeting of human needs, and offer opportunities for persons to share life with others.

At Vatican II, the bishops used different images and language to characterize the social vision of Catholicism than much of the pre-conciliar texts of Catholic social philosophy. Yet, the essential insight about the deeply communal nature of humanity was not abandoned. In paragraphs 23–32 of Chapter 2 of the *Pastoral Constitution on the Church in the Modern World,* the Council reflected upon Catholic teaching about society. They began with an acknowledgement of the social encyclicals of John XXIII written in 1961 and 1963: "Since rather recent documents of the Church's teaching authority have dealt at considerable length with Christian doctrine about human society, this council is merely going to call to mind some of the more basic truths, treating their foundations under the light of revelation."[121]

Among those "basic truths" to be called to mind, the bishops refer to human beings having been created as one family since all people come from a common origin, a loving Creator who is also the common destiny of all human life. For this reason, love of God and neighbor is the first and greatest commandment. In John's gospel, Jesus is portrayed as praying to his Father, "that all may be one . . . as we are one."[122] Implied in that prayer is "a certain likeness between the union of the divine Persons, and in the union of God's children in truth and charity."[123] That likeness is reflected in the communitarian nature of humankind. "This social life is not something added on" to men and women. Therefore, it becomes imperative that human societies are properly structured, that is, "the subject, and the goal of all social institutions is and must be the human person, which for its part and by its very nature stands completely in need of social life."[124] Respect for the communal nature of the person is thereby closely connected to the promotion of the common good. An obligation is placed on every social group to "take account of the needs and legitimate aspirations of other groups, and even the general welfare of the entire human family."[125]

The bishops are convinced that "Christian revelation contributes greatly to the promotion of this communion between persons, and at the same time leads us to a deeper understanding of the laws of social life which the Creator has written into man's moral and spiritual nature."[126] That leads to the claim that the Lord Jesus, when He prayed to the Father, 'that all may be one . . . as we are one' (John 17:21–22) opened up vistas closed to human reason, for He implied a certain likeness between the union of the divine Persons, and the unity of God's sons [and daughters] in truth and charity. This likeness reveals that [the human person] who is the only creature on earth which God willed for itself, cannot fully find himself [or herself] except through a sincere gift of himself [or herself].[127]

Indeed, our "social nature makes it evident that the progress of the human person and the advance of society itself hinge on one another. From the beginning, the subject and the goal of all social institutions is and must be the human person which for its part and by its very nature stands completely in need of social life."[128] Consequently, promoting genuine community is a vital concern since it is through participation in the shared life of a community that persons are able to meet their responsibilities and attain their desired aim of human flourishing. The bishops also affirm "the common good, that is, the sum of those conditions of social life which allow social groups and their individual members relatively thorough and ready access to their own fulfillment," must be pursued both locally and globally.[129]

Because every human being is created in God's likeness and "since they have the same nature and origin, have been redeemed by Christ, and enjoy the same divine calling and destiny, the basic quality of all must receive increasingly greater recognition." Of course, the authors of the Pastoral Constitution acknowledge that not all are alike in every respect; there are differences in physical, intellectual, and moral resources, and these differences lead to actual differences among individuals and groups. Nevertheless, "although rightful differences exist between men, the equal dignity of persons demands that a more humane and just condition of life be brought about. . . . Human institutions, both private and public, must labor to minister to the dignity and purpose of persons."[130]

Another aspect of the social dimension of human dignity is the ability of each person to be an active member of those communities necessary for expression of his or her social nature. Within the Catholic social tradition, this is the theme of participation. If human beings not only desire but require communal bonds, then "the will to play one's role in common endeavors should be everywhere encouraged."[131] To act in accord with one's being made in the image and likeness of a God who is Trinity means that persons must have the opportunity to become a self-gift, to give oneself away to others as an expression of love of neighbor. Individuals and groups must be able to participate in communities so that the imago Dei may be actualized in the life of a person.

This line of thinking leads, then, to a final theme in Chapter 2 of *Gaudium et spes*: solidarity. "[F]rom the beginning of salvation history [God] has chosen persons not just as individuals but as members of a certain community." Recalling the creation narrative from Genesis, the bishops declared that "God did not create humankind for life in isolation, but for the formation of social unity." They go on to observe that the life of Jesus makes clear that the Redeemer in his ministry willingly sought ties with people of various backgrounds and vocations. "He commanded his apostles to preach to all peoples the gospel message so that the human race might become the family of God, in which the fullness of the Law would be love."[132] Through the working of his Spirit, a new community, the church, was begun so that the bonds of faith and love might exemplify the solidarity to which all people are called.

POST-CONCILIAR THOUGHT
ON COMMUNITARIANISM

A prominent and influential book on Catholic social thought published in Germany when Vatican II was beginning went through eight subsequent updated editions and was published in six languages besides the original German. The author, Bishop Joseph Höffner, later archbishop and cardinal, maintained "all personal being essentially strives toward giving and sharing, so that personal being is of its essence ordered to the 'thou' of the other and to society." When discussing the social nature of the human, Höffner stated, "it seems obvious to emphasize first of all his dependence on the other and on society."[133] No other animal on earth requires the amount of time and assistance in being nurtured to survive as does the human animal. This simple fact demonstrates the essentially interdependent nature of the human. Höffner's point was an argument drawn from a natural law standpoint, and he did not refer to a theological foundation for the social nature of the human.

A more recent essay moves from the claim of interdependence to the theological warrant of Trinity. James Hanvey refers to "the deeper insights of the Trinitarian *imago*, namely that the dignity of the human person is ultimately grounded in relationality: first to God, and then to each other."[134] For Hanvey, it is the image of the Trinity that marks each person and which "discloses the dynamic of love at the centre of the person." Hanvey employs a theological formulation, traced back to Augustine, to explain why human beings are both sacred and social. We are made for relationship and called to be a covenanted community that lives in fidelity with God and our fellow creatures.

Understanding the depth of the divine image in the process of creation has led to speculation about the nature of the universe. In a reflection upon the scientific evidence of the sheer size of the universe—the trillions of stars and billions of galaxies—the theologian Thomas O'Meara observes that stars, planets, and galaxies tend to gather in clusters, occupying perhaps as little as one or two percent of the space of the universe. With so much of space an empty void and so much matter drawn together, he wonders if "there may be a primal, underlying reality common to the universe and to its creator, something essential to what is both divinely infinite and creaturely finite."[135] O'Meara poses the question: "Do the structures of the cosmos suggest that being in all its variety is essentially communal?"[136] The evidence being accrued through astrophysics suggests that "being could hold within itself a dynamic, a tendency, or format of community." Such a perspective is "not so much a theology of the human being in God but of the divine in creatures."[137]

Given that "God is Father, Son and Holy Spirit in reciprocal communion" and that each has coexisted for eternity, it can be said that "in the beginning is not the solitude of a One, of an eternal being, alone and infinite," but from the "beginning is the communion of the three unique Ones."[138] So does all creation reflect this claim about the Creator? As O'Meara underscores, "God being somehow pluriform is not asserted as one possible mode for a supreme being. . . . Community is the ultimate reality of God. . . . The being that is divine can only be communal."[139] So then it would seem plausible to infer that if God's life as Trinity is foundational, "the basic pattern of the format of the universe" will reflect the nature of the Creator.[140]

Certainly, Catholic social thought has followed this theme of the communal nature of human existence. As one commentator has observed: "The basic storyline of the tradition is this: we are persons in communities, inhabitants of deep stories and creatures oriented toward interdependence and cooperation. We seek to associate, organize, create, care and be cared for and struggle to overcome all that isolates, fragments and destroys." And this reading of theological anthropology has clear social implications, "the social forms we create through institutions of government, social and economic exchange, leisure and culture are further dimensions" of the Catholic view of the human person.[141] Once it is recognized that the language of communion plays such a central role in Catholic social thought, that is, the "language of being-in-relation," then it becomes evident that "exchanges of relationality are *the* basic and most fundamental context for human being."[142]

There is in the Catholic social tradition an oft-used analogy to convey the essential sociality of humankind; it is that of an organism. It is an analogy that pre-dates Christianity, having been used by Plato and Aristotle, comparing society to an organism. Catholicism has used the organism analogy to combat individualistic views of society that undercut the common good or ignore bonds of solidarity. The danger of the analogy is that an individual cell is completely given to the service of the larger organism, but a human must not be used solely for the good of society. Each individual person has their own dignity and worth; they are not just a part of a body that is subservient to the overall need of the whole. In a genuine community the good of the individual is not lost sight of nor is the individual ever reduced to being a tool for the whole. In Catholic social teaching, the person is served by society, not dominated by it. Throughout history totalitarian regimes and authoritarian rulers have abused individual persons in the name of some greater good. So there is the risk that some language employed to express the social nature of the person can be misused to such an extent that the dignity of the person is violated.

This comment about the way that human sociality can be misunderstood and used against a person's well-being points to the reality of sin in the human situation. As Anna Rowlands has noted, we are "fallen beings who misrecognize the good, actively refuse it, disengage in fear, fall into forms of passivity and act as agents of direct individual and structural violence and harm." The social life we create can be directed to supporting and protecting what serves human dignity in community, but the social institutions and culture we create "are susceptible to the same processes of misrecognition and refusal that mark our individual journeys."[143]

Pope Francis has spoken of the social ills that frustrate the purposes of the Creator. "One of these is a distorted view of the person, a perspective that ignores the dignity and relational nature of the person." He referred to the "throw-away culture" where "we look at others as objects, to be used and discarded." Francis, on the other hand, recalls that "God looks at a man and a woman in another manner." We are made in the divine image with a unique dignity, "calling us to live in communion with Him, in communion with our sisters and brothers, with respect for all creation." For the pope it is a simple lesson of faith that "the human being, indeed, in his or her personal dignity, is a social being, created in the image of God, One and Triune. We are social beings."[144]

According to the International Theological Commission, that sense of humans as social beings also extends to a wider set of relations: "human beings have developed a heightened awareness that they are organically linked with other beings. Nature has come to be seen as a biosphere in which all living beings form a complex yet carefully organized network of life."[145] The Commission suggests that the Incarnation, or what it calls "God's 'hominization' is his act of solidarity, not only with creaturely persons, but with the entire created universe and its historical destiny."[146] Acknowledging that "theology will not be able to provide us with a technical recipe for the resolution of the ecological crisis," the ITC does avow that theology "can help us see our natural environment as God sees it, as the space of personal communion in which human beings, created in the image of God, must seek communion with one another."[147]

Over the years Catholic communitarianism has evolved in such a manner that it essentially entails a posture that stands between the individualism of an excessive liberalism and the collectivism of an excessive socialism. With regard to the latter, there is a rejection of group domination of individual interests; with regard to the former, there is a rejection of individual interests understood as independent of group well-being. Catholic communitarianism is not a fixed ideology but a perspective that sees the dignity of the individual as being realized only in a virtuous community. Concern for the well-being of the community, therefore, is not over and against individual well-being, but the context within which the person's well-being is brought about. This way of envisioning social reality flows from recognition of the way that community is fundamental to the human person. Promoting the true interests of the community is no more a threat to the individual person than promoting unpolluted water is a threat to fish; rather, it is securing the conditions within which the individual can flourish.

The papacy of Francis has enriched this emphasis on communitarianism in Catholic social thought. In his encyclical *Fratelli Tutti*, Francis states that his desire is to "contribute to the rebirth of a universal aspiration to fraternity."[148] In a reflection on Francis's use of the word *fraternity*, Carmen Nanko-Fernández suggests that the language of fraternity "might serve as a hyperlink to a larger world of meaning and solidarity."[149] And it is precisely that larger world that the philosopher Charles Taylor also observes in the writing of Francis. Suggesting that the Pope is not content to merely write about moral obligation in a global society, Taylor notes "the encyclical operates in another dimension, which we might describe as the fullness of humanity and how to reach it."[150] Both Nanko-Fernandez and Taylor are correct in their commentary on the agenda of Francis in the encyclical.

Carlos Calleja offers an important insight into the papal mind. He notes that Francis acknowledges that "one aspect" of fraternity is our common human nature irrespective of country of origin or religion; fraternity is in that sense a given. But, Calleja observes, fraternity "is also something that is actively wrought as we forge our relationships with others." He points to Francis's extended reflection on the parable of the Good Samaritan in Chapter 2 of *Fratelli Tutti* as providing a clue to Francis's thinking about fraternity. "The crux of that well-known parable is that Jesus turns the scribe's question on its head. Jesus does not answer the question, 'Who is my neighbor?' but instead invites the scribe to *become* a neighbor to the person in need."[151]

This, then, is what Taylor meant when he said that Francis wants to accentuate "another dimension" of fraternity, that of philosophical and theological anthropology. It is a vision whereby we are "realizing more fully our humanity through contact and exchange with people and cultures beyond our original comfort zone. Through these exchanges new creative possibilities are disclosed and human life is enriched." Taylor does not deny that Francis has a sense of the moral duties incumbent upon disciples, but "Francis is not just telling us that we have not lived up to our responsibilities; . . . beyond these moral demands the Gospel also calls on us to grow, to emerge from our cramped, fear-driven lives."[152]

What Francis is proposing in his encyclical is to fashion a new perspective that corrects the myopic vision of those cultures that do not see some others as truly human persons beloved by God and equal in dignity to all other persons. He uses "fraternity" as a code-word for that new alternative perspective. "If the conviction that all human beings are brothers and sisters is not to remain an abstract idea but to find concrete embodiment, then numerous related issues emerge, forcing us to see things in a new light and to develop new responses."[153]

Francis believes that we live in a world where far too many of us do not see or hear or recognize the presence of others in our world. He views globalization as one failed effort to provide a correct perspective. "We are more than ever in an increasingly massified world that promotes individual interests and weakens the communitarian dimension of life."[154] Francis cites his predecessor Benedict's assessment that, "as society becomes ever more globalized, it makes us neighbors, but does not make us brothers."[155] The Catholic social tradition envisions the human person who is made for community as capable of reciprocity with others and attaining mutual enrichment through the sharing of life. Benedict XVI made the point that love "is the principle not only of micro-relationships (with friends, with family members or within small groups) but also of macro-relationships (social, economic, and political ones)."[156] This is related to what Francis means by referring to the "law of *Ekstasis*,"[157] a phrase that he borrows from then Karol Wojtyla's 1960 book, *Love and Responsibility*; the idea is that persons who love go out of themselves in self-giving, only to find a fuller existence through the act of self-donation.

Although Pope Francis does not explicitly cite Francis of Assisi in this context, the influence of the medieval saint is evident throughout the encyclical and not only in the title of the letter. For Francis, the saint, the language of fraternity did at least two things. First, when people approach one another as a brother or sister, there is a nonhierarchical quality to the relationship; people encounter one another on level ground. Francis of Assisi deliberately avoided the already existing language of monasticism with its abbots and priors, and he spoke to all friars as his brothers, cleric or lay. There was no culture of clericalism or hierarchy among the early generations of Franciscans. Francis, the pope, has something of the instinct of Francis the saint, employing fraternity as the key word in his suggested social perspective is meant to undercut the tendency to create relationships of higher or lower status, in-group and out-group dynamics. As the German theologian Marianne Heimbach-Steins comments, fraternity functions as a remedy for the various power-asymmetries that misshape so many social projects.[158]

The second lesson regarding fraternity in the Franciscan tradition has to do with Francis's Final Testament, which he wrote as a farewell message to his friars. At one point, he recalls how he began his conversion in response to a personal call he received from God and that his original intent had nothing to do with beginning a religious movement or community. But, Francis wrote, "the Lord gave me some brothers." This was a key insight into Francis's life and ministry. Although he sometimes found the fraternity a source of disappointment and suffering, Francis maintained his belief that his fellow friars were a gift from God. The man who initially understood his calling as an individual never doubted that gratitude was the appropriate stance at the arrival of more and more would-be Franciscans. To see the other, one's brother and sister, as a gift to be valued and appreciated encourages an attitude of reciprocal care among members of a society. These two dimensions of fraternity in the Franciscan tradition may help us grasp the "something greater" that Pope Francis thinks fraternity brings to the language of liberty and equality.

In his encyclical, Francis observes that political ideologies on the right and left have stressed liberty and equality, but that neither has adequately addressed the third element of the triad, fraternity. "Fraternity is born not only of a climate of respect for individual liberties, or even of a certain administratively guaranteed equality. Fraternity necessarily calls for something greater, which in turn enhances freedom and equality."[159] Francis desires to see social friendship and universal fraternity that acknowledges the dignity and worth of each person and which creates communities that allow each person to give themselves to others and receive the gift of others.

CONCLUSION

This chapter has explored the Catholic understanding of human dignity and how the meaning of the term has evolved within the tradition. While various voices in the Catholic community have placed the emphasis on one or another aspect of dignity, there is a fairly constant situating of dignity within the experience of communion with God and others. Within the tradition, the language may be that of social friendship or fraternity or community, but what this chapter illustrates is that when the Catholic tradition uses the language of community as a root metaphor for social life, then the resultant social vision is communitarian. That is, it is a vision placing an emphasis on the relational or communal context for understanding the human person and for promoting and protecting the dignity of the person.

NOTES

1. Michael Rosen, *Dignity: Its History and Meaning*, 8.
2. Autiero, "Human Dignity in an Ethical Sense," 13.
3. Autiero, 14.
4. Autiero, 15.
5. Autiero, 15.
6. Müller, "Concepts and Dimensions," 23.
7. Müller, 24. She is quoting Konrad Hilpert, *Die Menschenrechte*, 189.
8. Müller, 24.
9. Darlene Fozard Weaver, "Dignity: A Catholic Perspective," 31–32.
10. Fozard Weaver, 32–33.
11. Fozard Weaver, 35–36.
12. Fozard Weaver, 37–38.
13. Fozard Weaver, 40.
14. See Müller, "Concepts and Dimensions," 45.
15. Autiero, "Human Dignity in an Ethical Sense," 11.
16. Rosen, *Dignity*, 11.
17. Rosen, 12.
18. Rosen, 12.
19. Rosen, 13.
20. Müller, "Concepts and Dimensions," 30–31.
21. Müller, 31.
22. Phan, *Social Thought*, 92.

23. Phan, 93.
26. Müller, "Concepts and Dimensions," 32.
27. Gregory of Nazianzus, "On the Love of the Poor," 25 in Phan, *Social Thought*, 125.
28. Gregory of Nazianzus, 26 in Phan, 126.
29. Phan, 122.
30. Phan, 127.
31. Müller, "Concepts and Dimensions," 35.
32. Müller, 35.
33. Augustine, "Letter 130 [to Proba]," 12 in Phan, *Social Thought*, 207.
34. Müller, "Concepts and Dimensions," 37.
35. Müller, 37.
36. Müller, 37–38.
37. Müller, 38
38. Thomas Aquinas, *Commentary on the Sentences*, III, distinction 35, q.1, art.5, solution 1c, as quoted in Rosen, *Dignity*, 16–17.
39. Rosen, 17.
40. Rosen, 15.
41. Rosen, 18. I have drawn upon Rosen's account for most of this paragraph and the preceding one.
42. The title is due to the evidence of active Christians in France already in the second century.
43. Leo XIII, *Quod apostolici muneris*, n.6.
44. Michael Schuck, *That They Be One*, 179.
45. James Hanvey faults Rosen's reading of Leo on dignity and equality as inadequate, failing to see that Leo spoke of dignity as both intrinsic and extrinsic. Yet Hanvey, though correct in challenging Rosen's interpretation of Leo, does not adequately acknowledge that Leo's treatment of dignity was insufficiently connected to social reality. One might say that Leo affirmed the "intrinsic" equal dignity of all before God but failed significantly to recognize the "extrinsic" political, economic, and social implications of his affirmation. It remained more of a religious perspective than a focus for social teaching or an engine for promoting social reform. One sees this in Leo's belief that workers should not try to move beyond their station in life since it was ordained by God that they should be there. See James Hanvey, "Dignity, Person, and *Imago Trinitatis*," 212–214, esp. fns. 12 and 13.
46. John Cronin, "Forty Years Later: Reflections and Reminiscences," 73. In this essay, Cronin reflects on the way that many Americans misinterpreted Pius's encyclical to place a stifling burden on the role of employers in establishing a just wage during economic crisis.
47. Pius XII, "Radio Message of His Holiness Pius XII to the People of the Entire World" (1944), https://www.vatican.va/content/pius-xii/en/speeches/1944/documents/hf_p-xii_spe_19441224_natale.html
48. John XXIII, *Mater et magistra*, n. 65.
49. John XXIII, *Pacem in terris*, n. 35.
50. John XXIII, n. 8–38.
51. John XXIII, n. 5.
52. Rosen, *Dignity*, 9.
53. I draw upon John Crosby, "Foreward" ix–xi in the paragraphs describing the situation of Catholic intellectuals at the time of the Great War.
54. Burgos, *Introduction to Personalism*, 8.

55. "Yet nothing can be more remote from the facts than the belief that 'personalism' is one school or doctrine. It is rather a phenomenon of reaction against two opposite errors," namely individualism and collectivism. Jacques Maritain, *The Person and the Common Good*, 12.

56. Burgos, *Introduction to Personalism*, 32.

57. Autiero, "Human Dignity in an Ethical Sense," 11.

58. Anna Rowlands, *Towards a Politics of Communion*, 53.

59. Lothar Roos, "The Human Person and Human Dignity as Basis of the Social Doctrine of the Church," 54.

60. Rowlands, *Towards a Politics of Communion*, 53.

61. John Dwyer, "Person, Dignity of," 733.

62. Vatican II, *Gaudium et spes*, n. 22.

63. David Hollenbach, "Human Dignity: Experience and History, Practical Reason and Faith," 123–139.

64. Hollenbach, 129. The phrase "obligating features of personhood" is from Margaret Farley, "A feminist version of respect for persons," *Journal of Feminist Studies in Religion* 9 (1993): 183–198.

65. Hollenbach, "Human Dignity: Experience and History," 130.

66. Hollenbach, 131.

67. Hollenbach, 132.

68. Roos, "The Human Person and Human Dignity," 57.

69. National Conference of Catholic Bishops, "A Pastoral Message: Economic Justice for All," n. 14.

70. James Keenan, *Moral Wisdom*, 95 (italic added).

71. Groome, *Faith for the Heart*, 190.

72. Daniel Finn, *Christian Economic Ethics*, 48.

73. John Donahue, *Seek Justice That You May Live*, 49.

74. Lohfink, *Jesus of Nazareth*, 60.

75. Lohfink, 60.

76. Lohfink, 61.

77. Lohfink, 67.

78. Lohfink, 69.

79. John Gager, *Kingdom and Community*, 83.

80. Luke Johnson, *Acts of the Apostles*, 9. I rely upon Johnson's commentary extensively in this sub-section.

81. This account of Pentecost is likely a telescoped version of events occurring over the course of a longer period of time. But Luke's narrative is important not for the historical details but for his account that a number of Jews accepted the Christian message and began a common life together in Jerusalem.

82. Johnson, *Acts*, 58.

83. Johnson, 62.

84. Murphy-O'Connor, *Paul*, 202.

85. Murphy-O'Connor, 11. I follow Murphy-O'Connor's narrative and interpretation of the clash at Antioch-on-Orontes; see 107–112.

86. Murphy-O'Connor, 42.

87. Murphy-O'Connor's point about the significance of table-fellowship to express community is strongly supported by the research of Kloppenborg on the central role of

eating and drinking in fostering connectivity and the performative nature of these banquets. See Kloppenborg, *Christ's Associations*, 209–244.

88. Murphy-O'Connor, 115.

89. Murphy-O'Connor, 136–37.

90. Murphy-O'Connor, 137.

91. Shepherd of Hermas, "Second Similitude," 5 in Phan, *Social Thought*, 53–54.

92. Justin Martyr, "First Apology," 14, 67, and "Dialogue with Trypho," 93 in Phan, 56–58.

93. Clement of Rome, "First Letter to the Corinthians," 37–38, in Phan, 47.

94. Clement of Alexandria, "The Tutor," 2.12.120, in Phan, 67.

95. Clement of Alexandria, 2.12.120, in Phan, 66–67.

96. Phan, 85.

97. Phan, 93.

98. Lactantius, *The Divine Institutes*, 6,11 in Phan, 96–97.

99. Lactantius, 6, 11 in Phan, 97.

100. Basil the Great, "The Long Rules," in Phan, 119.

101. Basil the Great, "I Will Pull Down My Barns," 2, in Phan, 114.

102. Gregory Nazianzus, "On the Love of the Poor," 39, in Phan, 126.

103. John Chrysostom, "On Lazarus," Homily II,4, in Phan, 137–38.

104. Ambrose of Milan, "On Naboth," 53, in Phan, 173–74.

105. Augustine of Hippo, *City of God*, XII, 28, in Phan, 233.

106. ITC, "Communion and Stewardship," n. 44.

107. Keenan, *Moral Wisdom*, 42.

108. Personal communication with the author.

109. Augustine of Hippo, *The Good of Marriage*, 7 in Phan, *Social Thought*, 195.

110. See Augustine of Hippo, Sermons 50, 4; 206, 2; and 178, 3–4, as cited in Phan, 197.

111. Finn, *Christian Economic Ethics*, 107.

112. Johnson, Acts, 16.

113. Jean-Yves Calvez and Jacques Perrin, *The Church and Social Justice*, 111.

114. Heinrich Rommen, *The State in Catholic Thought*, 138.

115. Rommen, *The State*, 77.

116. Rommen, 138.

117. Calvez and Perrin, *Church and Social Justice*, 112.

118. Vatican II, *Lumen gentium*, n.1.

119. Johannes Messner, *Social Ethics*, 101.

120. Messner, 103.

121. Vatican II, *Gaudium et spes*, 23. The encyclicals of John were *Mater et magistra* (1961) and *Pacem in terris* (1963).

122. John 17:21–22.

123. Vatican II, *Gaudium et spes*, n. 24.

124. Vatican II, n. 25.

125. Vatican II, n. 26.

126. Vatican II, n. 23.

127. Vatican II, n. 24.

128. Vatican II, n. 25

129. Vatican II, n. 26.

130. Vatican II, n. 29.

131. Vatican II, n. 31.

132. Vatican II, n. 32.

133. Joseph Höffner, *Christian Social Teaching*, 22.

134. Hanvey, "Dignity, Person, and *Imago Trinitatis*," 221.

135. Thomas O'Meara, "Community as Primal Reality," 435.

136. O'Meara, 436.

137. O'Meara, 440.

138. Leonardo Boff, *Holy Trinity, Perfect Community* (Maryknoll: Orbis, 2000), 3; as quoted in O'Meara, "Community as Primal Reality," 440.

139. O'Meara, 442.

140. O'Meara, 443.

141. Rowlands, *Towards a Politics of Communion*, 6.

142. Rowlands, 9.

143. Rowlands, 6.

144. All quotes taken from Pope Francis's remarks at a General Audience, "Faith and Human Dignity."

145. ITC, "Communion and Stewardship," n. 71.

146. ITC, n. 75.

147. ITC, n. 78.

148. Francis, *Fratelli tutti*, n. 8

149. Carmen Nanko-Fernandez, "What Francis Means by 'Fratelli Tutti,'" *Commonweal* (9/24/2020) at https://www.commonwealmagazine.org/about-title

150. Charles Taylor, "Freedom and Equality Aren't Enough," *Commonweal* (12/2020) at https://www.commonwealmagazine.org/freedom-equality-arent-enough

151. Carlos Calleja, "To understand Pope Francis, you have to know what he actually means by the word 'fraternity,'" *America* (2/4/2021) at https://www.americamagazine.org/faith/2021/02/04/pope-francis-fratelli-tutti-friendship-fraternity-239916

152. Taylor, "Freedom and Equality Aren't Enough."

153. Francis, *Fratelli tutti*, n. 128.

154. Francis, n. 12.

155. Benedict XVI, *Caritas in veritate*, n. 19.

156. Benedict XVI, n. 2.

157. Francis, *Fratelli tutti*, n. 49.

158. Marianne Heimbach-Steins, "Pope Francis' Encyclical Letter Fratelli tutti—Focal Points and Aspects from the Discussion in Germany," *Catholic Theological Ethics in the World Church*, (12/1/2020) at https://catholicethics.com/forum/fratelli-tutti-germany/

159. Francis, *Fratelli tutti*, n. 103.

5

THE HUMAN PERSON ADEQUATELY CONSIDERED

While the twin foundations of the anthropology of Catholic social teaching—the sacred and social nature of the person—are crucial to understanding the tradition, these foundations can and must be expanded upon to understand the way that the tradition views the human person. Chapter 4 drew out two implications of the twin foundations: that we are creatures of dignity and worth, and that human dignity is attained within the context of genuine community. In this chapter the Catholic vision of the person will be further examined by presenting several key themes that have been given extensive treatment in Catholic theology. While these themes can only be summarized here, the aim is to further flesh out an understanding of the human person in the Catholic tradition.

As noted in Chapter 3, the idea of what characteristic of the human best reflects the presence of the imago Dei has been an ongoing conversation over the centuries. Various qualities—reason, free will, conscience, relationality—have been proposed as the key element. In this chapter I will mainly draw upon two sources for understanding the human person in the Catholic tradition: a significant text of the Second Vatican Council and an important reflection on the written record of the Council's discussions on the human person.

GAUDIUM ET SPES: WHAT DOES THE CHURCH THINK OF THE HUMAN PERSON?

The Pastoral Constitution on the Church in the Modern World was one of the last documents approved at Vatican II and is the longest conciliar document in the history of the Catholic church. Of special concern here are Chapters 1 and 2 of Part 1, which take up the topics of human dignity and community.

As we saw previously in this volume, there have been voices within the Catholic tradition that have proposed one or another feature of the human person as being the expression of the imago Dei. *Gaudium et spes* does not deny basic dimensions of the human person, but it did not endorse any single quality as definitive of the human, offering instead an array of human characteristics linked to the dignity of the person.

The authors of the document acknowledge several facets that are integral to the experience of human dignity in community, among which is the unity of the human person, that is, the human as an embodied spirit. The spiritual and material dimensions of human existence are not to be separated nor seen as being in conflict. While humans transcend the material world through our vocation to be in relationship with God, we remain material beings, and our dignity can be debased and violated by material conditions that are unworthy of our embodiment, such as torture, violence, and destitution. Each person is to regard his or her body "as good and honorable since God created it and will raise it up on the last day."[1]

Human dignity is connected with the gift of reason for through our intellect we share "in the light of the divine mind." Through the use of reason, humanity "has indeed made progress in the practical sciences, technology, and the liberal arts." But reason can go even further in the search for wisdom: "For wisdom gently attracts the mind of the person to a quest and a love for what is true and good." By wisdom we are "humanized" and grow into the ability to contemplate and appreciate God's activity in the world.[2]

The ability to seek truth and goodness leads to another essential aspect of the human condition, the phenomenon of conscience. The human capacity to seek the good as well as the true is integral to a person. Men and women mature in discovering and formulating a set of moral values which guide and direct the formation of character and practical choices of appropriate behavior. Children may experience a moral code as a set of rules imposed by parents or other authority. But mature persons develop values and standards through the exercise of conscience in a dialogue between the individual and those communities to which he or she has loyalty.

This last point naturally leads to another essential facet of the human person: human freedom. The search for truth and goodness requires freedom, "For God has willed that a person be left 'in the hand of his own counsel'" in the quest for the God who is truth and goodness. Human dignity "demands that a person act according to a knowing and free choice. Such a choice is personally motivated and prompted from within." When human beings act without external pressure or by blind impulse but freely, then such freedom is, indeed, "an exceptional sign" of the imago Dei.[3]

Freedom, however, has another side when people choose not virtue but vice in their lives. As the bishops at the Council acknowledged, "Although made by God in a state of holiness, from the very dawn of history humans abused their liberty." The Genesis story of creation makes clear that the reality of evil was not part of God's plan but came about due to human choice. "Often refusing to acknowledge God as his beginning, a person has disrupted also his proper relationship to his own ultimate goal. At the same time the person became out of harmony with himself, with others, and with all created things." Because of sin, "all of human life, whether individual or collective, shows itself to be a dramatic struggle between good and evil."[4]

So, in Chapter 1 of the Pastoral Constitution, we find the bishops proposing the unity of body and spirit, reason, conscience, and freedom as all intimately connected to human dignity. They acknowledge that despite these qualities, another aspect of the human condition, sin, can blind a person to the dignity of others as well as one's own dignity. The bishops noted that sin marks humanity both individually and collectively, which is only to be expected since we are essentially relational. Just as no one element of the human person can be simply identified with the image of God, there is no single basis for human dignity. Rather, the Pastoral Constitution named an array of qualities that are essential to any adequate rendering of the human.

THE PERSON INTEGRALLY AND ADEQUATELY CONSIDERED

A commission working on the chapter dealing with marriage and family life in *Gaudium et spes* sought to address the issue of a couple wanting to harmonize the dual goods of expressing conjugal love and responsible parenthood. While the draft of the text was undergoing revision there was concern that sexual intercourse not be treated solely as a biological or physical act but as a *personal* act, with the multiple dimensions that should suggest. The official record of the discussion stated a proposed revision was to "express the idea that the acts being spoken about here are not reducible to their mere biological aspects but actually refer to those activities of the human person integrally and adequately considered."[5]

Years after the conclusion of the Council, the Belgian theologian Louis Janssens authored an essay that included an extended commentary on the phrase "the human person integrally and adequately considered."[6] At the outset, Janssens made clear the official commentary indicated this expression, "the human person integrally and adequately considered," was "a general principle" and applicable not only to marriage and sexuality but to "the entire domain of human activity." In the author's words, "in order to determine whether or not an act is worthy of man or morally good, one must apply the criterion of 'the human person adequately considered,' i.e., in all his essential aspects or constitutive elements."[7]

Janssens then turned to elaborating those essential, constant, and constitutive aspects and proposed eight such elements in any adequate portrayal of the human person.

1. "*The human person is a subject,* not an object as are the things of the world." This claim entails consideration of a person as "one who is competent to act knowingly and willfully and as such is the principle of his acts or in control of his conduct."[8]

2. "*The person is a subject in corporeality.*" This means "that our body forms a part of the integrated subject that we are: corporeal and spiritual, nonetheless a singular being."[9]

3. "*Our body forms* not only a part of the subject who we are, but also, as corporeal, *a part of the material world....* Because we are corporeal, we need the things of the world. . . . We must make the world continuously more liveable for human persons."[10]

4. "*Human persons are essentially directed toward each other....* This is so true that a child can only progress toward being a moral subject with and through others. . . . Only in relation with a Thou can man become an I."[11]

5. "*Human persons* are not only essentially social beings because they are open to each other in the I–Thou relationship, but also because they *need to live in social groups* and thus in appropriate structures and institutions. We must live in society."[12]

6. "*Created in the image of God, the human person is called to know and worship Him and to glorify him in all his attitudes and activities.*"[13]

7. "*The human person is a historical being* (historicity). The life of every human being is a history which, according to developmental psychology, we can speak of as successive stages of life."[14]

8. "*All human persons are fundamentally equal, but at the same time each is an originality*... we share in the same human nature ... we share

in the same fundamental situation. . . . Fundamental equality explains why moral demands are universalizable. . . . But *in this framework* and *on this basis* of fundamental equality each person is simultaneously an originality, a unique subject."[15]

For Janssens, "[t]he promotion of the humanum—that which promotes the human person, adequately considered—becomes a moral obligation." He then proposes his tripartite "personalist criterion" for morality that (1) "an act is morally good if it serves the humanum, human dignity, that is, if it in truth—according to reason enlightened by revelation—is beneficial to the human person adequately considered *in himself* (as personal subject in corporeality, points 1&2) and *in his relations* (in his openness to the world, to others, to social groups and to God, points 3,4,5, & 6)."[16] (2) This is not a one-time discernment process for due to "the historicity of the person (point 7) this criterion requires that we again and again reconsider which possibilities we have at our disposal at this point in history to serve the promotion of the human person." And (3) "in conjunction with this we must, in our acts, respect the originality of all as much as possible (point 8)."[17] In sum, an act is moral if it respects the humanum in its historicity and originality.

Since the publication of Janssens's essay, several other moral theologians have offered their own variation on his personalist criterion, not so much by way of substantive alteration as by way of more concise formulation or additional nuance. Richard Gula has captured the essence of Janssens's framework under four headings: the human person is a relational being, an embodied subject, an historical subject, and one who is fundamentally equal but uniquely original.[18]

1. To be relational is to be directed toward others. We are shaped by interaction with others and find our fulfillment in communion, not isolation. Besides other human individuals, objects of our relationships include God, groups of others, human culture, and the nonhuman world. As beings who are social by nature, we require social structures that reflect our personal dignity and the common good.

2. As embodied *subjects*, we are agents with a measure of autonomy and self-determination who should be able to act according to our conscience, which should be both free and informed. We have a relation with our own inner selves. As *embodied* subjects we are part of the material world and the basic goods of physical existence are necessary for all, while the risks to physical existence ought to be minimized. The experience that physical illness can have on our emotional or

spiritual state testifies that as embodied spirits, our bodily life cannot be divorced from our inner life. The person is a unity. Through our bodies we interact with other persons and with the wider natural world of creatures.

3. Historical subjects are subject to time and processes of development both individually and culturally. We cannot understand humans and their actions divorced from the cultural context in which they live. Nor can we understand the person apart from processes of maturation and growth that come with aging, education, and life experience.

4. Because we are fundamentally equal we incur moral obligations due to our basic equality since no one should be marginalized nor utilized as a mere instrument for others. Yet we are also each unique in a variety of ways: genetically, our unconscious, our social conditioning. Each of us develops a worldview that affects our way of viewing and understanding experience. This personal perspective sets limits upon what we can ask of each other; since no person sees things exactly the same way, we cannot presume that each person has the same ability to respond or act in a situation. We must take responsibility for developing our capabilities to the extent to which they can be altered.

A former student of Janssens, Mary Elsbernd, relies heavily on her teacher's insights but highlights how feminist thinking has an affinity with Janssens's proposed anthropology, while emphasizing certain points more vividly. Elsbernd suggests that feminist theology would emphasize "the essential *relationality* of human persons and those qualities that facilitate authentic relationship, namely participation, reciprocity and interdependence. She also underscores that "*human embodiment* must be integrated into anthropology," but in a way that "does not ascribe social roles, worth, and qualities on the basis of anatomy." "Concrete and particular human experience" must be a source for a genuine anthropology for "*social location* constitutes human persons." A fourth aspect of theological anthropology highlighted by feminist thought is that "difference" is not only to be tolerated but such diversity is to be celebrated "as constitutive of authentic human living."[19] This latter point requires "a plurality of voices in the formation of Catholic Social Teachings and an end to western European male domination of that process."[20] Finally, feminist contributions would re-describe Janssens's idea of subjectivity to include the following: "1) autonomy emerges from committed agency; 2) freedom evolves from accountability in relationships; 3) moral imagination is included along with human will and rationality; and 4) embodied subjectivity is historically constituted."[21]

For the foregoing reasons, Elsbernd values a term other than human nature, "which connotes a certain abstracted and generic understanding of human-ness. Human person denotes particularity but can also be understood in an individualistic manner." She prefers to use the term "authentic human living" in an "effort to avoid individualistic overtones and to highlight con-crete particularity."[22]

Like Elsbernd, Lisa Cahill, in a review essay of a book by Joseph Selling, another student and later colleague of Janssens, admires the insight that arises from reflection on the person "integrally and adequately considered." She adds to the conversation among Catholic moral theologians by propos-ing "it is time that we all turn greater attention to the social and political aspects of sex and gender, to the intersection of gender, race, class, and eco-nomic inequality; and, in particular, to the difference perspectives from the global South might make to our methods and conclusions."[23] Cahill does not reject the work of Janssens and others but wants to push the conversa-tion further to give more attention to the way that "agents are constituted by the communities and relationships in which they are born and raised to be deliberating, deciding, and acting social subjects."[24] She sees Janssens and others as having developed a promising trajectory with the empha-sis on the multidimensionality of the human person. Yet, because she is attuned to how much "moral discernment and agency are collective, induc-tive, and locally variable," Cahill posits that "in addition to the person, we need to consider traditions and communities 'integrally and adequately.'"[25] The Catholic tradition of ethical thought needs to be much more "cross-communal and dialogic" if we are to truly discern what we share in common across cultures and appreciate how we differ because of our diverse com-munal experiences.[26]

Whether it is the analysis of Janssens, Gula, Elsbernd, Cahill, or others, in their efforts to delineate the meaning of "the human person integrally and adequately considered" it is clear there is an evolving moral framework of persons in community that provides the foundation of moral reasoning in the Catholic tradition.[27] Thus Catholic social teaching sees theological anthropology, even as it continues to be recast and reformed, as the foun-dation for building a body of ethical reflection on social, political, and economic concerns. The Catholic tradition strives to avoid reductionistic views of humanity by its insistence on multiple features of the person as being essential and constant in human experience. At Vatican II and in the later writing of Catholic moral theologians, the multidimensional aspect of human existence provided additional content to the theme of human dignity as realized in community.

FURTHER REFLECTION ON *GAUDIUM ET SPES*

The Pastoral Constitution provided multiple warrants for its affirmation of human dignity. Chapter 1 of Part I referred to the person being created in the image of God and the redemption of humanity through the paschal mystery of Christ's death and resurrection. However, "it also affirmed non-theological warrants for this [human] dignity: the capacity of human beings to understand and know the truth, their ability to discern the good through conscience, and the freedom that is the precondition for the pursuit of goodness."[28] This point about nontheological grounds supportive of personal dignity is also noted by Anna Rowlands in her study of Catholic social teaching: "Catholic accounts of personhood emphasize free will, intellect, self-determination and the fundamentally social nature of the person."[29]

We have already discussed the social nature of the person at some length in Chapters 3 and 4, but further comment on reason, conscience, and freedom is warranted here, given the role these characteristics of the person have played in Catholic treatments of human dignity. Recall that although at different points in the history of the Catholic tradition one or the other of these qualities has been seen as being *the* sign of the imago Dei in the human; this is a mistake and not in accord with the biblical witness in Genesis. Yet, these three aspects of the human—reason, conscience, freedom—are essential and constant characteristics of human experience. And the reality of sin is a fourth constant experience of the human condition that requires comment.

REASON

Catholic theology has accorded a central place to human reason in the search for truth, even as it acknowledges belief in the necessity of divine revelation to attain the fullness of truth. Despite the presence of sin in the world and within the human condition, Catholic theology has maintained that human reasoning is capable of finding truth. Sin hinders our reasoning ability and complicates the search for truth but does not create insurmountable barriers to a person's power to reason rightly.

Epistemologically, the Catholic theological tradition, rooted as it was in the classical philosophy of Greece and Rome, thought that it was possible to see beyond all the differences that distinguish one human being from another, thereby permitting perception of what was deemed a universal human nature. More recently, given the impact of historical consciousness, there has been a turn away from abstract understandings that applied to every person and a movement toward multidimensional and interdisciplinary efforts to understand the actual persons that we encounter and experience. This latter method, now characteristic of the Catholic tradition, is called "critical realism." The approach is not naively realist in the sense that the real is simply what I can see or touch, nor is the real merely a clear and distinct idea as in the idealism of a Descartes. Rather, critical realism suggests the reality of the world is mediated to persons by reflective judgment and convictions as well as experience and ideas.[30] So Catholic theology continues to maintain that human knowing—more complex, inductive, and historically conscious than in the past—is still capable of coming to truth.

When reason has been employed in the realm of morality, the Catholic tradition often relied upon the tradition of natural law. Charles Curran helpfully distinguished the theological and philosophical aspects of natural law reasoning. "The theological aspect refers to the question of the sources of moral wisdom and knowledge for the Christian and explains how human reason is related to God."[31] Thus, the main theological concern is to explain the relationship of revelation (the supernatural realm) and reason (the natural realm). Whereas "the philosophical aspect of natural law considers the precise meaning of human nature and human reason."[32]

Theologically, the Catholic natural law tradition holds that human reason can know something of God's purposes for creation and particular creatures by virtue of examining and reflecting upon what the created world is like. Presupposed here is that God has created with a purpose and that a loving deity, such as the Trinitarian God of Christianity, wills for creation to attain its fulfillment by a state of loving union with the Creator. Without the revelation of the Bible it is not possible to know all that Christianity believes about God; but, as Bonaventure and other medieval theologians claimed, the book of nature can tell us something of the Creator. Further, what is revealed in the book of nature is not in contradiction to what we learn from the book of the Bible.

Another commitment of Catholic theology presupposed in the natural law framework is the commitment to what may be called the principle of sacramentality or mediation. God's revelation comes to us through the finite; all of reality is potentially a means to encounter God's presence. God is made manifest through persons, things, history, and nonhuman creation. The belief in the sacramentality (lowercase "s") of all creation is the backdrop for Catholic belief in those specific rituals of washing, anointing, eating, that are called Sacraments (uppercase "S"). So, if the infinite God is revealed to us through finite creation, as biblical history claims, there is good reason to hold that the finite reason of humans can be an important means by which we may encounter and learn something of God's presence and purposes.

Human beings, as created in the image of God, are creatures made to receive God's revelation through their relationships with others, their meditation on creation's wonders, their experience of time and space, and their use of the gift of reason in reflecting on God's revelation through the sacramentality of creation. Understanding the image of God in the human person leads us to use the gift of reason, an important dimension of the imago Dei, to pursue truth. Through the intellect, human beings have the capacity to see signs and indicators of God's purposes in the material world.

Philosophically, the very expression "natural law" is often a cause for misunderstanding. Natural law refers to the idea that critical reflection upon our human condition functions as a basic source for moral insight. So natural law is not a code of regulations to consult when faced with a moral problem; rather it is a process or method of reflection, and only secondarily the result of that reflection. Natural law thinking proposes we critically reflect upon the human person for what reason could tell us about ourselves. Indeed, many medieval theologians and philosophers, borrowing from Cicero, employed the term *recta ratio* or right reason instead of natural law, when reflecting upon our human condition.

Right reason is not arbitrary but aims to grasp what truly serves the well-being of a person. So natural law thinkers maintain that reason can provide insight into what it means to be truly human in order that we may promote a person's well-being or authentic self-realization. This is a baseline claim of Catholic morality, personal and social, that what is good and right for a person is not imposed from without, through custom, law, or sheer force, but the good and right are expressive of what is intrinsic to the person—that which genuinely helps the person to grow and prosper in fulfillment of the true self. This clearly suggests that natural law reasoning must be in conversation with all the arts and sciences that offer insight into the nature of the human person.

Of course, there is a challenge to the natural law tradition by those who would deny that there is any real ongoing structure to the human condition, preferring to see humanity and much of the created order as simply pliable and adaptable, limited only by the state of science and available technology. Those who subscribe to some measure of the natural law tradition, however, maintain there is some recurring structure and consistency in human life and try to name and understand it. There are basic goods, as well as patterns of growth and development that point to enduring and universal characteristics of human beings. One sees this conviction in a thinker like Janssens.

Still, it must be admitted that the use of the natural law in Catholic social thought does present difficulties. The first is that the Church has often taught by appeal to natural law as if there was unanimity within the tradition. The tradition is very broad, however, and we need to be cautious about speaking as if all who support natural law reasoning (the theological aspect) support a particular conclusion based on natural law (the philosophical component). Criticism of a particular teaching based on natural law may stem from the inadequacy of a given theory of natural law rather than the entire tradition.

Related to the foregoing is the philosophical rendering of human nature in each theory. Often, the natural law is spoken of as being engraved on our hearts. However, many times natural law theorists do not read that in the holistic way it should be understood. The human person is not considered in all his or her totality, that is, integrally and adequately. Rather, one aspect of the human person is singled out as the source for understanding God's will as expressed in human nature. This leads to another concern regarding natural law.

Some past Roman Catholic appeals to natural law expressed an overly confident certitude regarding our ability to grasp the truths available to reason. There was a too easy belief that one could know the essence of a given thing so that circumstances, intentionality, and other aspects of human activity could be put aside as "accidents" that do not alter the unchanging substance. More recent efforts to formulate theories of natural law reflect what Bernard Lonergan called a shift from a classicist worldview to historical consciousness; that is, we think in terms of growth and development, not unchanging essences.[33] We see life and reality as in process, not static but dynamic. As a result, the epistemological method in contemporary natural law theories tends to be more inductive than deductive. We still can derive moral guidance and norms from the nature of human beings, but that nature is more complex and changing than the Catholic social tradition had previously supposed.[34]

Within the older deductive approach of neoscholasticism there was the tendency to ignore Thomas Aquinas's caution that as one moved from the general to the specific, we also needed to move from certitude to a more tentative conclusion. We simply cannot speak with the same confidence about concrete particulars than we can when dealing in the abstract. For example, the social tradition speaks often and with conviction about the obligation to assist the poor. However, determining what is the precise nature of the obligation of an individual or a society to the poor in a specific moment in history requires careful discernment. Determining what social welfare programs best serve the poor or what personal acts of compassion are most effective in helping the needy neighbor cannot be done with the same confidence as accepting that there is a general obligation to render assistance. Aquinas and other medieval thinkers would distinguish between the operations of speculative and practical reasoning. The truths which are learned from natural law are fundamental truths that can guide our living, but how these basic truths are to be applied to specific cases requires study, testing, assessment, and prudential judgment.[35]

One final challenge to the natural law is the issue of sin. Many Protestant theologians have expressed concern that the Catholic theological tradition tended to downplay how human sinfulness can pervert the gift of reason. This concern is reinforced when one finds in the social teaching of the Catholic community the identification of a particular societal custom or cultural rule with the "law" of human nature, for example, torture, slavery, or the second-class status of women. In our day one can find Christians arguing from some concept of what is human nature in defense of an ideology that is, in fact, at odds with the Gospel and right reason. A strong dose of intellectual humility is a necessary accompaniment to specific moral choices based on concepts of a fixed human nature, or a tendency to assume a particular custom is normative for all, such as treating European culture as a universal standard.

While considering such difficulties with the use of natural law, it is important that we also appreciate the reasons why Catholic social thought has, by and large, remained within the tradition of natural law. The first point to recall is that when we talk about natural law, we are discussing a *tradition*, but it is often the case that we actually have in mind *a particular theory* within the tradition. And a particular theory may or may not reflect the best of a tradition. In other words, we should avoid equating a theory with an entire tradition. One may be a critic of Augustine or Aquinas, Luther or Calvin, while remaining within the Christian tradition. So, too, one can criticize some versions of natural law without stepping outside the natural law tradition.

In its broadest sense natural law refers to the view that "morality derives from the nature of human beings." There are various theories of natural law because folks may disagree about the method (differing views "about the use of reason to discover God's designs for human beings") or the content (differing "accounts of what human nature is" and "how you derive morality from such an account"), but what the theories share is the belief that the foundation of morality is human nature.[36] Lisa Cahill has described belief in natural law as "a conviction that basic moral values are 'objective' and are shared among culturally different human beings (moral realism); a moral epistemology of inductive, experience-based, critical practical reasoning (a connection between the 'is' and the 'ought'), in which contingent contexts are highly influential in discerning priorities among goods and concrete choices about them."[37] So a first asset to natural law thinking is that morality is grounded in our understanding (however limited) of being; there is a foundation for moral reflection that cannot be reduced to personal whim, majority rule, or private opinion. Given our best understanding of what we are like, something either is or is not beneficial to human beings.

A second point that makes natural law appealing to the Catholic social tradition is that morality is also founded upon a doctrine of God, namely the view that God is the creator of all things, including human reason. The Catholic view is that humans can grasp aspects of divine revelation as they are mediated through the created order. It is important to note for the purposes of ecumenical dialogue that the natural law is not over and above a sovereign God, rather it is an effort to discern God's purposes as expressed within the mystery of creation.

Third, because all people may participate in the search for insights about the nature of creation and creatures, the natural law tradition encourages dialogue with all people of good will whether or not they subscribe to the Christian creed. Explicit faith in Christian revelation is not the only way to attain moral wisdom. The ability of human reason to grasp truth provides a rationale for why the Catholic social tradition can and should engage with many cultures and the physical and social sciences as well as humanistic disciplines in the effort to formulate an ethical framework for social life.

Fourth, the natural law tradition can also explain why those outside the Christian community may match or surpass the wisdom and conduct of Christians, since there is common ground for both attaining moral wisdom and formulating moral standards, namely understanding the nature of the human person. This, in turn, also permits the Catholic social tradition to emphasize that some moral teachings are not restricted just to Christians but are applicable to all persons. As will be seen in the next chapter, this is one of the reasons that Catholic social teaching has become supportive of the human rights movement. There are moral rights to be enjoyed and duties that are obligatory for all persons.

Finally, the Catholic social tradition upholds a theological basis for the natural law. In Paul's reflections on Gentiles and their moral guilt, he does not present a theory of natural law, but he does maintain that non-Jews who do not know the Mosaic law are still held to a moral code since by instinct they know right and wrong. Indeed, conscience serves as an internal guide that helps Gentile nonbelievers grasp what is right behavior, though Paul believes that such knowledge is insufficient to motivate the person to do the good (Rom 2:14–15). Yet reflection on created realities is a source of insight about God: "Ever since the creation of the world his eternal power and divine nature, invisible though they are, have been understood and seen through the things he has made" (Rom 1:20).

The natural law tradition also is coherent with other aspects of Catholic theology. For example, the encounter between the believing person and the revealing God is only possible because God makes use of "language" already familiar to us. Our ethical vocabulary is as broad as our moral experience, our moral consciousness. The human person is capable of hearing and giving intelligent belief to the ethical message of the New Testament because prior to the explicit revelation of God's Word, the person already grasps and expresses him- or herself as an ethical being. That is, in the realm of morality God can only communicate to us that moral insight which we already know, however inchoately, by means of the experience of ourselves as moral beings.[38] Thus, the operation of grace in the encounter with God's self-gift or revelation is not a contradiction to or dismissal of human experience but speaks to the depth of the human and finds a reception because God has already prepared us to accept a moral truth through our grasp of the moral law implanted in our hearts. This is an implication of being created in the image of God; we resonate with truth when it is spoken. Such an approach to the question of revelation is captured in the axiom of Karl Rahner that the condition for the possibility of revelation is a creature already constituted as a hearer of the Word.

Much contemporary Catholic Christology is premised on an understanding of the human as being open to the infinite; so that Jesus is seen as the incarnation of God but also the embodiment of authentic humanity. Such a view then leads to the claim that whenever human beings break through to the experience of the genuinely human, they become more truly the image of God in Christ; we become more Christ-like. So natural law refers to that inner drive toward authentic personhood. There is a stability and constancy to that drive, but more in the way of direction than an unchanging norm or law. Natural law is a pointer that orients us to the good, to the good of human life as we understand it. It helps us grasp what authentic human existence is all about. Natural law is not therefore some detailed blueprint for living, but an orientation toward authentic human personhood.

We can distill from this orientation some criteria for moral judgment. Moral values are not simply created by us or imposed on us but emerge out of our inner sense of selfhood, a self that is profoundly communal in its formation. We do not create the good but respond to it as we discover it. That is why natural law is said to be more fundamental than social or personal custom for it is the standard by which we determine whether a given individual or society is acting in accord with what is humanly good. Claims based on natural law are claims based on the very being of the person. As reflective beings capable of learning from our examination of experience, personal and social, we have some awareness of those actions which serve or violate the human person. In effect, contemporary Catholic social teaching may be better understood by not talking about natural law or the law of nature, but rather its understanding of the human person. Personhood, in its rich and multidimensional manner as described earlier, ought to be the focus of Catholic moral reasoning.

CONSCIENCE

In the Pastoral Constitution, the bishops stated, "Conscience is the most secret core and sanctuary of a person." And the bishops also affirm that "to obey it [conscience] is the very dignity of the person."[39] The idea of conscience has been a staple of Catholic moral theology, but the term has been used and understood in a variety of ways through the centuries. James Keenan has pointed out that the horrors of World War II and the involvement of many Catholics in those horrors pushed European theologians to restore to prominence the role of conscience in Catholic teaching, while at the same time calling for a reconsideration of its meaning. Those efforts came to fruition in the Council's statement about conscience in *Gaudium et spes*.[40] Scholars like Odon Lottin, Bernard Häring, Louis Janssens, and Josef Fuchs spoke about conscience not simply as the ability to choose prudently but as the interiority of the person that is at the heart of morality.

Keenan suggests that at the time of the Council most Americans employed conscience to express dissent against authority, be it the US government's policy in Vietnam, the state and local authorities' use of Jim Crow laws and racial segregation, or papal authority and the teaching on artificial birth control—whereas the Europeans, coming out of the experience of Nazism and fascism, focused on the collective failure of moral communities and the need to restore a sense of moral agency and responsibility. The individualism of American culture also encouraged thinking about conscience as the act of an individual rejecting the dictates of authority. The European turn to conscience "was not a matter of giving Christians freedom to exercise prerogatives, even compelling ones against law; rather, it was to place before Christians the mindfulness that ultimately they would be judged and hopefully redeemed by God."[41]

An important quality regarding conscience in the writings of several of the European moral theologians is evident in the Latin term *conscientia*, which means "to know together." Although someone like Häring understands conscience, as the Council taught, to be at the core of the person, it is not meant to be viewed as a solitary or private reality. Rather it is "the 'place' and the 'means' whereby persons come to know themselves 'in confrontation with God and with fellowmen.'"[42] This is what Häring meant by "the reciprocity of consciences"; our consciences are formed and informed by the moral communities in which we participate. There is a self-correcting dynamic at work through active participation by the person in community.

The twentieth-century retrieval of the idea of conscience is just that, a retrieval of earlier insights that receded in the Catholic moral imagination as a more passive, obediential mindset became dominant in the eighteenth and nineteenth centuries. Today, the teaching of Vatican II has helped us realize it is no overstatement to say the theme of conscience is central to the Catholic theological tradition on morality. And yet, the word is nowhere to be found in the Old Testament nor anywhere in the gospels. Such silence, however, is deceiving.

Although there is no Hebrew word for conscience, the idea is present in the Old Testament. It is an idea which underwent development, initially referring to external obedience to the covenant law of Moses and then later, during the period of classical prophecy, shifting to a more internal code of morality. In the prophetic lexicon the word most near to the sense of conscience is "heart," which is *leb* in Hebrew and *kardis* in the Greek translation. The prophets have been called the "conscience of Israel"[43] because of their stress on the importance of interior disposition in morality. This is evident in the prophet Jeremiah's challenge to the people of the southern kingdom.

> For thus says the LORD to the people of Judah and to the inhabitants of Jerusalem:
>
> Break up your fallow ground,
>   and do not sow among thorns.
> Circumcise yourselves to the LORD;
>   remove the foreskin of your hearts,
>   O people of Judah and inhabitants of Jerusalem,
> or else my wrath will go forth like fire
>   and burn with no one to quench it,
>   because of the evil of your doings. (Jer 4:3–4)

And words of the prophet Joel follow in a similar vein with his call to conversion:

> Yet even now, says the LORD,
>   return to me with all your heart,
> with fasting, with weeping, and with mourning;
>   rend your hearts and not your clothing. (Joel 2:12–13)

In both cases we see glimmers of the idea that the heart (conscience) is the interior self, the inner life of the person striving to be morally good.

Jeremiah had previously pointed out the hardness of heart among the people of Jerusalem and Judah, their stubbornness in abandoning Yahweh their God. He called upon them to be renewed in the covenant, but the sign of that bond was not to be the physical sign of male circumcision, but the sign of a changed heart expressed in the metaphor of removing the foreskin of the heart. It is not external obedience to Mosaic law that signifies true covenant fidelity but the renewal of the inner life of the person.[44]

The prophet Joel writes to a post-exilic audience, a people brokenhearted and feeling abandoned after the crushing experience of Jerusalem's destruction and the exile in Babylon. He urges them to return to Yahweh, to give voice to their sorrow, and to seek a renewed bond with their God. They should show outer signs of grief (fasting, weeping) but not the rending of their garments, a traditional display of mourning in the Semitic culture. Instead, they are to rend their hearts, not clothes; they must return to Yahweh internally, not just externally. It is the inner life that must be different if the covenant is to be restored.[45]

In the gospels we find no use by Jesus of the word "conscience," although, like earlier prophets, he is clearly concerned with the moral reality of an interior life. Chapter 15 of Matthew's gospel relates a story of rabbis from Jerusalem approaching Jesus with the challenge that his disciples do not follow the stipulated rituals of washing their hands before eating. Jesus, in turn, reproaches the rabbis for their legalistic tactics that avoid caring for their parents by claiming their money is dedicated to God. He calls them hypocrites and then quotes another prophet.

> Isaiah prophesied rightly about you when he said:
> "This people honors me with their lips,
>   but their hearts are far from me;
> in vain do they worship me,
>   teaching human precepts as doctrines." (Matt 15:7–9)

According to Matthew, Jesus then calls out to the assembled crowd that defilement does not have to do with what goes into the mouth but what comes out of it. Peter and other disciples, however, seek clarification of Jesus's teaching and ask him to explain further. He replies, "Do you not see that whatever goes into the mouth enters the stomach and goes out into the sewer? But what comes out of the mouth proceeds from the heart, and this is what defiles. For out of the heart come evil intentions, murder, adultery, sexual immorality, theft, false witness, slander. These are what defile a person, but to eat with unwashed hands does not defile" (Matt 15:17–20). Clearly, Jesus follows the prophetic tradition in his teaching on morality; it is crucial that one's inner life—intent and motive—be correct and not just dutiful external behavior.

In Paul's writing we find a further development of the biblical teaching on conscience. In his letters he uses the word "conscience" more than twenty times. This is not surprising, since Paul was an educated man whose preaching and writing were addressed mainly to Gentiles and Jews of the diaspora—people who would have been more familiar with Greek and Roman culture than Hebraic customs and practice, and who would have spoken Greek, not Hebrew. The Greek language had a word, *syneidesis*, that was commonly used and a lesser used word, *synteresis*; the Latin language had *conscientia*. Quite naturally Paul uses the language and thought-forms of the people to whom he was preaching and writing. I will discuss the significance of these Greek terms in the subsequent sub-section.

A key passage for the Pauline sense of conscience is found in Romans:

> When gentiles, who do not possess the law, by nature do what the law requires, these, though not having the law, are a law to themselves. They show that what the law requires is written on their hearts, as their own conscience also bears witness, and their conflicting thoughts will accuse or perhaps excuse them on the day when, according to my gospel, God through Christ Jesus judges the secret thoughts of all. (Rom 2:14–16)

In this passage, Paul suggests conscience is an interior reality, he links it to the heart; it is not an exterior norm but a dimension of the self. This is fully in accord with the prophetic view. Conscience is neither the Torah nor is it personal whimsy or opinion. Rather it is the voice of God calling from a deep sense of the person's self-awareness. And Paul maintains all people, Gentile as well as Jew, have this sense.

A few verses later, Paul picks up on Jeremiah's theme of the heart in the context of his teaching about conscience. He refers to an image that would be familiar to anyone who had read Jeremiah.

> Circumcision indeed is of value if you obey the law, but if you are a transgressor of the law your circumcision has become uncircumcision. So, if the uncircumcised keep the requirements of the law, will not their uncircumcision be regarded as circumcision? Then the physically uncircumcised person who keeps the law will judge you who, though having the written code and circumcision, are a transgressor of the law. For a person is not a Jew who is one outwardly, nor is circumcision something external and physical. Rather, a person is a Jew who is one inwardly, and circumcision is a matter of the heart, by the Spirit, not the written code. (Rom 2:25–29a)

Paul links the Old Testament "heart" with the Greek notion of conscience; they are both referring to the inner self's moral understanding. This is an understanding that will continue to be developed throughout the Catholic theological tradition: the fundamental theme of conscience as an interior locale where one encounters moral truth.

If the conscience (or heart) is related to the truth that pertains to knowing one's true self, then the first object of a conscientious decision is not to decide about *something* but to decide about *oneself*. Just as within human reason there is an eros for truth, a hunger to grasp it, there is within the person also a moral drive to authenticity. There is a craving within us for the good, a need to articulate what one's life stands for and what is the good that we seek to embrace. We desire to come to terms ethically and spiritually, as well as intellectually, with a universe that can be both puzzling and challenging.

Confusion over Conscience

In the English-speaking world, we have used the one word *conscience* in two ways, and this has led to confusion. Medieval theologians, drawing upon the Greek language, called synteresis one form of conscience as well as the more often used syneidesis for a second sense of conscience.

Synteresis can be used for conscience in the sense of an inner call, that dynamic quest for the good that is found within a person. It corresponds to what today is sometimes called the subjective conscience. Syneidesis, the second sense of conscience, refers to the capacity for making judgments, for discerning which concrete choice serves the good. This was also the Latin *conscientia* for medieval scholastics; it was later called actual conscience by the moral theologians of the eighteenth and nineteenth centuries and is today called the objective conscience.

When using conscience in the first sense, as the inner call to moral goodness or the subjective conscience, it is true to say that the first task of a person is to be true to one's conscience, which is the same as saying be true to oneself. Understood in this way, to act unconscientiously is to betray the self. A person ought always to be loyal to the good as best it can be known. So in this sense we correctly say a person must always be true to their conscience. Provided the person has made an honest effort to learn about the matter under review, then he or she is bound to follow conscience about what is believed to be true. If the person does not know it to be wrong, but honestly believes the decision to be right, then one must opt for what decision is believed to serve the good. Hence, a person must act in "good" conscience, that is, be true to themselves, rather than act in "bad" conscience, which is to go against one's best sense of the moral good. Being faithful to the truth as best it can be known is the measure of being in good conscience. This was upheld by the teaching of Vatican II: "Always summoning him to love good and avoid evil, the voice of conscience when necessary speaks to his heart: do this, shun that. For man has in his heart a law written by God; to obey it is the very dignity of man; according to it he will be judged."[46] Our highest law is to be true to our conscience in the first sense of synteresis.[47]

The second sense of conscience, *syneidesis*, entails the capacity of analysis, evaluation, judgment—the ability to choose rightly in specific cases. Here one should talk of right and wrong, not good and bad. When we act wrongly it may be the case that we have not gone against our conscience in the first sense, but that we followed conscience, in the second sense, which was improperly formed. Conscience in the second sense is not an inner call to be honest with myself but the ability to make wise decisions. At this second level, people can make poor decisions without necessarily being dishonest or insincere in seeking what is good. It is not uncommon that a person acted with the best of intentions yet did wrong. They thought what they did was right, but it was not, yet we do not necessarily doubt their good intentions. We use an expression such as, "it was an honest mistake." In such cases another person may show me that I was in error in my judgment, that I was wrong at this second level of conscience (syneidesis); but I can still claim that I was acting in good conscience (synteresis) in the sense of being faithful to the truth as I knew it at the time.

Differentiating the two senses of conscience requires a second distinction, between the pairs of words good/bad and right/wrong. Good and bad refer to one's intention. Is the person honestly seeking the good? This is conscience in the first sense. Good and bad pertain to conscience 1, the inner call to moral truth, or the subjective conscience. Right and wrong refer to my ability to make a specific judgment about a given action. Was what I did the right thing to do? Here we have conscience in the second sense. Right and wrong pertain to conscience 2, the capacity for judgment or the objective conscience.

Conscience at the second level reminds us that an unhelpful metaphor for conscience is to think of it as moral radar always homing in on the correct judgment. Rather, the better metaphor is to think of it more like intelligence—we all have some of it, degrees of it vary greatly, and even possessing a lot of it does not mean we are always right.[48] The moral life can be confusing because sometimes people do the wrong thing while being in good conscience. Good people (subjectively) can do the wrong thing (objectively). So being true to myself is no guarantee that I am acting in a correct or right way. The ideal is, of course, to be acting in good conscience regarding my pursuit of a moral good (conscience 1) combined with a right-thinking conscience regarding making practical judgments about which specific choice best achieves the moral good (conscience 2).

A benefit of this way of discussing conscience is that it can help us keep our differences with others in proper perspective. When we are in dispute with people about the morality of a certain action, we need not doubt a person's goodness even as we challenge his or her judgment about the rightness of an action. Someone may do something we consider wrong, but we do not have to conclude that the person is thereby bad or evil. It is possible to disagree vigorously and yet be respectful in our relationship with another. The Catholic tradition uses the phrase "invincible ignorance" to designate instances where a person is not held to be at fault subjectively for failing to know the objectively wrong nature of the omission or commission of an action.

Now while we must always respect a person acting in good conscience, the claim to be in good conscience is not always persuasive. There are acts that are so manifestly wrong, for example, massacres of innocent civilians in a terror campaign, that it is hard to imagine anyone being sincere in claiming that they did not know the wrongfulness of the action. This is akin to the legal expression "willfully blind," and courts have ruled that in cases where people choose to remain blind to the facts, they are as culpable as those who have knowledge. Morally speaking, people are held to be culpable because they could easily have overcome their lack of knowledge (what the tradition calls "vincible ignorance") but refused to do so. In such a case, the person is not just at fault for being wrong but for acting in bad conscience. This treatment of conscience is endorsed in the Pastoral Constitution: "Conscience frequently errs from invincible ignorance without losing its dignity. The same cannot be said of a person who cares but little for truth and goodness, or of a conscience which by degrees grows practically sightless as a result of habitual sin."[49]

The distinctions between the subjective and objective conscience, and between the word pairs good/bad and right/wrong, can be of real benefit when applying Catholic social teaching in a diverse society. Accepting that there can be principled and sincere disagreement between people on a question of public morality does not mean that argument, even passionate argument, has no place in the public forum. But it does mean that disagreement at the level of judgments about what is right or wrong need not move to the level of assailing a person's character by questioning good intention or sincerity in seeking to do what is right. The language of the Catholic social tradition does not make civil debate less challenging, but it can serve the causes of democratic deliberation and public courtesy.

FREEDOM

When the bishops met at Vatican II, they were still quite conscious of the dark events of two world wars and their aftermath. Hence, as David Hollenbach has pointed out, they did not speak about human dignity in the abstract, but as a way of referring to identifiable characteristics of personhood that make concrete demands for respect from other persons and social institutions. Many of these characteristics were likely identified through their violation. So, the denial of freedoms of movement, thought, expression, conscience, religion, assembly, and self-determination all brought home to church leaders how central to human dignity is the exercise of freedom.[50]

In the text of the Pastoral Constitution one finds the notable statement, "authentic freedom is an exceptional sign of the divine image within the person."[51] It is safe to say, the Catholic social tradition's encounter with liberalism and its promotion of individual liberty led the Church to reconsider the importance of freedom in its understanding of the person.[52] And it did so to the point that freedom, properly understood, is considered "an exceptional sign" of the imago Dei in humanity.

Still, it must be said that Catholic social thought "has not simply taken over liberal ideas uncritically."[53] The modifier "authentic" in the conciliar text referring to freedom is important; true freedom cannot be understood simply as "the freedom of individuals to act as they please in a zone of privacy"[54] Persons must be free in the act of choice that is "personally motivated and prompted from within. It does not result from blind internal impulse nor from mere external pressure."[55] Persons are obliged to direct their freedom by their knowledge of what is truly good.

This understanding of freedom is called positive freedom, which is distinguished from the negative freedom concerned only with limiting constraints upon the person. "According to this account positive freedom—the freedom to act and shape our lives—exists for the sake of human excellence; this excellence is understood as the fulfilling of our nature and a partaking in the life of paschal mystery and communion."[56] Freedom, in this view, is the necessary precondition for a human being to pursue the good. It is essential that each person have the capability to choose self-realization through a free response to the good as it is apprehended by the self.

This moves the discussion of freedom to another level than the freedom of choice that tends to be equated with personal liberty. Theologians talk about transcendental or basic freedom that is related to freedom of choice yet is distinct from it. Freedom of choice involves the capacity to decide between option A or B, or numerous additional options. Popularly, people speak of having more freedom if they have more choices. The Catholic moral tradition, while acknowledging the importance of freedom of choice, talks about a more fundamental freedom that transcends a particular act of free choice; it is not only that a person is free to choose between specific options but is also able to determine his or her very self. This freedom for self-determination posits that there is only one choice to make at a fundamental level and that is to choose what sort of person one will be.

In summary, there is freedom to choose a particular option: I will go out tonight or I will stay home; I will wear a blue shirt or a white one. These acts of free choice are what theologians call categorical freedom. There is another freedom, however, about a choice that is larger than any particular exercise of freedom at the categorical level; it is basic or transcendental freedom. The influential German theologian Karl Rahner puts it this way: "Freedom never happens as merely an objective exercise, as a mere choice 'between' individual objects, but is the *self*-exercise of the one who chooses."[57] There is a basic freedom to be distinguished from freedom of choice. That basic freedom is akin to positive freedom, the ability to be self-determining.

Granted, this basic freedom is not absolute, any more than freedom of choice is absolute. Human freedom is always conditioned or limited both from within and from without. As creatures of time and space we are conditioned by our history, and our self-understanding is shaped by parents, siblings, friends, relatives, and the wider society. The institutions that constitute our social world also condition our freedom—economic standing, social status, educational opportunities, and the like. We are limited by the place we inhabit in the material universe and the time in which we inhabit it. We are also limited from within by our psychic world, a good deal of which is not even present to our conscious self but resides in the unconscious. So, talk about any aspect of human freedom must acknowledge we are discussing relative freedom, a conditioned freedom. The idea of basic or transcendental freedom refers to the relative ability we possess to be self-determining, to fashion the person I am.

There is another important point to make, and that is how transcendental and categorical freedom are not only distinct but related. Basic or transcendental freedom is not exercised directly but is always mediated through free choices at the categorical level. Rahner uses the image of a knife cutting through butter to make his point. The knife does not change as it slices through the butter, but that is unlike us. For through all the choices we make, we are being changed through those choices. Various acts of free choice will have different impacts upon us. Clearly the choice of career has a major impact upon a person. Who we befriend, who we marry or not marry, whether we will be a parent, where we will live, whether we will participate in a church community—these are all choices that will have significant impacts upon us. Other choices may be less important but still meaningful: how we spend our money, the use of free time, hobbies pursued, educational or training opportunities taken. Still other choices may not be all that important when seen as a single act but taken as a series of behaviors may become quite impactful: daily diet, exercise regimen, sleep patterns, interactions with acquaintances. In making these choices, some carefully and some rather casually, we are, unlike the butter knife, being affected by them. It is through freely made acts of categorical freedom that we are also fashioning a self, the exercise of transcendental freedom.

Another illustration may further clarify the relationship of basic freedom and freedom of choice. Suppose a person desires to become a musician; how does that happen? Certainly, a decision is made that being a musician is something the person wants to be. But that intention does not transform the person into a musician. Instead, that happens by consistently doing certain things: purchasing or renting an instrument, taking instructions in how to play the instrument, finding an appropriate locale to practice playing the instrument, spending considerable time on a regular basis in practice, maybe learning some music theory or how to sight-read music. In short, a fair number of decisions are made on an everyday or at least consistent basis such that at some point in time a person can justifiably state, "I am a musician." The identity of being a musician was not a single act of will that transformed the person from nonmusician to musician. Rather, it was countless practical choices about spending time, effort, money, study, and psychic energy that eventuated in a person altering to some degree his or her identity.

Ultimately, there is only one choice in the exercise of basic freedom: what sort of person am I to be? But that is not a single, one-off choice; rather, it is the determination of a self through the countless daily acts of free choice that make up one's life. Seen that way, it is really a matter of how we view the self: as an agent or as a person. As an agent the emphasis is on the doer of acts in a responsible and accountable way. As a person the emphasis is on the human being who precedes, grounds, and transcends human acts. The dual way of seeing the self, both important and fully legitimate, corresponds to the dual nature of freedom as transcendent or categorical, self-determination or choice between discrete options.

For the Catholic moral tradition, it is vital that we grasp the first understanding of freedom as self-determination. If we see ourselves only in terms of agency, then we atomize our individual acts. They are analyzed as a series of unrelated choices that flow from a neutral center that never changes, that is, like a butter knife. That is to lose sight of the issue of moral character, and it defies human experience for it fails to see how the agent choosing is also a person who develops over time. Freedom of personhood (transcendental or basic freedom) helps us see that the doer of an act is always also being fashioned into a certain kind of person. We have freedom, conditioned as it may be, not only to choose objects but also in regard to the subject, the person, who chooses. This is the meaning of *self*-determination.

So the basic freedom is freedom of being, not acting; but being only comes through doing, that is, the moral dimension of personhood is formed through acts of agency. The person never exercises basic freedom directly but only through the mediation of freedom of choice. "Basic freedom only exists in the concrete act."[58] The two kinds of freedom are not in conflict; they are to be distinguished but remain closely related. The deeper sense of freedom is the capacity for self-determination, and this is only possible because of securing freedom for men and women to make choices for themselves so that daily life is not simply regulated and directed by others. However, even in situations where one may have limited freedom of choice, in a prison or in seriously ill health, a person is still left with the freedom to decide how to respond to such limiting circumstances, for instance, with despair, in anger, with patience, graciously.

Freedom for Love

The result of this process of self-determination is the creation of a person who is open to a covenant relationship with God or turns aside from such an offer of relationship. Whether this is done with conscious intent or obliviousness, we are throughout our lives creating a self who is oriented to the God who is love or directing ourselves to some lesser aim or purpose. Thus, theologically, the root question for personal freedom is not to evaluate a particular act of freedom of choice but to inquire into the moral character of the person who performs the act. What is the emerging moral makeup of the self who is doing the specific deed? Is the person someone who is developing the qualities that lead to growth in a relationship with God and God's people? Or is this a person who is in a state of growing alienation from God and others, living in what the biblical prophets saw as covenant infidelity? As the theologian Richard McBrien wrote: "Freedom enters into the very definition of what it means to be human. To be free is to be present to oneself, to be in possession of oneself, to be conscious of oneself as a distinct, responsible being. Freedom does not so much allow us to *do something* as to *be someone*."[59]

Biblically, the someone we are called to be is consistent with the same invitation extended to men and women of faith throughout history: a person who keeps covenant with God, which, in turn, requires that we enter into loving relationships with our neighbors. The deeper meaning of freedom is the "freedom to give oneself away and to receive the gift of the Other and others."[60] We are most free when we are in love, when we undergo the transformation that occurs by making ourselves into a gift for others. Thus, we become our truest selves—creatures made for loving communion.

We become free by embracing covenant relationships of love, not by shirking off or avoiding commitments to others. "[T]he Bible does not regard freedom as autonomous independence; rather liberation is *from* bondage *into* community."[61] That is the lesson of the exodus narrative that tells of freed slaves who swear a covenant at Sinai with Yahweh and one another, and it is the lesson of Jesus's preaching about forgiveness. Consider the parable of the unforgiving servant who in Matthew's gospel has been freed from a huge burden of debt by his lord yet refuses to forgive a much smaller debt owed to him. Judgment is then passed on him for how he abused his newfound freedom (Matt 18:23–24). Or there is the prodigal son forgiven his arrogance and greed by his father so that he can be restored as a son and family member (Lk 15:11–32). People are given freedom in order that they may create new relationships with those around them. Some fail to do so and are judged accordingly, while others experience new life as a life together with others. This is altogether fitting, since "the self is inherently relational and achieves depth and solidity only be going beyond itself in solidarity and community."[62]

A final point to be noted regarding freedom and human personhood: human life is not static, but dynamic; we are persons who develop in time. "There is a sense in which the human person is a person becoming through the realization of their dignity." Therefore a "main element in the notion of person must be freedom."[63] This connection between human dignity and authentic freedom suggests a new dimension to dignity; it is not just protological—rooted in the creation accounts of Genesis—nor just Christological—rooted in the Incarnation—but eschatological or soteriological. That is, personal dignity within the Catholic theological tradition is "simultaneously something we *possess* and something we *become*."[64]

Catholic theological reflection on the nature of freedom as both basic and categorical must still be related to ideas about political, economic, and cultural freedom. Because of its belief in the centrality of freedom for self-determination, the Catholic social tradition has often criticized those notions of freedom which seem to equate it with what popes have seen as mere license. That is, because authentic freedom is the working out of one's self-identity as a person committed to covenant identity, the notion of freedom as simply having the liberty to do as one chooses appeared shallow and false. Thus, criticism of liberalism, as it was understood by popes of the nineteenth and early twentieth centuries, was aimed at a particular kind of liberalism that exalted personal liberty but spoke less about the common good, personal duties, and the formation of character. That many liberals of that same era looked upon the Catholic church as an enemy of individual freedom only further hindered fruitful interaction between the Catholic social tradition and liberalism.

Today, it is evident that Catholic teaching has learned from and borrowed ideas about the importance of personal liberties. It is also clear that many critics of liberalism beyond Catholicism have pushed for greater attention to the moral dimensions of the exercise of personal liberty. Clarifying the relationship between freedom for *self*-determination and freedom within the realms of politics, economics, and cultural life has been an ongoing dialogue between Catholic social teaching and proponents of liberalism. Catholicism maintains the exercise of political and economic freedom by individuals and groups is laced with moral implications because the deeper sense of freedom is ultimately about the sort of person one becomes and the sort of communities one creates, and is created by, through participation in social life. Hence, Catholic social teaching is central to the moral instruction and practice of Catholic men and women seeking to exercise freedom in a responsible manner.

SIN

How are we to understand the mystery of human sinfulness? That question has been at the center of religious reflection since the biblical age. Like grace, sin is a multifaceted human experience, and we struggle to find appropriate ways of describing the reality, calling upon a variety of images and analogies. Any fully adequate image must help us to acknowledge several dimensions of the mystery of sin: (1) that we inherit an involuntary situation where our relationship with God is not what it should be; (2) that we can use our freedom to turn from God; (3) that our freedom and knowledge is hampered by sin; (4) that our sinful condition finds expression in wrongful actions; and (5) that sin is present in the structures of social life. No one image or model of sin can express all these features adequately. Placing all these elements of the experience of human sinfulness under one rubric is near impossible, and so the Catholic tradition has employed a variety of terms when speaking of sin.

First, it is important to see that sin is a religious term. Unlike purely ethical terms, such as bad/wrong, or purely legal terms, such as crime, felony, or misdemeanor, the word *sin* puts things in a religious context. Sin is about a rift in our relationship with God.

A traditional image of sin and perhaps the most dominant one in the Catholic tradition is sin as a violation of a moral norm. With this metaphor, sin is viewed as an action willfully and freely chosen against the divine will. The one who sins is the individual, the sin is willful rebellion, and juridical or penal imagery is the context, that is, what is important is to determine if a violation has been committed, ascertain the culpability of the actor, and assign an appropriate penalty. Sin in this framework is violation of a commandment. It was the governing image for generations of Catholics who practiced auricular confession as the mandated form of the sacrament of penance.

There are serious limits to the usefulness of this legalistic approach to the moral life. For in this context God's grace and mercy can be overlooked as the image of God can be punitive. The power of sin can be underestimated while the freedom of the person is overestimated; and the focus on the individual can fail to note the social aspects of sin. Regarding the image of God, there is a tendency to view God as a judge imposing penalties on miscreants who have not followed divinely instituted laws. God is a divine tribunal who administers the terms of forgiveness, sometimes in a less than merciful way.

Regarding the freedom of the person and the power of sin, by focusing narrowly on the sinful act, the fabric of the actor's life often was left unexamined. Insufficient attention was given to the biography of the sinner, which might have significant influence on the ability of the person to avoid the wrongful act. Whatever biological, psychological, intellectual, relational, and cultural forces were at work in a person's life limiting his or her freedom in a given situation was, for the most part, ignored. This was not regularly considered because the spotlight was on the isolated action removed from the life context.

Finally, because sin was seen as a personal failing, the willful act of an individual, little concern was expressed about the societal context of the action and society's complicity in a person's sin. The important thing was to determine the individual's guilt or innocence, not to address the possible sinful aspects of the environment in which the person lived. And so, a woman's single act deemed sinful could be considered apart from any reflection on the societal position of women—the familial, economic, political, cultural, and religious forces impinging on her self-understanding, her options, and her resources to deal with an issue. A person's sinfulness was separated out from any analysis of the failings of the society in which she lived. The way to remedy a sin was to punish the person so that God's legal and moral order could be re-established.

If that model of sin is no longer as useful, what new models can help us recapture an appropriate understanding of sin in our experience today? To begin that task we can search the Bible for other models of sin.

Biblical Models of Sin

Three words for sin in the Old Testament provide insight into the development of sin in ancient Judaism. First, however, it is important to recall the proper biblical context for understanding a theology of sin is the covenant relationship. The word used to convey the bond brought about through covenant is *hesed*. The word can be variously translated as love, loyalty, devotion, or mercy. All those elements are involved in hesed; it is a faithful and gracious love. Yahweh called each of the chosen people to an intimate union and pledged fidelity to Israel with the offer of a covenant.

Usually, the biblical authors see the rejection of Yahweh as being achieved through the person's wrongful behavior toward God and others. God disapproves of the sinner primarily because of idolatry and immoral conduct toward others. Sin is indeed a violation of the covenant relationship with God, but such a condition usually is expressed through idol worship or specific sins against other persons. Nor is the sinner left untouched, for sin is a rejection of the call to live fully in relationship with God and others. Sin can therefore be seen as a threefold alienation from the God who loves us, from our neighbors and the rest of creation we are called to love, and from ourselves.

In the Hebrew scriptures there are more than fifty words used for sin. Nonetheless, there are three images that are especially helpful when trying to understand the ancient Hebrew sense: *hattah*, *pesha*, and *awon*. None of the three are exclusively religious words since they have secular meanings quite independent of their use as terms for sin. But the fact that they are words used to describe sin tells us something of the Semitic understanding.

Again, sin was a breaking of the covenant, a failure to maintain hesed in the relationship with Yahweh. When one fails to live up to the standards that a true relationship would require, there is a breach of the covenant. The experience of hattah (to miss the mark) is that I'm off-center; my commitment is not as focused as it should be. It is akin to Augustine's sense of disordered love: something else besides love of God has become the priority, be it love of self or love of the world. When the covenant relationship with Yahweh has to compete with another value, then our loyalty has become less than faithful. This is described by hattah.

With pesha we see a similar theme. Throughout the ancient Near East, a covenant was of two basic types. A parity covenant was one formed by equals, for example, a treaty between two neighboring kings promising mutual assistance against a third party. The second covenant relationship was that of a suzerain/vassal nature. Here there was a greater and lesser status between the parties, and the greater promised benefits to the lesser in return for fulfillment of obligations such as payment of taxes, military support, and local governance. When a vassal refused to recognize the relationship to the liege-lord and broke the covenant, such a vassal was engaged in pesha or rebellion. The relationship between the two was broken. When the Hebrew employed pesha for sin, we are being told there has been a disruption of relationship by one who refused to acknowledge duties toward one's Lord. The covenant bond was severed. A relationship which should be marked by reciprocal duties freely pledged is characterized by an obstinate refusal on the part of one party to live up to the responsibilities assigned. In this sense the tragedy of sin is not the performance of this or that specific act, but the reality of being estranged from the Lord, of violating the nature of the relationship specified in the covenant.

Awon refers to a physical deformity, a body that is crooked or lame in some manner. It pointed to a burden or defect with which a person had to live; it was a condition that prevented or severely hampered free movement. In its religious usage, awon suggests that sin is the experience of bearing a burden that had to be removed if a person was to walk upright and gracefully. Awon directs attention to how sin damages a person's life by preventing one from being able to move or act freely. Rather the sinner must struggle to be released from his or her burden. Sin is something that cripples us interiorly like a physical deformity does to the body. We are bound by something that prevents us from being free to observe the covenant.

What all these terms demonstrate is that biblical authors viewed sin as a rift or rupture in the covenant relationship with God. In the earliest writing this rift might be caused by an innocent mistake, an unintended violation of cultic law that violated some ritual or taboo. Today, we would think of such things as merely accidents. As the moral consciousness of Israel evolved, especially in the prophets, sin came to be seen as a willful violation of the covenant.

When we turn to the New Testament, there are still other images for sin. In his ministry as portrayed in the synoptic gospels Jesus manifests several beliefs about sin: (1) that it is a power with a hold over people; (2) people are called to conversion, a radical turning away from sin; (3) forgiveness of sin is both possible and readily available; and (4) one must be compassionate toward sinners. Perhaps no story better conveyed the attitude of Jesus than the parable in Luke 15:11–32, the parable of the prodigal son or, more accurately, the forgiving father.

Recall that the younger son tells the father: "Father I have sinned against God and you. I no longer deserve to be called your son." The sin is not viewed primarily as the squandering of money, his actions with prostitutes, or the shame on his own head. For him sin means the bond that once united him with his father has been violated so that he is no longer a son. There is the grim reality of sin: the other matters, while serious, are symptoms of the disease, a broken relationship.

There are other lessons regarding sin to be learned in the New Testament materials. Paul's image for sin is best represented by the Greek word *sarx* or flesh. This is not simply the physical flesh for Paul but the whole world of historical existence that is deaf to God's word. Sarx is the Pauline term for the world (material *and* spiritual) viewed from the perspective of its unredeemed condition. For Paul sin is a power that permeates the human condition and deprives humans of the ability to hear and act on God's word. Sin is more than individual actions; it is the foundation from which rebellious acts spring up. Reading his letter to the Romans, one finds the Pauline view that sin is like a virus which takes away the ability to act as we would wish.

> I do not understand my own actions. For I do not do what I want, but I do the very thing I hate. Now if I do what I do not want, I agree that the law is good. But in fact it is no longer I who do it but sin that dwells within me. For I know that the good does not dwell within me, that is, in my flesh. For the desire to do the good lies close at hand, but not the ability. For I do not do the good that I want, but the evil I do not want is what I do. Now if I do what I do not want it is no longer I who do it but sin that dwells with me. (Rom 7:15–20)

For Paul sin is a fact of our earthly existence, and we need to be freed from its power.

In the gospel of John, one finds talk about sin as a state of hostility between a stubborn, blind audience and Jesus. John uses the word *world* to describe that hard-hearted state of existence within which one becomes enmeshed upon entrance into life—life that is lived in darkness rather than the light. The lesson is that if we look at John, we find talk of sin just as often or even more often than talk of sins. Sin can be plural if we think in terms of actions or deeds because we can perform many deeds. But if we think in terms of relationship (covenant) then we talk of sin in the singular because either we are or are not in covenant with God. In the gospel of John, sin is experienced as a state of existence, being in the dark instead of the light by refusing to believe in Jesus.

The Language of Sin Today

If we employ some of the insights from the scriptures along with our own experience, there are several models of sin which may speak effectively today. I will mention four: sin as failed relationship, sin as state, sin as power, and sin as social.

When considering the first model, we can see how the biblical images of sin as a failure to maintain the covenant relationship aligns with the Catholic theology of freedom. Remember basic freedom is not a choice to do this or do that; it is a decision made over time about the kind of person I am to be. As the end-result of my exercise of self-determination, through all my acts of free choice, I become a particular self. Throughout our lives we are bringing about a certain degree of self-realization, becoming a certain type of man or woman. I am fashioning an identity as one who is in covenant with God or one without such a relationship. Here then is the deeper evil of sin—we do not simply choose a particular evil deed but over the course of time we may create an identity for ourselves as sinners, characterized by negative qualities such as bigotry, greed, meanness, and violence. Transcendental or basic freedom is the freedom to become a specific kind of individual. Sin is the misuse of that basic freedom of self-determination to become a person who lives in alienation from, rather than in covenant with, God. When sin is understood in this way, we can say that sinfulness is an identity I assume over time.

Hence, it is important to recognize that an individual action seen in isolation may not in itself seem serious, but a series of such actions will, little by little over a period of time, alter relationships. For example, over the course of a life friendships may change not due a great rift or dispute, but because persons do not make the effort to stay in touch, they lose touch with their friend's experience who may have a new job, gotten married, or had a child. Or again, a minor fault of insensitivity to the needs of others can grow in time into a consistent lack of considerateness toward others, which deepens into a self-centered apathy regarding the needs of others. What this underlines is the banality of evil. Sinfulness does not necessarily cause a troubled conscience since, as was suggested in paragraph 16 of *Gaudium et spes*, bit by bit we can muffle the call of conscience, "which by degrees grows practically sightless" through a process of minor failings. Racism, graft, lying, tax fraud—all these things can be rationalized away quite easily by people who slip into mindsets and ways of living that gradually blind us to moral obligations toward others.

If we use the Johannine theme of sin as a state of existence, we find a second useful theme for today. Seeing sin as a state of being has an important repercussion for our theological anthropology. There can be a lost sense of personal responsibility in our culture, that is, the tendency to say that people are mentally ill or victims of their environment rather than say they are selfish or mean or violent. Of course we have become more sensitive to the psychological and sociological factors that may profoundly impact our capacity for moral decision and action. That awareness is a positive development. Yet if we are constantly citing mitigating reasons for our actions—poor parenting, lousy school system, poor self-image, lack of peer group formation, inadequate housing, and so on—it is possible that we can lose a proper sense of personal responsibility.

A figure like Augustine would push back at avoidance of the language of sin and the tendency to explain all moral failing as due to psychological or sociological conditions. For Augustine when one looks at the human situation one finds peace, generosity, and love. But he also knew that is not all there is within our hearts. For there is hatred, envy, discord, and selfishness as well. We, too, are aware that there is darkness in each of us. This is what Augustine was getting at in his famous *Confessions* about his conversion. He faced himself in a way that many others often avoid—no easy excuses or transfer of blame to parents, society or bad luck. Augustine looked at himself and saw sin within. In the famous episode of stealing the pears in his youth, Augustine makes the point that he did not need the pears which he stole; he did not even want the pears. What he wanted was the pleasure of doing something forbidden and to share in the evil with others. He loved the wrong itself, not the pears which he stole but love of the mischief. This is reminiscent of the Hebrew experience of hattah; the heart is not always steadfastly in love with the true good.

A third important model or image of sin is that of power. Our acquaintance with sin tends to be repetitive; sin is experienced by many of us as a bad habit. This resonates with the Pauline experience which emphasizes sin as power. There is an element of the pathological to sin; it is like a cancer which grows and develops within us. Small failings have a way of growing into destructive lifestyles; little choices set the stage for more malicious decisions later. And my sin helps to create a sinful environment in which others now find it more difficult to resist sin, for example, violence breeds violence, the shouted curse which evokes anger from another, my selfishness which warns others to look out for themselves first in dealings with me. Sin is more dynamic than the language of relationship sometime conveys; it is a power or virus.

Habits describe human behavior not at the level of individual acts but at the level of character traits, typical qualities of spirit, attitude, and action. Habits are more indicative of a person's true character than one act. Vice is the word we have for bad habits, and the point of speaking about vice is that we all have flaws in our character which are not easily overcome. People caught up in vice experience themselves as unfree, as not being able to resist or overcome their failing. When speaking of sin, we can never simply presume that each of us has the same amount of freedom to reject sin. Some of us due to previous choices and decisions are much more inclined to sin than others.

Sin is progressive; it is captured in the biblical idea of a "hardening of the heart." Vice has its own dynamic, moving people to ever deeper and deeper levels of disintegration. Once caught up in a pattern of sin, a habit of wrongful choice, it becomes progressively harder to break the pattern. Asking someone not to curse or gossip is much more of a challenge if the person has a daily pattern of improper speech or conversation. It is a far greater task for a community that has used violence as an ordinary way of handling disputes to refrain from violence than would be the case for a community that has resisted employing violent force.

In short, talk of sin as a power reminds us that we can be too glib in our talk of human freedom, for there are degrees of freedom and vice, that is, a habit of sin can place limits upon our ability to choose the good. People are not nearly as in control of their inner lives as some naively think. The personal challenge of overcoming a repeated temptation is akin to sin as awon and should temper a too easy optimism about the possibilities of personal and social reform.

There is one more important aspect of the mystery of sin which we cannot overlook, for it broadens our image of sin as personal and interpersonal, and that is sin in a transpersonal sense.

In recent decades a fourth dimension of sin that has gained attention is the experience of what has been called social sin or structural sin. This language points to the phenomenon of sin in a transpersonal sense. We live in a society filled with structures compromised by sin, and our societal sin is more than the sum of the parts of our individual sins. This theme has undergone considerable development as theologians have engaged not only with the Christian tradition on sin but with social scientists to better understand the dynamics of individuals living in social groups and creating social practices and institutions.

The terms "social sin" and "sinful social structures" are part of contemporary theological discussion and debate within Catholicism. A major reason for this debate is that the Catholic tradition has been wary of any notion of sin that undercuts personal freedom and responsibility for sin. The centuries-old practice of auricular confession has demanded accountability of each individual penitent for the sins committed. This, however, has led to a neglect of the social dimensions of sin, as noted previously, as well as an exaggerated notion of personal freedom in many cases. Still, there is a value in the tradition's presumption of personal freedom and responsibility so that we do not succumb to a moral evasiveness that readily transfers blame to anyone but ourselves and avoids facing the harsh reality of our own sinfulness.

At the same time, Catholicism has used the word *sin* analogously by speaking of "original sin" as a reality for which the individual is not to be blamed. Thus, sin in the sense of original sin is not the same as sin in the sense of personal sin according to the Catholic tradition. It may be, then, that sin in the sense of social sin is different again from original and personal sin. It is analogous; that is, it points to the similarity amid the difference. All three usages are concerned with the mystery of evil in human life and the varied ways in which humans experience evil. Yet, the three terms—original, personal, social—highlight how evil is manifested in varied ways.

Structures of sin may be understood as a species of the genus social sin. The latter encompasses all kinds of social factors that induce individuals to sin. Structures of sin are one such kind of social factor.[65] For the purposes of this chapter, the idea of structural sin or structures of sin illustrates well the benefit of using a broader conceptualization of sin than sin as simply personal or interpersonal.

Two insights from social scientists help clarify understanding the idea of structural sin. The first of these insights comes from the sociology of knowledge and is captured in a dictum from Peter Berger and Thomas Luckmann: "Society is a human project. Society is an objective reality. The human person is a social product."[66] The very first thing to be clear about is that Berger and Luckmann are not proposing a deterministic formula, premises 1 and 2 with a conclusion. Rather each simple statement is of equal weight. Humans are a culture-producing animal. The performing arts, advertising, business practices, political institutions, legal systems, religious bodies—all these things are created by human beings. Once created, however, these are all things outside myself and stand apart from me and impact me. These things are all elements in a social world that are more than my personal ideas, desires, or creations. Taken together they help shape a collective entity, society, which envelops me. The person is shaped by the culture in which he or she lives—we are different because we live in the twentieth-first century in the United States rather than as a peasant in fifteenth-century Western Europe, or a farmer in ninth-century Southeast Asia, or hunter in second-century central Africa. Hence, society is a project created by humans; society includes many groups, institutions, practices, customs, and beliefs that are not simply extensions of the person but exist apart from an individual; and these social forces have an impact on how the individual thinks, values, and acts.

To use an illustration of the Berger-Luckmann viewpoint: what is in our hearts as human beings, say our racism, gets expressed in the society we create; political and economic institutions discriminate among races, images of beauty and refinement reflect the ideas of one race rather than another, and so on. (Society is a human project.) This culture now reinforces and externalizes the racism in our hearts such that the needed conversion is now not simply changing one's personal view but also having to change laws, customs, financial practices, educational systems, and so on. (Society is an objective reality.) If one is born into a culture that is racist, the evil is transmitted through formal and informal channels that teach one race is superior to another, one race is not to be trusted, and that interracial friendships and marriages are difficult if not perverse. Therefore, a child raised in such a society is highly likely to internalize some of the racism of the society. (The human person is a social product.)

With regard to social structures, the causal dimension is the relation between the various roles and positions of people that will present an array of restrictions, enablements, and incentives influencing choices and behaviors. To borrow an example from Daniel Finn, if one examines a university as a social structure, there are established roles—professor, student, dean—that will influence the way the individuals in those roles will act that would not be the case if the same persons happened to be together in another structure, for example a church assembly. Stepping into various roles or positions in various structures will influence behavior due to the differing incentives, restrictions, and enablements that accompany the roles and how they are related to one another in various structures. A student in a university with a widely respected honor code will be influenced on the question of cheating on an exam in a way that is different from a student taking an exam in a class where cheating is widely accepted as a way to improve grades. And if the professor in the latter example has stipulated that only 10 percent of the class will receive an "A" grade, that will add additional incentives for the student to act in a certain way.[67]

Sinful social structures remind us that we are social beings, and we are affected by the environments in which we are situated. Just as the likelihood of a flower coming to bloom is increased if it is growing in a well-maintained greenhouse, so too the likelihood is lessened if the flower is in the shade and the soil around it is dry. Sinful social structures stunt human flourishing by situating people in settings where incentives, restrictions, and enablements provided by the structure promote active cooperation or at least passive complicity with evil.

Even if we are not the persons or the generation that created the unjust policies and structures, we are among those who benefit and cooperate with them and help maintain them by indifference to efforts to reform them. Social sin refers both to the ways in which our personal sins become embodied in unjust social structures (a business climate where bribery is widely accepted and practiced) and to the ways in which these structures, having taken on a life of their own, make it harder to reform entrenched evils (a new business owner in order to compete must give bribes to public officials). This is a vicious cycle where sinful acts beget sinful structures and sinful structures beget sinful acts. We find sin on both the personal and communal levels.

Thus, if sin as failed relationship, or condition, or power is a useful way to think about personal and interpersonal sin today, and which illuminate aspects of human life better than sin as infraction or stain, it is by no means the case that these are the only ways to think about sin. For the experience of sin is too vast to be captured in any one model or short list of models. Social sin and structures of sin are recent terms used to convey the reality that we experience ourselves as immersed in sin not only of our choosing but also sin as our participation in and complicity with moral blindness and environments that stifle human development and flourishing.

CONCLUSION

The Catholic social tradition stresses the dignity and worth of each individual person. It also emphasizes the communal contexts within which human flourishing occurs. Both of these commitments to the sacred and social nature of the person have been fed by a theological tradition that speaks of Trinity, Incarnation, Body of Christ, imago Dei, and other religious expressions that have shaped the imagination of those formed by Catholicism. Because of that imaginative vision, the Catholic social tradition has resonated with claims about the dignity of the human person integrally and adequately considered and that human dignity is only realized in community. Vatican II gave expression to the revival of interest in personal dignity by placing the theme at the center of Catholic social teaching. The foundational claim of the sacredness and sociality of the person has the significant implication that each and every human being has a dignity that must be honored, promoted, and protected within community.

In this chapter we have seen that the understanding of the human person in Catholicism's theological anthropology is multidimensional. It is linked to certain essential features of personal experience, namely, reason, conscience, freedom, and sinfulness. The formal social teaching of the Church is built upon the theological foundation elaborated in the chapters up to now. In the next chapters we will move from consideration of the foundations of the social tradition to an identification and examination of several ethical themes which serve as "coordinates" that map the moral landscape of Catholic social teaching. The themes to be presented next are implications drawn from the explicitly theological claims made here and in previous chapters. Catholic social teaching, as articulated by the teaching office of the church since the late nineteenth century, has developed these ethical coordinates to understand and teach about a range of moral issues. They are inferences drawn from the broader theological vision of the human person as sacred and social. We will next treat two of the key ethical coordinates: the common good and the idea of human rights.

NOTES

1. Vatican II, *Gaudium et spes*, n. 14.
2. Vatican II, n. 15.
3. Vatican II, n. 17 (the internal quote is from Sirach 15:14).
4. Vatican II, n. 13.
5. EM, 104, *Acta Synodalia* 4, VII, p. 502, as cited by Joseph Selling, "Origin of the Concept of the HPAC," from his website (Catholic) Christian Ethics. https://theo.kuleuven.be /apps/christian-ethics/theory/origin.html.
6. Louis Janssens, "Artificial Insemination: Ethical Consideration," 3–29.
7. Janssens, 4.
8. Janssens, 5.
9. Janssens, 5.
10. Janssens, 6.
11. Janssens, 8.
12. Janssens, 9.
13. Janssens, 9.
14. Janssens, 10.
15. Janssens, 12.
16. Janssens, 13.
17. Janssens, 14.
18. Richard Gula, *Reason Informed by Faith*, 67–72. In the treatment of these headings, I borrow liberally from Gula's description.
19. Mary Elsbernd, "Authentic Human Living in Catholic Social Teachings: A Feminist Perspective," 3.
20. Elsbernd, 12.
21. Elsbernd, 3.
22. Elsbernd, 5–6, n. 9.
23. Lisa Sowle Cahill, "Reframing Catholic Ethics: Is the Person an Integral and Adequate Starting Point," 3.
24. Cahill, 3.
25. Cahill, 4.
26. Cahill, 6.
27. In addition to Janssens and Gula, several other Catholic moral theologians concur in the approach advocated in this section.
28. David Hollenbach, "A Communitarian Reconstruction of Human Rights: Contributions from the Catholic Tradition," 138.
29. Rowlands, *Towards a Politics of Communion*, 54.

30. Bernard Lonergan has summed up the method of critical realism in his "transcendental precepts" that operate in all acts of human knowing: be attentive; be rational; be reasonable; be responsible. While the transcendental precepts appear in numerous works of Lonergan, see his *Method in Theology*, 20.

31. Charles Curran, *Catholic Social Teaching, 1891–present*, 24.

32. Curran, 53.

33. Bernard Lonergan, "The Transition from a Classicist World View to Historical Mindedness," 126–33.

34. "I propose that knowledge of nature and the natural law requires inductive consensus building that includes experiences of God, takes into account cultural differences, corrects bias, and envisions the possibility of change in nature itself, in the moral requirements of nature, and especially in knowledge of those requirements." Lisa Sowle Cahill, *Global Justice, Christology and Christian Ethics*, 251–2.

35. "Knowledge of the natural law is always perspectival and partial, even when it is also true and accurate. Knowledge is never detached from the particular contexts, identities, and interests of knowing subjects. An inductive epistemology is demanded by the practical nature of moral knowledge, and if it is also collaborative, it will help counteract the ever-present reality of bias. Knowledge of human needs, good, and obligations approaches universality only to the extent that the reasoning process behind it is extensive, inclusive, and critical." Cahill, *Global Justice, Christology and Christian Ethics*, 265.

36. Gerard Hughes, "Natural law," 47.

37. Cahill, *Global Justice, Christology and Christian Ethics*, 250–51.

38. On the points made in the preceding two paragraphs, see Bruno Schüller, "Can Moral Theology Ignore Natural Law?" 94–99.

39. Vatican II, *Gaudium et spes*, n. 16.

40. James Keenan, "Redeeming Conscience," 129–47.

41. Keenan, 135.

42. Robert Smith, *Conscience and Catholicism*, 83 as cited in Keenan, "Redeeming Conscience," 139.

43. Bruce Vawter, *The Conscience of Israel*.

44. Benedetta Rossi, "Jeremiah."

45. Stacey Davis, "Joel."

46. Vatican II, *Gaudium et spes*, n. 16.

47. "Over the Pope as expression of the binding claim of ecclesiastical authority, there stands one's own conscience which must be obeyed before all else, even if necessary against the requirement of ecclesiastical authority. This emphasis on the individual, whose conscience confronts him with a supreme and ultimate tribunal, and one which in the last resort is beyond the claim of external social groups, even the official Church, also establishes a principle in opposition to increasing totalitarianism." Joseph Ratzinger, "Commentary on *Gaudium et spes*," 134.

48. Anne Patrick, *Liberating Conscience*, 35.

49. Vatican II, *Gaudium et spes*, n. 16.

50. David Hollenbach, "Human Dignity: Experience and History, Practical Reason and Faith," 123–39.

51. Vatican II, *Gaudium et spes*, n. 17.

52. Bernard Brady, *Essential Catholic Social Thought*, 80.

53. David Hollenbach, "Afterword: a community of freedom," 323.

54. Hollenbach, 326.

55. Vatican II, *Gaudium et spes*, n. 17.

56. Rowlands, *Towards a Politics of Communion*, 54.

57. Karl Rahner, "Theology of Freedom," *Theological Investigations* VI, 185.

58. Josef Fuchs, *Human Values and Christian Morality*, 97.

59. McBrien, *Catholicism*, 954.

60. Rowlands, *Towards a Politics of Communion*, 28.

61. Hollenbach, "A communitarian reconstruction," 141.

62. Hollenbach, "Afterward: a community of freedom," 340.

63. Hanvey, "Dignity, Person, and *Imago Trinitatis*," 221.

64. Rowlands, *Towards a Politics of Communion*, 55.

65. Conor Kelly, "The Nature and Operation of Structural Sin," 294.

66. Peter Berger and Thomas Luckmann, *The Social Construction of Reality*, 61.

67. Daniel Finn, "What Is a Sinful Social Structure," 150.

PART III
GUIDELINES FOR DISCERNMENT

6

COMMON GOOD AND HUMAN RIGHTS

Most treatments of Catholic social teaching speak of principles or norms. Rarely in the literature is the distinction made between formal and material principles and norms. Material norms direct action; for example, do not kill. Immediately one sees the challenge of material norms, for throughout history we have made countless exceptions to the norm "do not kill." And most people have accepted that a fair number of the exceptions, though not all, are plausible. So "do not kill except in self-defense" or "do not kill except to defend the innocent" have been accepted over time as reasonable moral norms that illustrate necessary refinement of the principle "do not kill." The other kind of norm, a formal norm, is not action-oriented as much as it is agent-oriented. That is, "Be just" or "Be compassionate" does not tell us what to do so much as tell us what we should strive to be like in our character. These norms are paranetic or exhortatory; they point out a value and put it in an imperative form. The norms can be in a positive or negative style: "Be kind" or "Don't be cruel." Such norms do not really tell us what to do but bring to mind the sort of persons we ought to be. They exhort and encourage us to embody certain virtues or reject certain vices.

Talk about Catholic social teaching using the language of norms can be misleading since many might expect that the tradition provides material norms that can be readily applied to specific, particular issues. Yet many principles or norms in Catholic social teaching are more formal than material. What we find in the body of literature called Catholic social teaching is like road signs or guidelines that call us to pay attention to this or that but do not mandate a specific choice of policy or decision to act. Even with knowledge of the teaching, discernment is needed for decision-making, and there may be several plausible options to consider. It is better to think about Catholic social teaching as an effort to articulate the wisdom resident in the wider social tradition and how it might provide guidance for people as we strive to build better societies in which to live.

For those who profess commitment to the Catholic social tradition, making a judgment about an issue of social policy entails more than reflecting upon the theological roots of the tradition. There is the necessary process of bringing vital empirical data into conversation with the moral values and ethical wisdom found in Catholic social thought. That conversation must flow in two directions. The tradition provides a lens by which to view and interpret the empirical data. That is one side of the conversation, but the particular context and circumstance that is being analyzed must also shape how best to utilize and apply the wisdom found in the tradition. That second side of the conversation is what drives development and change within Catholic social teaching. The first side of the conversation is what underscores that matters of social policy are not morally neutral and purely technical in nature. However, neither individuals nor communities can work through all one's experience and knowledge every time a social issue confronts us with making a choice. Instead, over time we develop a particular "take" on our reality, what some have called an "onlook," a distinctive vision of social life. Based on that perspective we distill certain key ideas that serve as a sort of short-hand summation of our social vision.

In this chapter I will look at two major implications of the theological foundation and anthropology outlined in Chapters 2 through 5, the common good and human rights. A well-respected commentator on Catholic social thought has written that "The concept of the common good is the centerpiece of Catholic social thought."[1] Another esteemed commentator on social Catholicism has described the common good as "an old idea with a new urgency."[2] The common good is, indeed, central to the Catholic social tradition, and it is an old and venerable idea, which is in need of revision and reformulation. Part of that revision and reformulation will be evident in the second half of this chapter when the topic of human rights is integrated with the common good. First, however, the historical background and meaning of the common good will be examined, along with criticisms and concerns about how the common good has been understood and how it has functioned in Catholic thought. After responding to the criticisms, there will also be consideration of proposed changes to the meaning of the common good in Catholic social thought. At the outset it should be acknowledged that modern Catholic social teaching, perhaps as much any other tradition of social thought, has maintained the common good theme in the contemporary era.

Then in the second half of the chapter, I will discuss the idea of human rights. We will examine how the past use of rights language emerged in

Catholic social thought and then how it came to be used in the modern era of Catholic social teaching. After these two major sub-sections there will be a third that illustrates how human rights are to be understood in a Catholic framework. The chapter will conclude with comments about the connection between the common good and human rights in Catholicism.

Following this chapter, the next two chapters will examine several additional points of wisdom distilled from Catholic social thought. Rather than employing terms like "principles," "axioms," or "norms" to describe the material to be examined in these remaining chapters, I prefer a slightly different description, one that reflects my belief that the Catholic social tradition offers a distinctive perspective from which to view and interpret social reality. The ethical insights distilled from the foundational vision function as a set of coordinates that allow adherents of the social tradition to map the moral landscape of their social world. Thus, I will present the wisdom of the tradition not as a set of principles or norms to apply to particular issues but as a framework for moral discernment when seeking to bring values within the tradition into dialogue with the manifold social contexts and issues that confront modern disciples of the Catholic faith. These ethical coordinates lay out signposts by which to navigate an individual's and a society's pilgrimage through our morally complex world in the quest for building societies where the dignity of the human person in community is achieved. But the guidance from the tradition only takes us so far along the way—the exact policy choices, the nature of the social institutions to be established, and the strategies for incarnating our values in the lives of the various communities we create will require intellectual humility, a measure of trial and error, and a commitment to ongoing public dialogue. The Catholic voice should be part of public decision processes without the presumption of having the final say in the matter at hand.

HISTORICAL FACETS OF THE COMMON GOOD

Although it is true that the origins of the common good in antiquity were philosophical, not theological, there is biblical support for the idea that precedes the Greek and Roman thinkers who first articulated the concept of the common good. For ancient Israelites, belief in and worship of Yahweh was tied up with a set of social values. "The laws of the Pentateuch are presented in the context of a covenant between the god Yahweh and the people Israel."[3] There were always horizontal relationships with others, as well as the vertical relationship with Yahweh that were embedded in the covenant between God and the Hebrew people. "The most fundamental principle of biblical ethics is the belief in the reality of a God who is Lord of the covenant," a covenant that had stipulations about human behavior.[4] For the command to love God was accompanied by a commandment to love the neighbor as oneself. That second commandment was basically a command to serve the common good. An illustration of this point is evident in the various stipulations that comprise the sabbatical laws of the Pentateuch.

The biblical scholar John Collins describes the impact of those laws. Acknowledging that we do not have certain knowledge about the practical implementation of the sabbatical laws, he observes that the objectives of the laws were important and a matter of concern for generations. The Pentateuchal laws suggested a social perspective that was vital if the problems of the poor and concern for future generations were to be addressed. "The landowners of ancient Israel were forbidden to think primarily in terms of their individual profits but were directed to think instead of the common good."[5] Collins goes on to note that something similar was the case with laws against slavery and lending money at interest to a fellow Israelite. While there was certainly variation in how the laws were interpreted and there was development within the tradition, there were general principles that perdured and were widely acknowledged. The laws placed "restrictions on the aggrandizement of individuals" and provided "protection for the weaker members of the society."[6]

A communitarian ethic was ingrained in the religious imagination of Israelite religion. There was no sense of putting the legitimate concerns of the individual in opposition to the good of the community. Rather "the good of the individual is always viewed in the context of the community. The welfare of the community determines the welfare of the individual."[7] According to the biblical laws, it was in the best interest of the individual to seek to promote the communal self-interest, for the individual person could only function within the context of a community that nurtured, protected, and affirmed the worth of its members.

This latter theme is evident in the teaching of the classical prophets. The Pentateuchal laws largely reflect the ethos of Israel prior to the rise of the monarchy. Different social patterns emerge with the age of kings, and the story of Naboth's vineyard in the twenty-first chapter of 1 Kings offers a view of the social ills of the era, when the poor are treated harshly by those avidly pursuing land and wealth. "The charge which Amos and Isaiah bring against the rich of their day is not only that they are doing wrong to the poor but that they are violating the common good," understood as what is ultimately in the best interests of all the people both rich and poor. "Specifically, they claimed that social injustice would cause the Assyrian invasions, which would lay waste both Israel and Judah."[8] The prophets, particularly Isaiah, see the rulers of Israel and Judah as provoking their neighbor Assyria by the pursuit of wealth and power, a pursuit that was followed to the neglect of the poor and vulnerable. In the prophetic view, "provision for the poor and the restraint and moderation in the pursuit of material goods are recommended because they ultimately enhance the peace and prosperity of all."[9]

The Hebrew understanding of covenant required that after God had graciously liberated a people there was still the need for the people to accept their election as Yahweh's chosen people and to freely choose to be part of a community that would shape their lives going forward. "Covenant is the free commitment to be a person in relation to others. . . . Theologically, being a covenant people . . . is radically to be a member of a community; religion is not merely vertical, 'me and God,' it is also radically horizontal. It is a community of mutually shared obligations, responsibilities, and gifts."[10]

That strong sense of communal belonging and mutuality continues in the New Testament where there is great emphasis in the gospels on the commandment to love the neighbor. It is crucial that the disciples of Jesus put aside the quest for self-gratification, power, and prestige and embrace the identity of servants. The followers of Jesus must think of the well-being of others and seek the goods that build up the community of disciples. The narrative of the last judgment in Matthew 25, Jesus's teaching on the great commandment in Mark 12:28ff, Luke's parable of the Good Samaritan in 10:25ff, and John's account of Jesus washing the feet of the disciples at the Last Supper in 13:1ff are all illustrative of the servant theme in the gospels.

In Paul we find the ideal of the common good transposed in another key. Paul used the language of the body of Christ in a variety of ways—sometimes referring to the historical flesh of Jesus, sometimes his eucharistic body, and at other times the church as the gathering of the disciples. "In the last sense it is a figurative way of expressing the corporate identity of Christians with Christ."[11] Though not used in the earliest letters, the image of the church as the body of Christ appears in 1 Corinthians when Paul addresses the divisions within the community. He argues that since Christ was not divided neither should there be factions within the church. "The symbol of unity is the figure of the body with its members."[12] In Chapter 12, he writes:

> For just as the body is one and has many members, and all the members of the body, though many, are one body, so it is with Christ. For in the one Spirit we were all baptized into one body—Jews or Greeks, slaves or free—and we were all made to drink of one Spirit. Indeed,

the body does not consist of one member but of many. If the foot would say, "Because I am not a hand, I do not belong to the body," that would not make it any less a part of the body. And if the ear would say, "Because I am not an eye, I do not belong to the body," that would not make it any less a part of the body. If the whole body were an eye, where would the hearing be? If the whole body were hearing, where would the sense of smell be? But as it is, God arranged the members in the body, each one of them, as he chose. If all were a single member, where would the body be? As it is, there are many members yet one body. The eye cannot say to the hand, "I have no need of you," nor again the head to the feet, "I have no need of you." On the contrary, the members of the body that seem to be weaker are indispensable, and those members of the body that we think less honorable we clothe with greater honor, and our less respectable members are treated with greater respect, whereas our more respectable members do not need this. But God has so arranged the body, giving the greater honor to the inferior member, that there may be no dissension within the body, but the members may have the same care for one another. If one member suffers, all suffer together with it; if one member is honored, all rejoice together with it. (1 Cor 12:12–26)

Just prior to this extended analogy of the church's members with the body of Christ, Paul had written, "To each is given the manifestation of the Spirit for the common good" (1 Cor 12:7). So, in his mind, the various gifts that different disciples bring to the community are all inspired by the Spirit, and Christians are to use those gifts for the building up of the common good, that is, for the betterment of the entire body of Christ.

Of course, Paul also wrote regarding the body of Christ in a way that transcended the moral union of people dedicated to a common objective. In his reflections on the eucharist he understood disciples who partake in the one cup and one loaf as being not only in moral union but somehow as being members of Christ himself. Over time that latter union came to be called "mystical," but, as noted in Chapter 3, that was not a term in Paul's writing. It was later theologians who referred to the *corpus mysticum* to imply a oneness that is more than cooperative behavior for a shared goal.[13]

In the description of the early Christian community in Luke's Acts of the Apostles we get an idealized portrait of the church. Luke imitates classical portrayals of utopian societies found in Greek and Roman authors describing early Athens or the "golden age" of the Republic. He wants to emphasize it is by the gift of the Spirit at Pentecost that a community is created that attains the hopes and aspirations of humanity: genuine unity, peace, joy, and worship of God.[14] Yet Luke is not alone in witnessing to the disciples' experience of shared concern for one another: Galatians 2:10, 1 Corinthians 16:1–4, Philippians 4:15–20, as well as extra-biblical sources such as the Didache 4:5–8 and the Letter of Barnabas 19:8 all provide evidence of the deep sense of community and level of concern for the common well-being in the life of the early church.[15] *Koinonia* or community was not just a spiritual communion but a commitment to material sharing of life as well.[16]

Hence, though the Bible does not use the term "common good" in the sense that Greek and Roman thinkers employed it, there was within the biblical tradition a clear sense that the vision of life to be adopted was one in which "the communal and social dimensions of human existence" were stressed.[17]

Classical Ideas of the Common Good

It was in the cultures of ancient Greek city-states and the republic of Rome that one finds the philosophical roots of the common good. A key presupposition in both cases is that the human good is best achieved in the setting of common life. That, in turn, moves the discussion into the realm of politics, for it is by living as a citizen, participating in the life of public discourse and decision-making which shaped the state, that one pursues the good life. It was widely accepted that the common good attained through active citizenship also redounded to the good of the person. So political thought in the West would be influenced for centuries by the belief "that citizens have a moral responsibility to act in ways that promote the common good of the larger society rather than simply pursuing their own individual goods."[18]

In general, the common good was the term employed by thinkers to express the proper relation between the flourishing of individuals and the communities to which they belong. It did not require universally shared values nor uniformity in outlook. Whose good was to count in the balancing of the individual and group was a disputed point (as it remains so today). Slaves, noncitizens, and women were among the many who did not factor into the discussion. But among those who did count, the common good was not seen as being apart from or opposed to the good of the individual.

Aristotle is the most commonly cited Greek thinker on the common good, and his approach would much later become influential within the Catholic tradition of social thought due his impact on the work of Thomas Aquinas. For Aristotle, human persons are necessarily social; that is, to use one of his most quoted statements: "the person is by nature a political animal (*zōon politikon*)."[19] It is not possible to attain individual flourishing on one's own. Humans are meant to partner and collaborate. For him, citizenship was an intrinsic good necessary to achieve human well-being.

Aristotle believed that we all seek happiness, not in the sense of a passing emotional state but rather *eudaimonia* or well-being as a stable state of existence that is somewhat objective. It is closer to what we think of today as a person's character rather than their mood. In accord with Socrates and Plato, Aristotle thought that to attain true well-being or happiness, one had to cultivate the life of virtue. The virtues must be developed through training and exercise, but the full array of human virtues can only be acquired by living in a good *polis*, or city.

Hence, the importance of being a citizen and the obligation to be active in playing out that role; without it one could not be fully virtuous and thus not truly experience human flourishing. It is only by being an active member of a city-state, working in concert with others for the common good of the *polis*, that a person can cultivate the virtues necessary for the achievement of happiness, human well-being.

Centuries later, Cicero would resort to many of Aristotle's ideas as he wrote his major political work, *The Republic*, during a time when he foresaw and lamented the evolving transformation of Rome from a republic to an empire. Cicero's contribution was to translate Aristotle's idea of citizenship in a way that would make sense in a context far broader and more diverse than the narrow and homogeneous Greek city-state. He created different levels of citizenship and also moved away from Aristotle's ideas of interpersonal acts of self-government within a small population. In place of the Greek ideal of personal direct participation in democratic decision-making, Cicero, the lawyer, called for the dutiful citizen to have a deep commitment to upholding the rule of law.

For Cicero a republic could be any group of persons, even a substantial number, who were united in agreement on the nature and norms of justice and were committed to the shared or common good of the public. This, of course, reflects the literal sense of *res publica*, the public's thing. And that "thing" was a system of laws that was extended to all who were citizens of Rome and protected the rights and mandated the duties of being a citizen. The reason for the existence of the state was to establish and maintain that system.

Catholic Thought on the Common Good

The early church fathers due to their strong communitarian leanings were able to adopt the theme of a common good from the classical pagan tradition and incorporate it into their social thought. "The teaching of the Pauline epistles and the Acts of the Apostles on gift, on reciprocity, on the status of the poor, on the harmony and plurality of the worshipping body provided a new focus for developing ideas about the common good."[20] Clement of Rome, at the end of the first century, speaks of organisms that are composed of different elements yet work together for the common good. Justin Martyr, a Gentile convert in the second century, witnesses to the level of sharing in the early Christian communities in Palestine. Clement of Alexandria, in the later stage of the second century, writes: "God himself has created human beings for communion or sharing with one another, by sharing himself first of all, and by sending his Word to all alike, and by making all things in common."[21] The Roman lawyer and Christian Tertullian recalls the common sharing of goods and writes about Christians as being one body bound together by a common faith, discipline, and hope.

Basil, the father of Eastern monasticism, writes in many places during the mid-300s that the human person is a social animal, and the ground of that sociability is nature itself, with an innate "inclination to live together with and love" other humans.[22] As the father of Eastern monasticism Basil made clear that he preferred monks to live in community devoted to a shared life rather than be hermits, for "nothing, indeed, is so compatible with our nature as living in society and in dependence upon one another."[23] The great patristic preacher John Chrysostom made the point clearly: "This is the rule of the most perfect Christianity, its most exact definition, its highest point, namely, the seeking of the common good."[24]

If one looks at the Western fathers of the church, the same openness to the language of sharing and the common good is evident. Ambrose of Milan says, "it is clear, then, that we should consider and admit that what benefits the individual is the common good and should judge nothing as useful unless it benefits all."[25] And similar to Basil in the East, Benedict of Nursia, the father of Western monasticism, moved monastic life away from isolation and individual asceticism to an approach designed in the first half of the sixth century for ordinary Christians. "Rather than envisioning a collection of individuals competing in the quest for perfection, Benedict stressed the role of community as a school for holiness."[26]

As significant and influential as these various voices were, and without demeaning the importance of Benedict for the history of monasticism, it was Augustine of Hippo writing in North Africa in the late fourth and early fifth century that shaped later Christian writers. Augustine quite consciously adopted and adapted the language of the common good that he found in the classical authors of Greece and Rome. He makes the point that the common good, a good of the earthly realm for Greek and Roman philosophers, actually transcends any historical political community, for true fulfillment is a communal life to be found beyond death. In short salvation is a social good, for it is a shared common life between all the blessed and the Trinity. That eternal state of fulfillment reaches far beyond the common good of temporal life but does not negate the achievement of establishing a common good within history.

Augustine has a darker view of the possibilities of human cooperation and political order than most of his predecessors. He accepted that the human person was naturally social and drawn to community; however, due to the consequences of the Fall, humans and their social institutions have become corrupted. Augustine also maintained that the number of those restored by grace was relatively small so that the majority of those living in the earthly kingdom would not be drawn by justice into service of the common good. The role of the state, therefore, was not, as with Cicero or Aristotle, the promotion of the common good so much as the imposition of restraints that make a semblance of social life bearable. The state, while a natural society, takes on a coercive and punitive role to restrain injustice and the sinful will to dominate (*libido dominandi*).

Yet there does remain a measure of justice within the earthly city, and Augustine is supportive of efforts by Rome to establish social order. There are degrees of justice, and Rome is to be accorded more respect than those invaders who threaten the imperial state. It is a lukewarm acknowledgement of Rome's role in contributing to a common good, but Augustine does grant it a proper role. Though lacking true justice, a state can enforce an earthly justice that has value. Despite flawed motives, the inhabitants of the earthly city can understand their plight and conclude that imposing a measure of restraint upon themselves and others may allow support for a common good that otherwise would be lost. When people accept a share of the common good and are willing and capable of preventing others from exceeding their share, the result is a state that has a semblance of civic peace and protection of a society's way of life.

Throughout the patristic era the impact of the biblical tradition upon the social views of the church fathers is evident. In particular, Luke's portrayal of the early Jerusalem community deeply shaped the patristic understanding of community and how Christians were to live with others in working for a common good. And Paul's letters espousing the imagery of the body of Christ and how the various members cohere to form one body encouraged thinking about the church and society using organic metaphors.

This latter point is seen in Augustine's claim that "order is the disposition of equal and unequal things in such a way as to give to each its proper place."[27] This definition has been described as "one of the truly great legacies of the Ancient World which through the authority of St. Augustine henceforth became the basic tenet of all social, legal, and political thinking of the Middle Ages."[28] For Augustine, every individual organism had its place in the universal order established by the Creator and also had its own specific role and make-up. There was an organic unity of humankind based on being created by God and loved by God. There was also an irrevocable and irreplaceable dignity and worth in every individual person reflecting the person's immortal soul and his or her creation in the image of God.

> The premise of all socio-political thinking of the Middle Ages, namely the idea of a single and uniform but nevertheless articulate whole, presupposed an organic interrelation between this divinely ordained universal whole and its equally divinely ordained parts, members, or individuals on the one hand; and between the various parts, members, or individuals themselves on the other hand.[29]

In short, every human person has been given its place in the created order as well as its appropriate relationship to all other persons and creatures. Because every part was analogous to the universal whole, the imagery of the body of Christ became central wherein each part had a distinctive and valued existence and was also a vital member of a single visible communion. This social union was the mystical body, as distinct from the physical body, of Christ.

Thomas Aquinas built upon this Pauline imagery. His is "a vision of flourishing rooted in seeking to exercise the particularity of personality and calling for the sake of, and within the context of, the building up of the whole community." There is a sense, then, that for Aquinas, "the common good can be understood as rightly ordered self-interest."[30] As with the parts of the body, just as it is not possible that the hand or foot could survive if cut off from the body, so too the individual person cannot attain his or her flourishing apart from the community. Yet it must be emphasized that where the analogy falters is thinking that the good of the body can be attained even without one of its parts. For Aquinas, "the common good is composed of the good of each particular person." After all, "the common good is only truly common if I am able to pursue private goods and personal flourishing" and cannot be common if I or others are excluded from participating in the shared good.[31]

In an insightful essay on the common good in the Catholic social tradition, Drew Christiansen pointed out that commentators on Thomas "have generally diverged over whether the common good in politics may be interpreted in personalist or corporatist terms." That is, "does the common good regard the individual as a person with an irreducible dignity . . . or does it treat the individual simply as a member (part) of the body politic?"[32] Christiansen believed that Thomas held both views, treating the human in terms of a person who had preeminence over the good of the group, and at other times seeing the common good as having priority over individual self-interest. What Thomas was doing, according to Christiansen, was looking for a way forward between "the older collectivist feudal model of society, on the one hand, and the emerging freedom of urban society, on the other."[33]

It is important to understand that the Christian social tradition employed the organism analogy as a way to reject an individualistic rendering of social life as well as to explain the concept of the common good. The analogy was not meant to express the proposition that the individual part of the body is submerged or swallowed up by the whole. For "the whole only existed and fulfilled its real purpose in and through its various parts or members which are in themselves wholes."[34] This last phrase is key; the individual parts are "themselves wholes" and cannot be treated as mere accessories in the pursuit of the good of the whole. No society that fails to recognize the dignity and value of each person can fulfill its pursuit of the common good by sacrificing the good of the persons making up the society. So, the organism analogy falters if one uses it too literally. The leaves and roots of a tree are not for themselves but are at the service of the whole tree. But the person is not simply a part of the whole deriving its worth from the society; the person is an end in him- or herself. As Pius XII made clear during the second world war, the risk with the organic analogy of society is that society "is not a physical being and individuals its parts"; rather society is a community of persons who come together for a shared purpose and take up collective action to seek that purpose.[35]

The medieval use of the body analogy brought two biases into the Catholic social tradition that were to be problematic. First, it strongly implied that the parts could be easily harmonized with one another and that any conflict was only a seeming conflict; the body was in harmony and all the parts should know their place and play their role. That this was not easily resolved ought to have been evident from Paul's experience with the Corinthian community. He wrote to them precisely because there were divisions with the church over roles and responsibilities, and the factions within the community did not disappear quickly after Paul's instruction. Nonetheless, there remained within Catholic social thinking a belief that harmony, not conflict, was the norm, and conflict was almost always seen as negative without acknowledging that conflict sometimes forged new social realities that improved upon the previous circumstances.

The second bias encouraged by the body analogy is the acceptance of a hierarchical social order in which some parts were accorded greater status and power than others. Though Paul spoke of all the parts of the body as being valuable and indispensable, there was a broader tradition of speaking of the body politic in ancient Greece and Rome that fed thinking of higher and lower standing in those unequal societies.

> As early as the fifth century BC, Menenius Agrippa is supposed to have reconciled the patricians and plebians of Rome with the fable of the divided members that nevertheless form one body in a solidary fashion. In *The Republic*, Plato compared the "well ordered state" with a body and its members. Aristotle made use of the organism analogy to gain knowledge of the structure and life of society. Seneca taught the "we are members of one great body," since nature has generated us as "relatives" and made us "social beings."[36]

Those sources of the body analogy were at least as influential as Paul among social philosophers in the late antiquity and early medieval eras.

Belief in the hierarchical structuring of society was a controlling perspective in much Catholic social thought after Aquinas. This was true within various contexts—political, economic, ecclesiastical, cultural. One analyst of the tradition, Todd Whitmore, has suggested that "the most fundamental change" in Catholic social thought has been "from a hierarchical to a relatively egalitarian ordering of society as the primary condition of fulfillment."[37] He considers a prudential judgment that grew in wider and wider acceptance within the Catholic social tradition as what best facilitates social harmony is relative equality. He proposes that it was with the papacy of Pius XI that the shift toward greater equality began to appear in the realm of economics. That shift in economic thinking was then continued under Pius XII and extended into the sphere of politics as well.

According to Christiansen, this shift in outlook evolved to the point that by the papacy of John XXIII in 1958 it was inequality that had to be explained as equality had become the accepted premise of social teaching. In this changed context Pope John "reinterpreted the ancient principle of *the common good*."[38] In his 1961 encyclical, *Mater et magistra*, John stated the common good "embraces the sum total of those conditions of social living, whereby persons are enabled more fully and more readily to achieve their own perfection."[39]

In 1963, however, John offered another take on the common good. During the first half of the twentieth century, many Catholic social theorists still operated within Thomistic premises, employing the language of personalism to uphold human dignity and the language of human rights. "In this sense human rights as features of the person remained in tension with the common good as the collective welfare of the community. . . . In an extraordinary turnabout, in *Pacem in terris* the pope insisted that the common good largely consists in the defense and promotion of those rights."[40] Toward the end of that later encyclical the Pope discusses the idea of a universal common good and says, that "like the common good of individual States," the universal common good must have as its aim the proper regard for the human person. Therefore, public authority, whether national or international, "must have as its fundamental objective the recognition, respect, safeguarding and promotion of the rights of the human person."[41]

Christiansen rightly observes that the two definitions are not in conflict with each other, but "the human rights formula does increase the weight placed on the development of individual persons in the articulation of the common good."[42] Because the Catholic social tradition does not understand society as created by the free consent of autonomous individuals but as a natural grouping of persons arising out of multiple relationships and bonds of connection, "providing the conditions of social living, therefore, means guaranteeing the resources, defending the liberties, relieving the impediments, and opening the opportunities to participate fully in society."[43] So social conditions are an important dimension of the common good, as the 1961 definition of the common good suggests. Human flourishing, after all, is a social phenomenon. Indeed, for the Catholic tradition "salvation—the highest form of fulfillment—itself is social, an ultimate communion with God and neighbor that images the communion between the persons of the trinity."[44] Still, in Christiansen's opinion, "conceiving of the common good as the general enjoyment of human rights in society offers a more comprehensive, accurate, and definitive understanding of the common good than the customary appeal to 'conditions of social living.'"[45]

This historical overview of thinking about the common good suggests several significant elements regarding the common good. The Old Testament places the good of the individual Israelite in the context of the good of the entire covenant community. Prophetic criticism of the monarchy and ruling class often centered upon rules that neglected the interests of all the people in favor of benefits for the few. The New Testament is filled with examples of Jesus's preaching and teaching that true disciples must think always of serving others and building up the good of the community. St. Paul used the imagery of the body of Christ to bring home the same point, and Luke portrayed an early church that was characterized by a deep sharing in common life. Classical Greek and Roman authors addressed the importance of individual citizens contributing to the good of the city-state or republic. Though the exact strategies for such action differed between writers such as Aristotle and Cicero, the shared belief was that there was a common good in which all citizens benefited and to which all should be committed. Later Christian writers extolled the importance of the common good and how it served as a moral norm for members of the church. Over time Augustine and other patristic writers saw the state as having a role in protecting and maintaining the common good. Medieval thinkers wrestled with the relationship of the individual person to the common good, but the main thrust of the tradition was to see the relationship as harmonious and defend the idea that the common good was not to be understood as denying or overriding the good of the individual person. The modern papacy has strongly defended the idea of the common good but has integrated it with the idea of human rights that safeguard the dignity of each person.

UNDERSTANDING THE COMMON GOOD IN MODERN CATHOLIC SOCIAL THOUGHT

Within Catholic social teaching the common good along with the dignity of the person "are correlative concepts that keep the individual and society in balance."[46] This is a vital role for the common good in the tradition; it "provides a conceptual organizing category" that seeks a balance between the excessive claims of individualism and collectivism in social theories. "It serves as a way of construing the relationship of the individual to society so that the limits and possibilities of both individual and communal well-being are preserved, and in which the appropriate responsibilities and obligations that exist among individuals are clarified and articulated."[47] In accord with its communitarian perspective, the common good in Catholic social thought has emphasized that only in the context of community can the individual attain true fulfillment. Influenced in the nineteenth and twentieth centuries by liberalism, the Catholic understanding of the common good has affirmed and developed the ideal of freedom in the development of the human person. The outcome of this effort at balancing the two perspectives has been a social vision that asserts "the protection of the dignity of every person is understood to be a social project."[48] That "vision accentuates an objective morality, including criteria of justice and of a good society that can be known by all reasonable persons."[49]

The points about objective morality and criteria of justice will be treated later in this chapter, but first it is crucial to discuss the criteria of a good society as belonging to the common good. When John XXIII defined the common good in paragraph 65 of *Mater in magistra* he did so in terms that were primarily structural: "It is not a summation of the goods of individual citizens, but a set of social conditions which facilitate the realization of personal good by individuals."[50]

The sociologist John Coleman draws out the implications of this approach. "To conceive of the common good properly, we have to be able to think in terms of institutions and systems; we have to see individuals as inexorably situated, embedded beings, enmeshed in institutions which both constrain and empower them. Institutions shape their behavior, imaginations and purposes."[51] So a good society requires not only individual persons dedicated to the common good, but social institutions and structures that foster and promote well-being. Thus, the common good must "be consciously willed and pursued in the design of social institutions and public policy."[52] Among other tasks, educational, financial, health, and governmental systems must be put into place that will guarantee the resources, secure the opportunities, eliminate the obstacles, and ensure the freedoms that allow persons to participate in, benefit from, and contribute to the social conditions that facilitate personal and group flourishing. Coleman, borrowing from Philip Selznick, sums up the issue: "the common good can be defined as a state of the system—the sum total of appropriate institutional arrangements"[53] put in place to bring about human well-being.

Coleman suggests that there are three ideas central to the common good in the Catholic social tradition. First, as noted previously, it is institutional; that is, some goods cannot be obtained by solitary individuals on their own. "Such goods accrue to individuals through their participation in the public life and institutions of society."[54] For example, even a seemingly personal good like health is dependent on multiple social structures like food and drug testing, environmental protection, medical training, and access to health care providers. So, the common good "imagines and enacts the institutional conditions and arrangements necessary . . . to lives of even minimal human dignity and flourishing."[55]

A second idea vital to the common good is the notion of public goods. These are goods that are necessarily or preferably enjoyed with others. Friendship, teamwork, a sense of belonging, pride or pleasure in the success of others—all these experiences add to human flourishing and cannot be attained by the lone individual. In addition, there are other goods that are available to the public and not restricted to private individuals—safe streets, clean air and water, police and fire protection, public health measures.

And the third dimension of the common good in Catholic thought is that it is personalistic. The common good only exists where personal freedoms are safeguarded and dignified treatment of the person is secured. Hence, human needs and human agency are included in the common good.[56] For the good to be genuinely common it must be inclusive, leaving no person out of the benefits of shared life. Any institutional or individual bias that denies a person or group a fair share in the goods of the community is a distortion of the common good.

When the Catholic social tradition refers to the common good, it does not mean the mere sum of individual goods in a society. Nor is it meant that the good of the group is distinct from the good of its members and superior to them. Rather, the Catholic treatment of the common good suggests the good of the community includes the good of individual members and also the good of the relationships among the members. The common good entails a wide range of goods—provisions for health, safety, physical and economic welfare; participation and enjoyment of the cultural heritage of the community through arts and education; maintenance of voluntary non-profit groups that permit a rich associational life; opportunities for intellectual, moral, and emotional education; support and encouragement of values of civic friendship, personal freedom, and social justice; exercise of religious belief. The aim of the common good is "to provide that societal context within which persons together and individually might perfect their created powers and fulfill their natural and supernatural destinies."[57] To act for the common good is to act for oneself and for others; as social beings we have common as well as private interests, and the common good consists of the *whole* good of *all* its members.[58]

Debating the Common Good

While the idea of a common good is a cornerstone of the Catholic social tradition, it is a debated topic, at times within the tradition, but certainly among social thinkers outside the tradition. The main objections can be grouped under two headings: substantive and procedural. The latter pertains to how members of a societal or global group are to determine the common good. The substantive heading refers to objections to the idea of a common good based on doubts that in diverse and pluralistic human societies there can ever be a *common* good upon which all would agree. The procedural objection has to do with the manner in which the common good is identified and formulated. The Catholic social tradition has undergone evolution and reform in order to respond to these substantive and procedural concerns. Without pretending that these developments within the tradition have satisfied all critics of the common good concept, it is possible to see how the social tradition is attempting to retrieve the common good theme in a way that makes it appear to be reasonable and, hopefully, persuasive.

Substantive Criticisms

Historical consciousness has forced social thinkers to acknowledge the contextual nature of knowledge. It is simply not reasonable to presume that the social contexts of ancient Greece and Rome are the same as our present situation. We cannot reference the common good as if there is a pre-existent model of the good society that is true for all places and times. In short, the common good is not some Platonic form of an ideal society that is changeless and knowable to all persons of good will.

Today, there is wide acceptance that knowledge is socially constructed and that talk of an "objective" common good that transcends social location is highly questionable. At the same time it is important to note that acknowledging the contextual nature of knowledge is not the same as endorsing relativism. Properly understood, the common good has never been determined apart from some effort to acknowledge the actual needs and goods that human beings experience. Although past efforts at analyzing and comparing human experience have been at fault for neglecting entire classes and segments of people when considering whose experience counts, it remains true that at least some efforts, however inadequate, were made.

Social theories were developed out of insights into what kind of social relationships promoted human welfare. Philosophers and theologians throughout the ancient, patristic, and medieval eras tried to identify elements of the common good by seeking to name broadly shared interests and virtues that fostered well-being for societies and their members. Precisely because common life is not private but visible and public, it was possible to enumerate the values, virtues, goods, and relationships that communities sought to pursue and uphold in their social organization. Anna Rowlands describes the Catholic philosopher Josef Piepers's way of thinking:

> to think about acts as various as conceptualizing the conditions of being, giving blood, forging deep friendships, volunteering in a contagion virus clinic, forming movements to resist social violence

or protect the environment, housing the displaced, forming deep attachments to place, disrupting the sale of arms, preserving a dying language: to talk about any of these things properly, even in a solely secular register, seems to send us in the direction of some kind of appeal to the language of the common good.[59]

That is not to deny that there will be debates about the precise content of the common good. It is to suggest, however, that we can compare various sets of values, analyze competing visions for what is a good society, and debate alternative interpretations of the common good. We can ask ourselves and others if one social system is more attractive or preferable than others. It is possible that the outcome will be a movement of convergence regarding certain basic ethical coordinates for constructing a good society.

A number of feminist scholars have "coined the term transversalism (rather than universalism) to denote what happens when identity politics are transcended without losing their own rootedness and values, and without homogenizing their dialogue partners or the group to which they belong."[60] For example, the theologian Mary Elsbernd acknowledged that her articulation of a feminist anthropology had clear affinities with Janssens's attempt to name the constitutive elements of the human person that were examined in Chapter 5.[61] Another illustration is the scholarship of the philosopher Martha Nussbaum in which she delineates certain essential capabilities that can be seen as elements of a common good that is sensitive to an array of cultural settings.[62] The contemporary human rights movement has sought to move beyond Western conceptualizations of human rights to embrace an approach that goes beyond one cultural expression of rights language.

Such examples still acknowledge the social context out of which one's own values and commitment to public goods have arisen, even as one seeks points of contact and overlap with the values and goods prized by others living in communities different than one's own. Again, accepting the social context of knowledge is not to be equated with relativism. But it does suggest that when seeking out the common good we are searching for a good that we may not yet fully know but about which we have criteria that allow us to recognize the promotion of social well-being and personal flourishing. It is a grasp of the common good that does not come out of idealistic deduction, but from a heuristic method of trial and error, a praxis arising from engagement in the work of fashioning a society that benefits all. "We cannot construct our worlds in just any haphazard way. There is something like an objective reality to which we have some access and which we recognize as something we 'discover' and not merely something we 'create' or 'manipulate.'"[63]

Catholic social thought has come to a deeper appreciation of the complexity of the common good and an acceptance of its different levels as well as the responsibilities they generate. Yet there remains a claim made by the tradition that we can have a grasp of what it means to talk reasonably about the well-being of a person and the nature of a good society. It may not be as specific and detailed as papal texts in the nineteenth century suggested, but there is a reality to be probed and articulated—that of the human person and the sorts of communities that permit the flourishing of the person. As the political theorist Jane Mansbridge puts it: "We can go beyond cultural relativism. We can find 'good enough' agreement on specific virtues and values, without demanding that citizens 'share a substantive common good.'" That is, "we do not need a moral concept of *the* good to achieve that agreement on a particular common good,"[64] even if the attainment of consensus on particular goods is itself a challenging ambition. But working together to attain that end is part of the common good.

Working toward consensus does not eliminate the likelihood of conflict, a topic that Catholic social thought has sometimes shied away from. Yet conflict arises not only because people may have different goals for political life, but also because there is a richness to the human good and there are limits to any society's resources, energy, and talents. Too often the Catholic tradition has related conflict to sin or evil. However, conflict can arise among good people seeking worthwhile aims. In any public debate over budgets there will be conflicts over priorities: More money for education can mean less for infrastructure, more for addressing climate change can mean less for Medicaid, more for scientific research may mean less for public parks. The possibility for conflict is abundant and to a degree inevitable, but the origin is not evil. Hence, conflict ought not always be treated in negative terms but understood as a dimension of dealing with the pluralism and diversity that enriches a society. It invites deeper reflection and expansion of one's horizons and not feelings of hostility toward those who see things differently.

Indeed, an important element in the common good is to engage in public discourse around questions regarding, "how do we wish to live?" and "what kind of society do we want to live within?" There will be debate around such questions, but that would be to participate in what David Hollenbach calls "intellectual solidarity," a commitment to engage one another in the work of serious conversation about the good life and the good society.[65] Such intellectual engagement is a public good that we share in as members of varied communities and as citizens of a republic. It is an intellectual task because "it calls for serious thinking by citizens about what their distinctive understandings of the good life imply for the life of a society made up of people with many different traditions." And it is a work of solidarity "because it can only occur in an active dialogue of mutual listening and speaking across the boundaries of religion and culture."[66] Intellectual solidarity steers our attention to the processes necessary for constructing an authentic politics of the common good.

Procedural Concerns

In Book VI of Plato's *Republic*, there is the famous allegory of the ship with a poor captain and incompetent crew. The metaphors of "ship of state" and of a "ship of fools" come from the story. Plato relates the story to express his lack of belief in democracy ever serving the people's good. For Plato what was needed was a special class, the guardians, who would be trained from their youth to be superior in knowledge and ability so that they could rule the rest. In fact, Plato even considered the possibility that the best form of government might be the rule of one, a philosopher-king, rather than an aristocracy of the elite.

In his *Politics*, Aristotle engaged in what today we might call comparative politics, examining how various peoples conceived of the political order. Throughout the book, Aristotle was keenly aware of the difference distinguishing good and bad governance—namely government for the sake of the well-being of those being ruled or governance that rules for the self-interest of the governors. For him the difference between monarchy or tyranny, aristocracy or oligarchy, polity or mob rule was determined precisely by whether it was rule for the good of all or for self-interest. It was in this context that he could speak of the common good. Like his mentor, Plato, Aristotle also harbored doubts about democracy as the best form of government and thought political authority was best placed in the hands of those wise enough to rule, an aristocracy of virtue.

Christian thinkers inherited the presumption that a wise individual or small elite would best care for the community. Augustine thought the state was best when some*one* was in charge. Aquinas in *De Regno* and in his treatise on law implied that it is the emperor, king, or prince who should be entrusted with authority to determine the common good. Put simply, Christianity operated with the presumption that someone knows what is the common good as well as the best path to reach it; that person was the ruler. Centuries later when Catholic social thought began to consider the possibility of less hierarchical arrangements of political governance, it stayed committed to the idea that the common good was knowable and that it could be fairly and readily deduced through natural law reasoning. It is this way of thinking about the common good that gives people pause about the very idea of it. As Rowlands, citing the Spanish author Íñigo Errejón, reminds us, "the idea of the common good can be co-opted and presented as a theory of natural order that tends to shore up established power relations and to deny plurality."[67]

In the past Catholic social thought left itself open to suspicion that its account of the common good was elitist and reflective of a narrow range of experience that ignored a variety of viewpoints. To remedy that failing and to make appeal to the common good more persuasive, there must be a method employed that is more inclusive and built from the ground up rather than deduced from abstract nature. A method that seeks insight into the good of each person and the good of the whole person must adequately take into account the pluralism existing at many levels of human experience. Because discussions about the common good can appear to be outmoded or even oppressive to those who champion pluralism and diversity in societies and globally, the Catholic social tradition must be in conversation with "voices and sources" that are "much more local, bottom-up, and diverse."[68]

Vatican II was a key moment for reconceptualizing the common good in Catholic social teaching. One sees this in Karl Rahner's reflection, "Towards a Fundamental Theological Interpretation of Vatican II," where he posits that it was at the Council that the Catholic church appeared to actualize "the essence of the Church as a world Church" by attempting to move its self-understanding and practice beyond the boundaries of Western European Christianity.[69] Or again in the work of Rahner's student Walbert Bühlmann and his thesis about *The Coming of the Third Church*[70] and Catholicism's move to transcend the legacy of Greek and Roman culture and European history, one sees the narrative at Vatican II that Catholicism confronted the plurality of global existence. That pluralism included a variety of ways to articulate the common good of a society.

Consequently, an acceptable rendering of the common good necessarily will entail what Hollenbach calls "dialogic universalism"; that is, an affirmation of Vatican II's "pursuit of the common good in a divided world while it simultaneously urged renewal of a distinctively Christian vision of the human good." The approach "is universalist, for it presumes that human beings are sufficiently alike in that they all share certain very general characteristics in common and that the same general outlines of well-being are shared in common as well."[71] It is a dialogic approach because "cultural differences are so significant that a shared vision of the common good can only be attained in a historically incremental way through deep encounter and intellectual exchange across traditions." It also is dialogic because it views serious "engagement with others across the boundaries of traditions as itself part of the common good."[72]

As the Catholic social tradition evolves, efforts to formulate a substantive description of the common good must be done through an inductive and dialogical, inclusive and transversal methodology. Elsbernd puts the challenge forthrightly: "the constitutive character of difference requires a plurality of voices in the formation of Catholic Social Teachings and an end to Western European male domination of that process. The reluctance to embrace the constitutive character of difference may well reflect an ideological character of Catholic Social Teachings rooted in universals, gendered social roles, and control of official teachings."[73]

That reluctance is fading, however, as can be seen in Vatican II's treatment of the common good in *Gaudium et spes*, the "Pastoral Constitution on the Church in the Modern World." In the paragraph discussing the common good, the Council fathers acknowledged that "the people who come together in the political community are many and diverse, and they have every right to prefer divergent solutions." The role of political authority is to "direct the energies of all citizens toward the common good," but this is to be done "not in a mechanical or despotic fashion." Further, the common good should be seen as "a dynamic concept" that is not frozen in time or place but sought in an ongoing way that requires revision and new formulations.[74] Charles Curran has pointed out that already prior to Vatican II "there was a recognition that the content of the common good is bound to change." He cited an article in the *New Catholic Encyclopedia* written before Vatican II, though published afterward, in which the author stated, "It is simply impossible to define the common good in a final way irrespective of the changing social conditions."[75] It was the impact of the personalist movement in the aftermath of World War II that led Catholicism to give greater emphasis to dignity, freedom, and personal rights in describing the common good. John XXIII in both *Mater et magistra* (1961) and *Pacem in terris* (1963) gives witness to this development. Curran suggests that moving away from a view of society and the common good as being "structured from the top down" to a view emphasizing "the dignity, freedom, and rights of the person" inevitably resulted in the common good taking on a different understanding.

It is also worth noting that in the paragraph immediately following the treatment of the common good in *Gaudium et spes* the conciliar bishops urge all citizens to "freely and actively" take part in establishing the foundations of the political order.[76] It is through widespread participation in the determination of the common good—recall Hollenbach's dialogic universalism—that a check is placed on self-serving descriptions of the common good by an elite who claim to speak for those marginalized from participation from public life.

CONCLUDING THOUGHTS ON THE COMMON GOOD

At this point a few summary remarks can be made about the common good in Catholic social thought. First, recalling John XXIII's description of the common good as "the sum total of those conditions of social living, whereby persons are enabled more fully and more readily to achieve their own perfection,"[77] we can further specify those social conditions as inclusive of the following: (1) guaranteed access to public goods, (2) opportunities to participate in the goods of social life, and (3) promotion of (at least) minimal human flourishing of each person in one's chosen or historically situated communities.[78]

Second, the idea of the common good, as it is presently understood, contributes several positive characteristics to the Catholic social tradition. It makes explicit that the goal of the political and social order is the promotion of human flourishing viewed inclusively and integrally. It also strongly affirms that human flourishing is intrinsically social and requires solidarity. It corrects any understanding of public goods that reduces shared goods as extrinsic or merely instrumental to human flourishing rather than treating them as constitutive of the common good. When interpreted within the personalist framework of Catholic anthropology, the common good resists the subordination of the individual to any utilitarian calculus of a collective good.

Third, the common good is not only a norm for social ethics but is a theological theme founded upon the Catholic tradition. "The vision of a universal brotherhood and sisterhood of humanity as children of the one God and the Trinitarian model of communion which emphasizes equality and mutuality" is the basis for the Catholic social tradition's commitment to the common good.[79] This is, I believe, what Cahill means by describing the common good as "an incipient form of life,"[80] a way of living into a future that seeks to find, or build where not found, those grassroots organizations and mediating structures that make possible the full development of the human person "integrally and adequately considered."

Fourth, the common good is not to be imposed upon a minority by an intolerant majority, nor is it a term of circumlocution for an authoritarian elite to work their will upon a powerless majority. Rather, it is a social ideal that is neither predetermined nor deduced abstractly; instead, it is the outcome of a deliberative and open process of moral conversation in the public sphere. Awareness of the twin aspirations of participation and equality that "persistently make themselves felt" in our time as essential to human dignity and freedom[81] means that an appropriate formulation of the common good demands the building of an incremental consensus in support of it.

When in his two social encyclicals (*Mater et magistra* and *Pacem in terris*) John XXIII emphasized human development and human rights in his formulation of the common good, he made a signal contribution. By the first emphasis he "undercut the objection that the priority of the common good in Catholic political thought subordinated the individual to the group." The second emphasis on human rights "reassured critics that appeals to the common good were no excuse for authoritarianism."[82]

The first emphasis has been addressed in the foregoing material. The second emphasis, the centrality of human rights in the Catholic social tradition, will be the topic for the remainder of this chapter.

HUMAN RIGHTS

Human rights in Catholic social teaching are closely connected with community and the common good, as will be explained subsequently. But the language of rights is also intimately linked to the doctrine of the imago Dei and human dignity. Recall that in Chapter 2, I noted the theologian Roger Ruston has pointed out that the doctrine of the imago Dei can be understood in both an active and a passive sense. The active meaning of the doctrine, which was commonly cited in the patristic era, promoted the idea that Christian disciples should behave in a certain manner. Believers were expected to act with dignity, bearing witness to the image of God within them. The passive sense of the doctrine expressed the belief that human persons should be treated a certain way, out of respect for their being bearers of God's image. Ruston suggested that this way of thinking about the imago Dei may have become popularized during the nineteenth-century abolitionist campaigns and that Leo XIII used it in this way in his antislavery encyclical.[83] Ruston also observed that by the twentieth century "it became routine in papal and conciliar documents to link the possession of rights with the image and likeness of God in all human beings."[84] In her study of the Christian tradition on human dignity, Sigrid Müller confirms that human dignity is related to "moral rights and duties" and refers to a "moral quality that entitles humans to be treated by others with respect (passive dimension) . . . there is a corresponding moral duty, namely, to act according to one's dignity, which means to respect other people's rights . . . (active dimension)."[85]

As we already have seen, the idea of the imago Dei is foundational to the Catholic viewpoint on theological anthropology. It should not be a surprise, therefore, that belief in the imago doctrine is closely tied to a central theme in Catholic social thought, the existence of human rights. This close tie is seen in twin dimensions of human dignity that must be held together in creative tension. "On the one hand, there is the substantive track, which goes back to the totality of the human person as a subject, without leading to an individualistic isolation of the human being. On the other hand, there is the relational path, which opens the subject into a network of belonging and cultivates in the person an inclusive and participatory lifestyle."[86] When both the dignity of the person as subject and as a person in communion with others is appreciated, then the language of rights emerges as expressive of these dimensions of human dignity.

> In the dignity of the person as an individual subject . . . fundamental rights to self-determination are anchored with regard to the way of organizing and structuring her life, to freedom of opinion, and to the choice of where and how to practice her profession. In the dignity of the person, as a holistic being . . . the inalienable rights to life, bodily integrity, and health are rooted. At the same time, right to conditions worthy of humanity . . . the right to housing, work, a healthy environment and a habitable planet . . . in the dignity of the person as a self-transcending being that is substantially constituted as capable of relationality . . . there emerges in the person's various relationships the fundamental rights to socialization, to forms of love, marriage and family relationships, as well as to participation in social life. Here we also have the fundamental right to religious freedom.[87]

There is little question that the language of human rights has become a significant way that the Catholic social tradition conveys its teaching. Critics recall that the Catholic church was slow to recognize many of the rights that were championed by the liberal revolutions of the eighteenth and nineteenth centuries. Hence, it is important to understand how the language of rights came to prominence in modern Catholic social teaching. While Leo XIII may have adopted the idea of rights in his teaching about slavery, there is a far longer and richer history to consider when discussing the evolution of thinking about rights within Catholic circles.

Rights Language in the Catholic Tradition

Human rights as we know of them today have a complicated historical development. While the biblical and patristic eras provided certain ideas that later thinkers would pick up, it was largely in the medieval period that one sees the origins of our present concept of human rights. It was the medieval concept of the organic unity of humankind, which was based on the solidarity of all persons as children of a loving and divine creator, that was foundational for rights language. At the same time, medieval thinkers viewed each single person as having an "irreducible dignity and spiritual worth" due to being a temple of the Holy Spirit and having an immortal soul made by God in the divine image.[88]

Consequently, a basic premise of social and political thought in the Middle Ages was the idea of a single social whole that was divinely authored and that was made up of equally divinely ordained parts or members who were interrelated. There was a divinely willed harmony between the parts with each other and each part with the whole.[89] This outlook was inspired by the Pauline metaphor of the body of Christ, which was designated the *corpus mysticum* to distinguish it from the physical body of Christ and the sacramental body of Christ in the eucharist. The mystical body was the entire family of humankind united as creatures of a loving God made in the image of the Son and among whom the Spirit dwells.

In the mid-1100s, John of Salisbury, author of *Policraticus* and considered the first comprehensive work of medieval political theory, developed the foregoing ideas. He claimed that a well-ordered society is one where there is a sound apportionment of the varied social tasks to the different members of society. Further, since the body politic is meant to function harmoniously, the various members with their head are to support and assist one another in performing their functions. For John and other medieval social theorists, the desired social harmony is simply each member of the body acting in accord with right reason.

The concept of a single whole also implied an integrated union of like and unlike, "a harmony of balance of contrasts and differences in rank, estate, profession, and general qualifications." That is, the individual members who make up the whole "were never considered as being equal to one another in the sense of arithmetical equality. For each individual was also thought of as an element of a distinct social class within a rigorously stratified organism."[90] This idea of social differentiation was also in keeping with the Pauline metaphor in 1 Corinthians where the various parts of the body are seen to have distinct roles and honor (12:12–31).

Out of this social framework, it was argued that each particular group, guild, or estate had a definite place and role within the hierarchical order that embraced the lowest and highest into a social unity. Medieval political theory evolved in a way whereby every individual group or member of the whole possessed certain rights in accord with being a part of the whole. This is the initial step in the emergence of rights language. In addition, the relationship "between the governing and the governed part of the whole was emphatically declared as a *sui generis* relationship which involves reciprocal or correlative rights and duties. For both the governing and the governed part had their distinct rights and clearly defined duties."[91] Consequently, those who governed were not seen as having absolute rule and privilege, for they were bound by duties to others and limited by the rights of those others. And the governed, while duty-bound to obedience, were only bound by rightful commands and laws; duty was not unconditional or apart from moral obligation. In addition, since right reason, the eternal law of God, was the basis for the social order and its distinct parts, the rights and duties of each group and individual were understood to be ultimately of divine origin.

The historian Brian Tierney, in a series of important writings, has persuasively shown that it was medieval thinkers who began the development of "the idea that all persons possess natural rights."[92] While the precise origin of the doctrine of natural rights is unclear as is its exact relation to the Christian tradition, Tierney has argued "the origin of the later natural rights theories is to be found in the Christian jurisprudence of the late twelfth century."[93] This was a period of significant renewal in legal theory, characterized by "the recovery of the whole corpus of classical Roman law, and by the first adequate codification of the accumulated canon law of the church" in the work of Gratian completed about 1140 CE.[94] As Tierney explains, the traditional phrase *ius naturale* had been understood in an objective sense as what is naturally right by virtue of God's purposes or plan known through reasoned reflection. But canonists writing in the 1200s began to read the classic texts in a way that led to ius naturale now being "defined in a subjective sense as a faculty, power, force, ability inhering in individual persons." From there "canonists went on to develop a considerable array of natural rights."[95] This was the second step in the evolving process of rights.

By the mid-thirteenth century Pope Innocent IV wrote that property ownership was a natural right and that even non-Christians enjoyed the right. Other natural rights that were claimed in this period included rights to liberty, self-defense, and "the right of the poor to support from the surplus wealth of the rich."[96] By the end of the century canonists had developed a framework to express an entire system of natural rights. Important to realize is that these early theories of natural rights entailed a moral claim; the rights claimed may not have been exercised in a given society, but they were rights that "ought to be recognized in all societies because they are necessary for the fulfillment of some basic human needs and purposes."[97] Already in the thirteenth century, many canonists were using the traditional language of ius naturale in two ways: "to define both a faculty or force of the human person and a 'neutral sphere of personal choice,' a 'zone of human autonomy.'"[98]

The foundation for such rights did not start out from nature as cosmos but from reflection on the nature of human beings who were perceived as exercising human rationality, which "included a capacity for moral discernment; and from this fact it followed, for them, that humans ought to do what they discerned to be right."[99] In sum, the subjective idea of natural right did not stem from Christian revelation specifically nor from a comprehensive theory of divinely instituted cosmic harmony. Rather, subjective natural rights arose "from an understanding of human nature as itself rational, self-aware, and morally responsible."[100]

The next step in the evolution of rights language was when the idea of natural rights was taken from the juridical context into the work of political philosophy. The key figure here was the Franciscan William of Ockham. Relying more on the work of the canonists than upon his own theory of nominalism, Ockham formulated theories of property, poverty, and natural rights in defense of the Franciscans' claim that they had a right to live in absolute poverty without individual or corporate ownership, disputing the views of Pope John XXII and other critics of the Franciscan order. As Tierney has observed, one of Ockham's major contributions was his reshaping "the scriptural idea of evangelical liberty into a doctrine of natural rights. When Paul wrote about Christian freedom, he meant freedom from the law of the Old Testament or freedom from sin, but Ockham used Paul's texts to argue for freedom from any tyrannical government, especially within the church."[101] Relying upon the work of the canonists, Ockham consistently appealed to right reason as the foundation for his argument concerning subjective natural rights. Although his core ideas were built upon canonical insights, Ockham was the person who translated them into philosophy. As a result, "the outcome of his argument may seem to us more like early modern political theory than like medieval jurisprudence."[102]

Following Ockham, it was the theologian Jean Gerson, writing at the beginning of the fifteenth century, who influenced later natural rights theories with his definition of ius as "a power or faculty belonging to each one in accordance with the dictate of right reason,"[103] which was not lost or forfeited even after the effects of sin. Gerson's ideas were transmitted into the early modern world due to being taken up by a number of Spanish theologians who employed them in controversies over the treatment of native Americans during the age of colonialism. Bartolomé de las Casas is perhaps the best known of these defenders of the natural rights of native Americans subjugated by Spanish and Portuguese colonialists, but there was also the writing of the influential Dominican friar Francisco de Vitoria and the Jesuits Luis de Molina and Francisco Suarez and others who made up what was known as the Salamanca school in the sixteenth and early seventeenth centuries. All of these figures refined and recast the language of natural rights before the work of Locke and other early theorists of classical liberalism. As Walter Kasper has observed when considering this heritage, there exists "a Christian tradition of the rights of the person that is relatively independent of the modern human rights tradition." Indeed, as Ruston stated,

> the secular world owes the Christian past a huge, unacknowledged debt. Beliefs in such things as human equality, natural liberty, the right of access of all human beings to the goods of the earth, just conduct in war, universal human rights: we have these now (if we do) because our religious predecessors found them to be implied by their belief in a Creator God. In no sense are they original discoveries of Enlightenment rationalism, which found them already quite far developed by theologians.[104]

This is not stated as a prideful boast for Ruston also acknowledges, "clearly, in the last two or three centuries Christians have had to do some learning as much as teaching. Theology may have provided the framework, but it was often secular thinkers who made the applications."[105] It did take time for the Catholic social tradition to appreciate some of its own insights and work out how the language of rights might be appropriated and applied in modern contexts of republicanism, democracy, free markets, globalization, decolonization, and various popular movements for freedom and liberation. That story is ongoing, but modern Catholic social teaching has made important strides to incorporate the language of human rights.

Human Rights and Modern Social Catholicism

During the nineteenth century, the Catholic church found itself in a situation somewhat similar to the sixteenth in regard to changing social conditions.

As Ruston points out, people across Europe and North America were being denied basic rights, just as indigenous people had been in the New World, and once again the church was viewed as being "aligned with an oppressive order." With Leo XIII the language of natural rights was employed in the face of injustice, the exploitation of the mass of people. "In both centuries, people were being treated not as ends in themselves, as the doctrine of the image of God demands, but as instruments in the creation of wealth to be enjoyed by a small minority of slave-masters."[106] In the nineteenth century the masters were those industrial capitalists who were reaping great profit from the labor of underpaid and ill-treated workers. *Rerum novarum* hearkened back to "a dictate of nature more imperious and more ancient than any bargain between man and man" to overrule the theory of free contracts unregulated by norms of distributive justice.[107] For Leo, a just wage was one of several natural rights that workers had, including rights regulating the hours of the work week, the use of child labor, and resort to worker associations and collective bargaining.

Papal support for the modern language of natural rights was a significant development. Earlier popes of the nineteenth century—Gregory XVI and Pius IX—resisted such language, mainly due to their opposition to the way that rights had been employed as part of the project of the Enlightenment. That conception of rights was premised on the individual person being an autonomous subject whose independence needed to be safeguarded from incursions by society, the state, or other institutions such as the church. Such a perspective had "its origins in the breakdown of medieval unity with its strong sense of community—a breakdown that ushered in the individualism that has remained a trademark of the modern world, at least in the West. The rationalism of the Enlightenment placed this autonomous subject at the center of a world that had been stripped of mystery and in which God was at best a somewhat benign if distant observer of the human scene."[108] Hence Gregory and Pius attacked many of the rights to modern liberties such as freedom of religion, which Gregory called absurd.

Leo's support for the idea of natural rights in the realm of economics—his strong defense of private property as well as worker rights—was not quickly translated into other realms of life. His immediate successor, Pius X, was not at all interested in advancing Leo's social program and Benedict XV, following him, was pope at a time when European thought was preoccupied by the great tragedy of World War I. Despite Leo's use of rights language the Vatican remained suspicious of the agenda of modernity even after *Rerum novarum*. Pius XI, however, did add to the social tradition a measure of openness to structural change if that was necessary for the common good.

It was during the papacy of Pius XII (1938–1958) that the earlier teaching about economic rights began to be transferred into the political realm. Much of the motivation for that shift stemmed from the rise of totalitarian regimes on the right and the left in European politics. With the end of the second great war, Pius was concerned to defend and promote democracy and had already begun to lay out his vision of democratic politics in a number of speeches and formal addresses during the war. In a series of radio addresses delivered at Christmas time, the pope made the case that citizen participation in the political process was necessary to forge a future that would be in accord with human dignity. In line with this development, Catholic intellectuals were advancing arguments for subjective natural rights the person had against the state that would not be seen in an atomistic way.[109] Many of those thinkers who had embraced some form of personalism desired to develop a Catholic theory that might elaborate a sociopolitical program while avoiding either individualism or collectivism. Part of that effort was the adoption of rights language founded upon a specific understanding of human dignity, one that saw the human person as being transcendent, having an irreplaceable value, and from that status deriving subjective natural rights. Pius XII in a June 1941 radio address expressly called for an international bill of rights rooted in the base of human dignity. That call advanced an idea that would eventuate in the U.N. Universal Declaration of Human Rights in December 1948.

Catholic legal scholar Mary Ann Glendon has pointed out that "several features of the Declaration set it apart from both Anglo-American and Soviet-bloc documents," citing "its pervasive emphasis on the 'inherent dignity' and 'worth of the human person'" as well as "the affirmation that the human person is 'endowed with reason and conscience'" along with the roster of political and socioeconomic human rights.[110] Glendon suggests that many ideas of the UN Declaration result from the agendas of Latin American and continental European nations that had political parties largely unknown in Britain, US and Soviet bloc politics, namely Christian Democratic and Christian Socialist parties. And those parties drew upon resources within the Catholic social tradition rather than the agenda of Enlightenment liberalism or Marxism.[111]

It was John XXIII who incorporated the broad range of rights—political, civil, social, and economic—as found in the UN Declaration into Catholic social teaching with his encyclical *Pacem in terris*. During the medieval period there was the movement from natural rights to subjective natural rights reflecting belief in rights that are powers or faculties inhering in a person; and in the twentieth century there was the movement from subjective natural rights to human rights. The reason for the latter shift was that natural rights were linked to certain epistemic properties and given a certain metaphysical status that not every political philosophy could endorse. Human rights seemed to be neutral in this regard.[112]

Events of the twentieth century had shown it was no longer the narrow rationalism or excessive individualism of Enlightenment liberalism that was the threat, but totalitarian governments on the right and the left. Hence, the Catholic church came to view the language of human rights as a useful way to promote and defend human dignity. Vatican II accepted this linkage of human dignity and human rights, but it did not merely take over the arguments used by UN diplomats and the secular human rights movement. Instead, it looked within the church's social tradition on the idea of rights for a rationale that is "relatively independent of the modern human rights tradition."[113] By so doing, "it was able to recognize the positive aspects of human rights and to differentiate them from historically conditioned and polemical, anti-clerical" assaults of various liberal revolutions of the eighteenth and nineteenth centuries.[114]

In the conciliar text *Gaudium et spes*, it is evident that the understanding of the person and human dignity is thoroughly theocentric, not anthropocentric. As we saw in Chapter 2, the Catholic social tradition sees human dignity as flowing from our relationship with God our creator, not as the result of some characteristic that the person has independent of God. For the dignity of the human being is based on the belief that each person is made in the image and likeness of God and called to be a partner in the dialogue between Creator and creation. Because we are material and temporal creatures the broad range of human rights claims can be readily accepted within the Catholic tradition. Because we are not simply material and temporal but embodied spirits with a transcendent dimension, the foundation of human rights claims must be rooted in the conviction that humans are called to communion with their maker.

The conciliar document helped to integrate rights language into the church's sense of its mission. In Chapter 4 of the first part of the Pastoral Constitution, the conciliar bishops discussed the role of the church in the modern world, a world in which "the earthly and the heavenly city penetrate each other."[115] The bishops see that humanity is engaged in "a growing discovery and vindication" of rights.[116] For its part, "by virtue of the gospel committed to her, the church proclaims the rights" of every person. Further, the church, it is stated, "greatly esteems the dynamic movements of today by which these rights are everywhere fostered."[117] Yet the church's mission does not entail being tied to a "particular form of human culture, nor to any political, economic, or social system."[118]

The papacies of Paul VI and John Paul II developed strategies for how Catholicism's social teaching might be promoted while respecting the diversity of a universal church and the pluralism of its global context. In a 1971 apostolic letter, *Octogesima adveniens*, Paul cited the diverse situations in which believers find themselves due to geographic "regions, sociopolitical systems and, and cultures."[119] He then offered an approach that reflected a modest method for addressing the challenge. "In the face of such widely varying situations it is difficult for us to utter a unified message and to put forward a solution which has universal validity." He stated that it was not his understanding of the papacy's role to attempt such a strategy. Instead, he proposed that "it is up to the Christian communities to analyze with objectivity the situation, which is proper to their own country, to shed on it the light of the Gospel's unalterable words and to draw principles of reflection, norms of judgment and directives for action from the social teaching of the Church."[120]

Paul then notes the social documents issued by his predecessors—Leo XIII, Pius XI, John XXIII—as well as the Vatican Council's Pastoral Constitution. He also cites his own social encyclical, *Populorum progressio* (On the Development of Peoples) from 1967. In that document Paul made extensive use of what he called "integral development," which promotes "the good of every person and the whole person."[121] In *Populorum progressio*, Paul was particularly focused on the need for integral development in the poorer nations of the world, but he emphasized that authentic development had to be holistic, that is, adequate to the many dimensions of human flourishing, and should not be reduced to economic development alone. Writing four years later, he makes the point that this is where the church can make a "specific contribution" to the cause of human advancement, "to help them [men and women] attain their full flowering, and that is why she offers humankind what she possesses as her characteristic attribute: a global vision of the person and of the human race."[122]

Just a few months after Paul's *Octogesima adveniens*, the 1971 Synod of Bishops issued a document, *Justitia in mundo* (Justice in the World), that picked up on Paul's vision of a church that witnessed to an authentic and integral development of the human person and community. The bishops at the synod proposed the social ideal of a "right to development," which "must be seen as a dynamic interpenetration of all those fundamental human rights upon which the aspirations of individuals and nations are based."[123] Not only did the bishops endorse the idea of integral ("dynamic interpenetration") development, but they also alluded to Paul's earlier reading of the signs of the times where he claimed "two aspirations persistently make themselves felt" in the world at the time: "the aspiration to equality and the aspiration to participation, two forms of humankind's dignity and freedom."[124] So the language of human rights was understood by the bishops to be an appropriate way to explain the social vision of Paul on human development as well as his reading of the signs of the times.

With the papacy of John Paul II, a step forward was taken in the employment of human rights in the church's social tradition. John Paul was sensitive to the diversity of the global church as well as the pluralism of social models that might be found around the world. However, he was not as content as Paul VI was to leave the task of articulating the church's social teaching to episcopal conferences and local churches. Instead, he saw a role for himself as a spokesperson for the universal church in a number of areas including social teaching. To do that without being able to claim a single normative political and economic order was the challenge. Human rights, understood as subjective rights that belong to a person, are moral claims that any and all social orders should endorse and promote. For John Paul, human rights provided a basic normative framework of goods that any acceptable social order must respect. There is no model of societal organization that is *the* Catholic model; pluralism is accepted, but there is a moral framework set by human rights that any society needs to establish.[125]

Already in his first encyclical, *Redemptor hominis* (Redeemer of Humankind), John Paul had set an agenda for his human rights work: "We cannot fail to recall at this point, with esteem and profound hope for the future, the magnificent effort made to give life to the United Nations Organization, an effort conducive to the definition and establishment of the person's objective and inviolable rights." He continued, "This commitment has been accepted and ratified by almost all present-day States, and this should constitute a guarantee that human rights will become throughout the world a fundamental principle of work for humanity's welfare."[126]

It was through John Paul's writing, along with his extensive travels and pastoral visits, where he utilized human rights language to speak to an array of audiences. In his papacy the church became an important force for human rights because of its transnational character. The Catholic social tradition could play a role in shaping a cultural consensus on human rights, as well as building support for human rights through various church-related movements and agencies.

Although a learned and impressive scholar, Benedict XVI was not known for his work in the area of Catholic social thought as much as his interest in doctrinal questions. Nonetheless, when he did address social issues, he did not shy away from the language of human rights. In his 2008 address to the UN General Assembly, he noted the year was the sixtieth anniversary of the UN Declaration and that "human rights are increasingly being presented as the common language and ethical substratum of international relations." For Benedict, "the universality, indivisibility and interdependence of human rights all serve as guarantees safeguarding human dignity." Human rights also "are measures for the common good that serve to evaluate the relationship between justice and injustice, development and poverty, security and conflict." Finally, "the promotion of human rights remains the most effective strategy for eliminating inequalities between countries and social groups, and for increasing security." On this last point about security, Benedict went so far as to defend the UN doctrine of the "responsibility to protect" when a nation is unwilling or unable to uphold the human rights of its citizens.[127] Given his concern for the unity and coherence of the Catholic tradition, it would have been surprising if Benedict's social teaching was not in line with the development of the tradition as developed in the writing of his recent predecessors.

Francis also employs the language of rights, both expanding and deepening the social tradition's usage. The expansion is seen clearly in the encyclical *Laudato Si'* where he discusses ready access to clean water as "a basic and universal human right" for people[128]—a view also held by John Paul II, Benedict, and the Pontifical Council for Justice and Peace—but he also has spoken of a right of the environment itself. Such a right exists for two reasons: "first, because we human beings are part of the environment. . . . Any harm done to the environment, therefore, is harm done to humanity." This reasoning would suggest that humans have a right to a healthy environment. Yet a second reason there is a right of the environment is "because every creature, particularly a living creature, has an intrinsic value, in its existence, its life, its beauty and its interdependence with other creatures."[129] This would seem to extend the language of rights beyond the human family.

Francis has also deepened the language of rights in the Catholic tradition by pointing beyond the claims of human rights to the obligations which stem from what Francis refers to as fraternity. Paul VI had already made the point in *Populorum progressio* that as important as respect for rights remains, the Catholic social tradition seeks to build a world of universal solidarity, where people live together not just as bearers of rights but as brothers and sisters.[130] The 1971 Synod also took up this theme: "Christian love of neighbor and justice cannot be separated. For love implies an absolute demand for justice, namely a recognition of the dignity and rights of one's neighbor. Justice attains its inner fullness only in love." Due to the fact that every person is "truly a visible image of the invisible God" and Christ is our brother, the disciple finds in every person "God's absolute demand for justice and love."[131]

In *Fratelli tutti*, Francis makes a similar point about the need to practice justice but also to transcend justice and enter into relationships with others marked by solidarity and love—what he refers to as fraternity. In the letter there is an extended reflection by Francis on the parable of the Good Samaritan, which Francis uses to propose that the state of the world is such that more is needed from Christians than respecting human rights, while not belittling their importance. The "more" that is necessary is "to express our innate sense of fraternity, to be Good Samaritans who bear the pain of other people's troubles."[132]

For Francis, the great slogan of the French Revolution—Liberté, Égalité, et Fraternité—has not been fully promoted. More attention has been directed to liberty and equality in political movements than fraternity, and that is problematic. "Fraternity is born not only of a climate of respect for individual liberties, or even of a certain administratively guaranteed equality. Fraternity necessarily calls for something greater, which in turn enhances freedom and equality."[133] Francis maintains there must be a "conscious and careful cultivation of fraternity"[134] since being a sibling "is more than a generic sense of solidarity based on the common recognition of a national identity, since it precedes and goes beyond the rights and duties on which civil coexistence is established."[135]

Again, it is important to stress that although Francis may speak about the need for more than rights when depicting a good society, he is by no means rejecting the turn to human rights language in the Catholic social tradition. Indeed, when discussing Vatican II's stress on inalienable human dignity due to the person being made in the image of God, Francis calls that belief "the foundation of all social life." He then goes on to say, "In modern culture the closest reference to the principles of inalienable dignity of the person is the Universal Declaration of Human Rights."[136]

Looking back on the use of rights language by popes of the modern era, we can see several stages of development. At first, the papacy was wary of the language of rights since they equated it with liberalism's use of rights in politics—the French Revolution and the various European revolutions in the mid-1800s—that upset the social order to which the papacy was accustomed. With Leo XIII in the final quarter of the nineteenth century we find him resorting to the idea of subjective natural rights in the realm of economics to both defend private property against Marxism and the rights of labor against laissez-faire capitalism. Then in the twentieth century Pius XII employs natural rights in the political realm as a way to defend human dignity against the regimes of communism, fascism, and Nazism that violated human dignity. It was John XXIII and Vatican II that embraced the idea of human rights expressed in the UN Universal Declaration of Human Rights. All subsequent popes in the twentieth and twenty-first centuries have staunchly defended human rights and widely employed the language of human rights to express their social teaching.

It is evident that the modern papacy has adopted the language of human rights as a valid and important way to articulate, if not the entirety of its social message, at least what is essential for the promotion and protection of human dignity in the present moment.

Further Catholic Reflections on Human Rights

The promotion of human rights has not occurred without resistance. Some of that opposition, quite expectedly, comes from rulers and elites who act in authoritarian ways and who want to discredit popular movements for civil and political liberties. Others in opposition resist putting social and economic benefits into the language of rights because that would imply there are moral obligations to assist those whose basic material needs are not being met. But some opposition is not simply self-interested; it has to do with concerns that rights language can lead to too great a role for the state in everyday life, or that the language of rights is foreign—the roots of rights language are too Western and ignore the experience of other cultures. Those criticisms arising from the self-interest of the powerful or wealthy need not detain us. The worry about the role of the state will be touched upon in the next chapter when the idea of subsidiarity is discussed. Here, however, the issue of the Western origin of rights language will be addressed.

As I hope to have demonstrated, the language of rights in the Catholic tradition is not founded upon a particular political ideology found in the West but in a theological anthropology that has biblical, Greek and Latin patristic, and medieval influences. It is an effort to articulate the benefits and obligations that are related to any human person living in any society. Of course, humans are situated in historically conditioned cultures, and those cultures provide language, experiences, and ideas by which people construct their view of the human. For that reason, formulations of human rights must be provisional and strategic, considering the actual setting and circumstances of people. Certainly, a right to education will look different in a twenty-first-century high-tech society than it did in an eighteenth-century agricultural community. But that persons are entitled to levels of education that permit them to attain a measure of human flourishing in their social life is a claim made out of concern for promoting the dignity of persons. It is a reading of the person—similar to what was provided in Chapters 4 and 5—relevant to human well-being and flourishing in any culture that Catholic social thought champions.

The alleged Western bias of human rights requires nuance. As noted previously, several Catholic philosophers and theologians formulated arguments for the rights of indigenous peoples who were being maltreated by European colonial powers. Human rights were used against the dominant ideology of European powers at the time. It was in 1815 that the Congress of Vienna issued a statement in support of worldwide abolitionism at a time when control of slavery was in the hands of European and North American interests. The legal historian Samuel Moyn has argued the modern human rights movement was influenced by anticolonial movements in the 1950s that sought to overcome their colonialist heritage and emerge as functioning independent states in Asia, Africa, and Latin America.[137] Such a development was preceded by the revolution in Haiti at the end of the eighteenth and beginning of the nineteenth centuries in which a view of rights was proposed that was distinct from the American and French revolutions. Another less well-known instance of rights language was the promulgation in 1920 of the "Declaration of Rights of Negro People of the World." Promoted by Marcus Garvey, the 1920 Declaration united civil and political liberties with social and economic goods almost three decades before the UN Declaration. While many of these examples have a Western connection, they all evidence that the language of human rights was not simply an instance of Western cultural imperialism but a source of criticism of Western culture and its treatment of people seen as marginal to the culture. Furthermore, that the origins of rights language is Western "does not in itself preclude the possibility that the underlying ideals and aspirations inherent in that language may prove to have a universal significance."[138]

Within the Catholic social tradition, dignity expresses "a value commitment of inclusive regard for the equal moral worth of fellow human beings and a corresponding responsibility to dignify our own and others' lives, especially the most vulnerable, by cultivating the human and common good."[139] To describe that "corresponding responsibility" of acknowledging human dignity, I will rely upon an essay by David Hollenbach, who refers to the requirements of respect for dignity as "obligating features of personhood" or obligating features of human dignity.[140] Recall from Chapter 4 he proposes three obligating features of personhood: freedom, understood as the capacity to be self-determining; relationality, viewed as essential relationships that permit a person to exist and thrive; and basic needs, that is, minimal subsistence levels for material life and other goods essential for physical well-being. Hollenbach maintains the importance of certain freedoms, relationships, and needs "as crucial features of personhood emerges from reflection on the experience of what it is to be human," even while taking into account the diversity of our experience across the globe.[141]

These features were ratified in the UN's Universal Declaration. Hollenbach suggests that many of the characteristics of persons that demand respect "were identified through their absence." Denials of essential freedoms because of religion, race, or ethnicity "led to the affirmation that respect for freedom and dignity is due to all persons." This, in turn, furthered reflection on those freedoms necessary for a person to be self-determining: "freedom from slavery or arbitrary arrest, freedom of movement, thought, conscience, religion, expression, and assembly." Many of those freedoms entail relationships "that enable people to participate actively in the interpersonal and social interactions that are necessary for the well-being both of individual persons and of the communities" to which they belong. And because we are not simply spiritual beings who transcend earthly matters, respect for personal dignity "requires securing basic levels of subsistence, meeting other bodily needs such as the requirements of basic health, and the protection of persons through respect for their bodily integrity."[142]

Perhaps an example of the sort of practical reason involved in making judgments about what freedoms, relationships, and goods are essential can be seen in the argument for moral and religious freedom as crucial to human dignity. As was seen in Chapter 4, the Catholic understanding of freedom is not mere license to do whatever one pleases, but freedom as the capacity to exercise self-determination. In *Gaudium et spes*, the bishops wrote that the human conscience is a person's "most secret core and sanctuary," it is that internal forum where the moral law is revealed, a law "inscribed by God" and "human dignity lies in observing this law."[143] The bishops continue, it is "only in freedom that the person can turn the self toward what is good."[144] Moral integrity necessarily entails personal freedom, for an individual cannot be a full moral subject if the good is imposed rather than chosen. Authentic moral development demands that the good is to be personally appropriated, not simply acknowledged notionally and externally obeyed. Moral growth requires the transformation of the self and that occurs as a person freely chooses to embrace and make the good one's own. Hence, there must be a sphere of freedom for persons to choose and act out of their interior convictions if there is to be moral development. The exercise of moral freedom is a human right, and attempts at coercion such as torture are violations of the person's interior freedom.

One can see a similar line of practical reasoning at work in the Council's endorsement of the right to religious freedom. The Council's "Declaration on Religious Freedom" made clear it is the dignity of the person that is the basis for the right. As with moral truth, the duty to seek religious truth is a duty of conscience. "But people cannot satisfy this obligation in a way that is in keeping with their own nature unless they enjoy both psychological freedom and immunity from external coercion."[145] The choice of truth, religious or moral, is an exercise of internal freedom. As the Council decree made clear, the necessity of preserving religious freedom in the search for truth is a requirement not only of human dignity, but it is also due to the nature of truth. "Truth can impose itself on the mind of the individual only in virtue of its own truth, which wins over the mind with both gentleness and power."[146]

Vatican II's defense of religious freedom in *Dignitatis humanae* is of a piece with the defense of the dignity and freedom of conscience in *Gaudium et spes*. If each person has the obligation or duty to seek truth, moral and religious, then the language of human rights concerning conscience and religious expression is an effort to specify those necessary conditions which enable people to satisfy their moral duties or obligations. The Catholic social tradition is concerned with the social order "inclusive of the human community within which the individual functions."[147] In that framework, the language of rights exists in order to establish the fundamental conditions that allow persons to attain their authentic development within their social setting. The particular details of how a given human rights claim is to be formulated are an act of practical reason, which allows for discussion and debate over the precise framing of the right. As social conditions evolve, both the content of the right and the strategy for implementing and protecting it will change as well. But the claim that there are fundamental freedoms, essential relationships, and basic needs that constitute the elements of human rights is supported by the theological anthropology of the Catholic social tradition.

Catholicism's theological reading of the human person affirms the equal dignity of all humans before God. It is that dignity that is the foundation for human rights in the Catholic social tradition. Go deeper in the tradition and it is the doctrine of the imago Dei that grounds the contemporary commitment to human rights in Catholic thought. The emergence of rights language has been a complex process, and even though the idea of human rights is of recent vintage in the mid-twentieth century, the foundations of the idea are scriptural and present for centuries within the Catholic tradition. So, the writing of John XXIII in *Mater et magistra* and *Pacem in terris* is not a break with the tradition, but as ratified by the Second Vatican Council's teaching, it is a development that took place due to the church's reading of the signs of the times.

Walter Kasper has outlined two methods for affirming human dignity and the language of rights. What he calls the "ascending" foundation is found in the natural law philosophy of pre-conciliar texts. It is the claim that men and women have dignity due to their nature as creatures endowed with reason and free will. "Through reason, women and men can penetrate into the deeper nature of the world and inquire into its ultimate cause; through freedom, in their conduct they are ultimately independent of worldly determinants."[148]

The "descending" foundation has two bases. It begins with a theology of creation and the significance of the human created in the image and likeness of God (Gen 1:26). Catholic theology maintains that despite the impact of sin on the human condition, the imago Dei is not destroyed or abolished. Kasper goes on to state, "The real theological foundation, however, is placed at the christological level. The church Fathers, especially Pope Leo the Great, repeatedly say that in the person of Jesus Christ God once and for all took on himself everything human and so bestowed unique dignity on human beings."[149]

It is the "descending" or more theological foundation that Kasper prefers to the natural law method. First, because he believes it has a better chance to build ecumenical support for human rights than a natural law argument that is not always welcomed in Protestant circles. Second, he also argues that the threats to humanity today are so great that "an appeal to a minimal consensus founded in natural law" will be insufficient. Instead, "we must respond with all the concrete fullness and the concentrated strength of our Christian faith" so as to counter the power of injustice, violence, and death.[150]

A lesson from the theological foundation of human rights in the Catholic social tradition is that from ancient times there has been a legitimate Christian humanism that predates modern forms of secular humanism. This older strand of humanism can serve as a worthy dialogue partner in forging consensus on the meaning of what truly serves the human person.

A second lesson is that human rights—while historically conditioned and revisable as human reason discerns the changing opportunities and obstacles that arise in the project of upholding and protecting human dignity—are ultimately founded upon central credal affirmations concerning God and God's purposes.

Third, because Christ is not only the revelation of God but the revelation of authentic humanity, it is evident that the meaning and fulfillment of human life is intimately bound up with love of neighbor. Human rights, therefore, must be employed as delineating what basic justice requires, yet they may also point toward what compassion, forgiveness, and love demand of persons and communities.

HUMAN RIGHTS AND COMMON GOOD

For those whose understanding of human rights is essentially rooted in the tradition of Western liberalism, it may seem odd that the Catholic social tradition accentuates the common good at the same time that it expresses support for human rights. Liberalism founded human rights on individual freedom, often understood as personal autonomy. So Western liberalism sees tension, even contradiction, in the Catholic effort to uphold the common good and human rights together. For Catholicism, rights language is not divorced from concern for the good of the community because the common good is not understood as something over and above the good of persons.

Recall that at Vatican II, the bishops endorsed the dignity of the human person as the foundation of human rights. In *Gaudium et spes* there were both theological and philosophical rationales offered for that claim: the imago Dei, the importance of reason, the capacity for freedom as self-determination, and the exercise of conscience.[151] There was also a clear affirmation of the social nature of the person.[152]

Perhaps the 1985 pastoral letter of the US bishops on economic life speaks most clearly about the Catholic rationale for seeing the common good and human rights as complementary, not contradictory. In that letter, human rights are seen as "the minimum conditions for life in the community."[153] The language of rights is a way to secure for each person the ability to participate in the life of a community, which is vital to attaining human dignity. Through such participation a person is able to both contribute to and benefit from shared life. The array of goods that make up the common good are not just material but include those goods that arise due to a person's relationality. The experience of sharing is itself such a good; the flourishing of the human personality and spirit that comes about as we build relationships marked by affection, enjoyment, intimacy, support, forgiveness, and reconciliation are part of the common good. The common good is not simply a practical or material good but a moral good that serves attainment of the fullness of a person.

It should be remembered that the imago Dei is not only something given to us through God's gracious creation, but also it is something to be attained.

People grow into their likeness to Christ, becoming transformed by cooperating with God's grace and so, despite the element of human sinfulness, more in keeping with God's plan for creation. Primarily, this is through ever deepening one's commitment to love of God and love of neighbor. Participation in the process of conversion that brings about a greater likeness to Christ takes place through our relationships with others. Both how we treat others and how they treat us become factors in the actualization of the image of God in our lives. Put another way, "the personal and inter-personal modes of the imago are profoundly related, but also distinct."[154] As inherently social, it is necessary for human persons to realize the image of God not only as individuals but also in community. We have a duty to assist others in becoming ever more authentic in witnessing to the image of God that is present in each of us.

The freedom of the person in Catholic thought is not merely freedom *from* interference from others but freedom *for* life in communities where personal dignity is secured and experienced. A person has rights in order to benefit from life with others and has duties to contribute to a community so that others also benefit from communal life. This reflects the Old Testament perspective noted at the beginning of this chapter. Rights language in the Catholic social tradition is not premised on the individualism of liberalism, but in accord with the common good, understood as the "sum of those conditions of social life which allow social groups and their individual members relatively thorough and ready access to their own fulfillment."[155] Human rights are an important means whereby the Catholic social tradition articulates what are the basic goods, necessary freedoms, and essential relationships that people ought to enjoy through the actualization of their social nature.

It is crucial to grasp that the common good in the Catholic tradition is not some organic body that is greater than and above human persons, thereby making it possible to violate the human rights of individual persons for the sake of a collective benefit. The common good is, rather, the ensemble of those goods that secure the ability of persons to live with others in a fashion that is expressive of the dignity of each member of the community. A person's human rights are not overridden by appeal to the common good; but in the name of the common good a person's human rights are to be secured. The details of the common good, as with those of human rights, are subject to development over time. However, the fundamental human rights of a person remain constitutive of the common good; they neither undermine nor do they override the common good.

CONCLUSION

We have seen in Chapters 2 and 3 how certain central religious beliefs gave rise to and shaped the Catholic social tradition. In Chapters 4 and 5 the anthropological implications of those beliefs were described. Those implications are crucial since if we get our view of the human person wrong, it will be near impossible to get our politics, economics, or culture right. In this chapter we have seen how the Catholic tradition, drawing upon the foundations presented previously, has developed two major building blocks for its social thought, the common good and human rights. In the next two chapters I provide further examples of what I call "ethical coordinates" that the tradition has formulated. These ethical coordinates provide a means for the Catholic social tradition to map out its vision of a good society. It may be argued that the material in these next chapters, as with this one, is derivative from the twin pillars of the tradition: human dignity and community.

NOTES

1. Lisa Sowle Cahill, "Globalization and the Common Good," 42.
2. John Coleman, "Pluralism and the Retrieval of a Catholic Sense of the Common Good," 1.
3. John Collins, "The Biblical Vision of the Common Good," 53.
4. Collins, 54.
5. Collins, 57.
6. Collins, 58.
7. Collins, 59.
8. Collins, 61.
9. Collins, 65.
10. John Donahue, *Seek Justice That You May Live*, 49.
11. Fitzmeyer, "Pauline Theology," 1409.
12. Fitzmeyer, 1409.
13. Fitzmeyer, 1410.
14. Johnson, *Acts of the Apostles*, 62.
15. Johnson, *Acts*, 62.
16. Johnson, *Acts*, 58, n. 42.
17. Charles Curran, "The Common Good and Official Catholic Social Teaching," 118.
18. David Hollenbach, "The Common Good and Issues in U.S. Politics: A Critical Catholic Approach," 34.
19. Aristotle, *Politics*, 1253a1.
20. Rowlands, *Towards a Politics of Communion*, 133–34.
21. Clement of Alexandria, "The Tutor," as quoted in Phan, *Social Thought*, 66–67.

22. Phan, 108.

23. Basil the Great, "The Long Rules," as quoted in Phan, 119.

24. John Chrysostom, "Homily XXV on First Corinthians," as quoted in Phan, 153.

25. Ambrose of Milan, "On the Duties of the Clergy," as quoted in Phan, 179.

26. Johnson, *Acts*, 16.

27. Augustine, *City of God*, Bk. 19, ch. 13, 938.

28. Anton-Hermann Chroust, "The Corporate Idea and the Body of Christ in the Middle Ages," 437.

29. Chroust, 424.

30. Rowlands, *Towards a Politics of Communion*, 140.

31. Rowlands, 140.

32. Drew Christiansen, "The Common Good and the Politics of Self-Interest," 60–61.

33. Christiansen, 61.

34. Chroust, "The Corporate Idea and the Body of Christ," 440.

35. Pius XII, "Speech to Italian Physicians," as quoted in J-Y. Calvez and J. Perrin, *The Church and Social Justice*, 129

36. Josef Höffner, *Christian Social Teaching*, 45.

37. Todd Whitmore, "Catholic Social Teaching: Starting with the Common Good."

38. Christiansen, "The Common Good and the Politics of Self-Interest," 55.

39. John XXIII, *Mater et magistra*, n. 65.

40. Christiansen, "The Common Good and the Politics of Self-Interest," 61.

41. John XXIII, *Pacem in terris*, n. 139.

42. Christiansen, "The Common Good and the Politics of Self-Interest," 63.

43. Christiansen, 64.

44. Whitmore, "Catholic Social Teaching: Starting with the Common Good," 62.

45. Christiansen, "The Common Good and the Politics of Self-Interest," 63.

46. Cahill, "Globalization and the Common Good," 47.

47. James Donahue, "Introduction," x.

48. Hollenbach, "The Common Good and Issues in U.S. Politics," 36.

49. Cahill, "Globalization and the Common Good," 42.

50. Hollenbach, *Claims in Conflict*, 64.

51. Coleman, "Pluralism and the Retrieval of a Catholic Sense of the Common Good," 2.

52. R. Bruce Douglass, "First Things First," 25.

53. Coleman, "Making the Connections," 16.

54. Coleman, "Pluralism and the Retrieval of a Catholic Sense of the Common Good," 6.

55. Coleman, 7.

56. Coleman, 7.

57. Douglas Sturm, "On Meanings of Public Good: An Exploration," 20. The entire paragraph is a paraphrase of Sturm's position.

58. Margaret Atkins, "Clarifying the 'Common Good,'" 6–7.

59. Rowlands, *Towards a Politics of Communion*, 120.

60. Cahill, "Globalization and the Common Good," 48.

61. Mary Elsbernd, "Authentic Human Living," 5.

62. Martha Nussbaum, *Creating Capabilities*.

63. Coleman, "Pluralism and the Retrieval of a Catholic Approach to the Common Good," 7.

64. Jane Mansbridge, "Response to 'Pluralism and the Retrieval of a Catholic Sense of the Common Good.'" 3.

65. Hollenbach, in *The Common Good and Christian Ethics*, describes it as the "common pursuit of a shared vision of the good life," 137.

66. Hollenbach, 137.

67. Rowlands, *Towards a Politics of Communion*, 112.

68. Cahill, "Social Justice and the Common Good: Improving the Catholic Social Teaching Framework," 108.

69. Karl Rahner, "Towards a Fundamental Theological Interpretation of Vatican II," 717.

70. Walbert Buhlmann, *The Coming of the Third Church*.

71. Hollenbach, *The Common Good and Christian Ethics*, 152.

72. Hollenbach, 153.

73. Elsbernd, "Authentic Human Living," 15.

74. Vatican II, *Gaudium et spes*, n. 74.

75. Charles Curran, "The Common Good and Official Catholic Social Teaching," 120; quoting A. Nemetz, "Common Good," *New Catholic Encyclopedia*, 1967, vol. IV, 15–19.

76. Vatican II, *Gaudium et spes*, n.75.

77. John XXIII, *Mater et magistra*, n.65.

78. The foregoing is a paraphrase of Coleman, "Retrieving or Re-inventing Social Catholicism," 289.

79. Randy Sachs, "God, Images of," 419.

80. Cahill, "Globalization and the Common Good," 54.

81. Paul VI, *Octogesima adveniens*, n. 22.

82. Christiansen, "The Common Good and the Politics of Self-Interest," 56.

83. Roger Ruston, *Human Rights and the Image of God*, 269.

84. Ruston, 270.

85. Sigrid Müller, "Concepts and Dimensions of Human Dignity in the Christian Tradition," 24.

86. Antonio Autiero, "Human Dignity in an Ethical Sense," 19.

87. Autiero, 18.

88. Chroust, "The Corporate Idea and the Body of Christ," 423.

89. "To every human being within the created universe is assigned its proper place as well as its proper relationship to all other things." Chroust, "The Corporate Idea and the Body of Christ," 425.

90. Chroust, "The Corporate Idea and the Body of Christ," 442.

91. Chroust, 444–448 at 448.

92. Brian Tierney, "Religious Rights: An Historical Perspective," 26.

93. Tierney, 27.

94. Tierney, 28.

95. Tierney, 28.

96. Tierney, 28.

97. Brian Tierney, *The Idea of Natural Rights*, 5.

98. Tierney, 77.

99. Tierney, 6.

100. Tierney, 76.

101. Tierney, "Religious Rights," 28.

102. Tierney, *The Idea of Natural Rights*, 203.

103. Tierney, "Religious Rights," 29.

104. Ruston, *Human Rights and the Image of God*, 286.

105. Ruston, 287

106. Ruston, 276.

107. Leo XIII, *Rerum novarum*, n. 34.

108. Dwyer, "Person, Dignity of," 725.

109. See Heinrich Rommen, *The State in Catholic Political Thought*, and Jacque Maritain, *Man and the State* as classic illustrations of a post-war but pre-conciliar style of Catholic social thought.

110. Mary Ann Glendon, "The sources of 'rights-talk': Some are Catholic."

111. Glendon, "Sources of 'rights-talk.'"

112. Joel Feinberg, *Social Philosophy*, 85.

113. Walter Kasper, "The theological foundations of human rights," 154.

114. Kasper, 156.

115. Vatican II, *Gaudium et spes*, n. 40.

116. Vatican II, n. 41.

117. Vatican II, n. 41.

118. Vatican II, n. 42. This acceptance of pluralism and rejection of any single "Catholic" social system is reinforced in another significant conciliar document, *Dignitatis Humanae* (Decree on Religious Freedom), where it is accepted that the church can work with a variety of political arrangements as long as religious freedom of all persons is respected.

119. Paul VI, *Octogesima adveniens*, n. 3.

120. Paul VI, n. 4.

121. Paul VI, *Populorum progressio*, n. 14. Recall the discussion of the person "integrally and adequately considered" in the previous chapter.

122. Paul VI, *Octogesima adveniens*, n. 40.

123. Synod of Bishops, *Justitia in mundo*, ch. 1.

124. Paul VI, *Octogesima adveniens*, n.22.

125. See Gerald Beyer, "John XXIII and John Paul II: The Human Rights Popes" for a fine analysis of John Paul's thinking on human rights prior to his papacy and thereafter.

126. John Paul II, *Redemptor hominis*, n. 17.

127. Benedict XVI, "Address to the U.N. General Assembly," 2008.

128. Francis, *Laudato Si'*, n. 30.

129. Francis, "Address to the U.N. General Assembly," 2015.

130. Paul VI, *Populorum progressio*, n. 43.

131. Synod of Bishops, *Justitia in mundo*, ch. 2.

132. Francis, *Fratelli Tutti*, n. 77.

133. Francis, n. 103.

134. Francis, n. 104.

135. Michael Czerny and Christian Barone, *Siblings All, Sign of the Times*, 105.

136. Francis, "Faith and Human Dignity," August 12, 2020.

137. Samuel Moyn, *Christian Human Rights*.

138. Tierney, *The Idea of Natural Rights*, 346.

139. Weaver, "Dignity: A Catholic Perspective," 32.

140. Hollenbach, "Human Dignity: Experience and History," 129; Hollenbach is quoting Margaret Farley, 187. See my comment and reference in Chapter 4, n. 64.

141. Hollenbach, "Human Dignity: Experience and History," 130.

142. Hollenbach, 131. The above paragraph simply summarizes main points of the author's explication of crucial freedoms, essential relationships, and basic needs.

143. Vatican II, *Gaudium et spes*, n. 16.

144. Vatican II, n. 17.

145. Vatican II, *Dignitatis humanae*, n. 2.

146. Vatican II, n. 1.

147. Lisa Sowle Cahill, "Toward a Christian Theory of Human Rights," 285.

148. Kasper, "Theological Foundations of Human Rights," 15.

149. Kasper, 158.

150. Kasper, 160.

151. Vatican II, *Gaudium et spes*, ns. 12–17.

152. Vatican II, ns. 24–25.

153. US Conference of Catholic Bishops, *Economic Justice for All*, n. 17.

154. Matthew Petrusek commenting on the ITC document "Communion and Stewardship," n. 41 in "The Image of God and Moral Action," 81.

155. Vatican II, n. 26.

7

SOLIDARITY AND SUBSIDIARITY

As has been emphasized throughout this book, at the heart of Catholic social teaching lies a theological foundation that supports a communitarian social ethic. That is, the human person is consistently defined relationally—the relationships he or she has with God, other persons, and other creatures. As Heinrich Rommen suggested in his classic text of Catholic political theory, sociality is as essential to our humanity as rationality.[1] Procedurally and substantively, this communitarian ethical vision is served by solidarity and subsidiarity. These two ethical coordinates suggest both a strategy and content for a social ethic shaped by Catholic social thought.

In a 1986 document, the International Theological Commission observed that solidarity and subsidiarity "are profoundly connected" to the foundation of human dignity.[2] Johann Verstraeten posits that these two themes are central to Catholic social thought because solidarity "refers to the social responsibility of humans and implies a rejection of individualism," while subsidiarity "refers to the responsibility of people and intermediary communities and implies a rejection of collectivism."[3] In this chapter we will examine both the meaning of these two crucial ethical coordinates as well as how they have been developed within the social tradition of Catholicism.

SOLIDARITY

The word *solidarity* was not first employed in theological or ecclesiastical discourse but was a term that was used in secular social theory. Among the earliest thinkers to use the term was Adam Ferguson, a member of the "Scottish Enlightenment" along with David Hume, Francis Hutcheson, Adam Smith, and others. In his *An Essay on Civil Society* published in 1767, solidarity expressed a sense of shared interests or sympathies that fostered a spirit of unity among groups or classes. In Ferguson's view, it was a unity among those who, despite the division of labor, saw themselves as one in the work process. Decades later in 1840, a French socialist thinker, Pierre Leroux, underscored the "ethical content" of solidarity by his claim that it included "an obligation of belonging together" or "the duty of mutual help."[4]

According to Anna Rowlands, "solidarity enters the modern lexicon on the slipstream of the revolutions of the eighteenth and nineteenth centuries, expressing what had been thought of over centuries in Christian usage as fraternity and friendship." She suggests that the "idiom of solidarity took these older ideas and wove them through with an emerging Enlightenment language. . . . The eventual outcome was Liberty, Equality, Fraternity."[5]

Writing after those liberal revolutions, Emile Durkheim, according to Verstraeten, offered "one of the most well-known definitions" with his distinction between "mechanical" and "organic" solidarities. The former refers to a "unity based on equality characteristic of primitive communities" and the latter is "characterized by a unity in diversity" such as the division of labor.[6] Durkheim's point was that in preindustrial societies there was cohesiveness due to shared beliefs, experiences, and activities, whereas in industrial societies unity arises not out of similarity but interdependence.

Rowland is correct that the value and attitude suggested by solidarity had long been part of the Christian heritage.[7] Numerous biblical texts in the Gospels—the parables of the rich man and Lazarus, the Good Samaritan, and the Last Judgment scene in Matthew 25, coupled with the writings of Paul on the church as the body of Christ, along with his reflections on the implications of eucharistic sharing—all point to the unity that transcends societal distinctions of class, gender, and ethnicity. After noting several instances in the biblical witness, Gerald Beyer summarizes his conclusion, "the Bible may not use the word solidarity, but numerous texts provide a foundation upon which modern Catholic social teaching is built."[8]

In the early church the text of the Shepherd of Hermas used the parable of the vine and branches to stress the bond of solidarity between rich and poor. Justin Martyr, also in the second century, wrote about the "social implications of the Christian law of love."[9] Later authors like Basil of Caesarea and Clement of Alexandria exhibit similar sensibilities about the duties of Christians to share and the obligations of justice toward the least well off. In the West, Ambrose of Milan, writing in the fourth century, emphasized both social solidarity and the universal purpose of the goods of creation that ought to inspire the wealthy to use their riches in a just manner by extensive sharing.[10] Christian teaching long presupposed that people are drawn together by instinct, but it was the church's teaching about the obligations of those with superfluous or even merely adequate goods to care for those with less that underscored there was more than a social nicety at stake; the issue was one of justice.[11] What Peter Phan writes about John Chrysostom could be applied to many early Christian authors: "At the heart of his social thought lies the double principle that sustains and nurtures common life: charity, which is embodied in compassion and sharing; and solidarity, which expresses itself in the mutual interdependence of all human beings."[12]

The historian Paul Misner, speaking of solidarity, maintains that "one can find it hidden almost wherever one looks, often under the term 'Catholicism' or 'social Catholicism' itself."[13] It emerged in the modern era as socially aware Catholics struggled for a humane political economy that was distinct from liberalism and socialism. At the outset, the struggle was largely against liberal capitalism that shunned regulation or oversight of free markets. "Later, when the potential benefits of modern capitalism could be discerned and distinguished from individualistic abuses, and when socialism" had become claimed by antireligious movements and theories, "the essential mutuality of human beings in their inner life and labor came to be called 'solidarity' and its theoretical underpinnings 'solidarism.'"[14]

A key figure in this narrative is Heinrich Pesch, a German Jesuit. Pesch did not invent the term *solidarism*; it had begun "as a school of thought in France. Pesch adopted it as the term for his interest in articulating an approach that was distinct from and critical of individualism and collectivism."[15] He cited the Spaniard Donoso Cortes and the Belgian Charles Perin as "theological progenitors of Christian solidarism."[16] The term derives from the Latin *solidus*, meaning "firm" or "whole," and solidarism was an effort to develop a systematic theory about solidarity. The latter has been defined as "the unity of a social group, producing and based upon a community of interests, objectives, and standards." Solidarism is then defined as "a social concept maintaining that the interdependence of the members of a society offers a basis for a social organization grounded upon solidarity of interests."[17]

Pesch was convinced that both socialism and individualism were misguided and mistaken about the nature of the human person and society. He thought "that our true nature, expressed in observable deep human practices of social cooperation is betrayed by narrow appeals to competitive individualism or overarching collectivism." As a corrective he sought to develop an economic theory "that took into account a cooperative understanding of human nature and the common good."[18] Pesch presented his approach to the economy in his 1904 textbook on national economics which helped spread the use of the term *solidarity* among Catholic thinkers in Europe.[19]

Most social Catholics viewed capitalism as tending to proclaim an "exalted sense of human freedom that was not balanced by any positive appreciation for solidarity with other persons in society at large."[20] As a consequence, these Catholics supported the idea of government intervention in the economy for the purpose of aiding the working class through legislation. For Pesch, this was only sensible, given his view of the person. He was "emphatic in insisting that human beings are not just accidentally, but inherently, connected with other persons in a common life, for which they are morally responsible agents." Solidarity meant that personal dignity was related to the recognition of the dignity and freedom of others. Thus, for Pesch, "mutual assistance both given and received is a law of human life."[21]

There were, according to Pesch, two key principles to be kept in mind. What he called the principle of economy proposed that "the dominant issue is marshaling and husbanding limited resources for maximum effective output," and this had to be "tempered by and subordinated to the principle of solidarity." He argued that just as in the political realm, where "weaker members may not be cut off or denied their rights" for the sake of a more effective state, so, too, "weaker economic participants may not be put at further disadvantage in the name of higher productivity or greater gross national product."[22] Solidarity must correct and balance the principle of economy.

It is important to grasp that for Pesch and the other German Jesuits who followed him, solidarism was first and foremost a philosophy and not a program.[23] It was an articulation of a theological anthropology that emphasized how humanity's essential sociality called forth contributions to, and sharing in, the benefits of communal life. The aim was to transpose "pre-modern understandings of natural law, of the human being as essentially social, and of society itself as organic and cooperative, into the modern contexts of industrialized societies."[24]

Development of Solidarity in Catholic Social Teaching

Pesch's influence on the Catholic social tradition and papal social teaching continued through one of his students, Oswald von Nell-Breuning, another German Jesuit. Nell-Breuning provided a three-fold distinction regarding solidarity that has remained within the social tradition; that is, solidarity as a factual claim about human beings being interdependent, solidarity as an ethical norm governing interpersonal relations, and solidarity as a principle that should help order institutions of society, politics, and economics.[25] Nell-Breuning assisted Pius XI in the writing of the encyclical *Quadragesimo anno* in 1931, a document that promoted the idea that humans have a proclivity to cooperate and develop shared interests. Pius XI also "stressed universal human kinship set against attempts to place priority on solidarity within ethnic, national groups and consequent claims to racial superiority."[26] This was aimed at the positions of National Socialism in Germany and other ethnocentric ideologies. However Pius XI used the traditional expression "social charity" instead of solidarity to describe the contrasting papal outlook. In this he was in line with Leo XIII, who had expressed his appreciation for the idea of solidarity using terms like "friendship" and "social charity" without employing the word *solidarity*.

It was Pius XII who first used the term *solidarity* in papal writing. While serving in the Vatican diplomatic corps, Pius had lived in Bavaria and was aware of the work of Pesch and Nell-Breuning prior to becoming pope. *Summi pontificatus*, published in 1939, was the first encyclical of Pius XII, and it focused on the unity of human society while lamenting the outbreak of World War II in the previous month. For Pius the war was an outgrowth of several "pernicious errors," the first of which was "forgetfulness of that law of human solidarity and charity which is dictated and imposed by our common origin and by the equality of rational nature in all men, to whatever people they belong."[27] Pius went on to cite biblical texts from Genesis, the Acts of the Apostles, several Pauline letters, and the Gospel of John to show that solidarity is at the heart of the Christian view of the person and society. He concluded his biblical reflection with the words, "In the light of this unity of all humankind, which exists in law and in fact, individuals do not feel themselves isolated units, like grains of sand, but united by the very force of their nature and by their internal destiny, into an organic, harmonious mutual relationship which varies with the changing of times."[28] For Pius this should translate into citizens and governments being devoted to a sense of the common good and not the violence and destruction of war.

Following the war Europe saw the rise of Christian Democracy movements and political parties. The Italian Alcide de Gasperi, the German Konrad Adenauer, and in France Robert Schuman were all builders of postwar European democratic life. They took inspiration from the political thought of Jacques Maritain who, like the German solidarists, maintained that one's personal development came through taking responsibility for others in society as well as one's family. These political leaders and those who followed their vision "stressed the instinct and the need for all members of society to respect and help each other, and for all organizations and associations" within a society "to harmonize their functions in the service" of a common good that was inclusive.[29]

Commentators have noted that during John XXIII's papacy the foundation and meaning of solidarity underwent change.[30] Regarding the foundation, "there is a remarkable shift in emphasis from an ontological to a personalist vision."[31] This is evidence for the influence of Maritain and Mounier on Catholic social thought. Verstraeten points out that no longer is the starting point an ontological natural law, but rather the dignity of the person. Human persons are understood as beings who must become more truly human through their moral agency: "a calling to actualize themselves as people in a life for others."[32] This approach is coupled with a shift to a more sociological foundation when discussing the communal dimension of personhood.[33] People are seen to be increasingly interdependent, and this growth in the extent and complexity of mutual interdependence has led to an increased role for the state in societal affairs since there is more need for oversight and governance that promotes the common good.[34] Rowlands observes that John also shifted discussion of solidarity away from the concentration upon capital and labor in the industrial economy and gave attention to "the realities of being a global church" in a world that was radically unequal between rich and poor nations. John expanded the focus to "the challenges and need for solidarity *between*, as well as *within*, nation states."[35]

Although the term *solidarity* was not prominent in the *Pastoral Constitution on the Church in the Modern World*, it was closely related to much of the document's message expressed in other language regarding the communitarian nature of the person and duty to love the neighbor, the interdependence of persons in society and promotion of the common good, the equality of all people and the obligations of social justice, and the importance of responsibility for and participation in the common life.[36] The bishops made clear that all these themes are "developed and consummated in the work of Jesus Christ. For the very Word made flesh willed to share in the human fellowship." Jesus founded a new community "composed of all those who receive him in faith and in love." He did this "through his Body which is the Church," where "everyone, as members one of the other, would render mutual service according to the different gifts" that each person possesses. The bishops conclude this passage by urging that "this solidarity must be constantly increased" till the day when it will be perfected.[37] In other places in the document the eucharist is described as "a meal of brotherly solidarity," while the church is described as a "sign and an instrument of intimate union with God, and of the unity of all" people.[38]

Following the Council, Paul VI's document on human development, *Populorum progressio*, drew attention to the plight of the poorer nations and their populations. In the opening paragraph, Paul makes clear that the church must respond in a new and more vigorous way to the plight of the least well-off. He refers to "a renewed consciousness of the demands of the Gospel makes it her duty to put herself at the service of all, to help them grasp their serious problem in all its dimensions, and to convince them that solidarity in action at this turning point in human history is a matter of urgency."[39] Of course, any distribution of material goods that creates wide gaps between "haves" and "have nots" has long been a concern for the Catholic community; it is possible in the late 1960s, however, to see "a perceptible change toward a greater sense of urgency attached to the issue" than before.[40] Paul's 1967 encyclical was a catalyst for that change. In presenting his understanding of what authentic development entails, Paul observed that human beings greatly benefit from the work of those who have gone before as well as contemporaries. "For this reason we have obligations toward all, and we cannot refuse to interest ourselves in those who will come after us. . . . The reality of human solidarity, which is a benefit for us, also imposes a duty."[41] Note the twofold sense of solidarity in Paul's statement: solidarity is an empirical reality that enriches us, and it also has a moral meaning that imposes duties upon us. In Paul's thinking, the aim of development is to promote human self-realization, but "there can be no development" of humanity unless there is a "simultaneous development of all humanity in the spirit of solidarity."[42]

One year later the Conference of Latin American Bishops met in Medellin, Colombia, to provide a pastoral plan for the church in that region of the world. In the document on "Poverty of the Church," the assembled bishops decided to give a preference to providing resources for the poor and for the church to "come closer to the poor in sincerity and brotherhood." They went on to say, "we ought to sharpen the awareness of our duty of solidarity with the poor, to which charity leads us. This solidarity means that we make ours their problems and their struggles. . . . This has to be concretized in criticism of injustice and oppression, in the struggle against the intolerable situation which a poor person often has to tolerate."[43]

When the Synod of Bishops met in 1971, they described what they saw as a "crisis of universal solidarity." This was due to a "tremendous paradox" existing in the world situation. On the one hand, "never before have the forces working for bringing about a unified world society appeared so powerful and dynamic; they are rooted in the awareness of the full basic equality as well as of the human dignity of all." Yet "the paradox lies in the fact that within this perspective of unity the forces of division and antagonism seem today to be gaining in strength."[44] The episcopal document went on to analyze some of those negative forces while holding out hope for a solution that would promote the right of each person to authentic personal development that allows for human flourishing at the individual and societal levels. A major stumbling block along the road to such a future is the lack of solidarity whereby rich nations and their populations can remain indifferent to the needs and rights of poorer nations and populations.

Prior to his papacy, Karol Wojtyla was writing about solidarity due to his philosophical interest in the work of Max Scheler. Scheler had "defined solidarity as the co-responsibility of each individual for the moral well-being of all others."[45] At the same time that Paul VI was discussing the idea of solidarity, Wojtyla was writing about the theme from his perspective of philosophical anthropology in his book *The Acting Person* and in a series of essays that were later gathered into an anthology, *Toward a Philosophy of Praxis*. In the latter, Wojtyla proposed that "solidarity is a 'natural' consequence of the fact that a human being exists and acts together with others. Solidarity is also the foundation of a community in which the common good conditions and liberates participation, and participation serves the common good."[46]

By the time he writes in 1987 as John Paul II to commemorate Paul VI's *Populorum progressio*, Wojtyla has further developed his thoughts on solidarity and expanded its range to address global concerns. In the encyclical *Sollicitudo rei socialis*, John Paul acknowledges that interdependence is a fact, one that is evident in a globalized world. But the crucial issue is how one responds to that empirical reality of being interdependent. After all, people can be in relationships that are radically unequal and unjust. Nations may have mutual relations in trade, but those relations can lead to one nation being at a distinct disadvantage as it exports its raw materials cheaply but imports manufactured goods at a high price. Interdependence must be transformed into a "moral category." Once "interdependence becomes recognized in this way, the correlative response as a moral and social attitude, as a 'virtue,' is *solidarity*." As one might expect from someone who was concerned with a philosophy of praxis, John Paul was not content to leave the meaning of solidarity as a social attitude undefined. For him "solidarity is not a feeling of vague compassion or shallow distress at the misfortunes of so many people both near and far. On the contrary, it is a *firm and persevering determination* to commit oneself to the *common good*; that is to say to the good of all and each individual, because we are *all* really responsible for *all*."[47]

In John Paul II's ideas we can hear echoes of Heinrich Pesch. Solidarity is a natural tendency in the human as a social animal to respond positively to the experience of interdependence. That positive tendency can be cultivated into a virtue or abiding disposition to commit oneself to the equal dignity of each and every person in the human family. "The exercise of solidarity within each society is valid when its members recognize one another as persons."[48]

John Paul, however, takes his reflection to a more explicitly theological level than the early treatments of solidarity within the social tradition. He views solidarity as part of the Catholic understanding of the imago Dei and the Trinity. John Paul affirms the equality of all people and the human rights belonging to each person, but he goes on to state that faith offers us the ability to see the neighbor as "the living image of God the father," redeemed by Christ and sustained by the movement of the Holy Spirit. "Beyond human and natural bonds, already so close and strong, there is discerned in the light of faith a new model of the unity of the human race, which ultimately inspires our solidarity. This supreme model of unity, which is a reflection of the intimate life of God; one God in three persons is what we Christians mean by the word communion."[49] For the pope, then, it is the acceptance of the doctrine of creation and the imago Dei, as well as the belief that God is a Trinitarian communion of ongoing self-gift between Father, Son, and Spirit that is the ultimate foundation for solidarity. It is not simply an ethical response to the fact of interdependence but a recognition and acting out of theological beliefs that lay at the roots of the Catholic social tradition.

Benedict XVI's social encyclical *Caritas in veritate* looks at solidarity through theological reflection on *caritas* or love. That reflection was presented, prior to Benedict's 2009 social encyclical, in his first letter on the theme *God is Love* published on Christmas Day in 2005. In that initial letter, Benedict presented caritas as both "gift and demand, uniting love of God and love of neighbor."[50] That is, God offers love to all creatures, first by the very act of creation in which God's diffusive love moves out beyond the Trinitarian communion of love to the act of creation. Second, God offers the gift of covenant to creation, particularly human creatures, with the possibility of entering into a loving relationship between Creator and creature. Thus, God's presence is made manifest to human beings, and each person is necessarily called to respond to that presence. People can respond inappropriately by rejecting or ignoring the offer of covenant, but that is still a response. God's gift can be accepted, and people can grow into ever deeper covenant with God.

In paragraph twenty of *God is Love*, Benedict reflects upon the life of the early Christian community as portrayed in Chapter 2 of the Acts of the Apostles. There he points out that the members of the New Testament community of Jerusalem were "required to organize their love of neighbor so as to provide the conditions (material and spiritual) of a dignified life."[51] Benedict cites the Lukan parables of the rich man and Lazarus and the Good Samaritan, along with the final judgment in Matthew, to establish that the neighbor was understood to be universal, not just those who are within the community.[52] For Benedict, as for the author of the first letter of John, it is not possible to be in a loving relationship with God if one is not loving toward one's neighbor. "If anyone says, 'I love God,' and hates his brother, he is a liar; for he who does not love his brother whom he has seen, cannot love God whom he has not seen" (1 John 4:20). Thus, the gift of God's love comes with the demand to love the neighbor. For Benedict, this is foundational to a Christian understanding of the meaning of caritas.

When Benedict turned his attention to the writing of his social encyclical, he begins by asserting that caritas "is the principle not only of microrelationships (with friends, with family members or small groups) but also of macro-relationships (social, economic, and political ones)."[53] Thus, for Benedict, "charity is at the heart of the church's social doctrine."[54] This is so because the inherent dynamic of love—being received and given—means "as the objects of God's love, men and women become subjects of charity, they are called to make themselves instruments of grace, so as to pour forth God's charity and to weave networks of charity."[55] Benedict maintains, "this dynamic of charity received and given is what gives rise to the Church's social teaching, which is *caritas in veritate in re sociali*: the proclamation of the truth of Christ's love in society."[56] For the pope the element of love's demand means that one cannot simply shirk the obligations of care for the other to an impersonal governmental or economic system: "solidarity is first and foremost a sense of responsibility of everyone with regard to everyone."[57] Individual Christians must practice an active solidarity for that is the manner in which one demonstrates caritas. That is not to deny that active solidarity can and should work through organized caritas. "This is the institutional path—we might also call it the political path—of charity, no less excellent and effective than the kind of charity which encounters the neighbor directly."[58]

Within the first six months of his papacy Pope Francis issued an apostolic exhortation "On the Joy of the Gospel" in which he appealed to the importance of solidarity to overcome what he called a globalization of indifference. This phrase was used by his recent predecessors to describe a reality wherein people may acknowledge that they are interdependent due to globalization but refuse to act toward one another as brothers or sisters. There is a failure to acknowledge the moral duty that arises out of awareness of the linkages between people. For Francis this underscores the need for a genuine solidarity, what he and other popes have called the globalization of solidarity; it is the antidote to the globalization of indifference.[59]

Less than a year later Francis addressed the first ever gathering of the World Meetings of Popular Movements sponsored by the Vatican. The initial gathering brought together representatives of popular grassroots movements such as small farmers working for land reform, trade unions representing poor laborers, community organizers working with families denied safe and clean housing, and similar marginalized groups in the international economy. In his talk to the delegates Francis emphasized that among the many tasks to be addressed a major one was "the development of solidarity across all lines of demography, religion, and profession."[60] There must be intentional work done to build relationships that arise out of social projects that foster mutual regard and respect. In *Laudato Si'*, Francis's encyclical on the environment, he will further extend solidarity to include "intergenerational solidarity," a commitment to pass on to future generations a natural world that is sustainable and able to be a home for those not yet born.[61]

A final point concerning Francis and solidarity is that he often uses the word *fraternity* to express a similar point. His first World Day of Peace Message on January 1, 2014, was entitled "Fraternity, the Foundation and Pathway to Peace." According to Francis, "fraternity is an essential human quality, for we are relational beings. A lively awareness of our relatedness helps us to look upon and to treat each person as a true brother or sister." Standing in the way of this awareness is a globalization of indifference. "The many situations of inequality, poverty and injustice, are signs not only of a profound lack of fraternity, but also the absence of a culture of solidarity."[62] Again and again in this document and in other writing by Francis, one sees his use of fraternity and solidarity interchangeably. For Francis, it is a consciousness of the dignity and equality of the other that is crucial to the building of a better world, and that consciousness is fostered by people coming to see their shared origin and destiny as brothers and sisters under the care of a divine Father.[63] Once able to acknowledge that bond, it is possible to build a globalization of solidarity.

Understanding Solidarity

Solidarity betokens a moral disposition—not just a mental attitude but an orientation and motivation to action—that is also suggested by terms within the social tradition like social charity, fraternity, neighbor-love, and communion, or described in language of co-responsibility for others, or commitment to the common good, or recognition of the other as a person of equal dignity. There are various nuances to the way that solidarity has been used in papal teaching of the modern era, but behind it all is the belief that solidarity is meant to evoke the giving of oneself for the sake of the other. "Solidarity begins as an inner attitude and, when it has fully taken root within a person, expresses itself through numerous external activities that demonstrate a person's commitment to the well-being of others."[64] It is a moral quality that reflects the social tradition's bedrock conviction that the human person is social and that there is an obligation incumbent on all persons to contribute to the building up of a common good in social life that serves each and every person. In recent papacies there has been a deliberate effort to broaden our understanding of the common good as being global and not merely local or national. Solidarity entails more than merely acknowledging interdependence, for it demands an outreach to the other, understood as a moral obligation and also a spiritual necessity. The vision that develops out of solidarity reflects a social imagination that fosters ever better attempts at establishing institutions and structures that reflect the commitment to serve the well-being of all persons. While various church documents have offered guidance for what that commitment entails, it is not so much policy proposals that solidarity dictates as a moral will to overcome the indifference toward the suffering of the marginalized both near and far. As Lisa Cahill suggests, "solidarity imparts to other values . . . a distinctive character of altruism and compassion."[65]

Gerald Beyer has proposed that a survey of Catholic social teaching about solidarity reveals a three-fold dimension to the theme. First, solidarity is an "anthropological datum." This is similar to Pesch's point made in the nineteenth century that we are inherently and not accidently enmeshed in social relations and that our true nature as humans is to be cooperative and mutually supportive. The second dimension of solidarity in the tradition is that it is "an ethical imperative." We should draw ethical "oughts" from our interdependence, engaging in reflection and analysis as to how to act wisely and compassionately "to eliminate the causes of the suffering of the other." We are to love the brothers and sisters. Finally, solidarity should be "a principle concretized in legislative policies and institutions." This third dimension is needed because "solidarity requires the sustained effort to go beyond short-term solutions and temporary aid toward long-term institutional change."[66] Solidarity is not simply a passing feeling of concern but a commitment to build a common good that serves the well-being of all.

Three Topics Related to Solidarity

When the topic of the common good was taken up in the previous chapter, the point was made that there is not a Platonic idea of the common good awaiting our discovery if we simply look for it. Rather, the common good is a project to be sought through dialogue and debate which takes seriously the pluralism of our society and our world. Catholic social teaching does not presume to impose a common good defined by a minority, but it does call for an honest and searching conversation among all people of good will who take up the intellectual challenge of public inquiry into what values and practices may achieve a consensus as being constitutive of a good society that protects and promotes human flourishing for all.

In a number of his writings, David Hollenbach has called for an "intellectual solidarity," that is, "a willingness to take other persons seriously enough to engage them in conversation and debate about what they think makes life worth living."[67] According to Hollenbach, much of liberalism has too often promoted the "tolerance of diversity" as the "premier cultural lesson to be learned."[68] He warns that if we are to achieve genuine political community, it is "engagement with the other, and not just tolerance" that is necessary. Tolerance is content simply not to interfere with the beliefs and lifestyles of others who may differ from us, whereas "intellectual solidarity entails engagement with the other through both listening and speaking, in the hope that understanding might replace incomprehension and that perhaps even agreement could result."[69]

Solidarity in this sense demonstrates a sincere respect for the dignity of the other, a willingness to engage with a person and an openness to learn as well as search together for areas of mutual accord. Too often what passes for tolerance in society is really indifference to the other, not taking others seriously enough to truly engage them. It is not a virtue so much as a vice, a form of intellectual sloth that cannot be bothered to do the hard work of dialogue that demands listening as well as speaking, along with the ideological openness to change in response to what may be learned.

Hollenbach also reminds us that intellectual solidarity suggests that if public dialogue is to be truly open, there cannot be any a priori refusal to permit individuals to bring the full range and depth of their convictions into the conversation. Therefore, religious convictions should not be ruled out of bounds. If such convictions, even if expressed using the distinctive language of a faith tradition, can still be correlated with broader themes of shared human experience, they may gain a hearing and enrich the search for the common good. If religious convictions are unable to effectively illuminate human experience of our common life, they will not gain a hearing. That determination, however, should be made only after the voice of the religious community is heard and welcomed with openness to listen to insights from whatever source. Intellectual solidarity is a true aspect of the quest to forge a common good that serves the best interests of all.

A second point related to solidarity in the Catholic social tradition is the threat posed by inequality. Throughout the tradition there has been a concern for the poor, that it is wrong for people to have inadequate resources to meet basic material needs. More recently in the tradition, there has grown interest in the issue of inequality. One of the factors addressing this is the emergence of what Paul VI called the aspiration to equality. People today are less willing to accept a hierarchical ordering of society that takes inequality for granted. Increasingly, there is a sense that while some differences between groups or classes may be legitimate, extreme gaps in income, wealth, and power hinder the possibility of forging stable communities and undercut the commitment to solidarity. The ability to have a sense of fraternity, in Francis's usage, or to develop communion between people is compromised when individuals have such widely varying life experiences of great wealth or profound economic insecurity.

Social scientists who study inequality may argue on the grounds of political stability, reduced crime and violence, or economic efficiency that grave inequality in a society or globally is problematic. This will confirm the view of the Catholic social tradition, but the theological objection is not founded on the social science but the conviction that solidarity loses any effective meaning if large segments of the human population live in social worlds that have only tenuous connections with each other. Solidarity holds out the promise of people living in communion with one another, and that hope becomes distant and vague when confronted with vast economic disparities or social castes. A reading of the modern encyclical tradition, particularly since Paul VI, demonstrates a central concern of Catholic social teaching has become the globalization of indifference that mocks talk of a globalization of solidarity.

A third aspect of solidarity that has become a major theme in the Catholic social tradition is what has come to be called the preferential option for the poor.[70] Many commentators on the social tradition treat this theme as its own subject, but here it will be treated as a dimension of the theme of solidarity. The preferential option for the poor is a reminder that the group most likely to be left on the margins of a community's or society's awareness is the poor and that special attention and care must be taken to ensure that the bonds of solidarity extend to them.

In one sense the preferential option for the poor is a relatively new theme in Catholic social teaching; it did not appear in any official church document until 1979 and in no social encyclical of a pope until 1987. Yet in another sense it would be hard to think of a theme in the social tradition that has been around longer. As has been noted in earlier chapters, both the Old and

New Testaments are filled with narratives, stories, speeches, and parables that exhort the faithful to remember the poor and vulnerable in their midst. Throughout the patristic era there were numerous sermons and writings that brought the face of the poor before the entire ecclesial community and urged generosity and compassion toward the less fortunate. It can rightly be argued that "the preferential option for the poor is putting into contemporary and even somewhat Biblical language a point which was enshrined in the older Thomistic tradition's notion of distributive justice," which made the case that a basic minimum of material goods was owed to all on the basis of the common good.[71] It would be hard to imagine any period in the history of the Catholic social tradition when concern for the poor was not a major theme. It was the meeting of the Latin American episcopacy in 1979 at Medellin, Colombia, that brought the exact phrase into the vocabulary of the social tradition. And it was John Paul II in 1987 who wrote of "an option, or a special form of primacy in the exercise of Christian charity, to which the whole tradition in the Church bears witness."[72]

The connection between solidarity and the preferential option for the poor stems from what Gerald Beyer noted previously regarding the second dimension of solidarity, the moral imperative that arises from our recognition of the interdependence of human beings. Once aware of the pain and suffering of others with whom we are linked, it is not possible to turn away like the rich man in the parable who ignores Lazarus at his door. The moral imperative is to love all our brothers and sisters, but there is an urgency and a priority to reach out to those in particular who are suffering and at risk. A lesson from the Incarnation is that God became a specific human person, one who entered into relationships with the marginal of his own society. The invitation to enter into God's reign was extended to all who would listen to his message, but Jesus made a special effort to welcome those in society who had been shunned by the elites and who were left outside the collective of leadership and decision-making in Jewish society at the time. As one who understood the prophetic tradition of his faith, Jesus demonstrated a distinctive concern in his preaching and actions for the "widows, orphans, and aliens" of his time. Solidarity directs attention to those who are too easily forgotten or overlooked in our world.

When the term "preferential option for the poor" first began to be used in church circles, there was concern on the part of some that the expression might mislead people into thinking that the church had become one-sided in its social concern. This misunderstanding was due to the confusion that "preferential" was to be understood as "exclusive." That, of course, would be to deny the tradition's emphasis on the common good, a good in which *all* share in both the benefits and the obligations. In a 1986 statement the Congregation for the Doctrine of the Faith, headed at that time by Joseph Ratzinger, later to become Benedict XVI, made clear: "This special option for the poor, far from being a sign of particularism or sectarianism, manifests the universality of the Church's being and mission; this option excludes no one."[73]

The point is quite simple: parents love all their children, but there are times when one child requires more attention and care than the others. It may be due to illness or some setback in school, some difficult transition that must be navigated, or a disability that creates unique obstacles, but there are times when parents will focus special love and care upon a child. That does not mean it is done to the exclusion of love for the other children in the family; it is the distinctive character of the moment that one family member is in special need. So, too, in the life of a community or society, there will be persons who are in greater need of assistance and concern than others at a given time. The tragic element is that some in special need have been in that situation for long periods of time, often due to past neglect by those capable of offering aid. The preferential option for the poor points to a basic truth about human association: we should judge the decency of a community or society not by asking how are the well-off doing but by asking how well are the weak, vulnerable, and poor of the group being treated.

Summing Up Solidarity

In a careful study of the theme of solidarity in the Catholic social tradition, Marie Vianney Bilgrien has distilled the richness of the idea into seven important elements:

1. Interdependence is a fact and solidarity emerged through the consciousness of that actuality.
2. Solidarity is based on the reality of our human equality and dignity.
3. Solidarity works for the common good of all.
4. Solidarity must be practiced with an awareness of the poor.
5. Solidarity must be a firm and persevering determination.
6. Solidarity is not just a virtue of individual persons but also of groups and nations.
7. Compassion, empathy, and mercy move solidarity into action and help sustain the disposition.[74]

In many ways the importance of solidarity in the Catholic social tradition is due to its intimate relationship with the foundational themes of human dignity in community. It is by including all people in the common good through promotion of their human rights that solidarity is served. As vital and central to the Catholic social tradition as is solidarity, there is another vital theme also linked closely to human dignity in community, and it is to the theme of subsidiarity that we now turn.

SUBSIDIARITY

Both in theory and in much of its practice social Catholicism sought to protect "intermediate, voluntary groups such as neighborhoods, regions, guilds, labor unions, social and familial groupings of all kinds from the encroachment or suppression" by the expansion of both market and state in public life.[75] The word used in the social tradition to express this Catholic orientation to such "natural" communities or groups is subsidiarity. According to de Jonge, subsidiarity "implies that the State should not monopolize all tasks, but on the contrary, should delegate as many as possible to the intermediary public bodies, seeking a middle road between the State's absorption of the economy and the economy's absorption of the State."[77] Yet another oft-cited commentary on Catholic social teaching describes subsidiarity as "a regulatory principle" regarding "the state's right to intervene" in social and economic affairs.[78] Finally, a more recent popular textbook on Catholic social teaching states, "Subsidiarity, then, means decentralization."[79] While there are common strands in these brief descriptions of subsidiarity, there remains more background and nuance to be added to our understanding of subsidiarity and once that is done the wisdom and insight contained in Catholicism's commitment to subsidiarity will be more readily apparent.

The English word *subsidiarity* derives from the Latin *subsidium*, which refers to help or assistance given from one's reserves. "In Roman military terminology, the reserve cohorts (*subsidiarii cohortes*), who stand prepared behind the lines, are contrasted to the cohorts fighting on the front." When the expression was transmuted into discussions of society, "subsidiarity designates the supplementary helping intervention of the larger social body in favor of individual people and of smaller circles."[80] More often than not, the larger social body was an agency, or the institution, of the state.

Höffner provides examples of medieval use of subsidiarity in Aquinas (*De Regno*) and Dante (*De Monarchia*). Aquinas warned that overdone conformity and standardization would threaten the existence of a body politic composed of different members in much the same way that "the symphony and harmony of voices disappear when all sing the same note." And Dante emphasized that "not every little regulation for every city" should be determined by the emperor, for "nations, states, and cities have their own internal concerns which require special laws."[81] During the late medieval period, the idea of subsidiarity was a major element in the disputes between curialists supporting a centralizing papacy and conciliarists favoring dispersal of ecclesiastical authority in councils and limiting the power of the papacy.

Wilhelm von Ketteler (d. 1877), bishop of Mainz in Germany, perhaps the strongest and most insightful episcopal voice for social Catholicism in the middle of the nineteenth century, offered a helpful formulation of subsidiarity.

> For me, the state is not a machine, but a living organism with living members in which every member has its own right, its own function, and shapes its own free life. Such members are for me the individual, the family, the community, and so on. Every lower member moves itself freely in its sphere and enjoys the right of the freest self-determination and self-government. Only where the lower member of this organism is itself no longer capable of achieving its end or of itself averting dangers that threaten its development does the higher member enter into action for it.[82]

This statement of von Ketteler illustrates the philosophy underlying the Catholic outlook on subsidiarity. It is an organic view that sees society as an interconnected web of "natural" communities supporting and sustaining the individual in dignity and freedom. Decades after von Ketteler, Heinrich Rommen summarized the view, which draws upon Aristotle's political philosophy as refined by Aquinas. It was the governing viewpoint of the Catholic social tradition on the nature of society.

> For the organic conception, the social process, as we have repeatedly said, develops in different stages. They are: individual persons, family, neighborhood (town, city), professional and vocational groups, religious, national, cultural, educational organizations, and finally the state as the *unitas ordinis*, itself again a member of the community of states or nations, humanity. All organizational forms have their intrinsic values and their objective ends, the upper form does not make the lower one superfluous; it must never abolish it, nor may it take over its functions or purposes. . . . Thus the social process shows the end values of the intermediary organizations and their right to

realize their ends in the *ordo* of the state. Thus it is once and for all established that the state may not substitute itself for these organizations because it then degenerates into the meddlesome, bureaucratic, and paternalistic state. . . . [It may happen] a distortion in the social organism may disturb the balanced functioning and welfare of the whole. If this should occur, the supreme protector of the order, whatever its form, the state in that significant sense, has the rights and the duty to intervene.[83]

Subsidiarity, therefore, can be understood as that directive that points the way to active involvement and participation at all the different levels of social life. While the actual word was not always used in the tradition, it is a viewpoint on society that Catholic social thought has long accepted.

Papal Teaching on Subsidiarity

The foregoing material provides the background for how the modern papacy has thought about subsidiarity. Leo XIII never mentions subsidiarity in *Rerum novarum*, but something of the idea is present in his concern for workers and their communities of family, neighborhood, and church, all of which appeared under stress if not outright siege in the economic order of laissez-faire capitalism. By his defense of workers' associations, family farms, and artisanal workers, as well as the independence of the church, he was acting out of the social view summarized by Rommen, although without labeling it "subsidiarity."

Leo's call for state intervention in regulating contracts and working conditions of laborers was, of course, a direct assault on the ideology of laissez faire that defined economic liberalism at the time. Leo's concern was the failure of governments to act responsibly in the face of threats to the common good. His argument in *Rerum novarum* was rather sweeping, calling upon the state "in general to do everything necessary for the general welfare which could not be handled as well by private interests."[84] Leo XIII's defense of the state's right to intervene in economic life was straightforward, and no subsequent pope has disagreed with the argument laid out in *Rerum novarum*.

What has followed in later teaching is an examination of the extent of the state's right. Since Leo's argument was made in the face of liberal resistance to an activist state, it is understandable that his interest was to establish the right to intervene. However, Leo's endorsement of state action did pose difficulties. "What place should small unions and associations have in the community? Nowhere does *Rerum novarum* provide a specific principle that sets safe limits to government intervention and at the same time specifies the reasonable autonomy and independence of groups within political communities."[85] It was left to later popes to articulate the limits of that right, and well known in this regard is Pius XI's formulation of the principle of subsidiarity forty years later.

In *Quadragesimo anno*, Pius did not rebut or dissent from Leo's teaching about the right of the state to intervene, but he did seek to nuance Leo by offering to bring more precision to the topic. One factor in Pius's teaching is that he did not need to push back against economic liberalism as much as he did the threatening growth of state activity under the "isms" of communism, fascism, and Nazism. He wanted to preserve the role of smaller social organizations and institutions in public life. To do this Pius sought to balance Leo's endorsement of state intervention with guidance about the limits of such intervention. He did so by formulating what he called the "principle of subsidiarity."[86] First, he acknowledged "history clearly shows, that owing to the change in social conditions much that was formerly done by small bodies can nowadays be accomplished only by large institutions." So there is no blanket dismissal of the necessity of state activity. He then continued,

> Nevertheless, it is a fundamental principle of social philosophy, fixed and unchangeable, that one should not withdraw from individuals and commit to the community what they can accomplish by their own enterprise and industry. So, too, it is an injustice and at the same time a grave evil and a disturbance of right order to transfer to the larger and higher collectivity functions which can be performed and provided for by lesser and subordinate bodies.[87]

There are two aspects to Pius's teaching on the subject. First is the positive dimension; the individual or the smaller group may expect aid and support from the larger community when it is necessary due to the smaller body's inability. Second is the negative dimension, meant to place a restriction on state intervention. It is a standard of nonintervention by the state in the rights of individuals and smaller associations.

There is a possible misreading of Pius's teaching due to more attention being given to the negative dimension. To suggest that the state should intervene as little as possible, as Calvez and Perrin write, "would be to return to a modernized version of the liberal thesis, or at least to conceive of the state's intervention in purely pragmatic terms." Rather, a proper understanding of subsidiarity is to propose that "whenever the state does intervene, it does so to help individuals and lesser societies, which is the same as to say that it should not intervene save when the common good and distributive justice require."[88] The Catholic social tradition views the state as having "an authentic and natural function" which is to protect and promote the common good; the concern of Calvez and Perrin is that positive role can be overlooked if subsidiarity is reduced to the least amount of government as possible.

It should also be remembered that the influence of the German solidarist school, initiated by Pesch, had a role in the crafting of Pius XI's encyclical. Besides Nell-Breuning's role in drafting the text, Gustave Gundlach, a fellow German Jesuit, was often consulted in the writing process. It was Gundlach who elaborated upon the axiom that smaller social units in society had a necessary role and larger social units ought not simply usurp that role. "The idea was not new, but Gundlach gave it its own name."[89] When he originally did so, the context was a prevailing individualism that gave little attention to intermediate bodies within society. In *Quadragesimo anno* in 1931, the idea was used in the context of the growing power of authoritarian states. Hence, it was the negative dimension of subsidiarity that got attention at the time. However, Nell-Breuning saw it differently, describing subsidiarity not as a principle "but a *subsidiarium officium*, a duty of the community to be helpful to its members in the fullest sense of the word."[90] Just what that might entail will inevitably vary, given the historical context and one's reading of the corrective that subsidiarity can provide. Simply put, then, subsidiarity "is about the proper division of labor among human institutions"[91] that aim to serve the common good and the flourishing of the person.

One can see the varying emphases in subsidiarity in the teaching of popes after Pius XI. Like his predecessor, Pius XII served during a time when authoritarian, even totalitarian, states were on the international scene. Consequently, he tended to stress the limits of state power and the need to protect civil society independent of the state. Nonetheless, Pius XII did not lose sight of the positive role of the state: "it is the noble prerogative and function of the State to control, aid and direct the private and individual activities of national life that they converge harmoniously towards the common good." The key is that the "common good can neither be defined according to arbitrary ideas nor can it accept for its standard primarily the material prosperity of society," but rather the common good is what serves the well-being and development of the human person.[92]

John XXIII in his 1961 social encyclical quotes Pius XI on subsidiarity approvingly, but then immediately adds, "recent developments of science and technology provide additional reasons why, to a greater extent than heretofore, it is within the power of public authorities to reduce imbalances, whether these be between various sectors of economic life, or between different regions of the same nation, or even between different peoples of the world as a whole." Add to this theme John's comment about "socialization," the "daily more complex interdependence of citizens,"[93] and it can be understood why John acknowledges "the growing intervention of public authorities," even as he indicates this trend bears watching.[94] In *Pacem in terris*, John employs subsidiarity as a means to propose the need for a greater public authority in international affairs since the global common good is not being adequately served by individual autonomous states. There is need for a corresponding institution to do for the global common good what the state is tasked to do for a nation's common good.[95] Paul VI in *Populorum progressio* and John Paul II in *Sollicitudo rei socialis* both follow John's use of subsidiarity to make a case for a greater role for an international authority and use of international organizations to secure the global common good.[96]

In a later encyclical, John Paul II cast some doubt upon the role of what he called the "social assistance" state. Due to his experience in Poland under a communist regime, "he warns that the underestimation of the subsidiarity principle and of the right to economic initiative leads to serious social problems." John Paul acknowledged that state intervention in the economy can be necessary in order to address monopolies and unfair business practices, as well as to assist in "remedying forms of poverty and deprivation unworthy of the human person." In a passage often cited by critics of contemporary social welfare states, the pope went on to write, "the range of such intervention has vastly expanded, to the point of creating a new type of state, the so-called 'welfare state.'" For John Paul, the "malfunctions and defects in the social assistance state are the result of an inadequate understanding of the tasks proper to the state," and he is clear that "the principle of subsidiarity must be respected." When that does not happen, there is "a loss of human energies and an inordinate increase in public agencies, which are dominated more by bureaucratic ways of thinking than by concern for serving their clients, and which are accompanied by an enormous increase in spending."[97] Without question, John Paul underscores the negative emphasis of subsidiarity in these remarks.

In a speech two years later in Riga, Latvia, the pope seemed to strike a balance, one that many neoliberals ignored by championing his critique of the welfare state. Without denying that "society cannot be conceived as a shapeless mass which ends up being absorbed by the state" and which requires a range of intermediary groups to achieve the common good,[98] John Paul also underscored the positive role of the state when subsidiarity is properly understood. "A balanced concept of the state" is one that "emphasizes its value and necessity." It should include "a social state which offers everyone the legal guarantees of an orderly existence and assures the most vulnerable the support they need in order not to succumb to the arrogance and indifference of the powerful."[99] He concluded his speech by observing "the church's social teaching does not concern the concrete organizational expressions of society, but the inspirational principles which must give it direction in order that it should be worthy of humankind."[100]

Reading the papal speech in tandem with his 1991 encyclical, several things are evident. First, John Paul did not want to be interpreted as taking sides in policy debates in countries like the United States where the size and extent of social welfare programs sponsored by the federal and state governments are an ongoing topic of political debate. Second, he maintained that Catholic social teaching had something to contribute at the level of principle, though not the specifics of public policy. In the case of subsidiarity, that contribution is to hold up the values captured in both the positive and negative aspects of the idea. Third, given his formative experience under a repressive communist regime, John Paul was especially sensitive to how a large state can undercut the diversity, participation, and contribution of smaller communities. At the same time, one cannot imagine that a pope who was such an effective advocate for social and economic rights wished to denigrate government programs that are truly needed to help all members of a nation benefit from the common good.

I believe the papal outlook is nicely captured by the social theorist Philip Selznick in his search for an appropriate style of state intervention in social life.

> The alternative is not a rejection of government. . . . Rather, it is for the architects of the welfare state to transform their vision of how governments fulfill their responsibilities. Two strategies are appropriate. If the government will pay more attention to communal values and civil society, it will more clearly perceive and more adequately protect the needs of individual persons. And if it will adopt post-bureaucratic modes of organization, the welfare state can become more limited, more accountable, and more humane.[101]

Benedict XVI continues along the same path as John Paul II in his concern that subsidiarity be practiced in governance and social organization so that people are able to engage in self-giving and practice cooperation with others in mutual care and assistance. "Subsidiarity respects personal dignity by recognizing in the person a subject who is always capable of giving something to others." This promotion of reciprocity in human relationships implies that "subsidiarity is the most effective antidote against any form of all-encompassing welfare state." Benedict explicitly makes the point that subsidiarity is a necessary practice for governance in any scheme of globalization to avoid producing "a dangerous universal power of a tyrannical nature."[102]

At the same time, Benedict affirms that "the principle of subsidiarity must remain closely linked to the principle of solidarity and vice versa, since the former without the latter gives way to social privatism, while the latter without the former gives way to paternalist social assistance that is demeaning to those in need."[103] One can readily see Benedict shares John Paul's aim to find the proper balance in developing social policies that offer assistance to those in need, the goal being to provide genuine aid in an effective manner while avoiding approaches where the state undercuts or eliminates the role of intermediary groups and associations being part of the network of services and providers offering help to those who are vulnerable and suffering.

Pope Francis has provided his own nuances to the theme of subsidiarity. For one thing, he "had been as concerned to initiate the process of ecclesial subsidiarity as political-social."[104] For Francis, subsidiarity is an important principle of church governance; this was not an element in either John Paul II or Benedict XVI's thinking about subsidiarity. It is also the case that Francis has given much greater attention to the insights of regional and local churches in formulating social teaching. Simply to look at the reference notes in his encyclicals reveals a willingness to cite the documents of various bishops' conferences around the globe. As a large global institution the church must be as attentive to subsidiarity as it asks the state to be.

Another development in Francis's use of subsidiarity is its application to processes of listening to voices that have often been muted in formulating social teaching. "Francis describes subsidiarity as a principle with a double movement, from 'top to bottom and bottom to top.'" For him it becomes an expression of the option for the poor, an effort to bring about the participation of the least well-off and most vulnerable in reflecting on the social meaning of the faith. In an address at one of his weekly general audiences, he posed the questions, "Who is listened to? Who is seen as an expert on poverty, migration, climate change and so forth?" For Francis, "Any action that sees itself as promoting subsidiarity must be simultaneously an option for the poor—both privileging a listening process to the most marginalized communities and enabling the initiative and contribution of all." As Anna Rowlands puts it, "Francis argues that there is no solidarity without subsidiarity."[105]

One can sum up the treatment of subsidiarity in papal teaching in the following manner. Subsidiarity functions as both a theory of the responsibilities of the state and of citizens acting through the state to protect and promote the common good, often by offering help (*subsidum*) to those who are not benefiting appropriately from the common good of a society. This is its positive element. Subsidiarity also functions as a norm of restraint upon treating the state as the "default" preference for giving expression to solidarity. Instead, there is a preference for keeping practices of solidarity rooted in the closest communities to where the need is present. It may be that there will be a need to move up a ladder of higher and higher levels of social organization to address a need, either because lower levels are unable or unwilling to act, but the need for rising to higher levels needs to be persuasively demonstrated. The judgment about what subsidiarity requires is context-specific and ought not be determined by abstract political ideologies but by dialogue with those in need as well as knowledge of the empirical situation.

Clarifying Subsidiarity: Society, State, and Mediating Institutions

It is vital to grasp that subsidiarity is a central theme in the Catholic social tradition because it is not first of all a principle regulating the state, although it is often presented that way. Rather, it is an idea closely related to the health of civil society. When Pius XI spoke of society in *Quadragesimo anno*, he quoted Thomas Aquinas on the notion of "order," which is defined as "unity arising from the apt arrangement of a plurality of objects."[106] For the Catholic social tradition, uniformity is not the aim of social life; rather it is order amid a diversity that enriches, delights, and fulfills persons. Pluralism is both recognized and welcomed in social life. The aim of community is to find unity that bonds people together but does not ask people to sacrifice their personal uniqueness and talents. It is diversity that enriches common life and prevents it from being a stultifying similarity rather than, to use Pauline imagery, a body with many members and gifts (1 Cor 12:4–26). Without a shared sense of unity—we are one body—there cannot be communal life; but without many members with gifts that differ, there cannot be the pluralism that avoids a monochromatic picture of social life. For this reason, the Catholic social tradition has fostered the freedom of people to form groups and communities within civil society as fundamental rights of the person.

John XXIII in *Pacem in terris* made clear that because "human beings are by nature social, there arises the right of assembly and association."[107] He affirmed "it is by all means necessary that a great variety of organizations and intermediate groups be established which are capable of achieving a goal which an individual cannot effectively attain by a lone self. These societies and organizations must be considered the indispensable means to safeguard the dignity of the human person and freedom."[108] Again, John XXIII appeals to a society of mutual collaboration in the project of building a society worthy of a person's dignity. Since people are "social by nature they are meant to live with others and to work for one another's welfare." A society that is well-ordered requires that persons "recognize and observe their mutual rights and duties. It also demands that each contribute generously to the establishment of a civic order in which rights and duties are more sincerely and effectively acknowledged and fulfilled."[109]

The organic metaphor that the Catholic social tradition has used to describe social life entails a view of society as an ordered collection of smaller societies and groupings. This viewpoint perdures throughout the tradition and finds support among multiple papal statements. Writing three decades after John XXIII, John Paul sums it up this way: "According to *Rerum novarum* and the whole social doctrine of the church, the social nature of the person is not completely fulfilled in the state, but is realized in various intermediary groups . . . which stem from human nature itself and have their own autonomy, always with a view to the common good."[110] It is the wide variety of intermediary groups, ranging from family to business, cultural to political, social to recreational that constitutes the pluralism of civil society. This broad array of associations allows for various levels of participation in the life of a society, and such participation is essential for the full development of the human person.

Civil society is the locale where people establish their families, enjoy the company of friends, meet neighbors, educate children, and practice their religion. It is constituted by the churches, schools, community centers, labor unions, recreational groups, libraries, social clubs, and the vast array of other voluntary associations where people come together for the purpose of living in communion with others. It is where persons get in touch with their basic humanity—the realm of personal relationships that are governed by values of love, care, trust, responsibility, and solidarity. In the Catholic social tradition there is ample evidence that a robust and vital civil society is crucial to the attainment of human flourishing. Subsidiarity is Catholic shorthand for the practice of fostering, protecting, and assisting the multiple mediating institutions that stand between private life and the larger institutions of state and market.

Precisely because these smaller groups exist with limited resources and power despite their centrality to human well-being and the common good, those organizations with higher levels of resources and power should provide assistance in order to sustain the lower-level groups and enable them to play their role in encouraging human flourishing. At the same time, these groups serve to remind the larger institutions of politics and economics—the state and the market—of their fundamental purpose. Subsidiarity is a way to remind ourselves that what is essential to human life is far more than power and money. When these become ends in themselves, we see the corruption of social and personal life.

So the first important issue that subsidiarity raises up is the distinction between society and the state. The latter is an absolutely vital institution and not to be disparaged, but it is not all of social life. Society is greater than this one essential social institution. Subsidiarity underscores that point within the Catholic social tradition. The vision of public life that is encoded by the language of subsidiarity "is pluralistic in that it assumes no single form of human community is capable of embodying the full human good. It encourages, instead, active participation in multiple forms of human association."[111] That ability to participate in a diverse and rich social life is put at risk whenever any one institution accrues enough power to dominate all other social sectors, be that institution the state or the market.

A healthy society will always be home to a wide range of intermediary groups and associations that permit participation in social life without the interference of state power. Encouragement of a pluralistic civil society, however, is not the same as denigrating the utility of the state. National and regional governance is essential for some aspects of the common good to be protected. Subsidiarity stipulates that the state should support and expand local efforts in serving the common good and personal dignity without stepping away from its own necessary role.

By its own inner logic, civil society moves to political action in the state. This is because civil society is devoted to the building up and expression of the common good, but "there are needs of the common good which it cannot itself fulfill. Conflicts of interest need to be settled and positive steps for the development of society need to be taken which the less formal civil organization cannot undertake."[112] So even in domestic affairs there is a vital role for the state to serve the common good. Furthermore, historical experience reveals some issues must be resolved by resorting to large-scale operations that only a national government, or even international alliances, can adequately address.

A neoliberalism that simply exalts intermediate or mediating institutions, like business corporations, is a misguided effort "to pull subsidiarity into the liberal capitalist ideological camp," and that "would seem as little founded as would an effort to see it as a blueprint for state socialism." Within the Catholic social tradition the appeal to subsidiarity is "not to weaken the responsibility of the state, but to strengthen it by using it not to usurp functions it cannot usefully perform but to support and sometimes create those structures which can."[113] The distinction between society and state should be kept clear even as their dependence upon each other is acknowledged.

The understanding of the state in the Catholic framework is an outgrowth of the communitarian vision of the human person and society. The state is related to the social nature of the person, for it is an institution that gives shape and form to the virtue of solidarity; that is, the state provides public order for the multiplicity of social groupings—families, professional associations, religious communities, economic corporations, social clubs, and the like. From this perspective the state "proceeds by inner moral necessity from the social nature" of the person as a means of developing a rich social life of mutuality and cooperation, which, in turn, permits the full realization of individual personality.[114] The Catholic social tradition sees the state's purpose is to protect and promote the common good. This responsibility, the very reason for the state's existence, is ordained by God who has created humankind in such a way that persons are social; therefore, we have an obligation to contribute to the common good, and this good requires a political institution to protect and promote that goal. Such an understanding of the state's purpose and its consequences is readily distinguished from the classical liberal position where the duty to contribute to a common end is dimly perceived since the state's role is interpreted as merely a convenience which facilitates the individual pursuit of self-interest.

Finally, when discussing subsidiarity it is also important not to consider it as uncritical support for all intermediate groups or mediating institutions. Just as with the state and market, the large mega-institutions of society, so with the smaller ones—all are held to the obligation to contribute to the common good of society. While the Catholic social tradition does not specify what that entails, four sensible guidelines can be proposed.

1. An important aspect of the plight of the poor is often their location on the margins of society; they lack organizational ties, and we should not assume that the poor are participating in existing voluntary associations. Often what is needed at a local level is for existing mediating institutions to reach out to marginal people in the community to welcome them, or, in some cases, to create new locally based organizations which engage the poor.

2. The viability of a mediating institution cannot be presumed simply because it continues to exist. There are both geographic and historical variations in this regard. A group that is powerful in one region may not have the same strength and influence in another locale. There was a time when local parish churches may have been a sponsor or home to a variety of neighborhood organizations. With the decline in church-going populations and the closing of many churches in urban centers and rural areas, there may need to be new mediating institutions established.

3. Groups that move beyond particularity are preferable to those that do not. The aim ought not be simply to promote self-interest groups at the local level but to support forms of association that permit a participant to transcend self-interest, to act on the duty of solidarity. Without ignoring the role of self-interest in getting a person engaged, there should also be an element which expands the outlook of participants beyond their initial interest. At stake is the ability to engage citizens in the task of building community, fostering cooperation, resolving disputes amicably, and contributing to the common good.

4. We must be willing to evaluate the way that a mediating structure relates to the broader values of the society. We need to ethically assess the communal attachments we develop. A Catholic communitarian vision does not assume a live-and-let-live posture which refuses to distinguish between the local chapters of the Aryan Nation or Catholic Charities. Not all mediating structures are created equal, and we must develop criteria for determining those groups and organizations that merit inclusion under subsidiarity as understood in the Catholic social tradition.

CONCLUSION

As has been emphasized throughout this volume, at the same time that it upholds the dignity and uniqueness of the person, the Catholic tradition understands that the perfection of the self is realized only in community. Human beings achieve their self-development through involvement in a dense web of overlapping relationships that create a variety of communal experiences. Classical liberalism's emphasis on the unencumbered individual freely calculating the benefit of entering into a social contract is judged to be neither empirically accurate nor morally desirable. Thus, the liberal model of society as a social contract between independent individuals is opposed on behalf of a viewpoint which emphasizes reciprocity and mutuality.

A collectivist vision is also judged unworthy. While never denying the communal nature of the person, there is the emphasis on the dignity and uniqueness of the person in Catholic social teaching. Treating humankind as one great mass of people, without attention to the uniqueness of personal existence, is not an acceptable alternative to the failings of liberal theory. The social vision of Catholicism demands the individual person not become a mere numerical concept but be given attention within his or her concrete situation, thereby demanding a healthy respect for the particular relationships and communities that nourish the unique human personality. The human person was made for community, and society is a community of communities organically related to one another. It is through participation in a variety of communities that the human person flourishes.

Substantively, solidarity affirms the communitarian understanding that the development of the self is realized only in community. Human beings achieve well-being through involvement in a variety of communal experiences. As an ethical coordinate by which persons may find guidance in building societies that nurture human beings through promoting the common good, solidarity requires persons to dedicate themselves in charity and justice to what Paul VI called "a civilization of love."[115] Solidarity demands pursuit of the good that can only be found in a common life.

While the goods of political community are essential, they are insufficient to encompass all that the common good entails. The goods of family, friendships, and religion are also key components of human life. To presuppose that one undifferentiated community of humankind is adequate to realize the good of each person is to run the risk of creating what Pius XII called "the masses" whose depersonalization leads to the growth of the bureaucratic state.[116] In contrast, the Catholic social tradition strongly supports a rich variety of associations that give life and color to personal and communal experience.

Subsidiarity appears in Catholic social teaching precisely to prohibit the reduction of the richness of human association to one form. In Pius XI's formulation, subsidiarity provided a refinement of the argument of Leo XIII espoused in *Rerum novarum* that the state had not only the right but the duty to intervene in the marketplace and public square. State intervention ought not be approved without guidance, however, and Pius employed subsidiarity to distinguish Catholic social teaching from a collectivist or totalitarian outlook supportive of a state dominating all other forms of communal life.

Subsidiarity must be understood not only in the historical context of past Catholic social teaching but also in the context of contemporary public life and the threats to human welfare, community, and the common good that one finds there. Only if we determine what forces endanger the basic goods held up in the Catholic social tradition can we then grasp what subsidiarity and solidarity ask of us in the present. Surely, Pius XI was correct that the government of a nation-state can put the goods of human dignity and community at risk by overwhelming the institutions of civil society. Yet other forces may also effectively block participation in communal life and thereby deny a person's ability to contribute to and benefit from the common good. The state cannot protect civil society by simply abandoning the mediating institutions of that society to the self-interested forces of the market.

Solidarity and subsidiarity derive from the Catholic social tradition's commitment to the common good and human rights as essential elements of a good society. Solidarity and subsidiarity function as ethical coordinates to guide people in building such a society. In the concluding chapter, we will examine several remaining coordinates that offer insight into what it means to talk of bringing about authentic human development in our present age.

NOTES

1. Rommen, *The State in Catholic Social Thought*, 138.
2. Congregation for the Doctrine of the Faith, *Libertatis Conscientia*, n. 73.
3. Johann Verstraeten, "Solidarity and Subsidiarity," 133.
4. Verstraeten, 134.
5. Anna Rowlands, *Towards a Politics of Communion*, 240.
6. Verstraeten, "Solidarity and Subsidiarity," 134.
7. Recall the discussion of the early church's practice of fraternity and sorority in chapter 3.
8. Gerald Beyer, "The Meaning of Solidarity in Catholic Social Teaching," 12.
9. Rodger Charles, *Christian Social Witness and Teaching*, vol.1, 74.
10. Charles, 91.
11. Charles, 209.
12. Phan, *Social Thought*, 136.
13. Paul Misner, *Social Catholicism in Europe*, 324. As Beyer astutely puts it, "long before becoming a theme of theological reflection, solidarity had been Christian praxis." See, Beyer, "Solidarity in Catholic Social Teaching," 9.
14. Misner, *Social Catholicism*, 325.
15. Franz Mueller, "Solidarism," 906.
16. Mueller, 907.
17. Mueller, 907.
18. Rowlands, *Towards a Politics of Communion*, 244–45.

19. Beyer, "Solidarity in Catholic Social Teaching," 13.
20. Paul Misner, *Catholic Labor Movements in Europe*, 63.
21. Misner, 71.
22. Misner, 72.
23. Mueller, "Solidarism," 907.
24. Matthew Lamb, "Solidarity," 908.
25. Beyer, "Solidarity in Catholic Social Teaching," 13.
26. Rowlands, *Towards a Politics of Communion*, 249.
27. Pius XII, *Summi pontificatus*, n. 35.
28. Pius XII, n. 42.
29. Charles, "Christian Social Witness," vol. 2, 130.
30. Both Verstraeten and Rowlands discuss changes in how solidarity is presented in John's *Mater et magistra*.
31. Verstraeten, "Solidarity and Subsidiarity," 137.
32. Verstraeten, 137.
33. Verstraeten, 137.
34. The word that John XXIII used to identify this sociological process of growing mutual interdependence was "socializzazione" in Italian. Out of concern that it would be misunderstood as approval of socialism, the English translation referred to "an increase in social relationships." See *Mater et magistra*, n. 59.
35. Rowlands, *Towards a Politics of Communion*, 251.
36. Vatican II, *Gaudium et spes*, ns. 24, 25, 26, 29, 31 in particular.
37. Vatican II, n. 32.
38. Vatican II, ns. 38 and 42, respectively. In n. 42 the bishops quote themselves from *Lumen gentium*, n. 1.
39. Paul VI, *Populorum progressio*, n. 1.
40. Albino Barrera, *Modern Catholic Social Documents*, 42.
41. Paul VI, *Populorum progressio*, n. 17.
42. Paul VI, n. 43.
43. CELAM, "Poverty of the Church," n. 10.
44. Synod of Bishops, *Justitia in mundo*, ch. 1.
45. Beyer, "Solidarity in Catholic Social Teaching," 13.
46. Karol Wojtyla, *Towards a Philosophy of Praxis*, 47.
47. John Paul II, *Sollicitudo rei socialis*, n. 38.
48. John Paul II, n. 39.
49. John Paul II, n. 40.
50. Meghan Clark, *The Vision of Catholic Social Thought*, 34.
51. Clark, 35.
52. Benedict XVI, *Deus caritas est*, n. 15.
53. Benedict XVI, *Caritas in veritate*, n. 2.
54. Benedict XVI, n. 2.
55. Benedict XVI, n. 5.
56. Benedict XVI, n. 5.
57. Benedict XVI, n. 38.
58. Benedict XVI, n. 7.
59. Thomas Massaro, *Mercy in Action*, 19.
60. Massaro, 54.

61. Francis, *Laudato Si'*, ns. 159–62.

62. Francis, "Fraternity, the Foundation and Pathway to Peace," n. 1.

63. "Solidarity is rooted in the oneness of the human family with God as our common parent." J. Milburn Thompson, *Introducing Catholic Social Thought*, 60.

64. Thomas Massaro, *Living Justice*, 87.

65. Lisa Cahill, "Globalization and the Common Good," 51.

66. All quotes in the paragraph are from Beyer, "Solidarity in Catholic Social Teaching," 15.

67. Hollenbach, "Afterword: a community of freedom," 334.

68. Hollenbach, 335.

69. Hollenbach, 334.

70. An in-depth treatment of this theme in Catholic social teaching can be found in the work of Donal Dorr, *Option for the Poor and Option for the Earth*.

71. Curran, "The Common Good and Official Catholic Social Teaching," 126.

72. John Paul II, *Sollicitudo rei socialis*, n. 42.

73. Congregation for the Doctrine of the Faith, "Instruction on Christian Freedom and Liberation," n. 68.

74. Marie Vianney Bilgrien, *Solidarity: A Principle, an Attitude, a Duty or the Virtue for an Independent World?*, 105–6.

75. Robert Bellah, "On the Importance of 'Subsidiarity' as a Theme in Catholic Social Teaching," 4; quoting John Coleman, "Neither Liberal nor Socialist: The Originality of Catholic Social Teaching," 17.

77. De Jonge, "Participation in Historical Perspective," 173.

78. Calvez and Perrin, *The Church and Social Justice*, 328.

79. Thompson, *Introducing Catholic Social Teaching*, 61.

80. Höffner, *Christian Social Teaching*, 33.

81. As quoted in Höffner, 33.

82. Wilhelm Emmanuel von Ketteler, as quoted in Höffner, 33.

83. Rommen, *The State*, 301–303.

84. Richard Camp, *The Papal Ideology of Social Reform*, 141,

85. Michael Allsop, "Subsidiarity, Principle of," 928.

86. Pius XI, *Quadragesimo anno*, n. 80.

87. Pius XI, n. 79.

88. Calvez and Perrin, *The Church and Social Justice*, 332.

89. Misner, *Catholic Labor Movements in Europe*, 216.

90. Verstraeten, "Solidarity and Subsidiarity," 135.

91. Massaro, *Living Justice*, 93.

92. Pius XII, *Summi pontificatus*, n. 59.

93. John XXIII, *Mater et magistra*, n. 59.

94. John XXIII, n. 60.

95. John XXIII, *Pacem in terris*, ns. 140–41.

96. See Paul VI, *Populorum progressio*, n. 78 and John Paul II, *Sollicitudo rei socialis*, n.26.

97. All quotes in the paragraph are from John Paul II, *Centesimus annus*, n. 48.

98. John Paul II, "Address at the University of Latvia," n. 4.

99. John Paul II, n. 5.

100. John Paul II, n. 6.

101. Philip Selznick, *The Moral Commonwealth*, 513. Another noted social theorist, Robert Putnam, agrees: "Conservatives are right to emphasize the value of intermediary

associations, but they misunderstand the potential synergy between private organization and the government. *Social capital is not a substitute for effective public policy but rather a prerequisite for it and, in part, a consequence of it.* "The Prosperous Community," 42 (italics in original).

102. Both quotes in the paragraph are from Benedict XVI, *Caritas in veritate*, n. 57.

103. Benedict XVI, n. 58.

104. Rowlands, *Towards a Politics of Communion*, 235.

105. All quotes in the paragraph are taken from Rowlands, *Towards a Politics of Communion*, 235. Lisa Sowle Cahill has noted that subsidiarity is commonly envisioned as entailing vertical relationships, as Pope Francis spoke of top to bottom and bottom-up. Cahill makes the important point that we need to think of subsidiarity as horizontal as well as vertical, reaching out to an array of institutions in a manner that entails power-sharing, information sharing, and cross-cultural encounter. See Cahill, "Globalization and the Common Good," 50.

106. Pius XI, *Quadragesimo anno*, n. 84.

107. John XXIII, *Pacem in terris*, n. 24.

108. John XXIII, n. 25.

109. John XXIII, n. 31.

110. John Paul II, *Centesimus annus*, n. 13.

111. Hollenbach, "Afterword," 331.

112. Charles, *Christian Social Witness*, vol. 2, 393.

113. Bellah, "On the Importance of Subsidiarity," 13.

114. Rommen, *The State in Catholic Social Thought*, 137.

115. Paul VI, "*Regina Coeli* Address for Pentecost" (May 17, 1970).

116. Pius XII, "Christmas Radio Address" (1944).

8

INTEGRAL, JUST, PARTICIPATORY, AND SUSTAINABLE DEVELOPMENT

The Catholic social tradition is concerned with promoting and protecting the development of the human person so that each person is able to attain a state of human flourishing. Of course, there are different paths for a person to thrive and achieve a state of human well-being. Some of the possible paths are really dead ends that effectively frustrate the goal of human flourishing. Hence, the tradition speaks of the *authentic* development of the person, whereby there is genuine growth and progress toward a fuller and richer experience of human life. In this era of modern Catholic social teaching, there have emerged four modifiers that have been employed to indicate a particularly salient aspect of authentic human development. When taken together, these four modifiers of development provide a description of how the Catholic social tradition articulates what authentic human development entails. The four modifiers are integral, just, participatory, and sustainable. In this chapter, we will examine the background and meaning of these four terms that describe authentic human development as understood by the social tradition.

INTEGRAL DEVELOPMENT

On August 17, 2016, Pope Francis issued a formal pronouncement creating a new office (dicastery) within the church's administration.[1] The new office was titled the Dicastery for Promoting Integral Human Development, and with its creation several previously existing administrative bodies, including the Pontifical Council for Justice and Peace and the Pontifical Council *Cor Unam* (One Heart) among others, were merged into the new entity. *Cor Unam* oversaw the Vatican's programs to aid the world's needy, mainly

258

through humanitarian relief efforts globally; the Justice and Peace Council's primary work was "to engage in action-oriented studies based on both the papal and episcopal social teaching of the Church."[2] It is telling that the pope decided to bring the main Vatican branches of the church's social mission into a new body, which began its work on January 1, 2017, under the title of integral human development.

In 1961 when John XXIII called for increased financial aid packages for poor nations in his encyclical *Mater et magistra*, he was aware that the plight of the poorer nations and peoples had to be addressed in a new way. That same year the United Nations had declared the 1960s to be a United Nations Development Decade. John proposed three basic norms for development in his encyclical. First, poor nations should reform their internal governance and operations to ensure both efficiency and fairness.[3] Second, wealthier nations must avoid aid programs that are culturally imperialistic and ignore the experience of the recipient nations.[4] Finally, any new program of aid should not lead to an economic colonialism that replaces the older political colonialism practiced by richer nations.[5]

Six years later, Paul VI issued his major social encyclical *Populorum progressio* (On the Development of Peoples), in which he was concerned that more be said about the global process of development. For him, it was important to clarify the Catholic perspective on development as a goal. This was because he believed that too much of the literature emerging in the decade of the 1960s on the topic of development was reductionistic, focusing only on economic development and on a narrow approach even to that one element. The pope stressed in his encyclical that "development cannot be limited to mere economic growth. In order to be authentic, it must be complete: integral, that is, it has to promote the good of every person and the whole person."[6]

For Paul, the emphasis on economic growth in some development strategies was misguided, not because economic well-being is unimportant but because it can be a trap if individuals or societies turn economic goods into the supreme good of development. Early in his letter, the pope made clear what he thought integral development meant. Every human being is called by God to seek self-fulfillment. At our birth we are endowed with "certain aptitudes and abilities in germinal form, and these qualities are to be cultivated so that they may bear fruit." With the help of others as well as personal effort, through formal and informal educational processes a person moves "toward the goal set for him by the Creator." Individuals may be helped or hindered by external forces, yet each of us is responsible for growing in our humanity and seeking perfection of the self.[7]

Self-development is not to be viewed as an option since just as God's creation was done with a divine purpose, so too does each individual human being have a purpose in accord with God's plan. We ought to use our freedom and reason to gain understanding of that purpose and to seek it of our own accord. "Human self-fulfillment may be said to sum up our obligations" and, as one might expect from a papal teaching, for Paul the "highest goal of human self-fulfillment" is union "with the life-giving Christ."[8] The religious dimension of the human person must not be overlooked in the quest for authentic development.

Another point that one would expect from Catholic social teaching is that the pope follows his thoughts on self-development with the additional comment that each of us "is also a member of society," hence we belong "to the community of humankind." We are "called to further the development of human society as a whole." Each of us has reaped benefits from contemporaries as well as those who have gone before us; therefore, we cannot disregard the welfare of others in our own time as well as "those who will come after us."[9]

For Paul there are stages that lead to authentic development. "The passage from misery toward the possession of necessities, victory over social scourges, the growth of knowledge, the acquisition of culture" are all seen as essential first steps in achieving development. In addition, there is need for "increased esteem for the dignity of others, the turning toward the spirit of poverty, cooperation for the common good, the will and desire for peace." Here we see Paul suggesting higher moral aspects of development that follow, once basic material needs are addressed, along with fundamental socializing processes begun in the first stage. Then a third stage is "the acknowledgement by the person of supreme values, and of God their source and their finality." All these prior stages come to a climax with "faith, a gift of God accepted by the good will of the individual, and unity in the charity of Christ," which permits the person to share in the very life of God.[10] In sum, human development is inevitably a *spiritual* and *moral* project, of which the economic dimension is simply one piece.

Subsequent popes have stayed on the same path as Paul when treating the topic. John Paul II agreed that development has a richer meaning than the single goal of economic improvement. For him it was important that human development not be equated with the myth of progress in the West, and particularly that it not be identified with consumerism, by which he meant excessive consumption of material goods. Like his predecessor, John Paul II was not antimaterialistic; he knew there was an important economic dimension to human development. Yet, like Paul VI, John Paul wanted to emphasize that authentic or genuine development was integral; there were political, cultural, moral, and spiritual dimensions along with the economic. "[T]here is better understanding today that the *mere accumulation* of goods and services, even for the benefit of the majority, is not enough for the realization of human happiness." In fact, for John Paul, the temptation to equate development with material gain alone has led to another human evil; for alongside underdevelopment—the denial of even basic material goods to many—there is the phenomenon of "superdevelopment." This is defined as "an excessive availability of every kind of material goods for the benefit of certain social groups," that "easily makes people slaves of 'possession' and of immediate gratification." This is the very essence of a "civilization of 'consumption' or 'consumerism,' which involves so much 'throwing-away' and 'waste.'"[11] Later in this chapter, we will see that the latter point about "throwing away" will be a key theme in Pope Francis's criticism of the culture of wealthy nations.

To understand Catholic social teaching on this point, it is important not to equate the critique of superdevelopment with the material element proper to genuine development. "The evil does not consist in 'having' as such, but when a desire for 'having' overwhelms the call of 'being' the kind of person who is of high moral character."[12] John Paul cites Paul VI in this regard, that there are stages or levels of development, and that material development is both necessary and good but not a sufficient end in itself, if authentic development is to be achieved. The attainment of development that is true to the vocation of the human person must be in accord with the "*interior dimension*" of men and women; it must be integral development, not ignoring material goods but not solely focused on that one dimension.[13] The interior dimension is what is specific to humans who are "created by God in his image and likeness." The imago Dei theme recalled by John Paul reminds the reader that, according to the Genesis accounts, a human person has both a bodily and spiritual nature, symbolized by being created both from the earth and by the breath of life which God breathed into our nostrils.[14]

Benedict XVI added his voice to that of his predecessors in advocating on behalf of an integral development that does not reduce the human person to *homo economicus,* concerned mainly with maximizing self-interest. His encyclical *Caritas in veritate* has as its English subtitle "On Integral Development in Charity and Truth," and Benedict noted that just as John Paul II issued *Sollicitudo rei socialis* to commemorate *Populorum progressio* by Paul VI, he too wishes to commemorate that document. Benedict even expressed the "conviction that *Populorum progressio* deserves to be considered 'the *Rerum novarum* of the present age.'"[15]

According to his reading of Paul's text, there are two important truths to be drawn from the social vision developed in *Populorum progressio*. "The first is that *the whole Church, in all her being and acting—when she proclaims, when she celebrates, when she performs works of charity—is engaged in promoting integral human development*." So, this element of the social tradition is at the very heart of the nature and mission of the church. "The second truth is that *authentic human development concerns the whole of the person in every single dimension*." Here Benedict reiterates the insight of Paul that authentic development must be integral, that is, attending to the multidimensional nature of the human person. Benedict then asserts, using language similar to John Paul II, "integral human development is primarily a vocation, and therefore it involves a free assumption of responsibility in solidarity on the part of everyone."

With the language of vocation and responsibility, Benedict highlighted the vital importance of the religious and moral dimensions of the person in attaining integral development. Without these dimensions humanity "loses the courage to be at the service of higher goods." By the use of the word "vocation," Benedict maintains his predecessors acknowledged that integral human development is a project, "on the one hand that derives from a transcendent call, and on the other hand that it is incapable on its own, of supplying its ultimate meaning."[15] Within the Catholic social tradition, integral human development is a way to speak about the aim of the moral life: to employ the gift of freedom in such a way that a person grows into the image and likeness of God as found most fully and clearly in the human nature of Jesus of Nazareth. Only an integral development that gives appropriate weight to the moral and religious aspects of the person can be an authentic human development.

In the teaching of Pope Francis, the idea of integral development plays a role similar to Benedict's viewpoint. Francis maintains that the church must speak about integral development because the religious mission of evangelization must be addressed to human beings who are not just spiritual but material. Evangelization cannot be restricted to "the private sphere" nor treated as if "it exists only to prepare souls for heaven."[16] The social tradition of Catholicism, and the papal teaching based upon it, is not an appendage to gospel faith; Francis, like his predecessors, sees integral development as a vital and necessary dimension of the church's life and work.

Furthermore, Francis connects this ecclesial commitment to the witness of its Lord, "Our faith in Christ, who became poor, and was always close to the poor and outcast, is the basis of our concern for the integral development of society's most neglected members."[17] While Francis does not break new ground by citing a particular concern for the poor, his emphatic calls for the church to be close to the least advantaged in the world is noteworthy. It reflects how central the option for the poor has become in papal social teaching of recent times. This focus entails both "working to eliminate the structural causes of poverty and to promote the integral development of the poor, as well as small daily acts of solidarity in meeting the real needs which we encounter."[18]

Again, striking a note first articulated by Paul VI, Francis faults those who see development in terms that are reducible to economic growth with little regard for the distribution of material benefits or the broader range of goods that constitute authentic development. He calls for better economic policies to serve human dignity and the common good. "Human dignity is protected only by promoting the development of the whole human being, by realizing his or her potential for knowledge, responsibility, and freedom in every area of life—political, social, and economic—in such a way that these areas are not merely instrumental in attaining human dignity but become an integral part of the process."[19] Yet, Francis laments that such moral concerns too often "seem to be a mere addendum" and the result is "a political discourse lacking in perspectives or plans for true and integral development."[20]

Where Francis brings a new emphasis in Catholic teaching on development is his discussion of the close connection between human development and our relationship to the natural world. Again and again throughout his landmark encyclical *Laudato Si'*, Francis makes the point that "everything is interconnected."[21] For him, "nature cannot be regarded as something separate from ourselves or as a mere setting in which we live. We are part of nature, included in it and thus in constant interaction with it."[22] Any strategy for development that ignores humanity's shared creatureliness with the rest of nature will distort the human. As he posits, "human life is grounded in three fundamental and closely intertwined relationships: with God, with our neighbor and with the earth itself."[23] A rupture in any one of these relationships will lead inevitably to a rupture with the other two. Hence, he quotes approvingly the 1992 Rio Declaration from a UN sponsored conference: "The protection of the environment is in fact 'an integral part of the development process and cannot be considered in isolation from it.'"[24] This central element in Francis's vision of integral development should be seen as an expansion of Janssen's anthropological framework, discussed in chapter 5, of the human person integrally and adequately considered. Human persons are essentially social, and any adequate understanding of that claim extends to our relations with nonhuman creatures as well as with God and other persons.

To bring this sub-section on integral development in Catholic social teaching to a close, three things should be highlighted. First, the religious life of the human person and the transcendent destiny of the person is intimately linked to their material, social, and cultural flourishing. Salvation is meant for the whole person, not just their disembodied souls. The demeaning and unjust material deprivation that men and women experience in their lives is an obstacle to their flourishing as God's creatures. Second, human development cannot be understood on a purely economic level alone. Authentic development must be integral development, attending to all those conditions that characterize the flourishing of a human person integrally and adequately considered. Among those conditions are the quality of the relationship between the person and the rest of the created order. The social nature of the human extends to an inclusive community with all creation. Third, no one is to be excluded from the process of integral human development. Given the equal dignity of all persons, it would be a failure in justice if whole classes of people or entire groups of nations were prevented from contributing to and benefiting from the fruits of authentic development. This final point leads to the second modifier of development in Catholic social teaching, namely, besides being integral any process and goal of development must be just.

JUST DEVELOPMENT

As Charles Curran has written, "behind the references to justice in papal documents is the Thomistic and neo-scholastic approach to justice with its three different types: commutative, distributive, and legal."[25] Of course, the Thomistic approach to justice was heavily reliant upon the Aristotelian treatment of justice, where the influential distinction between the different parts of the virtue of justice was made. Ever since Aristotle's *Nichomachean Ethics*, "the Western tradition has distinguished three fundamental forms of justice according to the three fundamental social relationships: the relation of equal legal partners to one another, the relation of the social body to its members, and the relation of the members to the social body."[26]

Justice is what orders social life for Aristotle. Distributive justice is what apportions the benefits of the common good so that each person is allowed to develop humanly. Since, according to Aristotle, not all persons or groups participate in the common good in the same way, distributive justice must be proportionate in its equality. Some may have greater merit, or some other basis by which to determine the formula for allocation from the common good.[27] Whereas, when citizens encounter one another on an equal level, for instance in contracts or commerce in the marketplace, the standard of commutative justice is arithmetical, that is, it is equivalent for one-to-one relationships. Finally, because social bodies also have standing as bearers of rights, there is the category of legal justice governing what individuals owe to the common good, how people should be oriented to contributing to the good of the city-state or other collective body.[28]

Following in the Aristotelian tradition, Catholic theology saw justice as a virtue that gives to each person what is due them. It is readily imaginable that a person might meet the external obligation of justice, give to someone what is their due, while lacking the proper internal disposition. However, as a virtue, justice in the true sense requires that one's inner intention be in harmony with the outer behavior. One must have the proper interior orientation to the other as well as perform the appropriate external act. Catholic thought on justice adopted Aristotle's position that justice is the highest of the moral virtues because it is always directed *ad alterum*, to the other; the inner will is properly oriented to care for another beyond the self. Thus, in the Catholic vision of the moral life the human being, social by nature and called to communion, is consistently attuned to others. Justice is the virtue that in its three forms—legal, distributive, and commutative—governs those relationships with others. The virtue of justice calls the person out of a mindset of self-absorption and self-serving behavior to attend to the God and community that calls him or her into covenant.

When Thomas Aquinas treats the idea of legal justice he views it as the justice of the common good. "Its concern is the laws which govern the life of the community and the state towards the actualization of the common good."[29] For Thomas, legal justice is essentially the equivalent of what Aristotle had called general justice. Eventually it took on a narrower meaning so that "'legal' referred primarily to the obligations to obey the just laws of society as the minimal requirement of the common good."[30] Because the common political structure was hierarchical with a single ruler, be it king or prince, Thomists saw legal justice as largely the responsibility of the ruler to see to it that the common good was served by the laws of the land.

Thus, the Catholic social tradition continued with an understanding of justice that was largely Aristotelian but revised by Thomas and later commentators to relate it with the theological virtues, especially charity. That understanding was shaped by a view of the person as oriented to the other, embedded in communal ties, and, to some measure, responsible for the common good of all. The tripartite division of the virtue of justice was the prevailing view; it was not a view informed by scripture so much as by

Aristotle, Thomas, and the natural law reasoning of scholasticism. There was, however, one clear influence on the thinking about justice that stemmed from the biblical witness. Both the Old Testament and the Gospels reveal a God who had a special concern for the poor and vulnerable. The biblical triad of the widow, orphan, and alien in the land remained a moral challenge to Christians throughout the patristic and medieval periods to care for the poor. The teaching and ministry of Jesus underscored that prophetic strand in the biblical tradition, and it led the Catholic social tradition to focus on justice for the poor, which, in turn, led to Catholic social thought's emphasis on distributive justice. Each person should have a minimally decent share in the material goods necessary for a humane life.

Leo XIII and Pius XI

During the pontificate of Leo (1878–1903), it became apparent that many European Catholics of the industrial working class were attracted to socialism's critique of capitalism as they experienced it: low wages, long workdays, little opportunity for advancement, no power to negotiate with management. It was Leo's desire to acknowledge the plight of the worker, what was called at the time the social question. In 1891, in his important encyclical *Rerum novarum*, Leo addressed the social question and acknowledged the legitimacy of the workers' complaints. The pope, however, wanted to provide an alternate strategy than the socialists to secure justice for the working class: not to abolish private ownership of property but to make it possible for workers to acquire property.

Leo's analysis of the situation was that there had been a failure on the part of the state to secure distributive justice for many laborers who were denied adequate benefits from the common good.[31] Part of the solution also entailed recourse to commutative justice, for in Leo's analysis he saw an unfavorable balance of power in the relationship between owner and laborer. Whereas commutative justice presupposed a reasonable equality and freedom of both parties entering into a contract, the actual inequality between capital and labor in the industrial economy of the late nineteenth century made commutative justice impossible. In effect, the situation had evolved to the point that workers were essentially coerced into accepting unfavorable wages and contracts due to the lack of equal standing in the negotiating process.[32] Faced with that situation, Leo was not simply content to exhort the capitalist ownership class to be more generous; he accepted the need for workers to have collective bargaining through membership in labor unions and for the state to accept such arrangements.[33] This was a necessary step to protect the dignity of labor and permit workers to acquire the goods to which they were entitled as contributors to, and sharers in, the common good. Leo sought to level strong criticism against the liberal capitalism of his day without resorting to a socialist solution. He appealed to classic tenets of justice in Catholic social thought for the argument contained in his encyclical.

Important as Leo's letter was for the practice of papal social teaching, it was rather narrowly focused on the "social question" of the time. As Thomas Massaro has observed, "Two key questions that Leo left to be worked out by subsequent church leaders are these: How much inequality is allowable? And what measures should Christians recommend to address excessive inequality?"[34] Leo's immediate successors, Pius X and Benedict XV, did little to advance a response to those questions, but eventually Pius XI (1922–1939) had to face larger questions regarding economic justice due to the crisis of the worldwide depression that began in 1929 and continued through the decade of the 1930s.

In his 1931 letter, *Quadragesimo anno*, Pius introduced a new term to explain his assessment of the economic situation. In paragraph 88 of the encyclical, Pius discussed liberal economics and the emphasis on free markets. He acknowledged that free competition has its place and can be justified, but that it can also give way to an economic individualism that is dangerous for workers and others without power in the marketplace. Pius stated it is "very necessary that economic affairs be once more subjected to and governed by a true and effective guiding principle." He then cited "social justice and social charity" as "lofty and noble principles" to regulate economic life.[35]

Oswald von Nell-Breuning, one of the secret drafters of the papal letter, offered a commentary on the document several years later. About paragraph 88, he wrote that Pius gave "a clear answer" to the question of how "social justice may be implanted into economic society as a regulating force."[36] He cited the document, "The institutions of public and social life must be imbued with the spirit of justice, and this justice must above all be truly operative. It must build up a juridical and social order able to pervade all economic activity."[37] Then von Nell-Breuning commented, "the pope attaches first importance to governmental and social institutions" in bringing this about.[38] According to von Nell-Breuning's reading (again, as one of the unacknowledged drafters of the text), "Social justice is a spiritual and intellectual guiding rule which does not act through itself, but assisted by a power. This power, according to Leo XIII and Pius XI, is the *state*. The right social and economic order is established by the *supreme* authority in society, which in turn is bound by the demands of social justice from which it draws all its legal authority to direct and regulate." A few lines later, von Nell-Breuning made the point that the state should "look first of all to social legislation; it shall bring about a legal social order that will *result in the proper economic order*."[39]

A more recent commentary on *Quadragesimo anno* makes a further contribution in our understanding of Pius XI's viewpoint by noting that "social justice received a fuller official description in Pius XI's 1937 encyclical on atheistic communism, *Divini redemptoris*."[40]

> Now it is of the very essence of social justice to demand for each individual all that is necessary for the common good. But just as in the living organism it is impossible to provide for the good of the whole unless each single part and each individual member is given what it needs for the exercise of its proper functions, so it is impossible to care for the social organism and the good of society as a unit unless each single part and each individual member—that is to say, each individual person in the dignity of their human personality—is supplied with all that is necessary for the exercise of one's social functions.[41]

Pius XI's use of the term "social justice" was an innovation in the tradition.[42] Leo XIII did not use the term in *Rerum novarum*. Leo's immediate successor, Pius X, did use it once to describe Pope Gregory the Great, from the eleventh century, as a great defender of social justice. And Cardinal Pietro Gasparri, Pius XI's Secretary of State, in personal correspondence mentions a solution in the spirit of social justice. Pius XI used the term more formally than these earlier examples in an official letter about a disputed occupation in the Ruhr Valley after World War I and the punitive levying of war reparations. He reminded the victors that in the name of social justice the defeated ought not be strained beyond their capability to pay back war reparations.[43] Then in *Quadragesimo anno* he used the expression again, suggesting, in Bernd Kettern's apt description, that "social justice must strive for the actualization of the common good."[44]

The distinguished church historian Roger Aubert has written that by the twentieth century there was widespread acceptance of the view that concern for workers was not just a matter of charity but also justice. He noted, however, that "theologians and philosophers continued to argue" about what aspect of justice generated the obligation to address the 'social question.'[45]

Many asked why it was necessary to depart from the Thomistic language that had been enshrined in the social tradition. A number of Catholic scholars maintained that social justice was simply another term for the old Thomistic notion of legal justice.[46] Because Pius XI had given approval to the term by his use of it in a formal teaching document of the church, Catholic scholars could not simply ignore the innovation. Yet the term "was not only new in the vocabulary of the popes; it was also new to the common vocabulary of traditional Catholic moral theology."[47]

It will be helpful to know some of the background to Pius's choice of the term before examining how it has evolved as a key modifier, along with integral, for discussing authentic human development. It may seem odd that papal social teaching often addresses specific issues that touch upon justice or even profoundly involve the virtue, yet nowhere does the papal literature deal in a comprehensive way with the meaning of justice. Mainly, this is because the wider tradition of Catholic social thought, like the formal papal social teaching, had presumed that the Thomistic presentation of justice was adequate. There were, however, discussions dating from the nineteenth century among Catholic scholars about the concept of justice. These provide the historical context for understanding what Pius meant when he wrote of social justice.

The Meaning of Social Justice

It was an Italian Jesuit, Luigi Taparelli, who in 1840 coined the term "social justice." Although part of the effort to revive Thomism in the nineteenth century, Taparelli was not a strict follower of Thomas on all matters. For Taparelli, social justice was "first and foremost a personal virtue with regard to the disposition to protect and promote the exercise of the rights and the fulfillment of the duties of others in society."[48] Social justice, therefore, referred "not only to an individual virtue but to a state of affairs that embodies what virtuous people would do and that is conducive to the formation of personal virtue."[49] This secondary meaning of "a state of affairs" has been described by Thomas Behr as "a socioeconomic and political order, the actual arrangement of institutions, laws, and policies that operate to protect and promote the same exercise of rights and duties of individuals who make up that society."[50] Taparelli apparently used social justice to distinguish his view from that of legal justice. According to Normand Paulus, by the nineteenth century the traditional term of Thomas had been narrowed down (misleadingly) to mean obedience to properly enacted laws.[51] The more accurate understanding of legal justice in Thomas was that of Aristotle's general justice, that is, that form of justice which directs all the other virtues to the common good. Thomas called that legal justice because for him a proper law directs our action to the common good. Understood in that manner, law for Thomas entailed not just civil law but the natural and eternal law as well.[52] Taparelli's social justice would therefore be quite similar to what Thomas meant by legal justice.

While Taparelli's term did not catch on immediately or widely within Catholicism, it did get used, although throughout the nineteenth century there was always a suspicion that social justice had something to do with socialism.[53] In 1905 during the papacy of Pius X, a time when Rome was even more unfriendly to anyone or anything being cast as socialist, the German Jesuit Heinrich Pesch used *Soziale Gerechtigkeit* in his writings. Pesch was an influential figure among German Catholics, and from this point on most German Catholic authors used "social justice" but took care to identify it with legal justice.[54] Recall that among the disciples of Pesch was another German Jesuit, Oswald von Nell-Breuning, who was central to the writing of *Quadragesimo anno*. According to Aubert, on the matter of social justice, "Basically, what we are talking about here is the rediscovery of a long-forgotten aspect of traditional Thomist doctrine, but henceforward presented under the veil of a new expression."[55]

Nonetheless, there remained questions about just what Pius XI's exact aim was in using the term.[56] If one examines Pius's explanation in *Divini redemptoris*, written six years after *Quadragesimo anno*, it is evident that the pope saw social justice as demanding from each person what is necessary for the promotion of the common good. In that sense he is linking it to the category of legal justice in Thomas. However, the economic experience of the twentieth century led Pius to bring a new inflection to the notion of legal justice as Thomas had explained it in the thirteenth century. If legal or social justice was to promote the common good, there must be greater attention than in the past to the challenge of structural or institutional change and not simply the duties of the individual.

As noted earlier, paragraph 88 of *Quadragesimo anno* includes Pius's comment about how the institutions of social life must be "imbued with the spirit of justice" and that justice must be made operative throughout society by means of social legislation enacted by the state. Social justice becomes the guiding principle of state activity as it regulates and orientates the economic order to the common good. Later in that document, Pius summarizes the remedies he sees as necessary to overcome the social evils of the time: "The public institutions of the nations should be such as to make all human society conform to the requirements of the common good, that is, the norm of social justice."[57] This theme of structural change as an element in the idea of social justice is a departure from the more static view of social order that

Leo and previous popes had held. Pius XI's legacy of social justice is that it "concerns itself with the institutions that structure and facilitate the good of the whole social order. When such institutions fail to promote the common good, social justice calls for change and restructuring which enhanced both the good of the human persons and the common good."[58]

An important point to add regarding Pius and social justice is that although the common good cannot be complete without social justice, it is also true that more is required. For "justice must be leavened and enlivened by the virtue of social charity and love."[59] Put simply, "social justice removed obstacles" to the common good, "while social charity perfected the unity of the human family. Social justice was about structures."[60]

Social Justice in Recent Church Statements

In his 1967 encyclical *Populorum progressio*, Paul VI put the issue of social justice into a global context. He maintained that "local and individual undertakings are no longer enough. The present situation of the world demands concerted action based on a clear vision of all economic, social, cultural, and spiritual aspects."[61] The sheer scope of the new social question—the plight of the world's poor—demanded, in Paul's mind, that the remedies be adequate to the problem. For him that meant the obligations that had been talked about in the past for individuals to contribute to the common good now applied also to nations contributing to a global common good.[62]

It was 1961 when John XXIII in *Mater et magistra* called attention to the "demands of the common good, on both the national and world levels."[63] He then added that perhaps the most pressing question of our day "concerns the relationship between the economically advanced commonwealths and those that are in process of development."[64] Two years later in *Pacem in terris,* John wrote of the "universal common good," making an appeal in the hope that each individual nation, "whilst conscious of its own individual rights and duties, will work in a relationship of equality towards the attainment of the universal common good."[65] As with earlier papal descriptions of the common good at local and national levels, social or general justice is an essential part of the universal common good.[66]

Within the context of a universal or global common good, Paul VI introduced a new topic in Catholic social teaching, the ethics of international trade. Pointing out the similarity between the situation of owners and laborers in Leo XIII's time with the failure of commutative justice in trade relations, Paul wrote "the teaching of Leo XIII in *Rerum novarum* is always valid: if the positions of the contracting parties are too unequal, the consent of the parties does not suffice to guarantee the justice of their contract." He went on to insist that "what was true of the just wage for the individual is also true of international contracts."[67] The solution to the problem of a situation where commutative justice is not possible due to dramatic inequality between the parties is to turn to social justice to alter the structure of international trade. "In trade between developed and under-developed economies, conditions are too disparate and the degrees of genuine freedom available too unequal. In order that international trade be human and moral, social justice requires that it restore to the participants a certain equality of opportunity."[68]

This perspective was also characteristic of the document *Justice in the World*, which emerged out of the Synod of Bishops that took place in 1971. At that gathering in Rome, the assembled bishops proposed that confronted by international structures of domination the cause of justice depends on a commitment to genuine development. The bishops stated that this commitment is "expressed in awareness of the right to development," which should be understood "as a dynamic interpenetration of all those fundamental human rights upon which the aspiration of individuals and nations are based." Furthermore, the right to development demands "that the general condition of being marginal in society be overcome, so that an end will be put to the systematic barriers" that oppose the full development of individuals and entire nations.[69] The justice that requires transformation of systems and structures for the sake of the common good—locally, nationally, globally—is what falls under the title of social justice.

In the *Compendium of the Social Doctrine of the Church*, published by the Vatican in 2004, one finds this summation:

> The Church's social Magisterium constantly calls for the most classical forms of justice to be respected: *commutative, distributive* and *legal justice*. Ever greater importance has been given to social justice, which represents a real development in *general justice*, the justice that regulates social relationships according to the criterion of observance of the *law. Social justice*, a requirement related to the *social question* which today is worldwide in scope, concerns the social, political and economic aspects and, above all, the structural dimension of problems and their respective solutions.[70]

Social Justice, Distributive Justice, and Equality

One final remark about justice, particularly social justice, in Catholic social teaching should be made. Pius XI in *Quadragesimo anno* seemed to include distributive justice within social justice. Beginning in paragraph 56 of the encyclical, the pope discusses the guiding principle of just distribution. He begins by observing that the goods of the earth are meant for all, but that does not abolish the right of people to own private property. Yet, private property cannot become so concentrated among one class that other classes are effectively denied the possibility of ownership or the use of goods sufficient to maintain human dignity. The individual's right of private property still must serve the overall common good. Pius then writes, "By these principles of social justice one class is forbidden to exclude the other from a share in the profits. This law is violated by an irresponsible wealthy class who, in their good fortune, deem it a just state of things that they should receive everything and the laborer nothing."[71]

On the other hand, and to distinguish between the Catholic position and socialism, as Pius understood it, the law of social justice "is violated by the propertyless class, when, strongly aroused because justice is ignored . . . they demand for themselves all the fruits of production."[72] Pius wanted to steer between the extremes of an absolute right to private property with no regulation on ownership and the abolition of private property and the rights of those who own and invest capital. He concluded his comment on just distribution with the following: "Each class, then, must receive its due share, and the distribution of created goods must be brought into conformity with the demands of the common good and social justice."[73]

Calvez and Perrin believe that social justice in Pius XI had to do with "presiding over the division of wealth which has been produced by human activity." They also show that Pius XII, in a speech to a Catholic Action group in Italy, reflected a similar understanding when he said that in the name of social justice the church opposed "the accumulation of wealth in the hands of a relatively small number of exceedingly rich people, while vast numbers are condemned to pauperism." And on another occasion when speaking to a group of German bishops in the late 1940s, Pius XII said social justice ought "to regulate suitably the sharing and the using of wealth, so that it is not concentrated excessively in one place while it is lacking entirely in another."[74] So in the minds of both Pius XI and Pius XII social justice is closely linked with distributive justice when wealth inequality becomes so excessive that it threatens the integrity of the common good. In his close examination of the language of social justice in Catholic thought, Paulus maintains that this usage was correct for it employed social justice "to command the acts of distributive justice in the name of the common good."[75]

The question of distributive justice or of structuring the economic order so as to secure a decent measure of material well-being for all, as social justice would require, raises the issue of equality and how much inequality is morally acceptable. At Vatican II, the bishops of the Catholic church announced that "the basic equality of all must receive increasingly greater recognition." While basing the claim of fundamental equality of all persons on the belief in divine creation, the imago Dei, redemption in Christ, and the offer of eternal life as part of each person's existence, the bishops acknowledge that all people are not equal "from the point of view of varying physical power and the diversity of intellectual and moral resources." Yet, "although rightful differences exist," the equal dignity of persons demands that "a more humane and just condition of life be brought about." This is necessary because "excessive economic and social differences between the members of the one human family or population groups cause scandal, and militate against social justice, equity, the dignity of the human person, as well as social and international peace."[76]

Recall the two questions cited earlier that Thomas Massaro posed regarding Leo's call for justice for the industrial worker. What Leo left out were answers regarding how much inequality is too much and what Christians should advocate in reaction to excessive inequality. It is evident that leaving basic needs unaddressed violates the norm of social justice in a society. One hundred years after Leo's encyclical, John Paul II issued a reflection on the heritage of papal social teaching and, while endorsing free markets, went on to state, "there are many human needs which find no place on the market. It is a strict duty of justice and truth not to allow fundamental human needs to remain unsatisfied, and not to allow those burdened by such needs to perish." This is so because "even prior to the logic of fair exchange of goods and the forms of justice appropriate to it, there exists something which is due to persons because they are persons, by reason of their lofty dignity."[77]

Unlike other eras in time, ours is not one where the economy is strained to provide mere subsistence. Rather, there is genuine abundance available, enough for all, if there were less inequality in our world. It is evident that our aim should not be a right to subsistence but a right to authentic development. That entails goods and services that permit each person to flourish as a human being. Obviously, what is required for human flourishing is more historically and culturally conditioned than the more constant biological needs of mere subsistence. In this modern era of Catholic social teaching one finds a concern for people that goes beyond simple physical existence. When Leo XIII expressed his interest in the lives of workers in an industrial economy he wanted to see decent wages, safe working conditions, opportunities for securing access to health care, good housing, and basic education. Subsequent popes have pressed for even more expansive agendas that permit human flourishing as Paul VI's description of integral development demonstrates, and as

John XXIII and John Paul II's list of human rights attests.[78] The concept of the common good is seen in the Catholic social tradition as requiring members of a society to meet the demands of social justice, which includes sacrifice on the part of the privileged in order to secure benefits for those whose situations are precarious. Authentic development is more than an aspiration; it is a right, and as such it imposes duties on individuals and societies.[79]

The duties that derive from a right to development do not lead to an unqualifiedly egalitarian society or world. There are other aspects to distributive justice that ought to be included in addition to that of need.[80] There is little question that distributive justice, as understood within the tradition, requires a measure of economic equality if the common good is to be respected; yet the equality to be sought is not a strict equality applied to all persons in all cases, but a relative equality that permits differences in wealth for reasons that also serve the common good, for instance matters of effort or concern for productivity. A contemporary theorist of Catholic social thought acknowledges the "major challenge" that is entailed in "bridging the gap between the ideals of the Christian principle of equal dignity, on the one hand, and the blatant perennial differences of wealth and privilege that divide people into distinct social classes, on the other hand."[81]

We might label the dominant outlook of the Catholic social tradition, a view articulated in many recent papal documents, to be a position of relative egalitarianism. Following Drew Christiansen, the modifier "relative" is crucial to understanding the Catholic viewpoint. The equality being sought is not an absolute leveling by which everyone receives the exact same benefit and shares the exact same burden. *Rather, it points to a situation in which inequalities are held within a defined range set by moral limits.*[82] The range of moral limits is set by the demands of social justice. This, of course, "is not a magic formula out there somewhere, waiting to be applied automatically to concrete situations."[83] As Normand Paulus puts it: "all appeals to the concept of social justice must be supported by cogent rational arguments that show why the common good requires such and such an act in these specific circumstances.... Social justice imposes on each of us the stringent duty to fulfill our obligations to the whole and, in this way, to achieve our own highest proper good."[84]

PARTICIPATORY DEVELOPMENT

The assembled bishops at the 1971 Synod spoke about "liberation through development." By this expression they sought to point out that true development had to avoid a situation where wealthier nations dictated both the goal and means of the development process and that poorer nations were left in a state of passive acceptance, reflecting a "new form of colonialism."[85] Instead, the bishops insisted "it is impossible to conceive true progress without recognizing the necessity—within the political system chosen—of a development composed both of economic growth and participation."[86] That last word, participation, quickly became significant, joining "integral" and "just" as a third modifier of development within the Catholic social tradition. What the bishops sought were processes of development that were not controlled by economic elites living either in the rich or poor nations. They were opposing development as a "top down" process, instead envisioning development as an inclusive process to be directed, at least in part, by the poor themselves. Communal life is "one marked by participation, which is the optimal inclusion of all involved voices in a decision and in the sharing of the burden as well as the benefits of life together in a given locality."[87] This suggests participation is not just any sort of role in a community, some sort of insignificant procedural task; rather it must contribute to the subject's process of authentic human development. As Barrera states, "The principle of participation can be defined as the equitable allotment of the burdens and gains of community life—a balanced sharing that affords everyone a meaningful chance to contribute to and benefit from the common life."[88]

This idea of "participation" as central to authentic development has a background in the social tradition's emphasis on the role and dignity of work. As Catholic social thought evolved during the age of industrialization in Europe and North America, there was a growth in awareness that workers were becoming interchangeable cogs in a wheel, often reduced to rather mindless repetition of a segment within the production process. Since it is through labor that the vast majority of people participate in the economic life of a community, the alterations in the experience of labor in the industrial age led Catholics concerned about social issues to reflect upon the nature of work.

The French nobleman and parliamentary leader Alban de Villeneuve-Bargemont was, according to at least one French historian, "the true initiator of social Catholicism," at least in France.[89] He was a conservative Catholic who supported the restoration of the Bourbon dynasty, but unlike many of his aristocratic peers, he was deeply concerned about the working classes. Villeneuve-Bargemont provided a conservative critique of industrial capitalism. Against those supporters of laissez-faire economics, he "saw a role for the state in alleviating economic distress" and also "pointed to the necessity for involving the working population in the conduct of their own activity, at least to the extent of changing the laws to encourage mutual aid societies and something like credit unions run by workers." While these were small steps, it was Villeneuve-Bargemont who "raised for the first time the issue of emancipation, the participation of the lower classes in self-administered associations."[90]

An interesting illustration of how participation entered into the Catholic social tradition is found in the story of the Women's Trade Union League (WTUL) in the United States, described by a labor historian as "the most effective source of labor support for women in the early twentieth century."[91] The WTUL represented a different understanding of the role of a labor union than what became the norm during the twentieth century as the American Federation of Labor (AFL) became dominant. "The rise of the AFL in the 1890s signaled a turn from political and economic reform to trade unionism 'pure and simple.' Unions associated with the AFL generally opposed broad programs of social reconstruction."[92] Samuel Gompers, the head of the AFL, was a strong advocate of such trade unionism "pure and simple," that is, the task of a union was to negotiate the best possible package of wages and benefits for workers in the union. Essentially, it was organized labor as an interest group focused narrowly on the economic self-interest of union members, whereas the WTUL was foremost among those labor associations that promoted a broader civic vision. For this group, the idea of freedom was not simply the ability to enter into voluntary contracts negotiated by the union. Instead, for the leaders of the WTUL "freedom was equated with participation in self-government, which required, in turn, the possession of certain habits, dispositions, qualities of character."[93] Mary Kenney O'Sullivan and Agnes Nestor were two Catholic women who were principal leaders of the WTUL as well as related labor associations. The former saw a trade union not only as a vehicle for better wages and working conditions but believed that trade unionism was a necessary "context for forming women in virtues of self-initiative, courage, and solidarity."[94] Agnes Nestor "envisioned the trade union as a 'training school' of civic virtues which could provide the opportunity for members to learn, not only the rights, but responsibilities of citizenship, and to consider matters from the point of view of the common good."[95] She helped establish the first residential training institute for union leadership and was a proponent of extending democracy in political life into industry as well, maintaining that "women have a fundamental right to have a voice regarding the conditions under which they work with the opportunity for self-government and self-protection."[96]

Perhaps the best-known figure in American Catholic social thought in the first half of the twentieth century was Rev. John Ryan. His first major initiative was a book published in 1906 on the idea of a living wage that had been his doctoral dissertation at the Catholic University of America. Ryan was interested in promoting ties between Catholics and the politics of the Progressive era prior to World War I. During this time Ryan began to advocate not only for a living wage but also a change in the status of workers, and this became the second part of his social reform package. Though published under the name of the American bishops in 1919, the "Bishops Program for Reconstruction" was essentially a memorandum drafted by Ryan to propose a social agenda for the US episcopacy after the war. Part of that agenda was to promote greater sharing in the workplace at three levels: in management, in profits, in ownership. Sharing in ownership meant partial ownership through stock-sharing arrangements; sharing in profits meant changing the practice of all profits going to owners after expenses were paid; and sharing in management meant shared decision-making in areas that directly affect the worker—shop conditions, discipline, installation of new machinery, or production techniques. The aim was to revise the workplace along the lines of industrial democracy rather than what Ryan saw as the feudalism of the existing system.

Ryan argued that the vast majority of workers were not children but adults and "share in some degree the desire which is native in every adult human being to have some voice in determining the material conditions in which he lives and works. They have the desire which inheres in all normal persons to be something more than dependent instruments." When such desires are frustrated, Ryan argued, it becomes difficult for a worker to achieve that maturation of the person to which individuals are called as free and responsible beings. The flaw in the present managerial approach is that a worker "remains merely an executor of orders imposed by somebody else. His creative faculties, directive faculties, whether they be great or small, get absolutely no opportunity for expression." For Ryan this was an unacceptable state of affairs, "either for the individuals directly concerned or for society, to have large masses of men acting merely as the obedient instruments of other men, without any opportunity of exercising those higher faculties, those directive faculties, which all of us like to exercise to some extent."[97]

These examples of Catholic leaders in the Women's Trade Union League and the writing of Catholic theorists like Ryan are early hints at how the idea of participation came into the Catholic social imagination. As the WTUL and Ryan made clear, participation was important for the status and development of the individual worker, but also it was for the good of society to have people capable of exercising judgment and using their capabilities to contribute to the common good not only of a business enterprise but of a democratic nation.

It was not only in the United States, however, that the idea of participation became associated with the Catholic concern for industrial workers. At the end of the nineteenth century and again after World War I, there was talk of fostering worker participation in the industrial setting. Then in the post–World War II period there arose the demand for what in Germany was called *Mitbestimmung* or co-determination in the workplace. This demand was also found in France, Belgium, and the Netherlands. Legislation was proposed and often passed with regard to the creation of workplace councils.[98] A leading Catholic proponent of *Mitbestimmung* was the Jesuit Oswald von Nell-Bruening, mentioned earlier in regard to Pius XI and the topic of social justice. Nell-Bruening argued on two grounds for employee participation in the workplace. "According to him, the first and foremost argument is that workers who can participate in forms of co-administration no longer will be used as a pure means of production like raw materials, half-spent products, machines, and fossil fuels. . . . Working people have the right not to be treated as pure receivers of orders."[99] The second argument made by Nell-Bruening about the industrial worker is "they want to be treated in a dignified manner, but also they want to play a full-fledged role in the enterprise according to their capacity and competence. They do not want to be a simple subject, but want to face the employer as sensible and responsible humans and be treated as such, not as immature children." It is easy to hear echoes of Ryan in these arguments.

During this same period, one sees the participation theme migrate from economics, specifically work and workers, to politics, specifically democracy. During World War II, Pius XII and other Vatican leaders began to turn their attention to reconstructing a post-war European order. With the threat of the fascists and Nazis turned away, the remaining danger was Soviet communism. While there were varying formulations of what was meant by and hoped for in a democratic Europe, there was strong interest in supporting a political order that could withstand the efforts of communists to expand their power into European countries not already under the shadow of Soviet imperialism. Hence, Pius XII began to uphold the virtues of democratic politics. "In his Christmas address of 1944 he initiated a new development in papal thinking by arguing that the power to participate in the political process and thus to shape one's own future was essential to the preservation and development of human dignity."[100]

Participation in Recent Papal Teaching

John XXIII in *Mater et magistra* stayed with the economic order when he wrote of participation, but he did so with an appreciation for the various work settings and diverse kinds of business organizations existing in the modern age.[101] At the outset of the section treating worker participation, John made clear it was important that "justice be observed not merely in the distribution of wealth, but also in regard to the conditions under which workers engaged in productive activity have an opportunity to assume responsibility and to perfect themselves by their efforts.[102] The pope discussed worker cooperatives, family farms, and artisan enterprises, besides medium-size and large scale enterprises, acknowledging that it is not possible to present detailed norms for workplace partnership applicable to each sort of business. "Nevertheless," he continued, "we do not doubt that employees should have an active part in the affairs of the enterprise wherein they work, whether these be private or public."[103] And later he repeated his conviction, "it should be emphasized how necessary, or at least very appropriate, it is to give workers an opportunity to exert influence outside the limits of the individual productive unit, and indeed within all ranks of the commonwealth."[104]

That latter phrase of the foregoing quote hints at John's thoughts about participation in political as well as economic life. In *Pacem in terris,* he observed, "workers all over the world refuse to be treated as if they were irrational objects without freedom, to be used at the arbitrary disposition of others. They insist that they be always regarded as people with a share in *every* sector of human society."[105] In part two of his letter, John discussed the relationship between the citizen and the state where he simply declared: "It is in keeping with their dignity as persons that human beings should take an active part in government. . . . People will find new and extensive advantages in the fact that they are allowed to participate in government."[106]

At Vatican II the topic of participation also received attention. In Chapter 2 of Part One of the Pastoral Constitution, the bishops discuss the Catholic vision of life in society. One of the governing principles for a humane society is "the will to play one's role in common endeavors should be everywhere encouraged. Praise is due to those national procedures which allow the largest possible number of citizens to participate in public affairs with genuine freedom."[107] The bishops comment on participation again when they address economic life and political life in the second part of the document. The world of work is a world where persons "work together, that is, free and independent human beings created in the image of God. Therefore the active participation of everyone in the running of an enterprise should be promoted."[108] On the matter of participation in the political realm there is likewise a clear statement of support for active participation.[109]

In the spring of 1971, prior to the meeting of the Synod of Bishops in the fall of that year, Paul VI issued an apostolic letter to commemorate the eightieth anniversary of *Rerum novarum. Octogesima adveniens* allowed Paul to offer his reflections on the pressing issue of global justice after having attended the historic meeting of the bishops of Latin America in Medellín, Colombia where they issued important statements on justice, poverty, and peace. In a valuable contribution to the Catholic social tradition, Paul observed that in the present situation "two aspirations persistently make themselves felt" in the modern world and "they grow stronger to the extent" that people today become "better informed and better educated: the aspiration to equality and the aspiration to participation, two forms of a person's dignity and freedom."[110] These aspirations are fundamental, given their connection to dignity and freedom. But they have taken shape over the course of history, amid the evolving conditions of human existence, in a way that would not have been intelligible to premodern men and women.

For Paul it is important to recognize that claims about "progress" must be examined since some understandings of the word fall prey to economic reductionism and do not respect the integral nature of true human development. "The quality and the truth of human relations, the degree of participation and of responsibility, are no less significant and important for the future of society than the quantity and variety of the goods produced and consumed."[111] Particularly significant for Paul is that a "need is felt to pass from economic to politics."[112] Here Paul moves beyond John's treatment focused mainly on economic life in *Mater et magistra*. This move by Paul is due to people demanding a larger share in responsibility and decision-making regarding their lives. Paul agrees such responsibility should extend to the social and political spheres. Although he recognized that many decisions in the sociopolitical realm are complex, "these obstacles must not slow down the giving of wider participation in working out decisions, making choices and putting them into practice."[113]

At the 1971 Synod the attending bishops provided a much-quoted statement at the outset of their document. "Action on behalf of justice and participation in the transformation of the world fully appear to us as a constitutive dimension of the preaching of the Gospel, or, in other words, of the Church's mission for the redemption of the human race and its liberation from every oppressive situation."[114] Cited often in discussions of ecclesiology and the nature of the church's social mission, it is also significant for our purpose to note that the bishops see participation in social transformation as central to Christian faith. This clearly demonstrates that the idea of participation has moved beyond the economic arena to be applicable to the whole range of activities that are social and political.[115]

The Congregation for the Doctrine of the Faith issued a document in 1986 titled "Instruction about Christian Freedom and Liberation," which gave strong support to the theme of participation in Catholic social teaching: "participation is a necessity which beyond just sharing in the fruits of work must accept a true communal dimension on the level of projects, businesses, and responsibilities."[116] That statement came in the same year the American bishops issued their pastoral letter on the economy which addressed participation as central for understanding social justice. *"Basic justice demands the establishment of minimum levels of participation in the life of the human community for all persons.* The ultimate injustice is for a person or group to be treated actively or abandoned passively as if they were nonmembers of the human race."[117] The bishops then go on to say,

> Recent Catholic social thought regards the task of overcoming these patterns of exclusion and powerlessness as a most basic demand of justice. Stated positively, justice demands that social institutions be ordered in a way that guarantees all persons the ability to participate actively in the economic, political, and cultural life of society. The level of participation may legitimately be greater for some persons than for others, but there is a basic level of access that must be made available for all. Such participation is an essential expression of the social nature of human beings and of their communitarian vocation.[118]

The very next year, 1987, John Paul II issued his encyclical, *Sollicitudo rei socialis,* commemorating the twentieth anniversary of Paul VI's letter on development, *Populorum progressio.* When John Paul discussed the nature of authentic development, he noted several characteristics, among which was "development either becomes shared in *common* by every part of the world or it undergoes a *process of regression* even in zones marked by constant progress. This tell us a great deal about the nature of *authentic* development: either *all* the nations of the world participate, or it will not be true development."[119] Towards the end of the encyclical, the pope points out that development requires "a spirit of initiative on the part of the countries which need it."[120] Part of that initiative is that the poorer *"nations themselves* will have to identify their own *priorities* and clearly recognize their own needs, according to the particular conditions of their people, their geographical setting and their cultural traditions." He suggests for some nations the emphasis will be on food production, for other nations it might be literacy and basic education, perhaps others require access to a broader culture and easy access to information. He then states that there will be nations in need of reform of unjust structures, "and in particular their *political institutions*, in order to replace corrupt, dictatorial, and authoritarian forms of government by *democratic* and *participatory* ones." After all, he concludes, "the 'health' of a political community" is measured by "the free and responsible participation of all citizens in public affairs, in the rule of the law and in respect for the promotion of human rights."

While the idea of participation has clearly transferred over to social and political life since its early appearance in writing focused on industrial workers, that latter concern has not been forgotten. In the *Compendium* of Catholic social teaching published in 2004 there is a vital paragraph on the right to participate as it applies to work, which states this topic deserves "greater consideration." Citing John Paul's encyclical *Laborem exercens*, it is said that "each person is fully entitled to consider himself a part owner of the great workbench" where he or she labors.[121] This entails strategies for worker ownership of capital and worker associations with the freedom to make decisions about the common good of the workplace.[122]

To sum up this survey of the idea of participation in Catholic social teaching, we might say that it began as an element in the defense of the rights of workers in the industrial era, moved to being a theme in discussions about the value of political democracy, and eventually to a broader application relevant to political and social life as well as economics. In so doing participation became a central idea for understanding the nature of authentic development in the lives of persons as well as within and between nation-states.

Conclusion to Participation as an Element
in Authentic Development

When the Catholic social tradition speaks of the freedom to participate, the freedom in question is the right to share in decisions that structure political, social, and economic life since these are vital to human dignity and community. People mature and develop by using their freedom and intelligence to exercise moral agency and accepting the correlative responsibilities that accompany life in communion with others. The freedom to participate is really the freedom to be a contributing member of a community, and community, as explained in chapters 3 and 4, is intrinsically connected to the experience of human dignity.

To contribute to the common good of a community or society is one of the duties arising from social justice; hence, participation is an important way for a person to fulfill the expectations that come with being a member of a group. It is a vehicle whereby a person actualizes the responsibility that comes with the task of building communities where one can attain human flourishing and also assist others to advance that same end for themselves. From a faith perspective, the goal of the Christian life is to give oneself away to others in loving service. Dying to self through generous acts of self-donation that enrich the lives of others is a clear gospel mandate: "Very truly, I tell you, unless a grain of wheat falls into the earth and dies, it remains just a single grain; but if it dies, it bears much fruit" (John 12:24). The opportunity to participate is the opportunity for a person to enter into relationships with others so that the process of self-giving can happen and the grace of mutual self-giving take place. Hence, within the Catholic social tradition, participation is essential to the vocation of discipleship, and societies can be assessed by the way in which they facilitate or frustrate a person's ability to participate in the life of the group.

In sum, in Catholic theology participation is intimately related to freedom for self-determination, the attainment of justice in a community or society, the promotion of the common good, and the opportunity for a person to both give themselves away and receive the self-gift of others.

SUSTAINABLE DEVELOPMENT

The fourth element of development besides it being integral, just, and participatory is that it be sustainable. In Catholic social thought, the idea of sustainable development addresses a dual concern: that development be sustainable for all people, especially the poor; and that development be sustainable for the integrity of the earth. This linkage of what might be called human ecology with natural ecology has been emphasized by Pope Francis. In the encyclical *Laudato Si'*, the pope places the human in a relational context, emphasizing the communitarian nature of the person. More than in the teaching of any previous pope, Francis expands the range of relationships to include not only the present human community but relations with nonhuman nature. For Francis the absolutely vital task is to get the relationships right.[123] As he states in his encyclical, "It cannot be emphasized enough how everything is interconnected."[124] The following quote makes clear his outlook: "We are faced not with two separate crises, one environmental and the other social, but with one complex crisis which is both social and environmental. Strategies for a solution demand an integrated approach to combating poverty, restoring dignity to the excluded, and at the same time protecting nature."[125]

In *Laudato Si'* Francis uses the term "integral ecology" to capture his insight. While not an entirely new term as the International Theological Commission had used it in a 2009 document,[126] it is Francis who has made it central to a Catholic approach to the environment. He used the expression eight different times in his encyclical. The term "combines our concern for natural ecology and human ecology"; it is to prevent "viewing either one in isolation."[127] For Francis, what is needed is a recapturing of the proper biblical vision of creation and humanity's role in the Creator's plan. Only by reimagining our theological anthropology to avoid a destructive anthropocentrism can we hope to develop an integral ecology that will be sustainable for both humans and all the rest of creation. To begin that work, Francis provides a reflection on the Old Testament that is in tune with recent biblical scholarship.

Chapter 26 of the book of Deuteronomy contains a succinct statement of the historical faith of the Israelite people. The context for the passage is an instruction as to how to celebrate in thanksgiving for a successful harvest. Each household head is to go to the designated place of worship and present a basket of the first fruits of the harvest to the priest in office at the time. After the basket is accepted, the believer is told to declare in the presence of God:

> A wandering Aramean was my ancestor; he went down into Egypt and lived there as an alien, few in number, and there he became a great nation, mighty and populous. When the Egyptians treated us harshly and afflicted us, by imposing hard labor on us, we cried to the Lord, the God of our ancestors; the Lord heard our voice and saw our affliction, our toil, and our oppression. The Lord brought us out of Egypt with a mighty hand and an outstretched arm, with a terrifying display of power, and with signs and wonders; and he brought us into this place and gave us this land, a land flowing with milk and honey. (Deut 24:5b–9)

Over time the conviction grew that Yahweh was not simply the tribal god of Israel, but the God who was the creator of all the world. By the time of the Babylonian exile this conviction had become accepted to the point that in the final part of the book of Isaiah, written at the time of the exile's end, there was a belief that all people will be brought to Jerusalem to worship at the Temple and "their burnt offerings and their sacrifices will be acceptable on my altar, for my house shall be called a house of prayer for all peoples" (Isaiah 56:7). It is about this time in Israel's history that the Genesis accounts of creation were put into final form, and they reflect this sensibility of one God who is Creator of all.

In the first creation account, Genesis 1:1–2:4, one finds the refrain that after contemplating what has been created God sees that it is good (1:10, 12, 18, 21, 25). These pronouncements all refer to creation prior to the creation of humankind in verses 26–27. And as the narrative of creation moves toward its end with the sabbath on the seventh day, the reader finds the summary, "God saw *everything* that he had made, and indeed, it was very good" (1:31, emphasis added). All of creation has a goodness and worth in God's eyes, not only the human male and female.

Pope Francis is, of course, aware that this same creation story gives to the first humans "dominion over the fish of the sea and over the birds of the air and over the cattle and over all the wild animals of the earth and over every creeping thing that creeps upon the earth" (1:26). He also knows that this passage "has encouraged the unbridled exploitation of nature," but Francis maintains "this is not a correct interpretation of the Bible." He goes on to say that "nowadays we must forcefully reject the notion that our being created in God's image and given dominion over the earth justifies absolute domination over other creatures."[128] Turning his attention to the second creation account (Gen 2:4–25), Francis sees the command by God for humans to live in the garden of Eden and "to till it and keep it" as a corrective to the exploitative mentality of some readings of Genesis. "'Tilling' refers to cultivating, ploughing or working, while 'keeping' means caring, protecting, overseeing and preserving. This implies a relationship of mutual responsibility between human beings and nature."[129]

For Francis, the scriptural narrative of Genesis and the theological doctrine of creation alter the way that one sees the environmental crisis. "Nature is never just 'nature' but retains a sacred quality as 'creation,' something made and sustained by God."[130] What the belief in creation entails is a conviction that there is an ongoing "relationship of the world to its transcendent ground; it is the conviction that everything that exists must have an ultimate unity and community."[131] It is to place the human person in a relationship with nonhuman creation and so evoke a mindset different than a pure utilitarian approach to the natural world as just so much "stuff" for humans to use as they wish. The community of creatures all share the same origin: the diffusive love of a Trinitarian God who creates in order to share love, and that love continues to sustain all creatures in existence.

Belief that the human person is in a unique way the image of God in the created order need not, and should not, be discarded or downplayed. But it is essential that the imago Dei be properly understood. To be created in the image of God means that humans are made for relationship, not dominance. As the International Theological Commission affirmed, "the fundamental truth that visible creation is itself a divine gift, the 'original gift,' that establishes a 'space' of personal communion."[132] Humans as creatures are companions with all other creaturely entities, for everything that is creaturely is innately poor, incapable of calling itself into existence and of sustaining itself. All creation is graced by God's love and dependent on that love for existence, humans no less than other creatures. Humanity is the place where creation comes to consciousness of its creaturely state, but that is not a license to despoil the rest of the community of creation. Rather, it is a responsibility to "till and keep" creation in accord with God's love for all that is divinely made.

A Flawed Tradition

If the foregoing way of thinking is part of the Catholic social tradition, how is it that we heard too little of it, even within the social teaching of the church? Marvin Mich has suggested three elements of the Catholic theological tradition that have contributed to the relative paucity of attention to the natural environment compared to the human environment in the church's social teaching.

1. "Jews and Christians, in their radical monotheism, refused to identify God with nature and believed in God's power over nature. By separating God from nature, the earth may have become less holy to monotheists than it had been to pantheists."[133] The point is that by distinguishing God from the created order, the tradition went too far in dividing God from nature. Demystifying a world thought to be filled with spirits inhabiting woods and rivers, storm clouds and full moons, was necessary for Jewish and Christian believers who were well aware of the understandable tendency of ancient people to worship the elements of nature. The created order is, after all, awesome and beautiful, as well as essential to human life, safety, and security. So monotheism may well have had to distinguish itself from the nature religions that held the imaginations of people. Yet a downside of this was to lessen respect and appreciation for nature as being an expression of the sacred.

2. "The assumption that reality consists in dual realms: earth and heaven, time and eternity, matter and spirit, good and evil, the natural and supernatural, has been a constant temptation and heresy for Christians."[134] Throughout the centuries the Christian community has struggled to uphold the goodness of the created order, the embodied nature of human life, the truth of the incarnation, the goodness of bodily pleasure, along with the value of nonhuman creation. There have been a variety of heresies that undervalued or flatly denied the genuine humanity of Jesus, or the worth of sexual pleasure, or rightful enjoyment of food and drink. If worldly nature was a passing reality and our true home was beyond temporal existence, such a perspective might mistakenly come to devalue the goods of creation and fix our gaze not on the things of this world but only of eternity.

3. "The Christian church in its spirituality and its theology adopted a hierarchical worldview in which everything and every class of people are assigned a place. The higher levels control and direct the lower levels."[135] There are many reasons for why a hierarchical worldview became dominant in Catholic theology and practice—neoplatonism's impact on theology and philosophy, emulation of secular models of political structure and governance, patriarchal social orders, imperialism, ethnocentrism, and racism all shaped a worldview that saw some as superior to others. The Catholic church in its thinking and practice reflected such a hierarchical approach throughout many periods of its history.

One clear manifestation of how these undercurrents and, in some cases, major motifs played out in the Catholic social tradition was to place the human at the center of the created order. The unique nature of the human and the rightful upholding of human dignity are major contributions of the social tradition, but what was too often neglected, or poorly formulated, was the relationship of the person to the rest of creation. Without denying there have been leitmotifs within the tradition voiced by figures like Hildegard of Bingen or Francis of Assisi that spoke of creation in relational imagery, the major motif has focused upon the imagery of dominion. That metaphor gave way eventually in modern times to the metaphor of stewardship. Much of the modern Catholic social tradition still operates with that latter metaphor, but Pope Francis and other recent authors writing from within the Catholic social tradition now urge a move to a relational metaphor for articulating a proper understanding of an integral ecology that leads to sustainable development.

Catholic Teaching on the Environment Prior to Francis

There is no attention to the environment in the formal church documents on social questions until Vatican II. Even at the council the environment was not mentioned on the agenda during the four years of the council's sessions.[136] There are three brief references to the environment in *Gaudium et spes,* all of which reflect the dominion mindset. In the discussion of the imago Dei in Chapter 1 of the document it is asserted that humankind "was appointed by [God] as master of all earthly creatures" and this so that humans "might subdue them [other creatures] and use them to God's glory." Then in Chapter 3 of the text one finds the statement that "with the help of science and technology" the human person "has extended his mastery over nearly the whole of nature and continues to do so." The same passage observes that "many benefits once looked for, especially from heavenly powers" are "now enterprisingly procured" by human effort. This reflection on the value of human activity continues in the next paragraph where the imago Dei theme is invoked once again: "the human person, created to God's image, received a mandate to subject to [humanity] the earth and all that it contains, and to govern the world with justice and holiness."[137] While the last phrase softens the tone of dominance somewhat, it is evident that the conciliar bishops were impressed with the ability of science and technology to offer humanity mastery of the created order. The council's approach "portrays the natural world as a resource created by God and intended solely for the benefit of humans, who are its sole beneficiary."[138]

Six years after the Council, Paul VI issued the apostolic letter *Octogesima adveniens.* In that document the pope devoted a paragraph to the environment and, though hardly a major theme of the letter, his comment revealed an awareness by Paul that the issue is a daunting one. He referred to a "dramatic and *unexpected* consequence of human activity."[139] Paul observed that humankind "is suddenly becoming aware that by an ill-considered exploitation of nature" there is a risk of destroying it and humanity itself becoming "the victim of this degradation." He continued, "not only is the material environment becoming a permanent menace—pollution and refuse, new illnesses and absolute destructive capacity—but the human framework is no longer under [human] control, thus creating an environment for tomorrow which may well be intolerable." In Paul's view Christians must join with all the rest of the human family to address this new responsibility.

It has been suggested that one reason Paul designated his document as an apostolic letter and not an encyclical is that he did not wish to publish a more formal teaching just months before the 1971 Synod of Bishops was to take up many of the same social concerns.[140] Indeed, in his text the pope made reference to the upcoming synod with the theme of justice in the world.[141]

When the bishops met in Rome in the late fall of that year, there was a substantial presence of bishops from the developing nations who wanted to advance the church's engagement with the social issues that plagued many of their people. At the beginning of the first chapter of the Synod's statement, there is the comment that among the changes they perceive in the world is the dawning awareness that material "resources, as well as the precious treasures of air and water—without which there cannot be life—and the small delicate biosphere of the whole complex of all life on earth, are not infinite, but on the contrary must be saved and preserved."[142]

A few lines later the bishops linked their emerging ecological consciousness with the development issue: "such is the demand for resources and energy by the richer nations, whether capitalist or socialist, and such are the effects of dumping by them in the atmosphere and the sea that irreparable damage would be done to the essential elements of life on earth, such as air and water, if their high rates of consumption and pollution, which are constantly on the increase, were extended to the whole of humankind."[143] Here is an important aspect to note about the bishops' dissatisfaction with development—the way the Northern model of development exploits the earth's resources. This point gets at a significant difficulty for poorer nations. First, it becomes clear that the North's development is not repeatable in the South. Thus, the Global South's underdevelopment is not temporary but long-term under present conditions. Second, development is only available to those few who exploited the earth's resources first. Third, this is also an exploitation of the poor, for to use more than one's share of the goods of the earth is to exploit those who now have less resources to use for their own progress. Finally, therefore, the rich nations must share the benefits they have gained with those who have not been guilty of past exploitation of the resources of the planet.[144]

Two years later the Pontifical Commission *Justitia et Pax* addressed the environmental question in a brochure that was part of a series meant to explain and promote the teaching of the 1971 Synod. The text was written by the international development economist Barbara Ward, a friend of Paul VI, member of the Pontifical Commission, and invited expert at the Synod. The document cites dangers to three vital elements of our environment— soil, air, water—illustrating how humankind is threatening each of them. Increased population and food demand, fertilizer runoffs, excessive irrigation, and monoculture farming for the sake of higher cash crops are taking a toll on the soil. The destruction of rain forests (the "lungs" of the planet) along with the rise of air pollution due to plane and automobile use exemplify the danger to clean air. And "ultimately, all the waste and detritus and emissions of modern technology end in the oceans. All the soil's erosions wash down the rivers into the sea. So does industry's plastics and the cities' sewage. So do gas and exhausts and soot emitted into the air and passed onto the seas by precipitation."[145] These and other factors assault our rivers, seas, and oceans.

What is evident in this first stage of church teaching on the environment is that there is a critique of the "dominion" mentality that reflects a mistaken reading of the Genesis narrative. But the governing metaphor for the new mentality might be called "stewardship"; that is, "the focus of concern remained exclusively on protecting humans, not ecosystems and the nonhuman species with them, from harm." The aim of environmental concern is to limit "the potential boomerang effects on people" by the degradation of the natural world.[146] The stewardship approach, while a vast improvement on the dominion outlook's espousal of human mastery over creation, still maintained an instrumental viewpoint, failing to see any intrinsic value in nonhuman creation.

At the outset of his pontificate, John Paul II showed an awareness of environmental issues in his very first encyclical in 1979. The letter was a reflection on the centrality of Christ for a proper understanding of the human person, and the mission of the church as entailing a promotion and defense of what is truly human. At one point, discussing the various threats to the integrity of the person and human development, John Paul stated, "the moral character of development" cannot "exclude respect for the beings which constitute the natural world." Such respect has a threefold character. First, is to acquire "a growing awareness of the fact that one cannot use with impunity the different categories of beings, whether living or inanimate—animals, plants, the natural elements—simply as one wishes, according to one's economic needs." Rather, "one must take in account *the nature of each being* and of its *mutual connection* in an ordered system." Second, we all must realize "that *natural resources* are limited; some are not, as it is said, *renewable*. Using them as if they were inexhaustible, with *absolute dominion*, seriously endangers their availability not only for the present generation but above all for generations to come." Third, addressing the quality of life in the industrialized zones, "we all know that the direct or indirect result of industrialization is, ever more frequently, the pollution of the environment, with serious consequences for the health of the population."[147] This was a promising beginning to the new papacy.

However, John Paul's encyclical on human work in 1981 "was a missed opportunity" that failed to make connections between the dignity of labor and the dignity of creation and the moral responsibility to respect the natural environment in the labor process.[148] Yet by 1987 the issues surrounding care of the environment increased in prominence in the mind of John Paul II. In his encyclical commemorating the twentieth anniversary of Paul VI's *Populorum progressio*, the pope wrote a "a true concept of development cannot ignore the use of the elements of nature, the renewability of resources and the consequences of haphazard industrialization."[149] According to John Paul a growing awareness about "the need to respect the integrity and the cycles of nature" is one of the positive signs of the times.[150]

Four years later, in 1991, the pope suggested that "at the root of the senseless destruction of the natural environment lies an anthropological error," which is that people think they "can make arbitrary use of the earth . . . as though it did not have its own requisites and a prior God-given purpose."[151] Perhaps most significant was his World Day of Peace message in the previous year, where he developed an argument for the moral nature of the ecological crisis and pointed out the common responsibility all people have for preserving the integrity of creation.[152] This document was the first papal text devoted in its entirety to the topic of the environment, and it signaled the first halting steps of a new shift from the stewardship mentality to a relational model of thinking about creation. John Paul wrote of a "'cosmos' endowed with its own integrity, its own internal, dynamic balance. *This order must be respected.*"[153] There is a value and worth in natural creation that is acknowledged, yet the pope also falls back on arguments that the good of creation is "*a common heritage, the fruits of which are for the benefit of all.*" He then quotes *Gaudium et spes*, that God intends creation for the good of all people. The focus remains on what is beneficial to the human, even if it is a more inclusive understanding of the human that encompasses the poor and marginalized. John Paul remains anthropocentric in his perspective. Still, there is the call for rethinking the "relationship" between natural creation and the human and an appeal that the natural order within the cosmos be respected.

Care for the environment was a particular interest of Benedict XVI in his social teaching. Although he made a number of statements on environmental matters, his two most important statements are found in the 2009 encyclical *Caritas in veritate* and the 2010 World Day of Peace message, "If You Want to Cultivate Peace, Protect Creation." In his encyclical Benedict expresses wariness about "neo-paganism or a new pantheism," but he also warns against "the opposite position, which aims at total technical dominion over nature."[154] The former overvalues natural creation and the latter under-values it. At the foundation of Benedict's environmental approach is the belief that creation is a divine gift that God has entrusted to humankind: "nature is the wondrous work of the Creator, containing a 'grammar' which sets forth ends and criteria for its wise use, not its reckless exploitation." For Benedict, "Nature speaks to us of the Creator and his love for humanity" and must be treated with respect.

In his World Day of Peace message, Benedict used several themes of the Catholic social tradition (e.g., solidarity, subsidiarity, option for the poor, authentic development) to point toward criteria for an environmental ethic. He noted the close link between development and the obligations that humanity has due to its relationship with the natural environment. "The environment must be seen as God's gift to all people, and the use we make of it entails a shared responsibility for all humanity, especially the poor and future generations."[155]

Three aspects of Benedict's environmentalism are worth noting. First is his theistic approach. Benedict sees three general perspectives on ecology, each of which reflects a cultural outlook. There is an anthropocentric per-spective that reflects a secular/scientific outlook in its view of nature as having no value except its instrumental usefulness to human beings who are free to exploit the material resources of nature in whatever manner benefits human-kind. A second perspective is biocentric, and this reflects a pantheistic view that reverences nature itself as divine or quasi-divine. This is the outlook of those who romanticize nature and see humanity as spoiling nature and not being part of the natural created order. And then there is Benedict's preferred theistic approach that treats nature as a gift of the Creator to be used for the common good of the human family, both present and future generations, and that also appreciates the value of all created entities as being more than instrumental since they, too, are creatures of God. Creation may be used responsibly to meet legitimate human needs, material or otherwise, but there is an order of creation worthy of respect for its intrinsic value. Bene-dict maintains that Christianity is not the underlying cause of the ecological crisis, but the true solution to the crisis.

The second aspect of Benedict's environmentalism is its connection to natural law philosophy. According to him, problems like climate change, deforestation, and pollution prove that the natural law is real, not some false set of universalist claims made by the church. Rather, there really is a natural moral order that reflects God's purposes to be found in the "grammar" of creation. For Benedict the environmental crisis illustrates that there is an order to creation that humanity ignores to its peril.

And the third dimension of Benedict's environmentalism is its placement within a broad pro-life framework. He sees attitudes toward a range of life issues—conception, embryo research, assisted euthanasia, abortion—as interrelated with attitudes toward nonhuman life. "*The way humanity treats the environment influences the way it treats itself, and vice versa.*" Needed is a "human ecology," a phrase he borrows from his predecessor, that is, "the culture that shapes human coexistence." And with regard to this human ecology, "*the decisive issue is the overall moral tenor of society.*" The pope maintains that "*when 'human ecology' is respected within society, environmental ecology also benefits.*"[156]

For too long the Catholic social tradition, despite its resources, failed to adequately address the emerging environmental issue. While hardly alone as a community that was late in coming to ecological awareness, the Catholic church had resources that it did not mine, which might have fostered a better and earlier response to the crisis of nature's despoliation. The writings of recent popes have been a step forward, certainly in the decisive movement away from a model of dominance in thinking about the environment. Yet, "for all their contributions to Catholic ecological awareness, Popes John Paul II and Benedict XVI continued to draw a sharp distinction between human (or social) ecology and environmental (or natural) ecology."[157] They remained within an anthropocentric worldview, however attentive to the value and beauty of nature. The outlook remained "decidedly human centered, as if all the goods of the planet are meant only for human beings."[158] Certainly, these popes had reason to underline "the uniqueness of humankind among all other creatures,"[159] but that belief could be safeguarded even as the social tradition moves beyond the stewardship model.

A theological anthropology that prizes human dignity remains at the heart of the Catholic social tradition, but the tradition need not be anthropocentric. The human person is fundamentally relational, and that emphasis suggests the tradition needs to become more attuned to the implications of a creation-centered perspective; a viewpoint that situates the person amid his or her relationships with nonhuman as well as human creatures. It is the contribution of Pope Francis that he "clearly affirms the special place of humans in the universe" while also proposing "the framework of integral ecology as a corrective."[160]

Chapter 2 of *Laudato Si'* describes how humans ought to relate to the rest of creation. Especially in his interpretation of the creation narratives of Genesis, Francis reflects on the three vital relationships (God, neighbor, earth) and how sin ruptured each of those relations by seeking to make humans dominant. What is hoped is that humans move beyond the individualism and self-interest that blocks viewing human life properly. By adopting a relational framework, humanity will come to see the aim is not to dominate nature but to live in harmony with God, neighbor and the earth.[161]

A major cause of the error of anthropocentrism was the misguided faith in a view of progress that grew out of the Industrial Revolution. For Francis, what he calls the technological paradigm is the viewpoint that human societies and individuals have made scientific advance and economic growth ends in themselves instead of means that may be useful to other goals. Too much emphasis is given to the "how" of technological advance and too little to the "why" that would place it within the broader framework of what serves authentic human development. That, in turn, requires keeping the three vital relationships at the center. It is not that science or technology are evil but they are meant to be situated within a broader and richer ecology, one that attends to the necessary relationships with God, neighbor, and the earth. For Francis, the failure to monitor the harm we have done to the earth is the most glaring example of pursuing science and technology unconstrained by concerns for what is happening to our common home.

Francis also picks up on a theme we have seen before in *Populorum progressio*, *Centesimus annus*, and *Caritas in veritate*, the idea that we are defining economic progress in terms of having more and judging the market only in terms of whether we are getting more things from it. Francis, like his predecessors, asks that we realize market forces do not necessarily lead to human flourishing nor the just treatment of all. The argument in a nutshell is that profit cannot be the sole criterion of a good economy; politics ought not be subject to the logic of the technocratic paradigm. What is needed is a politics and economics that takes seriously the need to reflect upon what truly serves the common good.[162] For this to happen there will need to be structural changes as well as individual reform. Right now we are living in a "throwaway culture" that entails excessive consumerism and disrespect for the needs of earth's ecology.[163]

When Catholic social teaching uses the term "ecology," it is not the same ecology as used in the environmental sciences. In Catholic social teaching integral ecology is a summons to a new responsibility to create a global politics and economics that serves the well-being of all creation. In Chapter 4, Francis describes integral ecology as "a receptive awareness of the interconnectedness of all created things. Woven a priori through creation, this interconnection is divinely intended and a social reality that must be actively forged by co-creative human action."[164]

For the scientist, ecology is the study of the relationship between living organisms and the environment in which they develop.[165] For Francis, an integral ecology is not just a matter of understanding environmental interactions but includes an economic ecology that appeals to a broader reality than economic growth and profit maximization. Cultural ecology requires greater attention to the treasures of a community's heritage and the need to study local cultures when studying environmental problems. The ecology of daily life has to do with home design, public spaces, transportation systems, and aesthetics. It also has to do with our bodies and whether we respect the nature of our embodied selves and how that shapes our lives. An ecology of the common good raises the issue of whether we are sensitive to the flourishing of the poor when we discuss the environment; do we pay heed to concerns about environmental justice? Finally, an ecology of generational justice is also needed to secure intergenerational justice as well as intragenerational justice, so that we have a way of life individually and societally that is sustainable.[166]

Throughout his letter Francis stresses protecting our common home through a sustainable development must also include the challenge to achieve an integral development inclusive of all persons. This is what he means by the claim that we need "to hear *both the cry of the earth and the cry of the poor.*"[167] To do so, it will be necessary to transform mindsets away from one-dimensional ideas of development and purely anthropocentric readings of humanity's place in the mystery of creation. He believes that the Catholic social tradition, at least in some of its historical mediations, provides the resources for such transformation. At the outset of his letter, he reflects upon the example of Francis of Assisi.

> His response to the world around him was so much more than intellectual appreciation or economic calculus, for to him each and every creature was a sister united to him by bonds of affection. . . . Such a conviction cannot be written off as naïve romanticism, for it affects the choices which determine our behavior. If we approach nature and the environment without this openness to awe and wonder, if we no longer speak the language of fraternity and beauty in our relationship with the world, our attitude will be that of masters, consumers, ruthless exploiters, unable to set limits on their immediate needs. . . . The poverty and austerity of Saint Francis were no mere veneer of asceticism, but something much more radical: a refusal to turn reality into an object simply to be used and controlled.[168]

The saint of Assisi showed that the way to understand nature was to see it through the prism of the doctrine of creation. We are only in the early stages of Catholic social teaching in retrieving the environmental implications of our theological tradition. It is no betrayal of the tradition to move away from mentalities of dominion or even stewardship to a vision of humanity in relationship with the rest of creation, united by the fact of being creatures. Only by integrating that theological claim about the created order into our environmental vision will we be able to shape a future that is sustainable for the authentic development of all creatures.

CONCLUSION

When the Catholic social tradition attempts to delineate what authentic human development looks like, it has adopted four modifying terms to convey the breadth and depth of the idea. *Integral* development entails achieving the proper balance between material goods and other aspects of human well-being. *Just* development means concern for establishing fairness among the nations of the world and between all members of a society in the distribution of the benefits of the common good. *Participatory* development requires that poor people and nations be considered agents capable of self-determination and of advancing their own development and contributing to the common good for others. Finally, *sustainable* development calls attention to the challenge of promoting human flourishing in sync with the protection of the dignity of the rest of all the created order. These four adjectives describe a view of human development within the Catholic social tradition that constitutes authentic development and offers guidance for building societies that permit and promote human flourishing.

NOTES

1. Pope Francis, "Apostolic Letter issued Motu Proprio instituting the Dicastery for promoting Integral Human Development," https://www.humandevelopment.va/en/il -dicastero/motu-proprio.html
2. Pontifical Council for Justice and Peace, https://www.vatican.va/roman_curia /pontifical_councils/justpeace/documents/rc_pc_justpeace_pro_20011004_en.html
3. John XXIII, *Mater et magistra*, ns. 167–68.
4. John XXIII, ns. 169–71.
5. John XXIII, n. 172.
6. Paul VI, *Progressio populorum*, n. 14. Although John XXIII did not use the term "integral development," he was aware that economic development alone was insufficient and must be accompanied by "a corresponding social development" so that all persons could develop as fully as possible. See *Mater et magistra*, n. 73.

7. Paul VI, *Populorum progressio*, n. 15.

8. Paul VI, , n. 16.

9. Paul VI, , n. 17.

10. The stages of development as summarized are laid out by Paul in n. 21.

11. John Paul II, *Sollicitudo rei socialis*, n. 28.

12. This quotation and all those in the previous paragraph are from John Paul II, n. 28.

13. John Paul II, n. 29.

14. John Paul II, n. 29.

15. Benedict XVI, *Caritas in veritate*, n. 8.

16. This quotation and all those in the previous paragraph are from Benedict XVI, n. 11.

17. Francis, *Evangelii gaudium*, n. 182.

18. Francis, n. 186

19. Francis, n. 188.

20. Dwyer, "Person, Dignity of," 726–27.

21. Francis, *Evangelii gaudium*, n. 203

22. Francis, *Laudato Si'*, n. 70; see also ns. 91, 111, 117, 240.

23. Francis, 66.

24. Francis, n. 141, quoting the *Rio Declaration on Environment and Development* (June 14, 1992), Principle 4.

25. Curran, *Catholic Social Teaching 1891–present*, 188.

26. Höffner, *Christian Social Teaching*, 42.

27. Proportionate distribution based on merit was also adopted by Aquinas; today, as we shall see, it is often need that is the basis for using proportionality in distributive justice.

28. Höffner, 43.

29. Kettern, "The Development of the Concept 'Iustitia' From Thomas Aquinas through the Social Encyclicals," 88.

30. Curran, *Catholic Social Teaching*, 190.

31. Leo XIII, *Rerum novarum*, n. 27.

32. Leo XIII, n. 34.

33. Leo XIII, n. 36.

34. Massaro, *Mercy in Action*, 35.

35. Pius XI, *Quadragesimo anno*, n. 88.

36. Oswald von Nell-Breuning, *Reorganization of Social Economy*, 249.

37. Pius, XI, *Quadragesimo anno*, n. 88.

38. Nell-Bruening, *Reorganization of Social Economy*, 249–50.

39. Nell-Breuning, 250.

40. Christine Firer Hinze, "Commentary on *Quadragesimo anno*," 174.

41. Pius XI, *Divini redemptoris*, n. 51.

42. Curran, *Catholic Social Teaching*, 189.

43. Kettern, "The Development of the Concept 'Iustitia,'" 92.

44. Kettern, 93.

45. Roger Aubert, "Development of the Social Teaching of the Church in Europe from Leo XIII to Pius XI," in *Catholic Social Teaching: An Historical Perspective*, 174.

46. Aubert, "Development of the Social Teaching," 174.

47. Calvez and Perrin, *The Church and Social Justice*, 138–39.

48. Thomas Behr, *Social Justice and Subsidiarity: Luigi Taparelli and the Origins of Modern Catholic Social Thought*, 149.

49. William Collinge, "Review of Social Justice and Subsidiarity: Luigi Taparelli and the Origins of Modern Catholic Social Thought," 172.
50. Behr, *Social Justice and Subsidiarity*, 150.
51. Normand Paulus, "Uses and Misuses of the Term 'Social Justice' in the Roman Catholic Tradition," 268.
52. Collinge, "Review of Social Justice," 172.
53. Antonio Rosmini, a priest, philosopher, and Italian patriot, published a book, *Civil Constitution according to Social Justice*, which was put on the church's Index of Forbidden Books in 1849 during the pontificate of Pius IX. Then 1893 a French cleric, Paul Naudet, the leader of a movement called the "abbé democrats," started a weekly journal *La Justice sociale* to promote Christian Democracy in France during the papacy of Leo XIII (see Paul Misner, *Social Catholicism in Europe*, 325). In 1895 another French priest, Fr. De la Bégassière, wrote a pamphlet "The Notion of Social Justice." He wanted to distinguish the idea from any sort of socialist ideology, which was a common mistake made by Catholic critics of Taparelli and Rosmini. Social justice, De la Bégassière wrote, is nothing less than "that justice whose object is the social good and the common good of all" (as quoted in Aubert, "Development of the Social Teaching," 175). A Jesuit student of De la Bégassière, Charles Antoine, wrote a widely used textbook on social economics that further emphasized social justice was to be distinguished from socialism and also described social justice in a way that was close to legal justice, properly understood (Calvez and Perrin, *Church and Social Justice*, 147).
54. Calvez and Perrin, 147.
55. Aubert, "Development of the Social Teaching," 175.
56. Curran in *Catholic Social Teaching* observes: "Following the encyclical, a cottage industry arose among Catholic scholars in an attempt to understand the exact meaning of social justice and its relationship to the neoscholastic understanding of justice," 189.
57. Pius XI, *Quadragesimo anno*, n. 110.
58. Mary Elsbernd and Reimund Bieringer, *When Love Is Not Enough*, 95.
59. Hinze, "Commentary on *Quadragesimo anno*," 175.
60. Elsbernd and Bieringer, *When Love is Not Enough*, 95.
61. Paul VI, *Populorum progressio*, n. 13.
62. Paul VI, n. 48, quoting Vatican II, *Gaudium et spes*, n. 86.
63. John XXIII, *Mater et magistra*, n. 81.
64. John XXIII, n. 157.
65. John XXIII, *Pacem in terris*, n. 125.
66. John XXIII, n. 91.
67. Paul VI, *Populorum progressio*, n. 59.
68. Paul VI, n. 60.
69. All quotations in the paragraph are from Synod of Bishops, *Justitia in Mundo*, chap. 1, "Justice and World Society."
70. Pontifical Council for Justice and Peace (PCJP), *Compendium of the Social Doctrine of the Church*, n. 201.
71. Pius XI, *Quadragesimo anno*, n. 57.
72. Pius XI, n. 57.
73. Pius XI, n. 58.
74. Both quotes of Pius XII are found in Calvez and Perrin, *Church and Social Justice*, 149.
75. Paulus, "Uses and Misuses," 273.

76. All quotations in the paragraph are from Vatican II, *Gaudium et spes*, n. 29.

77. All quotations in the paragraph are from John Paul II, *Centesimus annus*, n. 34.

78. For John XXIII, see *Pacem in terris*, ns. 11–27 and for John Paul II, see his speech at the UN General Assembly in October, 1979, n. 13.

79. Pontifical Council for Justice and Peace, *Compendium*, n. 446.

80. For example in one of his major works, John Ryan, a prominent advisor to several generations of American Catholic bishops, wrote about what he called "canons of distributive justice": arithmetical equality; proportional needs; efforts and sacrifices; comparative productivity; relative scarcity. All these factors, he maintained, had to be weighed when determining a just system of remuneration for workers. This is but one example of the complexity of justice as developed in the Catholic social tradition. See Ryan, *Distributive Justice*, 243.

81. Massaro, *Living Justice*, 85.

82. Drew Christiansen, "On Relative Equality," 653–54.

83. Paulus, "Uses and Misuses," 277.

84. Paulus, 278.

85. Synod of Bishops, *Justitia in mundo*, chap. 1.

86. Synod of Bishops, chap. 1.

87. Judith Merkle, *From the Heart of the Church*, 246.

88. Barrera, *Modern Catholic Social Documents and Political Economy*, 218.

89. Jean Baptiste Duroselle, *Les débuts du catholicisme social en France (1822–1870)*, 70.

90. Misner, *Social Catholicism in Europe*, 51–2.

91. Philip Foner, *Women and the American Labor Movement*, 290.

92. Patricia Lamoureux, "Irish Catholic Women and the Labor Movement," 26.

93. Lamoureux, 26.

94. Lamoureux, 36.

95. Lamoureux, 41.

96. Lamoureux, 41.

97. John Ryan, "Labor Sharing in Management," 143.

98. Eugene De Jonge, "Participation in Historical Perspective," 157.

99. De Jonge, 157.

100. Dwyer, "Person, Dignity of," 726.

101. John XXIII, *Mater et magistra*, ns. 82–103.

102. John XXIII, n. 82.

103. John XXIII, n. 91.

104. John XXIII, n. 97.

105. John XXIII, *Pacem in terris*, n. 40 (italics added).

106. John XXIII, ns. 73 and 74, respectively.

107. Vatican II, *Gaudium et spes*, n. 31.

108. Vatican II, n. 68. Footnote 144 in the document follows the sentence quoted previously and cites *Mater et magistra* on this point but also mentions allocutions by Pius XII in 1950 and Paul VI in 1964 to illustrate "the evolution of the question."

109. "It is in full accord with human nature that juridical-political structures should, with ever better success and without any discrimination, afford all their citizens the chance to participate freely and actively in establishing the constitutional bases of a political community, governing the state, determining the scope and purpose of various institutions, and choosing leaders." Vatican II, *Gaudium et spes*, n. 75.

110. Paul VI, *Octogesima adveniens*, n. 22.

111. Paul VI, n. 41.

112. Paul VI, n. 46.

113. Paul VI, n. 47.

114. Synod of Bishops, *Justitia in mundo*, Introduction.

115. "Participation constitutes a right which is to be applied both in the economic and in the social and political field." *Justitia in mundo*, chap. 1

116. Congregation for the Doctrine of the Faith, "Instruction about Christian Freedom and Liberation," n. 86.

117. National Conference of Catholic Bishops (NCCB), *Economic Justice for All*, n. 77.

118. NCCB, n. 78.

119. John Paul II, *Sollicitudo rei socialis*, n. 17.

120. This and all following quotations in the paragraph are from John Paul II, n. 44.

121. PCJP, *Compendium*, n. 281 quoting John Paul II, *Centesimus annus*, n. 41.

122. PCJP, n. 281 quoting John Paul II, *Laborem exercens*, n. 14. The quotation continues: "the new ways that work is organized, where knowledge is of greater account than the mere ownership of the means of production, concretely shows that work, because of its subjective character, entails the right to participate."

123. Massaro, *Mercy in Action*, 79.

124. Francis, *Laudato Si'*, n. 138.

125. Francis, n. 139.

126. International Theological Commission, "In Search of a Universal Ethic," n. 82.

127. Massaro, *Mercy in Action*, 79.

128. Francis, *Laudato Si'*, n. 67.

129. Francis, n. 67.

130. Charles Murphy, *At Home on Earth*, 26.

131. Murphy, 51.

132. International Theological Commission, "Communion and Stewardship," n. 74.

133. Marvin Mich, *Catholic Social Teaching and Movements*, 396.

134. Mich, 397.

135. Mich, 397.

136. Mich, 386.

137. All quotes from *Gaudium et spes*, ns. 12, 33, and 34, respectively.

138. Massaro, *Mercy in Action*, 73.

139. Paul VI, *Octogesima adveniens*, n. 21, emphasis added. All remaining quotes in the paragraph are from the same source.

140. Christine Gudorf, "Commentary on *Octogesima adveniens*," 329–30.

141. "It will moreover be for the forthcoming synod of bishops itself to study more closely and to examine in greater detail the Church's mission in the face of grave issues raised today by the question of justice in the world." *Octogesima adveniens*, n. 6.

142. 1971 Synod of Bishops, *Justitia in mundo*, Ch. 1.

143. Synod of Bishops, Ch. 1.

144. The Synod statement is an important one, but it is one of many episcopal statements on the environment that began to emerge in the 1970s and 1980s. No doubt this was a response to Paul VI's call for local churches to assume responsibility for discerning how the Catholic social tradition was to be applied to various situations. *Octogesima adveniens*, n. 4 was viewed as a "magna carta" for individual bishops and regional bodies

of bishops to address the distinctive contexts of their churches. See the many instances of such statements in Drew Christiansen, ed., *And God Saw that It Was Good*.
145. Barbara Ward, *A New Creation? Reflections on the Environmental Issue*, 32. (Vatican City: Pontifical Commission Justice and Peace, 1973).
146. Massaro, *Mercy in Action*, 74.
147. All quotations in the paragraph are from John Paul II, *Redemptor hominis*, n. 34.
148. Mich, *Catholic Social Teaching and Movements*, 389.
149. John Paul II, *Sollicitudo rei socialis*, n. 34.
150. John Paul II, n. 26.
151. John Paul II, *Centesimus annus*, n. 37.
152. John Paul II, "Peace with God the Creator, Peace with All of Creation," n. 5.
153. John Paul II, n. 8.
154. All quotations in the paragraph are from Benedict XVI, *Caritas in veritate*, n. 48.
155. Benedict XVI, "If You Want to Cultivate Peace, Protect Creation," n. 2.
156. All quotes in the foregoing paragraph are from Benedict XVI, *Caritas in veritate*, n. 51.
157. Massaro, *Mercy in Action*, 80.
158. Sean McDonagh, "Theological and Historical Background of *Laudato Si'*," 6.
159. Massaro, *Mercy in Action*, 80.
160. Massaro, 80.
161. Francis, *Laudato Si'*, ns. 67–8.
162. Francis, ns. 187, 189.
163. Francis, n. 22.
164. Anna Rowlands, *Towards A Politics of Communion*, 270.
165. Francis, *Laudato Si'*, n. 138.
166. Francis treats these elements of integral ecology in chapter 4 of *Laudato Si'*, ns. 137–62.
167. Francis, n. 49.
168. Francis, n. 11.

AFTERWORD

The divine Persons are subsistent relations, and the world, created according to the divine model, is a web of relationships. Creatures tend towards God, and in turn it is proper to every living being to tend towards other things, so that throughout the universe we can find any number of constant and secretly interwoven relationships. This leads us not only to marvel at the manifold connection existing among creatures, but also to discover a key to our own fulfilment. The human person grows more, matures more and is sanctified more to the extent that he or she enters into relationships, going out from themselves to live in communion with God, with others and with all creatures. In this way, they make their own that trinitarian dynamism which God imprinted in them when they were created. Everything is interconnected, and this invites us to develop a spirituality of that global solidarity which flows from the mystery of the Trinity.[1]

In the foregoing paragraph Pope Francis admirably captures a good deal of the underlying vision that animates the Catholic social tradition and the formal teaching that has been derived from that tradition. As persons we are sacred because we are creatures made in the image of God; our God is Trinitarian and so as persons we are social, made for community where we can develop and grow into the persons God intends us to be. In the previous pages I have sought to demonstrate how the claims of being sacred and social have shaped the tradition and how the tradition has given rise to an imaginative vision expressed in documents of formal teaching since the latter part of the nineteenth century. That teaching seeks to capture what authentic human life in community looks like.

The teaching, however, did not arise from nowhere, but from within faith communities founded upon the revelation given to the people of Israel and embodied in the life of one particular Jewish prophet, Jesus of Nazareth. Those communities sought to plumb the riches of that revelation as new experiences and new contexts came about over the course of time. Fairly quickly, Christianity moved beyond its Semitic roots to engage with the Gentile world of Greece and Rome, which was then followed by encounters with Germanic tribes and other peoples of the European and near Asian lands. As the church expanded along with European colonialists it remained relatively fixed in its European culture, bringing it into non-European settings. It is only in the latter half of the twentieth century that Catholicism truly adopted a more global perspective and permitted regional churches to engage with other cultures on their own terms rather than as European outposts.

Despite the slow embrace of pluralism the church's social tradition did continue to develop a fundamentally humanistic outlook that reacted against those ills seen as dehumanizing. While the initial assessments were not always on target, the social tradition does demonstrate an ability to learn from hindsight and even provide insight into contemporary issues. Catholic social teaching, despite its initial antipathy, did come to acknowledge that not all socialist programs were destructively collectivist and not all liberal freedoms were dehumanizing by their undermining of community bonds. And the learning occurred on both sides of the dialogues. There were excesses in many nineteenth-century social ideologies and practices, on both the right and left in economics, politics, and culture. By the latter I mean the "set of meanings and values that informs a people's way of life."[2] Catholic social teaching was right to oppose those excesses, even if it did on several occasions go too far in lumping useful and worthwhile social changes into the category of excesses.

IMPLICATIONS

There are some people—and I am one of them—who think that the most practical and important thing about a person is still his view of the universe. We think that for a landlady considering a lodger, it is important to know his income, but still more important to know his philosophy. We think that for a general about to fight an enemy, it is important to know the enemy's numbers, but still more important to know the enemy's philosophy. We think the question is not whether

*the theory of the cosmos affects matters, but whether, in the long run,
anything else affects them.*[3]

As G. K. Chesterton suggests in the foregoing quote, a person's foundational
perspective does have practical import. There are practical implications to
be drawn from the theological commitments in the Catholic social tradition
as the tradition is brought into engagement with particular issues in specific
contexts. It is not that one easily and simply moves from a concern for the
dignity of workers to the specific policy of a federal minimum wage, no less
a specific figure for what that wage ought to be. For the tradition's insights
must be mediated through a theory of justice, an economic analysis of a
given labor market, scrutiny of the effectiveness of federal mandates rather
than alternatives, and other such exercises of practical reason. Yet the Catholic social tradition does, through its ethical coordinates, provide guidance in
discerning a way forward in social policy.

Because the teaching did not just come out of nowhere, it was not teaching addressed to any time and any place. Catholic social teaching was formulated in response to particular issues and concerns in a historical moment.
The modern era of Catholic social teaching was initially articulated at a time
when many European people were experiencing work in a new way—it
was industrial, it was urban-based, it entailed wages, it was set in a capitalist
framework and in a culture that embraced liberal ideas in political and personal life. And so the first stage of the church's modern social teaching was
attentive to the situation of workers in Europe, and eventually North America, as liberal capitalism grew in dominance. The teaching did not dismiss a
fundamental tenet of liberal capitalism, the right to own private property,
but it did challenge a basic economic belief popular at the time, the idea of
free contract. That is, many economic liberals maintained that if an employer
and employee agreed to a given wage for a job, then such a freely determined
contract was, by the fact that both sides agreed to the terms, a fair arrangement. Leo XIII took direct aim at that liberal presumption when he wrote
that there was a higher and older norm than free consent and that was justice; every laborer is due remuneration that enables a person to live in "reasonable and frugal comfort." Further, "if through necessity or fear or a worse
evil, the worker accepts harder conditions because an employer or contrac-
tor will give no better, the worker is the victim of force and injustice."[4]

By this claim Leo put Catholic social teaching squarely on the side of
the industrial workers who often toiled for long hours, at low pay, under
harsh conditions. For Leo the "dictate of nature" that overrules the claim of
"free consent" is justice. It is not right that individual workers must accept

substandard labor contracts because they are in a power dynamic with employers that is so unequal that they are effectively coerced and unable to bargain freely. To correct such an imbalance, Leo insisted on a variety of measures to secure basic justice for the new class of industrial workers. Measures that entailed interventions in the labor marketplace went against the rubrics of laissez-faire capitalism. While there would continue to be reasonable debates about the wisdom of particular market interventions by the state or other entities, there could be no debate that Catholic social teaching insisted on the propriety, indeed necessity, of institutional regulation of economic life. The arguments of social Darwinists like Herbert Spencer or William Sumner and economic libertarians such as Ayn Rand are not reconcilable with fundamental norms of Catholic social teaching.

In time, as has been discussed in Chapter 6, the Catholic social tradition, which for a long time employed the language of natural rights and duties, came to endorse the modern idiom of human rights to articulate the obligations of promoting human dignity. Included in a human rights regime are certain socioeconomic rights that even now are not yet formally recognized in the American legal system, but which Catholic teaching supports. While the ethical coordinate of subsidiarity cautions against too readily assuming that the federal government must always be the agent to promote human rights, the parallel coordinate of solidarity insists there must be provision made for effectively protecting basic rights for all to health care, housing, food, and other essential material goods. Fidelity to the tradition's mandate of the option for the poor also requires that the basic needs of the poor must not be neglected to satisfy the wants and desires of the rich.

The coordinate of participation as an element in authentic human development suggests the Catholic tradition's attitude toward the activity of work. For most of us, work is an ordinary way to participate in economic life. Being able not only to draw upon but to contribute to the economy suggests that work should not be seen as a curse or a burden for people. Instead it is a blessing for by it we our able to add to the material well-being of others as well as ourselves. The Catholic tradition views human labor as an activity whereby a person develops skills, uses their talents, learns to cooperate with others, finds self-esteem in making a contribution to the common good, and enjoys the mutual enrichment of adding to as well as drawing upon the prosperity of a society. Hence unemployment, especially chronic or long-term unemployment, is the real curse. In effect, being out of the workforce for a significant period is a message that an individual's contribution to the common good is not needed. Unemployment marginalizes people and prevents their full participation in the economic life of a community. A proper economy strives for full employment as well as fair treatment of workers. In short, what the foregoing underscores is that while Catholic social teaching does not endorse one single strategy for constructing and maintaining a just and sustainable economy, there are practical economic implications that follow by accepting the vision of the Catholic social tradition.

A similar point may be made in the realm of politics. A central claim of the church's social tradition is that politics is meant to serve the common good. Centuries before the Christian era, Aristotle proposed that the difference between good government and bad government is whether a government serves the well-being of the governed or the governors. As he writes in the *Politics*, "governments which have a regard to the common interest are constituted in accordance with strict principles of justice, and are therefore true forms; but those which regard only the interest of the rulers are all defective and perverted forms."[5] This distinction is what differentiates the constitution of a true monarchy versus a tyranny, an aristocracy versus an oligarchy. The Catholic social tradition came to terms with a plurality of forms of government in the course of history, but it adopted Aristotle's viewpoint that politics, whatever its constitutional form, is to serve the common good. Certainly it has been true over the course of history that at times the church engaged in power politics and narrowly pursued the self-interest of the institution. Yet, even when its performance did not match its own teaching, there has been at the heart of the church's social tradition a commitment to seeing politics as a noble arena wherein the common good is to be served, and the state is the institution that has as its *raison d'etre* the promotion of the common good. As with the economy, there is no single form of government that is *the* Catholic position, but whatever its constitutional arrangement, the state exists for the sake of the common good.

This implies that those who would see only a negative role for the state, playing the role of a night-watchman having little to do other than maintain law and order, are not in accord with the vision of Catholic social teaching. For example, if participation is a legitimate aspiration of people, as Paul VI maintained,[6] then state systems that are open and transparent, allowing citizens entry into the realm of political power, are necessary. Popes ever since Pius XII have been explicit that democracy appears to be the most apt form of government in the present age, without ruling out the possibilities of other constitutional forms.[7] The major reason for Pius promoting democracy was his belief that it was the future direction of peoples toward self-government. He felt the modern state was so large and inevitably intrusive in individuals' affairs that it was natural for people to want more say in their government. Democracy offered that opportunity. So for Pius democracy was the form of government that best fit the mood of the times. His argument was not metaphysical or premised on some ahistorical theory of natural law principles but was a realistic assessment of what seemed appropriate to the situation. This approach of supporting democracy had repercussions for the East-West conflict since it put the church at odds with the Soviet bloc.

The extensive agenda of human rights endorsed by John XXIII included many civil and political liberties that facilitate citizen participation in political decisions of self-determination. And the teaching has made the point that self-determination requires a commitment to inclusivity in determining a citizen's right to be politically active. There is a clear implication in Catholic social teaching that efforts to restrict voting rights and disenfranchise segments of a population on the basis of unsubstantiated and exaggerated claims of voter fraud are wrong. Elections ought to be monitored, but absent clear evidence of abuse, there should be sincere efforts to extend political participation to all eligible citizens. In many societies this will also entail a government's duty to promote literacy and accessible educational opportunities to marginalized populations. There are important social conditions implied in the Catholic tradition's embrace of political self-determination just as there are implications in the case of advocating economic justice.

These comments do not come close to exhausting the practical implications of the Catholic social tradition and its formal teaching, but I make them simply to underscore that such implications exist and can be readily distilled through critical reflection that engages the teaching in one's historical context.

Solidarity and the central place it has come to have in the Catholic social tradition indicates the communitarian bias of the Catholic imagination, for relationality and community are essential to the authentic development of persons. Solidarity in many ways is a contemporary retrieval of the organic body metaphor so central in premodern theologies.

On the other hand, the very existence of gaps between rich and poor, Black and white, new immigrants and established citizens, Anglo and Latino/a, male and female, marginalized and powerful, humankind and other creatures—all these and more suggest that solidarity is markedly absent in much of what we experience as human beings living in the present moment. Hence, I think that solidarity should be a central element to be promoted by the Catholic church in our society for it is very much needed in order to close the divides among us.

Overcoming the divisions that are characteristic of our social existence is a vital ministry and will entail strategies for reconciliation, forgiveness, inclusive participation, just allocation of resources, and conflict resolution. Also a comprehensive and integrated vision of the good we hold in common must be articulated persuasively so that people can understand what solidarity is meant to promote—a dedication to work for the common good of the entire human family and the earth as our shared home. Overcoming division ought not be equated with eradicating difference, however. The metaphor for the human family is not the puree of baby food but a rich stew with distinctive ingredients. What is needed is a social theology that adequately celebrates and honors difference without allowing "otherness" to become a rationale for injustice or violence.

Before ending this volume, I wish to add a comment on the social theology we need for the life of the ecclesial community.

FASHIONING A CATHOLIC SOCIAL THEOLOGY

A genuine social theology should lead the Catholic community into conversion. A genuine social theology should be presented in transformative discourse that induces change. And this conversion is not confined to the personal; a true social conversion, one that addresses sinful social structures, is required in our time. In order for conversion to occur, however, it must be experienced as needed.

Recall the paradigmatic prophetic call to conversion that is found in 2 Samuel, Chapter 12 where the prophet Nathan reveals David's sin by having David himself pronounce upon its evil after hearing Nathan's parable of the abusive rich man's treatment of his poor neighbor. When Nathan uttered, "you are the man" there was an experience of profound recognition by David. Hence, his immediate desire to repent and change. Conversion demands self-knowledge and personal acknowledgement of sinfulness. Has the Catholic church in the United States found a parable or narrative whereby its people recognize themselves and their failings in a manner similar to Nathan's confrontation with David?

Luke's parable of Lazarus and the rich man, as a culture of winners and losers, unfeeling rich and destitute poor, may capture the painful social reality that is present in some cultures. But does such stark division, such broad categories, capture the experience of working-class and middle-class Catholics in the United States? While rhetorically powerful, the language of John Paul II about a "culture of death" and a "culture of life" is not analytically helpful.

Take a moment to imagine a working couple who own a modest home with a mortgage to pay off; their two grown children are saving money by attending community college and hoping to transfer to a major state university for the final years of college. This couple has friends who care about them, and they are able to enjoy a week's vacation at a lake resort most summers. The couple is worried about aging parents who are less and less able to live independently. While the couple can put food on the table each night, they rarely attend any recreational or cultural event that requires admission fees. They get by on one car purchased several years ago and only recently paid off. They both work at jobs where they mostly take orders from bosses and exercise little discretionary authority over anyone else at their workplace. The neighborhood where they live is relatively free of street crime, and the parish they attend satisfies the few expectations they have of the church.

Are these people Lazarus? Or are they the rich man? Do they embody the culture of death? The culture of life? Would they consider themselves fairly judged by anyone who placed them in either category? The point is that any social theology must be adequate to the actual experience of the people it seeks to address. If people do not recognize themselves in the stories and parables of a theological tradition, then it will not be a tradition that inspires conversion. The overall stance of a social theology ought to be one that takes seriously "the duty of scrutinizing the signs of the times and of interpreting them in the light of the Gospel."[8] The fact that "the signs" have to be scrutinized and interpreted means that not everything we see is revelatory of the Gospel. The deep mores and values of US society are not simply continuous with the Christian message, even if they may not be entirely discontinuous. There is a mixture of light and darkness in our nation, and no social theology can be exclusively a booster or a critic of US society.

What is needed is a theology that is able to intersect with those dimensions of society that reveal traces of God's reign at work and stand against those negative realities that illustrate the absence of God's reign. The Catholic social tradition must foster a theology that upholds personal freedom, political equality, economic security, the rule of law, and other aspects of US society at its best. It must be a theology that stands against the racism, violence, sexism, nationalism, and exceptionalism that are deeply embedded in our national history and current practice.

To fashion such a theological project, the Catholic church must be genuinely dialogical in two senses. First, the church must be dialogical with the people and realities of its local context; thus it must practice subsidiarity. Second, a local church must be dialogical with other regional churches and the universal church, thereby demonstrating a solidarity that is global.

With regard to the first sense, consider certain realities of US Catholicism. By the latter half of the twentieth century the consequences of two public policies enacted in the first half of the century came to be seen. With the immigration reform act of 1924 sponsored by the nativist congressman Albert Johnson, there was the establishment for the first time of a quota on European immigration. Consequently, the Catholic church in this country saw the constant flow of new immigrants from Catholic countries of Europe slow to a trickle compared to the century from 1820–1920. As second- and third-generation immigrants began to advance their economic and social standing, there was not a substantial generation of new arrivals coming along to maintain the American Catholic church's image as being a church of immigrants. Gradually within the span of several decades the Catholic community had dramatically rising metrics for per capita income and years of formal education.

The second public policy was the G.I. Bill after World War II that provided many Catholic veterans with the means to go to college, greatly expanding the number and size of Catholic institutions of higher education. The new law also provided access to financing for home mortgages, at least among white veterans living in the North, that led to the shift of Catholics from ethnic enclaves in major urban areas to assimilation within the vast suburban tracts being developed in the post-war decades of the 1950s and 1960s. The face of the Catholic church was becoming markedly different from the blue-collar ethnics of the industrial heartland.

What this means is that sitting in many of our parish pews are people who are now more likely to sit on management's side of the table than labor's, who are as likely to attend elite universities as they are community colleges, and who are at least as well-educated as the priests preaching to them from pulpits. American Catholics need an experience of church that is broadly participatory, consultative, and which employs methods of communication and education that reflect the changed social status of the Catholic laity. Unless the church becomes a place where believers can find suitable opportunities for the formation of conscience and the cultivation of character, it will never be able to promote a social theology that actually has adherents beyond a scattering of academic theologians and social activists. The church must become a community of serious moral discourse that does not short-circuit adult formation by practices that undercut honest questioning, genuine searching, and critical reflection.

A few other items for consideration in a social theology that is in dialogue with the local context is that US culture is pluralistic, secular, diffuse, and free. American Catholics live within an environment that requires they negotiate the values and practices of public life with hundreds of millions of others who do not share their faith. The broad diversity of American culture inevitably produces people who are wary of far-reaching claims to authority and certainty. Having learned how to live and work with others on campuses, in the workplace, and at recreational and cultural gatherings, it is difficult not to transfer the learned behaviors of forbearance and openness to the realms of religion and morality. The Catholic community in the United States will be skeptical of any social theology that is not deeply respectful of the pluralism in our society.

As a secular society the United States is not a society that opposes religion, but it is a society that limits organized religion's power over other segments of social life. A sound social theology should inform and shape our political, economic, judicial, educational, and cultural institutions. But none of these arenas can be made subject to religion for they have their legitimate autonomy. A social theology must engage these realms by speaking insightfully and persuasively about the nature of a good society and the shape of a virtuous life.

We are living in a period of significant concentration of power and control of communication at the corporate level, with a few companies becoming conglomerates of formerly independent organizations. Yet at the same time we see a remarkable diffusion of voices through new means of communication. Consider the emergence of artificial intelligence, blogging, YouTube, and Tik Tok videos that compete with the ever present "spin doctors" and PR flaks for shaping the nation's discourse. The ways in which people communicate and learn today are constantly shifting and being recast. In order to promote a social theology for our regional church, we will need to become more adept in the use of new media. Lengthy encyclicals and pastoral letters likely will not be the best mode of communication within the church or between the church and the public square.

A final attribute of a local theology to mention is the level of individual freedom people have with regard to church membership. Our culture does not pressure people on the issue of church participation. Few people today suffer discrimination at the workplace, ostracism from family, or marginalization in social life because they drop out of church. If people belong to a church community, it is increasingly a matter of personal preference and choice rather than family, peer, or cultural coercion. In large part this will mean that the church will have to demonstrate that active involvement in a religious community is an effective path toward authentic human development and flourishing so that people will wish to join and participate. This does not mean that churches should become therapy groups or associations for self-actualization. It does mean that calls to sacrifice, invitations to service, and prophetic challenges to change will need to be integrated into a theology that offers a comprehensive vision of what genuine personhood and community look like.

For a social theology to be successful it must promote hope for historical change, build alliances across differences for the sake of attaining shared goods, and pledge to work with diverse individuals and institutions in a cooperative manner to achieve those common goods. This is in reference to its external mission; internally the church must continue to be a community that gathers to hear the Word of God and celebrate the sacramental life. It will also need to create structures and spaces that allow for all segments of the church to participate and deliberate in creating and receiving the Catholic social tradition.

As part of a universal church, the various regional theologies that developed must take us to another place, one that transcends the region not by ignoring the local but by bringing it into dialogue with other regional churches of the one body of Christ. The challenge ahead is to avoid extremes. We can formulate a social theology so prophetic and countercultural that we become a church that marginalizes itself and loses members who do not see their own moral experience captured by an overly radical critique of American institutions and practices. We can also develop a social theology that is so thoroughly assimilationist that it is little more than an echo of the jingoism and arrogance of defenders of American capitalism and exceptionalism, thereby losing a vision of the Gospel. We can forfeit a rooted social theology by merely parroting the theologies of other regional churches or the universal magisterium. We can also forsake our bonds with other churches and the universal church to become a self-absorbed community indifferent to our brothers and sisters around the globe.

What is needed is a path that forges a social theology, guided by the Spirit of God, that pushes us out of our sanctuaries and into the public spaces of our nation. That same Spirit can open our minds and hearts to listen to the voices of our brothers and sisters in faith who are articulating their experience of the Gospel in their locales. Then the hope is that we will know a new Pentecost, not where a theological Esperanto is spoken, but where each of us hears the Gospel message in our own language and yet all are able to hear and understand the message that unites us as people who are sacred and social, made for communion with God and one another.

NOTES

1. Francis, *Laudato Si'*, n. 240.
2. Bernard Lonergan, *Second Collection*, 232.
3. G.K. Chesterton, *Heretics*, 15–16.
4. Leo XIII, *Rerum novarum*, n. 34.
5. Aristotle, *Politics*, Bk. III.6.
6. Paul VI, *Octogesima adveniens*, n. 22.
7. Pius XII, *Christmas Message*, 1944.
8. Vatican II, *Gaudium et spes*, n. 4.

BIBLIOGRAPHY

Allsop, Michael. "Subsidiarity, Principle of." In *The New Dictionary of Catholic Social Thought*. Edited by Judith Dwyer, 927–29. Collegeville, MN: Liturgical Press, 1994.

Aquinas, Thomas. *Commentary on the Sentences*.

———. *Summa Theologica*.

Aristotle. *The Politics and The Constitution of Athens*. Edited by Stephen Everson. Cambridge: Cambridge University Press, 1996.

Atkins, Margaret. "Clarifying the Common Good." *Oikonomia* 4 no. 2 (2005): 14–25.

Aubert, Roger. "Development of the Social Teaching of the Church in Europe from Leo XIII to Pius XI." In Roger Aubert, *Catholic Social Teaching: An Historical Perspective*. Edited by David Boileau. Milwaukee: Marquette University Press, 2003.

Augustine. *The City of God against the Pagans*. Edited by R. W. Dyson. Cambridge: Cambridge University Press, 1998.

Autiero, Antonio. "Human Dignity in an Ethical Sense." *Interdisciplinary Journal for Religion and Transformation in Contemporary Society* 6 no. 1 (2020): 9–21.

Barrera, Albino. *Modern Catholic Social Documents and Political Economy*. Washington, DC: Georgetown University Press, 2021.

Behr, Thomas. *Social Justice and Subsidiarity: Luigi Taparelli and the Origins of Modern Catholic Social Thought*. Washington, DC: Catholic University Press, 2019.

Bell, Daniel. *Communitarianism and Its Critics*. Oxford: Clarendon Press, 1993.

Bellah, Robert, Richard Madsen, William Sullivan, Ann Swidler, and Steven Tipton. *Habits of the Heart: Individualism and Commitment in American Life*. Berkeley, CA: University of California Press, 1985.

———. "On the Importance of 'Subsidiarity' as a Theme in Catholic Social Teaching" (Paper Prepared for Conference on "100 Years of Catholic Social Thought.") University of San Francisco (June 26–29, 1991).

Benedict XVI. *Deus caritas est*. (December 25, 2005).

———. "Address to the U.N. General Assembly." (April 18, 2008).

———. *Caritas in veritate.* (June 29, 2009).

———. "If You Want to Cultivate Peace, Protect Creation." (December 8, 2009).

Berger, Peter and Thomas Luckmann. *The Social Construction of Reality.* New York: Doubleday, 1967.

Beyer, Gerald. "John XXIII and John Paul II: The Human Rights Popes." *Ethos* 27 no. 2 (2014): 50–91.

———. "The Meaning of Solidarity in Catholic Social Teaching." *Political Theology* 15 no. 1 (2014): 7–25.

Biechler, James. ed. *Law for Liberty.* Baltimore: Helicon Press, 1967.

Bilgrien, Marie Vianney. *Solidarity: A Principle, an Attitude, a Duty or the Virtue for an Interdependent World?* New York: Peter Lang, 1999.

Boff, Leonardo. *Holy Trinity, Perfect Community.* Maryknoll, NY: Orbis Books, 2000.

Brady, Bernard. *Essential Catholic Social Thought.* Maryknoll, NY: Orbis Books, 2008.

Buhlmann, Walbert. *The Coming of the Third Church.* Maryknoll, NY: Orbis Books, 1977.

Burgos, Juan Manuel. *Introduction to Personalism.* Washington, DC: Catholic University Press, 2018.

Cahill, Lisa Sowle. "Toward A Christian Theory of Human Rights." *Journal of Religious Ethics* 8 no. 2 (1980): 277–301.

———. *Global Justice, Christology and Christian Ethics.* Oxford: Clarendon Press, 1993.

———. "Globalization and the Common Good." In *Globalization and Catholic Social Thought.* Edited by John Coleman and William Ryan, 42–54. Maryknoll, NY: Orbis Books, 2005.

———. "Embodying God's Image." In *Humanity Before God.* Edited by William Schweiker, Michael Johnson and Kevin Jung, 55–77. Minneapolis: Fortress Press, 2006.

———. "Reframing Catholic Ethics: Is the Person an Integral and Adequate Starting Point." *Religions* 8 no. 10 (2017): https://doi.org/10.3390/rel8100215.

———. "Social Justice and the Common Good: Improving the Catholic Social Teaching Framework." *Journal of Moral Theology* 1 (2021): 106–18.

Calleja, Carlos. "To Understand Pope Francis, You Have to Know What He Actually Means by the Word 'Fraternity.' *America* (February 4, 2021): https://www.americamagazine.org/faith/2021/02/04/pope-francis-fratelli-tutti-friendship-fraternity-239916.

Calvez, Jean-Yves and Jacques Perrin, *The Church and Social Justice.* Chicago: Henry Regnery Company, 1961.

Camp, Richard. *The Papal Ideology of Social Reform.* Leiden: E.J. Brill, 1969.

Charles, Rodger. *Christian Social Witness and Teaching,* vols. 1 & 2. Herefordshire, UK: Gracewing, 1998.

Chesterton, Gilbert Keith. *Heretics.* New York: John Lane, 1905.

Christiansen, Drew. "On Relative Equality." *Theological Studies* 45 no. 4 (1984): 651–75.

———. "The Common Good and the Politics of Self-Interest: A Catholic Contribution to the Practice of Citizenship." In *Beyond Individualism: Toward a Retrieval of Moral Discourse in America*. Edited by Donald Gelpi, 54–86. Notre Dame, IN: University of Notre Dame Press, 1989.

———. and Walter Grazer. eds. *And God Saw that It Was Good*. Washington, DC: United States Catholic Conference, 1996.

Chroust, Anton-Hermann. "The Corporate Idea and the Body of Christ in the Middle Ages." *The Review of Politics* 9 no. 4 (1947): 423–52.

Clark, Meghan. *The Vision of Catholic Social Thought*. Minneapolis: Fortress Press, 2014.

Coleman, John. "Pluralism and the Retrieval of a Catholic Sense of the Common Good." *Commonweal* Colloquium on American Catholics and the Public Square. (New York, NY: May 12–14, 2000).

———. "Retrieving or Re-inventing Social Catholicism." In *Catholic Social Thought: Twilight or Renaissance?* Edited by J. Boswell, F. McHugh, and J. Verstraeten, 265–92. Leuven: Leuven University Press, 2000.

———. "Making the Connections." In *Globalization and Catholic Social Thought*. Edited by John Coleman and William Ryan, 9–27. Maryknoll, NY: Orbis Books, 2005.

Collinge, William. "Review of *Social Justice and Subsidiarity: Luigi Taparelli and the Origins of Modern Catholic Social Thought*." *The Journal of Social Encounters* 6 no. 2 (2022): 170–79.

Collins, John. "The Biblical Vision of the Common Good." In *The Common Good and U.S. Capitalism*. Edited by Oliver Williams and John Houck, 50–69. Lanham, MD: University Press of America, 1987.

Collste, Göran. *Is Human Life Special?* Bern: Peter Lang, 2000.

Congregation for the Doctrine of the Faith. "Instruction about Christian Freedom and Liberation." (March 22, 1986).

Consejo Episcopal Latinoamericano y Caribeno (CELAM). "Poverty of the Church." Medellin, Colombia: Second General Conference of Latin American Bishops, 1968.

Cronin, John. "Forty Years Later: Reflections and Reminiscences." In *Readings in Moral Theology, vol. 5: Official Catholic Social Teaching*. Edited by Charles Curran and Richard McCormick, 69–76. New York: Paulist Press, 1986.

Crosby, John. "Foreword." In Juan Manuel Burgos, ix–xii. *Introduction to Personalism*. Washington, DC: Catholic University Press, 2018.

Curran, Charles. "The Common Good and Official Catholic Social Teaching." In *The Common Good and U.S. Capitalism*. Edited by Oliver Williams and John Houck, 111–29. Lanham, MD: University Press of America, 1987.

———. *Catholic Social Teaching 1891–present*. Washington, DC: Georgetown University Press, 2002.

Czerny, Michael and Christian Barone. *Siblings All, Sign of the Times*. Maryknoll, NY: Orbis Books, 2022.

Davis, Stacey. "Joel." In *The Jerome Biblical Commentary for the Twenty-First Century*, 3rd ed. Edited by John Collins, Gina Hens-Piazza, Barbara Reid, and Donald Senior. London: T&T Clark, 2022. https://doi.org/10.5040/9781350182875.046

De Jonge, Eugene. "Participation in Historical Perspective." In *Principles of Catholic Social Teaching*. Edited by David Boileau, 119–32. Milwaukee: Marquette University Press, 1994.

Deneulin, Severine and Augusto Zampini Davies, "Life Lived to the Full." *The Tablet* (August 31, 2013): 10–12.

Donahue, James. "Introduction." In *Religion, Ethics, and the Common Good*. Edited by James Donahue and M. Theresa Moser, ix–xvii. Mystic, CT: 1996.

Donahue, John. *Seek Justice That You May Live*. New York: Paulist Press, 2014.

Dorr, Donal. *Option for the Poor and Option for the Earth*, rev. ed. Maryknoll: Orbis Books, 2016.

Douglass, R. Bruce. "First Things First: The Letter and the Common Good Tradition." In *The Deeper Meaning of Economic Life*. Edited by R. Bruce Douglass, 21–36. Washington, DC: Georgetown University Press, 1986.

Duroselle, Jean Baptiste. *Les débuts du catholicisme social en France (1822–1870)*. Paris: Presses universitaires de France, 1951.

Dwyer, John. "Person, Dignity of." In *The New Dictionary of Catholic Social Thought*. Edited by Judith Dwyer, 724–37. Collegeville, MN: Liturgical Press, 1994.

Elsbernd, Mary. "Authentic Human Living in Catholic Social Teachings: A Feminist Perspective." *Bijdragen* 64 no. 1 (2003): 3–19.

———— and Reimund Bieringer. *When Love Is Not Enough: A Theo-Ethic of Justice*. Collegeville, MN: Liturgical Press, 2002.

Eusebius of Caesarea. "From a Speech for the Thirtieth Anniversary of Constantine's Accession." In *From Irenaeus to Grotius*. Edited by Oliver O'Donovan and Joan Lockwood O'Donovan. Grand Rapids, MI: Eerdmans, 1999.

Feinberg, Joel. *Social Philosophy*. Englewood Cliffs, NJ: Prentice-Hall, 1973.

Finn, Daniel. *Christian Economic Ethics*. Minneapolis: Fortress Press, 2013.

————. "What Is a Sinful Social Structure?" *Theological Studies* 77 (2016): 136–64.

Fitzmyer, Joseph. "Pauline Theology." In *The New Jerome Biblical Commentary*. Edited by Raymond Brown, Joseph Fitzmyer, and Roland Murphy, 1382–1416. Englewood Cliffs, NJ: Prentice-Hall, 1990.

Foner, Philip. *Women and the American Labor Movement*. Madison, WI: University of Wisconsin Press, 1982.

Francis. *Evangelii Gaudium*. (November 24, 2013).

————. "Fraternity, the Foundation and Pathway to Peace." (December 8, 2013).

————. *Laudato Si'*. (May 24, 2015).

————. "Address to the U.N. General Assembly." (September 25, 2015).

———. "Apostolic Letter issued Motu Proprio instituting the Dicastery for promoting Integral Human Development." (August 17, 2016).

———. "Faith and Human Dignity." (August 12, 2020).

———. *Fratelli tutti.* (October 3, 2020).

Fuchs, Joseph. *Human Values and Christian Morality.* Dublin: Gill and Macmillan, 1970.

Gager, John. *Kingdom and Community: The Social World of Early Christianity.* Englewood Cliffs, NJ: Prentice-Hall, 1975.

Gaillardetz, Richard. *By What Authority?* rev. ed. Collegeville, MN: Liturgical Press, 2018.

Glendon, Mary Ann. "The Sources of 'Rights-Talk': Some Are Catholic." *Commonweal* (October 12, 2001): 11–13.

Greeley, Andrew. *No Bigger Than Necessary: An Alternative to Socialism, Capitalism, and* Anarchism. New York: Meridian Books, 1977.

———. *The Catholic Myth.* New York: Simon & Schuster, 1990.

———. *The Catholic Imagination.* Berkeley: University of California Press, 2000.

Groome, Thomas. *Faith for the Heart.* New York: Paulist Press, 2019.

Gudorf, Christine. "Commentary on *Octogesima adveniens.*" In *Modern Catholic Social Teaching: Commentaries and Interpretations* 2nd ed. Edited by Kenneth Himes, 326–344. Washington, DC: Georgetown University Press, 2018.

Gula, Richard. *Reason Informed by Faith.* New York: Paulist Press, 1989.

Hall, Douglas John. *Imaging God: Dominion as Stewardship.* Grand Rapids, MI: Eerdmans, 1986.

Hanvey, James. "Dignity, Person, and Imago Trinitatis." In *Understanding Human Dignity.* Edited by Christopher McCrudden, 209–28. Proceedings of the British Academy 192. Oxford: Oxford University Press, 2013.

Happel, Stephen and David Tracy, *A Catholic Vision.* Philadelphia: Fortress Press, 1984.

Heimbach-Steins, Marianne. "Pope Francis' Encyclical Letter Fratelli tutti—Focal Points and Aspects from the Discussion in Germany." *Catholic Theological Ethics in the World Church* (December 1, 2020). https://catholicethics.com/forum/fratelli-tutti-germany/

Himes, Michael. *Doing the Truth in Love.* New York: Paulist Press, 1995.

Hinze, Christine Firer. "Commentary on *Quadragesimo anno.*" In *Modern Catholic Social Teaching: Commentaries and Interpretations,* 2nd ed. Edited by Kenneth Himes, 158–82. Washington, DC: Georgetown University Press, 2018.

Höffner, Joseph. *Christian Social Teaching.* Cologne: Ordo Socialis, 1983,

Hollenbach, David. *Claims in Conflict.* New York: Paulist Press, 1979.

———. "A Communitarian Reconstruction of Human Rights: Contributions from the Catholic Tradition." In *Catholicism and Liberalism: Contributions to American Public Philosophy.* Edited by R. Bruce Douglass and David Hollenbach, 127–50. Cambridge: Cambridge University Press, 1994.

———. "Afterword: A Community of Freedom." In *Catholicism and Liberalism: Contributions to American Public Philosophy*. Edited by R. Bruce Douglass and David Hollenbach, 323–43. Cambridge: Cambridge University Press, 1994.

———. "The Common Good in the Postmodern Epoch: What Role for Theology?" In *Religion, Ethics, and the Common Good*. Edited by James Donahue and M. Theresa Moser, 3–22. Mystic, CT: Twenty-Third Publications, 1996.

———. *The Common Good and Christian Ethics*. Cambridge: Cambridge University Press, 2002.

———. "The Common Good and Issues in U.S. Politics." *Journal of Religion and Society* 4 (2008): 33–46.

———. "Human Dignity: Experience and History, Practical Reason and Faith." In *Understanding Human Dignity*. Edited by Christopher McCrudden, 123–39. Proceedings of the British Academy 192. Oxford: Oxford University Press, 2013.

———. "Human Dignity in Catholic Thought." In *The Cambridge Handbook of Human Dignity*. Edited by Marcus Düwell, Jens Braarvig, Roger Brownsword, and Dietmar Mieth, 250–59. Cambridge: Cambridge University Press, 2015.

———. "Commentary on *Gaudium et Spes*." In *Modern Catholic Social Teaching: Commentaries and Interpretations*, 2nd ed. Edited by Kenneth Himes, 275–301. Washington, DC: Georgetown University Press, 2018.

Hughes, Gerard. "Natural Law." In *Christian Ethics: An Introduction*. Edited by Bernard Hoose, 47–56. London: Continuum, 1998.

Hunt, Anne. *Trinity*. Maryknoll, NY: Orbis Books, 2005.

International Theological Commission. "Communion and Stewardship: Human Persons Created in the Image of God." (2004).

———. "In Search of a Universal Ethic." (2009).

———. "Religious Freedom for the Good of All." (2019).

Janssens, Louis. "Artificial Insemination: Ethical Considerations." *Louvain Studies* 8 (1980): 3–29.

John XXIII. *Mater et magistra*. (May 15, 1961).

———. *Pacem in terris*. (April 11, 1963).

John Paul II. *Redemptor hominis*. (March 4, 1979).

———. "Address to U.N. General Assembly. (October 2, 1979).

———. *Familiaris consortio*. (November 2, 1981).

———. *Sollicitudo rei socialis*. (December 30, 1987).

———. "Peace with God the Creator, Peace with All of Creation." (January 1, 1990).

———. *Centesimus annus*. (May 1, 1991).

———. "Address at the University of Latvia." (September 9, 1993).

Johnson, Luke. *The Acts of the Apostles*. Sacra Pagina vol. 5. Collegeville, MN: Liturgical Press, 1992.

Junker-Kenny, Maureen. "Human Dignity or Social Contract." *Interdisciplinary Journal for Religion and Transformation in Contemporary Society* 6 no. 1 (2020): 74–89.

Kasper, Walter. "The Theological Foundations of Human Rights." *The Jurist* 50 (1990): 148–66.

Keane, Philip. *Christian Ethics and Imagination*. New York: Paulist Press, 1984.

Keenan, James. *Moral Wisdom*, 3rd ed. Lanham, MD: Rowman & Littlefield, 2017.

———. "Redeeming Conscience." *Theological Studies* 76 no. 1 (2015): 129–47.

Kelly, Conor. "The Nature and Operation of Structural Sin." *Theological Studies* 80 no. 2 (2019): 293–327.

Kettern, Bernd. "The Development of the Concept 'Iustitia' from Thomas Aquinas through the Social Encyclicals." In *Principles of Catholic Social Teaching*. Edited by David Boileau, 85–101. Milwaukee: Marquette University Press, 1994.

Kloppenborg, John. *Christ's Associations: Connecting and Belonging in the Ancient City*. New Haven, CT: Yale University Press, 2019.

Lamoureux, Patricia. "Irish Catholic Women and the Labor Movement." *U.S. Catholic Historian* 16 no. 3 (1998): 24–44.

Leo XIII, *Quod apostolici muneris*. (December 28, 1878).

———. *Rerum novarum*. (May 15, 1891).

Lohfink, Gerhard. *Jesus of Nazareth*. Collegeville, MN: Liturgical Press, 2012.

Lonergan, Bernard. "The Transition from a Classicist World View to Historical Mindedness." In *Law for Liberty*. Edited by James Biechler, 126–33. Baltimore: Helicon Press, 1967.

———. *Method in Theology*. London: Darton, Longman, and Todd, 1971.

———. *A Second Collection*. Toronto: University of Toronto Press, 1974.

Lamb, Matthew. "Solidarity." In *The New Dictionary of Catholic Social Thought*. Edited by Judith Dwyer, 908–12. Collegeville, MN: Liturgical Press, 1994.

Maguire, Daniel. *The Moral Choice*. New York: Harper Collins, 1979.

Maly, Eugene. "Genesis." In *The Jerome Biblical Commentary*. Edited by Raymond Brown, Joseph Fitzmyer, and Roland Murphy, 7–46. Englewood Cliffs, NJ: Prentice-Hall, 1968.

Mansbridge, Jane. "Response to 'Pluralism and the Retrieval of a Catholic Sense of the Common Good.'" *Commonweal* Colloquium on American Catholics and the Public Square. (New York, NY: May 12–14, 2000).

Maritain, Jacques. *The Person and the Common Good*. Notre Dame, IN: University of Notre Dame Press, 1966.

Markus, R. A. "'Imago' and 'Similitudo' in Augustine." *Revue d'Etudes Augustiniennes et Patristique* 10 nos. 2–3 (1964): 125–44.

Massaro, Thomas. *Living Justice: Catholic Social Teaching in Action* 3rd ed. Lanham, MD: Rowman & Littlefield, 2016.

———. *Mercy in Action: The Social Teachings of Pope Francis*. Lanham, MD: Rowman & Littlefield, 2018.

McBrien, Richard. *Catholicism*, 2 vols. Minneapolis, MN: Winston Press, 1980.

McDonagh, Enda. *Gift and Call: Toward a Christian Theory of Morality*. St. Meinrad, IN: Abbey Press, 1975.

McDonagh, Sean. "Theological and Historical Background of *Laudato Si'*." In *On Care for Our Common Home: Laudato Si'*. Maryknoll, NY: Orbis Books, 2016.

McFadyen, Alastair. "Imaging God: A Theological Answer to the Anthropological Question?" *Zygon* 47 no. 4 (2012): 918–33.

McKeown, James. *Genesis*. Grand Rapids, MI: Eerdmans, 2008.

Meeks, Wayne. *The First Urban Christians*. New Haven, CT: Yale University Press, 1983.

———. *The Origins of Christian Morality*. New Haven, CT: Yale University Press, 1993.

Merkle, Judith. *From the Heart of the Church*. Collegeville, MN: Liturgical Press, 2004.

Messner, Johannes. *Social Ethics: Natural Law in the Modern World*. St. Louis: Herder Book Company, 1949.

Mich, Marvin. *Catholic Social Teaching and Movements*. Mystic, CT: Twenty-Third Publications, 1998.

Misner, Paul. *Social Catholicism in Europe*. New York: Crossroad Publishing, 1991.

———. *Catholic Labor Movements in Europe*. Washington, DC: Catholic University of America Press, 2015.

Moyn, Samuel. *Christian Human Rights*. Philadelphia: University of Pennsylvania Press, 2015.

Mueller, Franz. "Solidarism." In *The New Dictionary of Catholic Social Thought*. Edited by Judith Dwyer, 906–8. Collegeville, MN: Liturgical Press, 1994.

Müller, Sigrid. "Concepts and Dimensions of Human Dignity in the Christian Tradition." *Interdisciplinary Journal for Religion and Transformation in Contemporary Society* 6 no. 1 (2020): 22–55.

Murphy, Charles. *At Home on Earth: Foundations for a Catholic Ethic of the Environment*. New York: Crossroad Publishing, 1989.

Murphy-O'Connor, Jerome. *Paul: His Story*. Oxford: Oxford University Press, 2004.

Nanko-Fernandez, Carmen. "What Francis Means by 'Fratelli Tutti.'" *Commonweal* (September 24, 2020).

National Conference of Catholic Bishops. *Economic Justice for All*. (November 1986).

Nussbaum, Martha. *Creating Capabilities: The Human Development Approach*. Cambridge, MA: Belknap Press of Harvard University Press, 2011.

O'Collins, Gerald and David Braithwaite. "Tradition as Collective Memory: A Theological Task to Be Tackled." *Theological Studies* 76 no. 1 (2015): 29–42.

O'Donovan, Oliver and Joan Lockwood O'Donovan, eds. *From Irenaeus to Grotius*. Grand Rapids, MI: Eerdmans, 1999.

O'Meara, Thomas. "Community as Primal Reality." *Theological Studies* 78 no. 2 (2017): 435–46.

Orsy, Ladislas. "The Divine Dignity of the Human Person in *Dignitatis humanae*." *Theological Studies* 75 no. 1 (2014): 8–22.

Patrick, Anne. *Liberating Conscience*. New York: Continuum, 1997.

Paul VI. *Populorum progressio*. (March 26, 1967).

————. "*Regina coeli* Address for Pentecost" (May 17, 1970).

————. *Octogesima adveniens.* (May 14, 1971).

Paulus, Normand. "Uses and Misuses of the Term 'Social Justice' in the Roman Catholic Tradition." *Journal of Religious Ethics* 15 no. 2 (1987): 261–82.

Pelikan, Jaroslav. *The Vindication of Tradition.* New Haven, CT: Yale University Press, 1984.

Perkins, Pheme. "Reading Guide to John." In *The Catholic Study Bible.* Edited by Donald Senior, Mary Ann Getty, Carroll Stuhlmueller, and John Collins, RG 437–451. New York: Oxford University Press, 1990.

Petrusek, Matthew. "The Image of God and Moral Action." *Studies in Christian Ethics* 30 no. 1 (2016): 60–82.

Phan, Peter. *Social Thought.* Message of the Fathers of the Church vol. 20. Wilmington, DE: Michael Glazier, 1984.

Pharo, Lars Kirkhusmo. "The Council of Valladolid (1550–1551)." In *The Cambridge Handbook for Human Dignity.* Edited by Marcus Düwell, Jens Braarvig, Roger Brownsword, and Dietmar Mieth, 95–100. Cambridge: Cambridge University Press. 2014.

Pius XI. *Quadragesimo anno.* (May 15, 1931).

————. *Divini redemptoris.* (March 19, 1937).

Pius XII. "Christmas Radio Message of His Holiness Pius XII to the People of the Entire World." (December 24, 1944).

————. *Summi pontificatus.* (October 20, 1939).

Pontifical Council for Justice and Peace. *Compendium of the Social Doctrine of the Church.* Citta del Vaticano: Libreria Editrice Vaticana, 2004.

Putnam, Robert. "The Prosperous Community: Social Capital and Public Life." *The American Prospect* 4 no.13 (April 1, 1993): 35–42.

Rahner, Karl. "Theology of Freedom." *Theological Investigations* vol. 6. Baltimore: Helicon Press, 1961, 179–96.

————. "Towards a Fundamental Theological Interpretation of Vatican II." *Theological Studies* 40 no. 4. (1979): 716–27.

Ratzinger, Joseph. "*Gaudium et spes*: Part I The Church and Man's Calling; Chapter 1 The Dignity of the Human Person." In *Commentary on the Documents of the Second Vatican Council* vol. 5. Edited by Herbert Vormgrimler, 115–63. London: Burns and Oates, 1969.

Richardson, Alan. *Creeds in the Making.* New York: The Macmillan Company, 1969.

Ricoeur, Paul. *The Symbolism of Evil.* Boston: Beacon Press, 1967.

Rommen, Heinrich. *The State in Catholic Thought.* St. Louis: Herder Book Company, 1945.

Roos, Luther. "The Human Person and Human Dignity as Basis of the Social Doctrine of the Church." In *Principles of Catholic Social Teaching.* Edited by David Boileau, 53–70. Milwaukee: Marquette University Press, 1994.

Rosen, Michael. *Dignity: Its History and Meaning.* Cambridge, MA: Harvard University Press, 2012.

Rossi, Benedetta. "Jeremiah." In *The Jerome Biblical Commentary for the Twenty-First Century*, 3rd ed. Edited by John Collins, Gina Hens-Piazza, Barbara Reid, and Donald Senior. London: T&T Clark, 2022. https://doi.org/10.5040/9781350182875.039.

Rossi, Philip. "Community." In *The New Dictionary of Catholic Social Thought*. Edited by Judith Dwyer, 206–10. Collegeville, MN: Liturgical Press, 1994.

Rowlands, Anna. *Towards a Politics of Communion*. London: T&T Clark, 2021.

Ruston, Roger. *Human Rights and the Image of God*. London: SCM Press, 2004.

Ryan, John. *Distributive Justice*. New York: The Macmillan Company, 1916.

———. "Labor Sharing in Management and Profits." *Catholic Charities Review* 4 nos. 2–3 (1920): 46–49; 71–74.

Sachs, John. "God, Images of." In *The New Dictionary of Catholic Social Thought*. Edited by Judith Dwyer, 417–21. Collegeville, MN: Liturgical Press, 1994.

Schuck, Michael. *That They Be One: The Social Teaching of the Papal Encyclicals 1740–1989*. Washington, DC: Georgetown University Press, 1991.

Schüller, Bruno. "Can Moral Theology Ignore Natural Law?" *Theology Digest* 15 (1967): 94–99.

Selling, Joseph. "Origin of the Concept of the HPAC." https://theo.kuleuven.be/apps/christian-ethics/theory/origin.html.

Selznick, Philip. *The Moral Commonwealth*. Berkeley, CA: University of California Press, 1994.

Shannon, Thomas. "Bonaventure and Human Dignity." In *Franciscan Leadership and Ministry: Foundations in History, Theology and Spirituality*. Edited by Anthony Carrozzo, Vincent Cushing, and Kenneth Himes, 59–77. St. Bonaventure, NY: Franciscan Institute Publications, 1997.

Stark, Rodney. *The Rise of Christianity*. Princeton, NJ: Princeton University Press, 1996.

Sturm, Douglas. "On Meanings of Public Good: An Exploration." *Journal of Religion* 58 no. 1 (1978): 13–29.

Synod of Bishops. *Justitia in mundo*. (1971).

Taylor, Charles. "Freedom and Equality Aren't Enough," *Commonweal* (November 24, 2020).

Thompson, J. Milburn. *Introducing Catholic Social Thought*. Maryknoll, NY: Orbis Books, 2010.

Tierney, Brian. "Religious Rights: An Historical Perspective." In *Religious Human Rights in Global Perspective: Religious Perspectives*. Edited by John Witte, Jr. and Johan van der Vyver, 17–45. Leiden: Martinus Nijhoff Publishers, 1996.

———. *The Idea of Natural Rights*. Grand Rapids, MI: Eerdmans, 1997.

Tracy, David. *The Analogical Imagination*. New York: Herder and Herder, 1998.

Vatican II, *Gaudium et spes*. (1965).

———. *Dignitatis humanae*. (1965).

Vawter, Bruce. *The Conscience of Israel: Pre-exilic Prophets and Prophecy*. New York: Sheed and Ward, 1961.

Verstraeten, Johann. "Solidarity and Subsidiarity." In *Principles of Catholic Social Teaching*. Edited by David Boileau, 133–48. Milwaukee: Marquette University Press, 1994.

von Nell-Breuning, Oswald. *Reorganization of Social Economy*. Milwaukee: Bruce Publishing Company, 1939.

Ward, Barbara. *A New Creation? Reflections on the Environmental Issue*, 32. Vatican City: Pontifical Commission Justice and Peace, 1973.

Weaver, Darlene Fozard. "Dignity: A Catholic Perspective." In *Value and Vulnerability: An Interfaith Dialogue on Human Dignity*. Edited by Jonathan Rothchild and Matthew R. Petrusek, 31–54. Notre Dame, IN: University of Notre Dame Press, 2020.

Westerman, Claus. *Creation*. Philadelphia: Fortress Press, 1974.

———. *Genesis 1–11: A Commentary*. London: SPCK Press, 1984.

Whitmore, Todd. "Catholic Social Teaching: Starting with the Common Good." In *Living the Catholic Social Tradition*. Edited by Kathleen Maas Weigert and Alexia Kelley, 59–81. New York: Rowman & Littlefield, 2005.

Wojtyla, Karol. *Toward a Philosophy of Praxis*. New York: Crossroad Publishing, 1981.

Wolin, Sheldon. *Politics and Vision*. Princeton Classics Expanded Edition. Princeton, NJ: Princeton University Press, 2016.

INDEX

ABOUT THE AUTHOR

KENNETH R. HIMES, OFM, is a professor emeritus in the theology department at Boston College and resident Franciscan scholar at Siena College in Albany, NY. A former president of the Catholic Theological Society of America, he is the editor of *Modern Catholic Social Teaching*.